Rethinking the Western Tradition

*The volumes in this series
seek to address the present debate
over the Western tradition
by reprinting key works of
that tradition along with essays
that evaluate each text from
different perspectives.*

David Hume on Morals, Politics, and Society

Edited by
Angela Coventry and Andrew Valls
with an Introduction by
Andrew Valls
with essays by
Mark G. Spencer
Elizabeth S. Radcliffe
Frederick G. Whelan
Peter Vanderschraaf and Andrew Valls

Yale
UNIVERSITY PRESS

New Haven & London

Published with assistance from the Annie Burr Lewis Fund.

Published with assistance from the Mary Cady Tew Memorial Fund.

Yale University Press books may be purchased in quantity for educational,
business, or promotional use. For information, please e-mail
sales.press@yale.edu (U.S. office) or
sales@yaleup.co.uk (U.K. office).

Set in Times Roman type by
Newgen North America, Austin, Texas.
Printed in the United States of America.

Library of Congress Control Number: 2018938116

ISBN 978-0-300-20714-9 (paperback : alk. paper)

A catalogue record for this book is available from the British Library.

This paper meets the requirements of
ANSI/NISO z39.48-1992 (Permanence of Paper).

10 9 8 7 6 5 4 3 2 1

Contributors

Angela Coventry is Associate Professor of Philosophy at Portland State University.

Elizabeth S. Radcliffe is Professor of Philosophy at the College of William and Mary.

Mark G. Spencer is Professor of History at Brock University.

Andrew Valls is Associate Professor of Political Science at Oregon State University.

Peter Vanderschraaf is Professor of Philosophy at University of California Merced.

Frederick G. Whelan is Professor Emeritus of Political Science at University of Pittsburgh.

Contents

Essays

Acknowledgments

Many thanks to Gretchen Becker, Sione Filimoehala, and James Funston for their fine work on the text and Index of Names. We are grateful as well to Bill Frucht and two anonymous reviewers for very helpful comments on the manuscript, Margaret Otzel for her guidance in preparing the manuscript, and Margaret Hogan for her excellent copyediting. We also thank the Center for the Humanities, the College of Liberal Arts, and the School of Public Policy at Oregon State University for support for the Index through a Faculty Excellence Publication Support Grant.

Introduction

ANDREW VALLS

David Hume occupies an odd position in the history of moral and political theory. On the one hand, he is often considered one of the greatest philosophers in the Western tradition, and his works are widely read, studied, and taught. Philosophers and political theorists produce a steady stream of papers, articles, and books on Hume's thought, and these regularly appear or are discussed in academic journals and at professional conferences. Yet, on the other hand, scholars, particularly those interested in Hume's social, moral, and political thought, sometimes complain that he is neglected or underappreciated, and that, as Amartya Sen (2011, 23) puts it, "some of Hume's central but more iconoclastic ideas have not been brought adequately into contemporary discussions." According to some observers, this is partially because the radical and profound nature of Hume's thought is only now coming to be appreciated and absorbed. Russell Hardin (2007, vii) suggests that Hume's "moral psychology and his social science are highly original and are a couple of centuries ahead of their time in that almost no one grasped many of his theoretical claims until recent decades." While Hume scholarship is thriving, and recent theoretical developments put us in a better position to appreciate and engage his thought, at the same time he remains, among political theorists at least, consigned to a subordinate position in the pantheon of modern thinkers. Anthologies and textbooks that devote entire chapters to Thomas Hobbes, John Locke, and Jean-Jacques Rousseau often contain just a few brief references to Hume (for a recent example, see Ryan 2012).

For "Hume enthusiasts," as Annette C. Baier (1991, vii) calls those who deeply appreciate Hume's thought, this strange situation is somewhat distressing. Hume's philosophy provides a sophisticated and thoroughly empirical and secular account of social and political life. From the point of view of those who are persuaded that Hume's moral and political thought is profoundly *right* about a great many things, his relative neglect is unfortunate. It overlooks an extraordinarily rich set of texts that could otherwise inform and advance our understanding. This is part of the motivation

behind the present volume: Hume's work is experiencing renewed appreciation, and yet at present he still does not enjoy the status of a first-tier
thinker in modern moral and (especially) political thought. This seems a
propitious time to "rethink" Hume, and to (re)introduce him to students
and scholars alike.

Part of the reason for the situation that I have described may be that
Hume wrote no single work that contains the whole of his moral and political philosophy. Hume's first published work was his *A Treatise of Human
Nature,* written when he was still in his twenties and published in 1739–40.
The *Treatise* contains three books: Book 1, "Of the Understanding," offers
an account of Hume's theory of knowledge and the workings of the human mind. Central to this account is the role of the non-rational faculty of
the "imagination" in associating certain ideas with one another. Book 2,
"Of the Passions," contains Hume's theory of our emotional life, including
the important idea of sympathy, which is the mechanism by which people
come to share their emotional responses and hence their moral appraisals.
Book 3, "Of Morals," presents Hume's moral and political theory, including his account of justice.

The *Treatise* is very much the work of a young man anxious to make
his mark on the world. It is ambitious in scope and does not shy away from
announcing new ideas boldly. In its introduction, Hume writes that he will
"propose a compleat system of the sciences, built on a foundation almost
entirely new, and the only one upon which they can stand with any security" (2007, 4). The *Treatise* is also a long and dense book, and sometimes
seems to be making several arguments at once. Hume picks many fights
and purposely provokes his reader with startling pronouncements. Among
these are the famous (or, depending on one's point of view, infamous) as-
sertions that many of our most fundamental beliefs cannot be rationally
justified; that personal identity is a "fiction"; that pride is a virtue, and
not the vice that some Christian moralists would have it; that reason is the
slave of the passions; that moral distinctions are based not on reason but
on a non-rational "moral sense"; and that justice is an "artificial" virtue,
dependent not on God or reason but on human conventions.

As Mark G. Spencer describes in his essay, below, the *Treatise* did not
get the reception that Hume had hoped. In his autobiographical essay, "My
Own Life," Hume wrote that his *Treatise* "fell *dead-born from the press,*
without reaching such distinction, as even to excite a murmur among the
zealots" (1985b, xxxiv). This was an exaggeration. The *Treatise* was indeed read, reviewed, and commented on – both in the years immediately
following its publication and throughout the rest of Hume's life (Norton

and Norton 2007). Yet the response was clearly not what Hume had desired, both in its quantity and its substance. Much of the reaction was negative. Hume was indeed disappointed, but he concluded that the response to the *Treatise* was due "more from the manner than the matter" (1985b, xxxv) of its doctrines. That is, Hume was convinced that his philosophy would meet with a better reception if he presented it differently, while retaining its central arguments. He therefore set out to "cast . . . anew" the *Treatise.* He revised book 1 into the *Enquiry Concerning Human Understanding,* book 2 into the *Dissertation on the Passions,* and book 3 into the *Enquiry Concerning the Principles of Morals.* In addition, Hume turned to essays as a primary genre for communicating his ideas. Some of his essays present arguments that originally appeared in the *Treatise,* while others go well beyond anything contained there. Finally, Hume wrote a monumental six-volume history of England, which has recently received greater attention as yet another source of Hume's moral and political philosophy (see Sabl 2012 and Spencer 2015).

This volume brings together Hume's *Enquiry* on morals (often referred to as Hume's second *Enquiry*) and a selection of his most important political essays, along with four interpretive essays by contemporary Hume scholars. With only a single exception, these works by Hume were written and published by 1752, and yet Hume continued to revise them for successive editions that were published over the course of his life. The large number of revisions that Hume made reflect the care that he took with these works. While much of the text of Hume's *Enquiries* and essays remain the same across all of the editions, he never stopped correcting, rephrasing, and polishing these texts, right up to the last weeks of his life. Hume was clearly satisfied, on the whole, with his *Enquiries* and essays, even as he tried to improve them at every opportunity. He judged the second *Enquiry* to be "of all my writings, historical, philosophical, or literary, incomparably the best" (1985b, xxxvi).

These numerous editions reflect the fact that Hume achieved with his later works the success that eluded him with the *Treatise.* What he wished to do was to engage in philosophy in a way that would be accessible to a wide audience. To accomplish this, he eliminated some of his more controversial claims, especially where they were likely either to be misunderstood, to offend the sensibilities of his readers, or both, but not at the expense of his central arguments. Hume wrote to friends that, comparing the *Treatise* to the *Enquiry,* "The philosophical Principles are the same in both," and that they present "the same doctrines" (Beauchamp 1998, xiii). And as James A. Harris (2015, 250–65) describes in his recent intellectual biography of Hume, in order to reach and engage a wide audience Hume dropped what he considered to be inessential, to avoid distraction from his central ideas. For example, the distinction between natural and artificial virtues, which is sharply drawn in the *Treatise,* is merely implied in the *Enquiry.* The doctrine of sympathy, so central to the *Treatise,* is not nearly as explicit in the *Enquiry.* The *Treatise* more clearly lays out the machinery of Hume's philosophy, but the *Enquiry* retains the earlier work's essential ideas. Justice remains a matter of rules and conventions, and the mechanism of sympathy remains, albeit in somewhat muted form.

So Hume's later works are the product of his sustained efforts over the course of many decades to present his ideas to the public – an "expanding audience of general readers," as Mark G. Spencer puts it in his essay in this volume. (Spencer's essay provides much valuable biographical and contextual background on Hume's works.) The ways and extent to which Hume labored over these works stands in stark contrast to the *Treatise,* which by comparison was written hastily, as Hume himself suggested (and regretted). Now, this does not mean that the *Treatise* should be ignored. On the contrary, the very qualities that led to its reception, as described above, has made it a favorite among philosophers. Many Hume scholars are *Treatise*-lovers (myself included) and admire its elaborate and technical arguments. Ideally, anyone interested in Hume's philosophy would read both the *Treatise* and Hume's later works. This is precisely what Hume scholars do, often citing passages from both to support the same point. But students, many reading Hume for the first time, are unlikely to read both. In addition, teaching Hume's political philosophy by focusing on the *Treatise* is challenging, I have found, because the arguments in book 3 depend heavily on the ideas presented (at great length) in the earlier books. The *Enquiry,* on the other hand, is intended to be read on its own.

There are many fine editions of Hume's works, and some of these are appropriate for classroom use, but no other volume currently in print aims to present the combination of works that we do here. The preferred edition of the *Enquiry* among scholars is the Oxford edition, edited by Tom L. Beauchamp (Hume 1998), and the best edition of the essays remains the Liberty Classics edition edited by Eugene F. Miller (Hume 1985a). Although these volumes have been enormously helpful to us as we prepared the present volume, and contain much useful information for Hume scholars, they are not particularly suited to classroom use. There are many other editions of the *Enquiry* alone, but we believe that some of Hume's essays are essential to complete the picture of his moral and (particularly) his political thought. Similarly, we are convinced that fully understanding

Hume's thought requires attention to the *Enquiry* and not only his essays. Hence we do not duplicate Knud Haakonssen's (1994) admirable volume of Hume's political essays, which contains no excerpts from the second *Enquiry* (nor from the *Treatise*). We have also decided against following the example set by other editions that include excerpts from both the *Treatise* and the *Enquiry,* along with a (more or less extensive) selection of Hume's essays (see Aiken 1948; MacIntyre 1965; Sayre-McCord 2006; and Warner and Livingston 1994).

In constructing a volume that may be of use in teaching Hume, my co-editor, Angela Coventry, and I have attempted to collect works that present his mature views on moral and political philosophy. It is our hope that by presenting the *Enquiry* along with a selection of Hume's most important political essays, we offer the most complete picture of Hume's moral and political theory that can be achieved in a volume of this size. The four interpretive essays provide an additional resource to students and instructors alike. They synthesize large literatures that are focused on various aspects of Hume's philosophy: Mark Spencer on the composition and early reception of Hume's works; Elizabeth S. Radcliffe on Hume's moral psychology and moral epistemology; Frederick G. Whelan on the interplay of empirical political analysis and normative political theorizing in Hume; and Peter Vanderschraaf and I on the decision- and game-theory aspects of Hume's philosophy, including his accounts of coordination and justice. These essays provide helpful context for understanding Hume's ideas; they also show that Hume's philosophy remains the focus of lively debate among scholars today.

One of the ideas that Hume asserted starkly in the *Treatise,* and that may have shocked some of his contemporaries, was that moral judgments are based on sentiment rather than reason. But in fact a careful reading of the *Treatise* shows that, although the impetus for our moral judgments is the sentiments that actions and characters produce in us, reason does have a role to play. In the *Enquiry,* perhaps wanting to avoid misunderstanding and offense, Hume makes this much more explicit, avowing that reason and sentiment "concur in almost all moral determinations and conclusions" (EPM, 1.9). Still, it remains clear that, like the *Treatise* account, in the *Enquiry* sentiment plays the predominant role. Although Hume does not come to any firm conclusions on this issue in section 1 of the *Enquiry,* his understanding of the relation between reason and sentiment in producing moral judgment is elaborated in appendix 1, which can usefully be read immediately after reading section 1.

Some of Elizabeth Radcliffe's account of current debates over Hume's moral epistemology in her essay below focuses on section 1 and appendix 1 of the *Enquiry*. As Radcliffe shows, the broad outlines of Hume's view are clear: Hume argues that reason is inert in producing either motivation for action or moral judgment. The driving force of these is passion and sentiment. But reason still plays an essential role by informing us of matters of fact, including the likely consequences of actions. Many contemporary scholars accept this general view but argue about its precise specification – and hence Hume has spawned, or at least inspired, divergent schools in moral theory. But of course other scholars reject Hume's view entirely, often in favor of a Kantian view that reason can and must inform us not only of the means to our ends but also of what our ends should be. This divide between Humeans and Kantians on the nature and role of reason is one of the great debates in modern moral theory.

Another doctrine in the *Treatise* that came in for criticism was Hume's sharp distinction between natural and artificial virtues. The natural virtues, he argued, were those that are acted on spontaneously and are spontaneously approved of by observers. They are also those that, in each case of their exercise, are beneficial to those involved. Such is the case with benevolence. But artificial virtues like justice depend on human conventions and rules, and while the uniform observance of those rules is a virtue, not all such cases of rule-following are immediately beneficial. Rather, it is the whole scheme of rules that is generally beneficial. This view of justice as artificial may have led some readers to suppose that, for Hume, justice is not a real virtue at all. Thus in the *Enquiry* Hume largely drops this characterization, consigning the only instance of it to a footnote to an appendix (EPM, app. 3, note 2).

Instead of this sharp distinction between benevolence and justice, as natural and artificial virtues, we instead get, in sections 2 and 3 of the *Enquiry,* a treatment of the two virtues that emphasizes what they have in common. And what they have in common, first and foremost, is that they are *useful,* both to the possessors of the virtue and to others more generally. It is the consequences of characteristics and actions that constitute their moral status, Hume argued – not intention and not conformity to duty (let alone to the will of God) for its own sake. Therefore, in determining whether an action is virtuous, we must attend to its consequences. Giving alms to the poor, however well intentioned, is not virtuous if it turns out to do more harm than good to its intended beneficiaries (EPM, 2.18). This highlights a theme in Hume's thought that Frederick Whelan emphasizes in his account of Hume's political theory: the close connection between empirical analysis and normative theorizing. Sound moral judgments, for Hume, depend heavily on a sound and accurate causal understanding of the consequences of actions.

Hume's account of justice is one of the strikingly original aspects of his political philosophy. In essence, it is an account of the conventions, such as those regulating property, that emerge under specific though widespread conditions—which have come to be called "the circumstances of justice" (Rawls 1999, 109–12). The two primary components of these circumstances are moderately scarce resources and limited benevolence toward others. If resources were extremely abundant, Hume suggests, or if people were so generous as to immediately give to others what they themselves possessed but that others desired, then there would be little need for rules to determine who owns what. If, on the other hand, scarcity were severe, or if people were so selfish as to be unable to moderate the pursuit of their desires, then rules of justice would be useless. Moderate conditions between these extremes, along with the relative equality and interdependence of humans, give rise to the need for rules of justice. This account of justice as arising contingently, to meet a specific problem, contrasts sharply with the views of philosophers who believe justice to have more exalted origins, such as in natural law.

While the need for rules of justice is widespread (or even nearly universal) for Hume, the specific dictates that arise to meet this need can vary considerably. This is an implication of the fact that for Hume justice is a convention, a set of practices that enable people to cooperate with one another and coordinate their actions. While some such rules are needed, their content is contingent, and so rules can be different in different times and places—and yet all may do the job of facilitating cooperation. In general, the function of rules of justice is to increase the public welfare, and good rules of justice will be informed by the relevant empirical considerations, including "the nature and situation of man" (EPM, 3.27). Rules will therefore take account of things like incentive effects, which suggests that they will often permit private property since this "give[s] encouragement" to "useful habits and accomplishments" (EPM, 3.27). Hume, like Locke, thus endorses private property rights in things that are "improved by a man's art or industry," but for reasons other than those Locke provided (EPM, 3.28). Locke argued that natural law, a product of God's reason, sanctions private property in that with which one mixes one's labor. Locke's account is far too theistic and rationalistic for Hume. Indeed, Hume seems to delight in showing just how contingent and almost arbitrary some rules of property are. He does not wish to thereby undermine property rights but merely to elucidate their origins and reason for being. Hume compares many of the particular features of property rules to superstition, but he also emphasizes an important difference between the two – that rules of justice are useful, while superstition is "frivolous, useless, and burdensome" (EPM, 3.38).

Hume's views on justice are further elaborated in appendix 3, where he essentially affirms the *Treatise* position that justice is artificial. Here Hume also emphasizes again that "public utility" is the end of the rules of justice, but that their content is "often determined by very frivolous views and considerations" (EPM, app. 3n64) – that is, on the "imagination," that non-rational faculty of the mind that associates one idea with another. Central to this account of justice is that the rules that operate in a particular society are neither the result of rational decisions nor are they the result of explicit agreement. Rather, they "gradually *emerge*" (Warner and Livingston 1994, xii) over time as a result of trial and error, and they are (to use an anachronistic phrase that Hume did not use) path-dependent.

As Peter Vanderschraaf and I attempt to demonstrate in our essay below, the logic of Hume's account can be captured in terms of modern-day decision theory and rational choice theory. Hume's account of the respective roles of reason and passion in human motivation has strong resonances with later accounts of instrumental rationality. His account of cooperation and coordination have informed and inspired recent work in game theory, which generally confirms Hume's analysis. Hume shows that abiding by a convention that regulates cooperation is often rational, and that this alone is sufficient to account for and motivate such cooperation. In some cases, social cooperation takes the form of what is now called "pure coordination," where neither party has any incentive to depart from a practice. "Thus two men pull the oars of a boat by common convention, for common interest, without any promise or contract" (EPM, app. 3.8). In other cases that take the form of a prisoners' dilemma, while some parties may have a short-term incentive to not cooperate their longer-term interest lies in doing their part and keeping their promises. Hume's analysis suggests that Hobbes was mistaken to think that cooperation in a state of nature would not take place. Hume also rejects Hobbes's assumption that humans are only egoistically motivated (what Hume calls the doctrine of "self-love"), as demonstrated in Hume's response to a "knave" who is tempted to break promises and cheat others. Such a person, he urges in the final paragraph of the conclusion to the *Enquiry,* sacrifices far more than they can hope to gain by trading a clear conscience and honest intercourse with others for "worthless toys and gewgaws" (EPM, 9.25).

While Hume emphasized the roots of the rules of justice in human "imagination," he also tied justice strongly to "utility." Hume helped to inspire Jeremy Bentham to develop his highly calculative account of utilitarianism, but Hume himself was no utilitarian. Utilitarianism is a maximizing doctrine – it judges actions, rules, policies, or institutions (depending on the version of utilitarianism) by the standard of whether it maximizes the utility, or wellbeing, of all effected. As Fred Whelan says in his essay, for Hume "utility" is roughly a synonym for "public good." Our practices and institutions should promote the public good and general welfare, but Hume would have denied that we could ever know how to maximize wellbeing, or know whether we had done it.

Still, throughout the *Enquiry,* Hume characterizes virtue as a property of an individual that is either useful or agreeable, to its possessor or to others. As Annette C. Baier (2008) has emphasized, this account of virtue has implications that would have disturbed some of Hume's readers. It entails Hume's rejection of what he calls the "monkish virtues," which are endorsed by some versions of Christianity. Denying oneself pleasure, for example, is no virtue – unless it serves some other purpose. Hume's irreligious views were widely denounced in his time, even by those who otherwise admired him (as Mark Spencer shows). One important upshot of Hume's account of virtue in the *Enquiry* is that virtue must be judged in terms of the benefit and pleasure that human characteristics produce. A virtue that does no worldly good is inconceivable on Hume's account.

While cooperation, justice, and property are possible without a state, at some point a society becomes sufficiently large, complex, and anonymous to require a state. Under these conditions the state performs the function of helping to make it in everyone's interest to perform their obligations under justice, as well as specifying the details of what justice requires. While Hume alludes to these origins of the state at the beginning of section 4 of the *Enquiry,* to get the full account we must turn to some of his essays. In "Of the Origin of Government" Hume describes how government "oblige[s] men, however reluctant, to consult their own real and permanent interests" by enforcing the rules of justice, and how this gives rise to a "new duty" of obedience (Essay 4.3). Obedience, or "allegiance" to government, is a duty because government is essential to the public good, or utility, which is the ultimate sanction in Hume's political philosophy. Again, this is not to say that government maximizes utility but merely that government enforces the rules of justice, which facilitates social cooperation. Hence there is a certain conservatism built into Hume's view:

by virtue of existing and performing important functions (tolerably well), rules, practices, and institutions – including government – are entitled to deference and obedience. Hume was skeptical of the pursuit of some ideal system of government but focused his analysis instead on what exists and why. (In this respect the exercise that Hume undertakes in "The Idea of a Perfect Commonwealth," designing a set of institutions from scratch, is somewhat out of character – though the essay does demonstrate his republican sympathies.)

While his view has a degree of conservatism, Hume also makes clear that the state and its policies can be reformed and improved. Indeed, the fact that justice is a convention suggests that once the state is up and running, it may modify or augment the rules governing social cooperation. Hume had already made this point in the *Enquiry,* where he writes that "where it is impossible for reason alone to determine" the requirements of justice, "civil laws here supply the place of the natural code." He goes on to say that "all questions of property are subordinate to the authority of civil laws, which extend, restrain, modify and alter the rules of natural justice" (EPM, 3.33–34). This view contrasts with that of Locke, who held that natural law limits what the state may do, particularly in regulating private property rights. Hume's view has no room for such (potentially libertarian) implications. As he writes in the *Treatise,* once the state exists it takes on many functions – and this is a good thing: "Thus are bridges built; harbours open'd; ramparts rais'd; canals form'd; fleets equip'd; and armies disciplin'd; every where, by the care of government" (3.2.7.8).

While the state is an essential institution under modern circumstances, like the rules of justice it is the result of a slow evolutionary process and not a social contract – as Hume makes clear in his best-known political essay, "Of the Original Contract." This essay reflects many of the central themes in Hume's philosophy. He rejects the "speculative" doctrine that government is based on the consent of the governed, in part because nothing in the world "corresponds" to this idea (Essay 10.1, 7). Most governments come about through "usurpation or conquest," without any pretense to gaining the consent of those over whom they rule (Essay 10.9). Most people never consider obedience to government a choice, and even if they did, withdrawing consent (such as through emigration) is often difficult or impossible. But Hume's "more philosophical" refutation of the idea of a social contract relies on his analysis of conventions and artificial virtues (Essay 10.32). Contracts and promises to abide by them are conventions, as is government itself. The social contract view must hold that the obligation to abide by agreements is somehow prior to the obligation to obey government, and this foundational character of performing promises is usually provided by a theistic natural law view (Forbes 1975, 67). Hume of course rejects such a view and grounds both the obligation to uphold promises and the obligation to obey government on public utility.

The upshot of the view that government is based on the consent of the governed is that unjust governments may be resisted or overthrown. Hume acknowledges, in the companion essay "Of Passive Obedience," that this is the case. Most of the time, when a government is performing its functions tolerably well, there is no reason to resist or overthrow it. Everyone's interest is served by obedience (even while they may attempt to improve or reform). But in "extraordinary emergencies" people may resist oppressive governments. Hume, ever cautious, advises that such action be taken only "as the last refuge in desperate cases" (Essay 11.3). Conventions and established institutions should not be cast aside lightly, for, as we have seen, they are usually the product of a long process, and they are what makes social cooperation possible. Hume does not speak of a "right" of revolution – since his philosophy has no place for such a claim – and he denies that philosophers can state in advance the conditions under which resistance would be justified. He agrees with those who reject "passive obedience" and insist that resistance to oppressive government is sometimes justified. In the end, for Hume, while the public good underwrites the obligation to abide by conventions, people must (and will) judge for themselves where their interests lie, for better or worse. As Hume affirms in the essay "Of the First Principles of Government," "governors have nothing to support them but opinion" (Essay 3.1).

Hume was fortunate to live in a time and place of relative stability and increasing prosperity. Unlike Hobbes or Machiavelli, Hume was not preoccupied with the problem of establishing authority during times of political upheaval. Rather, much of his political thought is devoted to understanding (and defending) the fortunate circumstances that led to the political stability and general improvement that Britain experienced in the eighteenth century. As Frederick Whelan notes in his essay below, many of Hume's essays are devoted to this task and contain a mix of empirical explanation and normative recommendations. Hume tries to show that "politics may be reduced to a science" to the extent that institutions produce predictable results (Essay 2). On the whole, Hume approved of and defended the major political institutions and economic trends of his time: the "mixed" British constitution and the increase in trade with its concomitant increase of wealth and "luxury." In this, Whelan shows, Hume took recognizably liberal positions and thereby produced a distinctly "modernist" political theory. He eschews the kind of nostalgia for a more virtuous ancient republicanism found in Rousseau. Hume does, however, endorse a distinctly modern republicanism by supporting representative institutions – both in his essays on the British constitution and in the "Idea of a Perfect Commonwealth" (Essay 12).

Hume's moral and political philosophy, then, is a mixture of a number of distinct streams of thought. He is, as Elizabeth Radcliffe shows, a virtue theorist, yet he is also, as Peter Vanderschraaf and I try to demonstrate, a proto-game theorist. While not strictly speaking a utilitarian, Hume's work inspired later utilitarians, and his emphasis on the public good suggests a broadly consequentialist outlook. His conclusions are generally those of a classical liberal, but he does not attempt to place strict limits on state authority. His work also reflects a certain conservatism, but it is a conservatism grounded in an understanding of the importance of established conventions in making social cooperation possible. His thought is also broadly republican in that he endorses elective democracy and argues that republican institutions are compatible with large territory. As both Fred Whelan and Mark Spencer point out, this last position was one that James Madison took up in his defense of the American Constitution.

With all of these streams to be found in Hume, it is perhaps no surprise that divergent moral and political schools of thought lay claim to him. As L. A. Selby-Bigge noted in the late nineteenth century, Hume wrote so many different things that it "makes it easy to find all philosophies in Hume, or, by setting up one statement against another, none at all" (1975, vii). Still, while James Harris (2015, 25) is surely right that one should be cautious about attributing to Hume a single philosophical system that stretches across all of his works, Hume's moral and political philosophy, for all of its richness and diversity, hangs together remarkably well. Hume offers a clear and attractive alternative to many major modern moral and political philosophers. He avoids the egoism and the statism of Hobbes, the theism and social contract theory of Locke, the nostalgia for a small and virtuous republic of Rousseau, the rationalism of Immanuel Kant; and the false precision of Benthamite utilitarianism. What Hume offers instead is a deeply historically and empirically informed, theoretically sophisticated understanding of moral judgment, human motivation, social cooperation, and political institutions. In short, there is ample reason to read, reread, and rethink Hume.

NOTE

Many thanks to the following for invaluable comments on previous versions of this introduction: Angela Coventry, Mark Spencer, Elizabeth Radcliffe, Frederick Whelan, Peter Vanderschraaf, Bill Frucht, and two anonymous readers.

WORKS CITED

Aiken, Henry D., ed. 1948. *Hume's Moral and Political Philosophy*. New York: Hafner Press.

Baier, Annette C. 1991. *A Progress of Sentiments: Reflections on Hume's Treatise*. Cambridge, Mass.: Harvard University Press.

Baier, Annette C. 2008. "*Enquiry Concerning the Principles of Morals:* Incomparably the Best?" In *A Companion to Hume,* edited by Elizabeth S. Radcliffe, 293–320. Malden, Mass.: Wiley-Blackwell.

Beauchamp, Tom L. 1998. "Introduction: A History of the Enquiry on Morals." In David Hume, *An Enquiry Concerning the Principles of Morals,* edited by Tom L. Beauchamp, xi–lxxx. Oxford: Oxford University Press.

Forbes, Duncan. 1975. *Hume's Philosophical Politics*. Cambridge: Cambridge University Press.

Haakonssen, Knud, ed. 1994. *David Hume: Political Essays*. Cambridge: Cambridge University Press.

Hardin, Russell. 2007. *David Hume: Moral and Political Theorist*. Oxford: Oxford University Press.

Harris, James A. 2015. *Hume: An Intellectual Biography*. Cambridge: Cambridge University Press.

Hume, David. 1985a. *Essays Moral, Political, and Literary*. Edited by Eugene F. Miller. Indianapolis: Liberty Classics.

Hume, David. 1985b. "My Own Life." In *Essays Moral, Political, and Literary,* edited by Eugene F. Miller, xxxi–xli. Indianapolis: Liberty Classics.

Hume, David. 1998. *An Enquiry Concerning the Principles of Morals*. Edited by Tom L. Beauchamp. Oxford: Oxford University Press.

Hume, David. 2007. *A Treatise of Human Nature,* Volume 1. Edited by David Fate Norton and Mary J. Norton. Oxford: Clarendon Press.

MacIntyre, Alasdair, ed. 1965. *Hume's Ethical Writings: Selections from David Hume*. New York: Collier Books.

Norton, David Fate, and Mary J. Norton. 2007. "Historical Account of *A Treatise of Human Nature* from Its Beginnings to the Time of Hume's

Death." In David Hume, *A Treatise of Human Nature,* edited by David Fate Norton and Mary J. Norton. Volume 2: Editorial Material. Oxford: Clarendon Press, pp. 433–588.

Rawls, John. 1999. *A Theory of Justice.* Revised edition. Cambridge, Mass.: Harvard University Press.

Ryan, Alan. 2012. *On Politics: A History of Political Thought from Herodotus to the Present.* 2 vols. New York: Norton.

Sabl, Andrew. 2012. *Hume's Politics: Coordination and Crisis in the* History of England. Princeton, N.J.: Princeton University Press.

Sayre-McCord, Geoffrey, ed. 2006. *David Hume: Moral Philosophy.* Indianapolis: Hackett.

Selby-Bigge, L. A. 1975. "Editor's Introduction." In David Hume, *Enquiries Concerning Human Understanding and the Principles of Morals,* 3rd edition, edited by L. A. Selby-Bigge and P. H. Nidditch, vii–xxxi. Oxford: Oxford University Press.

Sen, Amartya. 2011. "The Boundaries of Justice: David Hume and Our World." *New Republic.* December 29, 23–26.

Spencer, Mark G., ed. 2015. *David Hume: Historical Thinker, Historical Writer.* University Park: Pennsylvania State University Press.

Warner, Stuart D., and Donald W. Livingston, eds. 1994. *David Hume: Political Writings.* Indianapolis: Hackett.

Index of Names

In this index, "EPM" designates *An Enquiry Concerning the Principles of Morals,* cited by section and paragraph number; appendixes to the EPM are designated by appendix number and paragraph number. "Dialogue" designates "A Dialogue" and is cited by paragraph number. "Essays" designates *Essays, Moral, Political and Literary,* cited by essay number and paragraph number.

Achæus (320–275 BCE), prince of Syria and the son of Seleucus I Nicator, king of Syria, and Apama of Baktria. Achæus married the daughter of Alexander the Great, king of Macedonia (EPM, appendix 4.9).

Aeschines (390–314 BCE), Greek statesman, orator. As a member of the embassies to Philip II, Aeschines advocated for a 346 BCE peace treaty of the Athenians and Macedonians after a ten-year war over Macedonia's expansion (EPM, appendix 4.20n89).

Agesilaus II (444–360 BCE), Greek king of Sparta (400–360 BCE). Ruled as the successful king of Sparta and commander in the Corinthian War, fought over Sparta's expansion in Asia Minor and northern Greece. His life was documented by his friend and Greek historian Xenophon in the biography *Agesilaus* (Essay 2.10n8).

Ajax. Hero in Greek mythology. Ajax (Aias) is a strong, courageous Greek hero in Homer's Iliad and the Epic Cycle poems about the Trojan War. In the Iliad, he fights Hector in two duels and successfully defends the Greek ships from Hector and the Trojan armies (EPM, 7.4).

Albinus (101–200 CE), Greek philosopher. A Middle Platonist philosopher, Albinus integrated schools of philosophy to analyze Plato in the work *Epitome,* organized in three sections – logical, theoretical, and practical. He also helped initiate the Neoplatonist movement (Essay 10.42).

Alcibiades (450–404 BCE), Greek statesman, orator, general. During the Peloponnesian War, Alcibiades served with Socrates and initiated an aggressive military expedition to Sicily, which ended in a decisive Athenian defeat that began the last phase of the war. He used brilliant negotiation tactics and treachery to conquer cities, and often gave political advice for his own benefit (EPM, 5.40n31; Essay 9.1n53).

Alexander the Great [Alexander III of Macedon] (356–323 BCE). Educated by Aristotle, Alexander ascended to the throne at age twenty, and by the age of thirty had amassed a vast empire stretching from Greece to northern India. Never facing defeat, Alexander is remembered as one of history's greatest military commanders (EPM, 7.5–6; Essay 2.10n8; Essay 6.32n38; Essay 9nn54, 55).

Alexander VI (1431–1503), Spanish pope. As pope during the Renaissance, Alexander VI was corrupt, ambitious, and broke the vow of celibacy to father several children. In response to a request of King Ferdinand and Queen Isabella, he issued the Treaty of Tordesillas, which gave Spain exclusive rights to explore and conquer the New World west of Cape Verde. His papacy contributed to the Protestant Reformation (EPM, appendix 4.18).

Antiochus III (242–187 BCE), Greek, Seleucid king of Syrian Empire (223–187 BCE). As king, he rebuilt the eastern Hellenistic Syrian Empire and initiated the Fourth Syrian War, which ended in the concession of what is now southern Syria and Palestine to Ptolemy IV (Essay 2.10n8).

Anthony, Mark (83–30 BCE), Roman politician, general. Mark Anthony was first appointed military commander by Julius Caesar in the Gallic Wars and then administrator of Italy. After Caesar's assassination in 44 BCE, Anthony joined Octavian and Marcus Lepidus to form the Second Triumvirate dictatorship and defeated Caesar's assassins. The three then divided the Roman Republic and assigned Anthony control over Rome's eastern provinces including the Ptolemaic Kingdom of Egypt (Essay 2.9).

Archimedes (287–212 BCE), Greek mathematician, engineer, scientist. Archimedes proved several geometric theorems, including the area of a circle, surface and volume relationship of a sphere, and the area under a parabola; formulated the hydrostatic principle of buoyancy; derived an approximation of pi; and laid the groundwork for calculus through his use of the concept of infinitesimals (Essay 6.6n28).

Ariaeus (401–394 BCE), Persian general. In Greek historian and soldier Xenophon's writings, Ariaeus fought with Prince Cyrus the Younger in attempts at overthrowing the Achaemenian throne in the Battle of Cunaxa. After Cyrus's death, he declined the throne and led the retreat out of Persia with the remaining Persian and Greek soldiers (Essay 2.10n8).

Aristotle (384–322 BCE), Greek philosopher, scientist. Aristotle's normative political theory demonstrated his interest in comparative politics, democracy, and monarchy. His works maintain the importance of constitutions and the role of the lawgivers who organize and govern city-states in its different forms, whether democratic or oligarchic. Throughout his *Politics,* Aristotle is highly critical of Plato's ideal constitution, arguing that each citizen possesses moral virtue and strives to attain a life of excellence and happiness (EPM, 6.2n34, 8.9, 8.9n62, appendix 4.12; Essay 6.31n37).

Armstrong, John (1709–1779), Scottish poet, physician. Author of the poem *The Art of Preserving Health* (1744). After establishing a medical practice in London, Armstrong became a literary celebrity of the time, writing *The Oeconomy of Love* (EPM, appendix 4.7n79).

Arrian [Lucius Flavius Arrianus] (c. 87–c. 146), Greek historian, senator. His *Anabasis of Alexander* is considered the best source on the campaigns of Alexander the Great. Due to the success of his work, he referred to himself as the second Xenophon (Essay 2.10n8; Essay 9.1).

Artachaeas [Artachaees] (5th century BCE), Persian engineer who supervised construction of a canal around Mt. Athos (Essay 2.10n8).

Artaxerxes (5th century BCE), king of Persia (465–24 BCE). Son of Xerxes I, Artaxerxes I was the fifth king of Persia during an Egyptian revolt. In 445 BCE, he sent his cupbearer Nehemiah to help rebuild Jerusalem's city walls and to construct the citadel for the Second Temple (Essay 2.10n8; Essay 6.32).

Atticus, Herodes (101–177 CE), Greek orator, author. Known for his works of the Second Sophistic movement of rhetoric, of which one speech remains: *On the Constitution,* which explores the history of Greek constitutions (EPM, appendix 2.3; appendix 4.10; 4.10n81).

Augustus (63 BCE–14 CE), Roman emperor (27 BCE–14 CE). Augustus (Octavius) was named Julius Caesar's adopted son and heir. With Mark Anthony and Marcus Lepidus, he formed the Second Triumvirate dictatorship. After its end, Augustus restored the former republic through autocratic rule as a military dictator (EPM, 7.27; Essay 7.7; Essay 9.1, 24; Essay 10.30, 43n67).

Bacon, Francis (1561–1626), English philosopher, scientist, orator, and essayist. An early empiricist, Bacon established inductive methods during the Scientific Revolution. His legal reform proposals influenced the Napoleonic Code and reforms by Sir Robert Peel, which served as the foundation of modern jurisprudence (EPM, 5.17; Essay 5.1; Essay 6.24; Essay 7.19, 19n45).

Bayle, Pierre (1647–1706), French philosopher, author. Himself a Protestant, Bayle wrote about religious tolerance, arguing that its promotion strengthens states, and organized an encyclopedia titled *Historical and Critical Dictionary* (1697). Bayle recognized the limits of human reason to discover true knowledge and supported reliance on conscience instead. Bayle's work later influenced the Enlightenment (EPM, 3.38n17).

Bentivoglio, Guido (1579–1644), Italian historian. As a historian, Bentivoglio's writings contained detailed political accounts of countries he visited. In 1621 he was made cardinal by Pope Paul V and in 1633 signed the papal condemnation of Galileo (Essay 6.25).

Berkeley, George (1685–1753), Anglo-Irish philosopher. In his works Berkeley advanced the theory of immaterialism, which denies the existence of material substances outside the minds of observers through their senses (Essay 6.24n33).

Boileau-Despréaux, Nicolas (1636–1711), French poet, literary critic. A critic of French and English literature, Boileau-Despréaux promoted the classical tradition. Beginning his writing career with political satire, he would later publish *L'Art poétique* in verse, outlining rules for poetry composition. These would later influence the English poet Alexander Pope (EPM, 7.7n49).

Boulainvilliers, Henri de (1658–1722), French historian, writer, nobleman. Friends with Pierre Bayle, Boulainvilliers wrote essays on philosophy and history, and published a French translation of Spinoza's *Ethics*. He became one of the first to argue that history should be used to analyze and interpret events in the present (Essay 10.45n68).

Brahe, Tycho (1546–1601), Danish astronomer. Brahe invented astronomical instruments and measured the positions of at least 777 stars, though without the assistance of a telescope. In his *On the New Star* (1573) he criticized Aristotle's celestial system of immutable celestial spheres by demonstrating the existence of supernova beyond the moon and measuring the movement of comets. Johannes Kepler used Brahe's data years later to posit his three laws of planetary motion (Essay 6.1).

Brutus, Marcus Junius (85–42 BCE), Roman politician. Brutus led the conspiracy to assassinate Julius Caesar in 44 BCE; he was later forced out of Rome by Mark Anthony along with Gaius Cassius Longinus. After defeat in the Battles of Philippi in 42 BCE, both Brutus and Longinus committed suicide (EPM, 2.19; EPM, Dialogue 15; Essay 2.19; Essay 9.9).

Burrhus [Sextus Afranius Burrus] (1–62 CE), Roman prefect, advisor. Burrus was an official of the Roman imperial guard, or a Praetorian prefect, and chief advisor to the emperor Nero (EPM, 5.40).

Busiris. Egyptian king in Greek mythology. Son of Poseidon, Busiris instituted an annual sacrifice of a foreigner to Zeus to end a nine-year period of famine. Later, he was killed by Heracles, who was brought into Egypt for this sacrifice (Essay 9.6).

Caesar, Gaius Julius (100–44 BCE), Roman general, statesman, dictator. Caesar amassed military power in the Gallic Wars and was instrumental in the rise of the Roman Empire. In 49 BCE, he refused an order by the Senate to return to Rome, and the resulting conflict sparked a civil war that ended with Caesar assuming control over the government. During his dictatorship, he was known for his skills of negotiation and ruthlessness, his rapid expansion of the Roman military, and several constitutional reforms (EPM, 7.3; EPM, Dialogue 15n92).

Camillus, Marcus Furius (446–365 BCE), Roman statesman, soldier, dictator. Known as the Second Founder of Rome, Camillus commanded the Roman Army during its conquest of the city of Veii and was appointed dictator five times during Rome's recovery in the years after the Gauls' assault on Rome. Despite his promotion of patrician class interests, he accepted the plebian Licinian-Sextian reforms to restore consular positions and limits to ownership rights for conquered lands (Essay 7.7).

Capet, Hugh (938–996), king of the Franks (987–996). Some historians have suggested that Capet's coronation marked the beginning of modern France, since he was the first king to rule from Paris. Despite his limited military power, he was unanimously elected as king, which meant he commanded strong moral authority during his reign (Essay 10.45n68).

Capitolinus, Julius. The collection of biographies in *Historia Augusta* covers the lives of Roman emperors and heirs and claims to have six authors, one of which is named "Julius Capitolinus." The collection, however, is now considered to be the plagiarized and forged work of one person (Essay 10.43n67).

Cassius [Gaius Cassius Longinus] (1st century BCE), Roman senator. During the civil war between Julius Caesar and Pompey in 50 BCE, Cassius sided with Pompey and commanded part of his fleet. He was overtaken by Caesar, who then made him a Roman general. Later, Cassius devised Caesar's assassination plot with Brutus. In the Battle of Philippi, he was defeated by Mark Anthony (EPM, 7.3; EPM, Dialogue 15).

Castiglione, Baldassare (1478–1529), Italian author, diplomat, courtier. Castiglione is remembered for his work *The Book of the Courtier,* which covers morality and etiquette expected of advisors serving the royal court, guided by humanism and a commitment to public service (EPM, 9.2).

Catiline [Lucius Sergius Catilina] (108–62 BCE), Roman senator. As a Roman senator, his political views were well received, including a proposal to cancel outstanding debts and oust wealthy citizens. In 63 BCE Catiline devised a plot to overthrow the Roman Republic, known as the second Catilinarian conspiracy. He fled after Cicero discovered his plan (EPM, appendix 1.16; Essay 8.6).

Cato, Marcus Porcius (95–46 BCE), Roman politician, statesman, orator. Cato (the Younger) led the Optimates, a group of patrician aristocrats, in efforts to preserve the Roman Republic. He was a follower of Stoicism and known for his moral integrity and opposition to corruption. His ongoing conflicts with Julius Caesar helped to organize the First Triumvirate coalition of Pompey, Caesar, and Marcus Licinius Crassus. Later, Cato joined Pompey in the civil war against Caesar and in defeat committed suicide (EPM, Appendix 4.6; EPM, Dialogue 40; Essay 2.19; Essay 8.6).

Cervantes [Miguel de Cervantes Saavedra] (1547–1616), Spanish novelist, poet, playwright. Author of *Don Quixote,* Cervantes is known as one of the most influential Spanish novelists. The masterpiece is in part a parody of chivalric romances but it also serves as a critique of Spain's history of imperialism (Essay 6.1).

Charles I (1600–1649), Scottish; king of Great Britain (1625–49). Charles's rule was considered excessively tyrannical by his people, especially his taxation policy implemented without the consent of the parliament. Widespread antipathy provoked a civil war, which resulted in his capture by the parliament. Refusing their demands for a constitutional monarchy, he was executed for high treason and the Commonwealth of England was formed (Essay 10.28; Essay 11.6).

Charles II (1661–1700), king of Spain (1665–1700). Charles suffered from physical, intellectual, and emotional disabilities, and failed to produce an heir. This led him to appoint his grandnephew Philip, Duke of Anjou, to succeed him. Because of Philip's relation to French king Louis XIV, many saw this as disruptive to the European balance of power. Following Charles's death, the War of Spanish Succession commenced (Essay 10.45).

Charles VIII (1470–1498), king of France (1483–98). Because he was considered foolish and inept, the first years of Charles VIII's reign was controlled by his sister Anne and her husband until he turned twenty-one. In 1495 he invaded and, virtually unopposed, conquered the Italian peninsula and was crowned king of Naples. These political acts resulted in over fifty years of war over the territory (Essay 8.8).

Charles XII (1682–1718), king of Sweden (1697–1718). Although Charles XII was an absolute monarch, he initiated several domestic reforms during the early Enlightenment. During his reign, Charles defended Sweden against the alliance of Denmark-Norway, Saxony-Poland-Lithuania (ruled by Augustus II), and Russia in the Great Northern War. While young and inexperienced, Charles led the Swedish Army in their efforts to dethrone Augustus II. Ultimately, however, the army faced destruction in Russia, and Charles was forced into exile (EPM, 7.24).

Cicero, Marcus Tullius (106–43 BCE), Roman statesman, writer, political theorist, orator. Known as the greatest Roman orator, Cicero outlined an early conceptualization of rights derived from ancient laws and introduced Greek philosophy to the Romans. His works would later influence Enlightenment thinkers such as John Locke and David Hume. Cicero defended republican principles during Julius Cæsar's dictatorship and the civil wars that ended the Roman Republic. He was executed by the Second Triumvirate in 43 BCE after criticizing Mark Anthony in a series of speeches (EPM, 2.3n4, 14n8; 3.1n15; 6.19n39; 8.10, 12; appendix 1.16; appendix 4.10, 11ns81–83; Essay 2.9; Essay 6.24; Essay 7.8n44).

Clarke, Samuel (1675–1729), English philosopher, theologian. A proponent of Newtonian physics and Isaac Newton's friend, Clarke argued that God and moral principles can be discovered through mathematical reasoning. Clarke is also known for his dispute with Gottfried Leibniz (1646–1716) on space, time, and God (EPM, 3.34n16).

Claudius [Tiberius Claudius Drusus Nero Germanicus] (10 BCE–54 CE), Roman emperor (41–54 CE). Succeeded to the Roman throne following the assassination of his nephew Caligula, Claudius was a sickly man, not seen as a threat by political rivals. As emperor, Claudius instituted an expansion of infrastructure. He was poisoned, likely by his final wife, Agrippina, in 54 CE (Essay 5.13n26).

Cleanthes (330–230 BCE), Greek philosopher. Cleanthes furthered Stoic perspectives within physics, materialism, and pantheism as Zeno's student and successor in the Stoic school in Athens. He rejected the passions of love, fear, and grief as against nature, weakening the soul, and as a threat to a life of reason and moral virtue (EPM, 9.2).

Clearchus (c. 450–401 BCE), Greek Spartan general. Clearchus was hired by Cyrus the Younger to assist his efforts to overthrow Artaxerxes II. Following Cyrus's death, Clearchus was betrayed by the remaining generals of Cyrus's forces and executed by Artaxerxes (Essay 2.10n8).

Columbus, Christopher (1451–1506), Italian maritime explorer, admiral. Sponsored by the Catholic monarchs of Spain Ferdinand II and Isabella I, Columbus led four transatlantic voyages between 1492 and 1504 to the Americas for the purpose of exploration and colonization (Essay 12.2).

Commodus [Marcus Aurelius Commodus Antoninus Augustus] (161–192 CE), Roman emperor (180–192 CE). Commodus often executed powerful and successful people he perceived to be a threat and was known for his increasingly capricious rule. Political and civil unrest became commonplace, and his own sister conspired with senators for his assassination, which was unsuccessful. Over time, his mental health worsened; he renamed Rome "Colonia Commodiana," claimed he was Hercules, and fought as a gladiator. In 192, his advisors ordered his death by strangulation at the hands of a wrestler (Essay 10.41).

Conde, Prince of [Louis II de Bourbon] (1621–1686), French general. During the Thirty Years' War (1618–48) Bourbon led an attack against the battle-hardened Spanish, earning battle prowess and the name le Grand Condé at the age of twenty-one. During the Fronde (1648–53), both sides attempted to gain his support (EPM, 7.6).

Corneille, Pierre (1606–1684), French poet, dramatist. He was the creator of the classical French tragedy and authored *Le Cid,* now known as the most important French drama in history. The first French classical tragedy, *Le Cid* explores tension between following love or preserving family loyalty (Essay 2.13n14).

Cotys I (d. 358 BCE), Odrysian king (384–358 BCE). Cotys allied with Athens, marrying his daughter to an Athenian general. His conquest of the Chersonese peninsula led him to conflict with Athens. During his conflict with the Athenians, Cotys allied with Macedonian king Philip II. Cotys was assassinated by Python and Heraclides, students of Plato (Essay 2.10n8).

Cromwell, Oliver (1599–1658), English military commander, statesman. As lord protector of the Commonwealth (1653–1658), Cromwell was a strong Puritan, talented military leader, and believer in religious toleration. He led the Commonwealth through the trial and execution of Charles I and the reemergence of his country as a European power (EPM, 6.8; Essay 12.67).

Cyrus II (6th century BCE), king of Persia (559–530 BCE). Also known as Cyrus the Great, he was the founder of the Achaemenid Empire and, in the Bible, he liberated the Jews in Babylonia. An ancient clay cylinder in the name of Cyrus the Great was found, inscribed with the earliest known declaration of human rights. During his rule, he led several expeditions and conquered the Median, Lydian, and Neo-Babylonian Empires, demonstrating considerable respect for their customs and religions. He governed with a centralized administration whose aim it was to work for the benefit of his subjects (EPM, appendix 3.4; Essay 9.1).

Cyrus the Younger (c. 423–401 BCE), Persian prince, general. Greatly loved by his people, he was killed in an attempt to wrest the Persian throne from his brother Artaxerxes II (Essay 6.32).

Darius I [Darius Hystaspes] (550–486 BCE), king of Persia (522–486 BCE). One of the greatest rulers of the Achaemenid Empire, Darius the Great divided it into provinces governed by satraps, implemented a unified monetary system, and emphasized large construction projects (EPM, 7.5, 25; Essay 3n115; Essay 6.32).

Datames (4th century BCE), Persian general, satrap. As military general, Datames exhibited great skill and courage. Goaded by his enemies in the Persian court, he abandoned his allegiance to the king and withdrew his troops in Egypt across the empire in the Satraps' Revolt (Essay 8.11).

David (1040–970 BCE), Israeli king of Judah (1010–1002 BCE), king of Israel (1002–970 BCE). The second Israeli king united Israel and established Jerusalem as its capital. He is regarded as a righteous, effective king in Judaism and Christianity, and a prophet in Islam (EPM, appendix 4.15).

De Retz [Jean Francois Paul de Gondi] (1613–1679), French priest, writer. He was a leader in the Fronde aristocratic rebellion against the growing power of monarchs, beginning under Louis XIII, but switched allegiances for personal gain. Although arrested after the rebels' defeat, he escaped and fought to retain his position as archbishop of Paris from exile. In retirement, he wrote a memoir covering his life and the events of the Fronde (EPM, 6.8; Essay 12.53).

was marked by the Black Death pandemic of the bubonic plague and the development and expansion of the English parliament (Essay 10.39).

Epaminondas (418–362 BCE), Greek general, statesman. As a Theban statesman, Epaminondas transformed and strengthened the city state of Thebes, leading it out of control by Spartans. He also liberated a group of Peloponnesian Greeks from the Spartans after over 230 years of slavery. He was highly regarded by Cicero, who called him the "first man of Greece" (EPM, 6.26n41).

Epictetus (55–135 CE), Greek philosopher. A Stoic philosopher, Epictetus considered philosophy to be a way of life, and that events beyond the disciplined acts of an individual are determined by fate and should be accepted. He was born a slave to Nero's secretary but was granted an education and freed after Nero's death (EPM, 7.17; appendix 4.14).

Epicurus (341–270 BCE), Greek philosopher. Epicurus is known for his hedonistic ethics, which promoted peace and absence of fear or pain, and materialistic metaphysics. He taught that neither death nor the gods should be feared, that the universe is infinite, and that natural phenomena could be explained by the interactions and motions of indivisible atoms (EPM, appendix 2.3).

Euclid (3rd century BCE), Greek mathematician. Known often as the father of geometry, his main work, *Elements,* wherein he described geometric principles, is one of the most important of the history of mathematics (EPM, appendix 1.14).

Euripides (484–406 BCE), Greek tragic dramatist. One of the three great Greek tragedians, Euripides's contributions to theater are significant and profound. His most famous works include *Medea* and *The Bacchae,* and portrayed mythical heroes as fallible, facing extraordinary circumstances. His plays included complex female characters and philosophical debates, and often explored emotional motivations such as revenge, suffering, or insanity (EPM, appendix 4.15n84).

Eurybiades (5th century BCE), Greek general. As the Spartan commander of the Greek Navy, he worked with Athenian general Themistocles at the Battle of Artemisium (480 BC), a naval battle in which the Greek forces were heavily outnumbered by Persian ships (EPM, Dialogue 16).

Evrémond [Charles de Marguetel de Saint-Denis] (1613–1703), French literary critic, essayist, soldier. Although the French critic's works were meant for his friends, not publication, many were published after his death, including essays promoting religious toleration and hedonism. He was exiled to England after attacking French policies leading up to the Treaty of the Pyrenees, which ended the Franco-Spanish War in 1659 (EPM, 6.9; 7.4n46).

Fabius [Quintus Fabius Maximus Verrucosus Cunctator] (280–203 BCE), Roman politician, general. His battle strategy, known as the Fabian Strategy, to slow enemies and force them into a war of attrition, earned him the agnomen Cunctator (Latin, delayer) (EPM, 6.9).

Fénelon [François de Salignac de La Mothe-Fénelon] (1651–1715), French archbishop, theologian, essayist, poet. Fénelon's liberal views on politics, education, and theology generated significant controversy; his public defense of the leading exponent of the Quietist school of prayer led to his work's condemnation by the pope and his subsequent exile to his diocese (EPM, 7.15).

Fontenelle [Bernard Le Bovier de Fontenelle] (1657–1757), French scientist, author. Fontenelle originated many ideas central to the Enlightenment period and was a religious critic and influential supporter of the Copernican model of heliocentrism. His *Dialogues of the Dead* and *History of the Oracles* popularized philosophy among the French public. A lunar crater was named after him in 1935 (EPM, appendix 2.7n72).

Germanicus [Germanicus Julius Caesar] (15 BCE–19 CE), Roman general. The adopted son of the Roman emperor Tiberius, he was a successful and popular general. According to the historian Tacitus, Germanicus promoted republican political principles (Essay 10.40).

Gordian III [Marcus Antonius Gordianus Pius Augustus] (225–244 CE), Roman emperor (238–244). He became emperor at the age of thirteen, and as such, was a figurehead for aristocratic families to manipulate. Gordian died under questionable circumstances (Essay 10.43n67).

Gratian [Flavius Gratianus Augustus] (359–383 CE), Roman emperor (367–383 CE). Gratian was the last emperor to lead a campaign across the Rhine to attack a neighboring tribe. A moderate, popular emperor and defender of the Christian church, his father's and uncle's deaths left almost the entire Roman Empire under his control (EPM, 9.2).

Grotius, Hugo (1583–1645), Dutch jurist, scholar, statesman, diplomat. Grotius was known as the "father of international law" for his most famous work, *On the Law of War and Peace,* grounded in secular natural law with the aim to limit bloodshed in war. His works spanned philology, drama, theology, and politics, and during his lifetime he was embedded in a political battle against the orthodox Calvinists, resulting in his imprisonment. With the help of his wife, he escaped in a chest of books in 1621 (EPM, appendix 3.8n74).

Guicciardini, Francesco (1483–1540), Italian historian, statesman, diplomat. One of the most influential political writers of the Renaissance, he was a critic of Machiavelli and developed a new style of historical analysis in *Storia d'Italia* (EPM, 5.33; appendix 4.18n87; Essay 8.8).

Hannibal [Hannibal Barca] (247–181 BCE), Carthaginian general. Commander of the Carthaginian forces against Rome during the Second Punic War (218–201 BCE), Hannibal was known for his military leadership, strategic tactics, and lifetime hostility against the Roman Republic (EPM, appendix 4.17).

Harrington, James (1611–1677), English political philosopher. Harrington's most influential work was *The Common-wealth of Oceana,* which outlined the basis of an ideal constitution for building a utopian republic and argued revolutions are a consequence of the separation of economic and political power. Many of these theories would later inspire Thomas Jefferson and have been linked with U.S. political developments such as written constitutions and the indirect election of presidents (Essay 3.4n21; Essay 12.5, 50).

Henry III (1551–1589), French king (1574–1589). Ruled during the Wars of Religion (1562–98), which devolved into a war of succession following Henry's inability to produce an heir. Henry was assassinated by a Catholic fanatic, Jacques Clèment (Essay 2.2).

Henry IV (1553–1610), French king (1589–1610). Remembered as Good King Henry, he improved agriculture, education, and public works. Henry also encouraged the arts by bringing all classes of artists to work on the Louvre (Essay 2.2; Essay 9.32n61).

Henry VIII (1491–1547), English king (1509–1547). Henry VIII separated England from the Roman Catholic Church and formed the Church of England. This move was done to secure a divorce from his then-wife Catherine of Aragon, who failed to produce a male heir (Essay 10.28).

Herodotus (5th century BCE), Greek historian. Herodotus is considered the "Father of History" for being the first known historian to develop a historiographic narrative organizing geographic and ethnographic evidence. His only known work, *The Histories,* explored the origins of the Greco-Persian Wars (EPM, 7.14n55).

Hobbes, Thomas (1588–1679), English political philosopher, historian, scientist. Author of the *Leviathan,* Hobbes's contributions to political philosophy have endured; his social contract theory influenced the likes of John Locke, Jean-Jacques Rousseau, and Immanuel Kant. Many of the essential concepts behind Western liberalism can be traced back to Hobbes and his promotion of individual rights, natural political and social equality, and representative political power (EPM, 3.15n15; appendix 2.3–4).

Homer (8th century BCE), Greek poet, speechwriter. Homer is the presumed author of the famous epic poems the *Iliad* and *Odyssey,* and is mentioned by Herodotus. Plato's *Republic* identifies him as the leader of Greek culture and "first teacher" of the tragedians (EPM, 6.26, 7.15; Essay 6.23).

Horace [Quintus Horatius Flaccus] (65–8 BCE), Roman poet. Horace was a lyric poet and satirist that explored philosophy, friendship, and love in his works *Odes* and *Epistles* through hexameter verse. He wrote during Rome's transition from a republic to an empire under emperor Augustus (EPM, 5.18n27, 30; 7.1; 9.8n68; appendix 2.3; appendix 4.20n89; Dialogue 36).

Hutchinson, Thomas (1711–1780), British colonial governor of Massachusetts, historian, businessman. A Loyalist politician of the province of Massachusetts Bay, Hutchinson's governorship was politically polarizing as he was a proponent of British taxation and the crown, and harbored open hostility to Samuel Adams. His political positions and policies stirred colonial unrest, which eventually led to the American Revolution (1775–83), including the events of the Boston Tea Party (1773). He was also the acting governor during the Boston Massacre (1770) (Essay 9.29).

Huygens, Christiaan (1629–1695), Dutch mathematician, scientist. During his lifetime, Huygens used his improvements in telescope lens to discover the shape of Saturn's rings, the usefulness of pendulums in clocks to regulate time, laws governing centrifugal force, and the wave theory of light among other remarkable scientific accomplishments. He also published his *Discourse on the Cause of Gravity,* which was a critique of Newton's theory, arguing instead for a mechanical explanation of gravitational force (Essay 12.2).

Iphicrates (418–353 BCE), Greek general. As an Athenian general, he successfully fended off the Spartans during the Corinthian War with his use of "peltasts," lightly armed soldiers with longer swords, and other strategic military reforms (EPM, 8.10).

Isocrates (436–338 BCE), Greek orator, rhetorician, teacher. Isocrates founded an alternative school of rhetoric to Plato's Academy, and his surviving works describe Athenian political and intellectual life. He claimed rhetoric leads to civilized life and stressed the ability of language to address practical issues (EPM, 7.25).

James II (1660–1701), king of Great Britain (1685–1688). Tensions between James's stated religious tolerance and his promotion of Roman Catholicism led to his deposition, the subsequent establishment of the legislative purview of parliament in England, and passage of the Bill of Rights in 1689 (Essay 11.6).

Julian [Flavius Claudius Julianus] (332–363 CE), Roman emperor (361–363 CE), philosopher. Julian's own troops proclaimed him as emperor, which resulted in the outbreak of civil war between Julian and emperor Constantius II. Julian was known as "the Apostate" for his public conversion to Neoplatonic paganism and was the last non-Christian Roman emperor. Wanting to return the empire to its earlier Hellenic culture, he tried to reintroduce earlier religious practices, place limits on what he saw as the corrupt and burdensome bureaucracy of the imperial administration, and thought an ideal ruler should live under the same laws as his subjects (Essay 10.42).

Juvenal (1st–2nd century CE), Roman poet, satirist. Not much is known about Juvenal's life, though his satiric poems skillfully address themes of corruption in Rome and human brutality with impressively clear, illustrative scenes. His works and satirical style are still studied and imitated (EPM, 2.4n5; Essay 6.24n35).

Laius. King of Thebes and divine hero in Greek mythology. In the mythological account of the founding of the city Thebes, King Laius was Oedipus's father. On his orders, Oedipus was left bound on a mountain to avoid an oracle from Delphi that Laius's son would kill Laius and marry his wife. The oracle was later fulfilled regardless; on the way to Thebes Oedipus had an altercation with Laius that ended with the king's death (EPM, appendix 1.12).

Livy [Titus Livius] (d. 17 CE), Roman historian. His history of Rome, from early legends until Emperor Augustus, and reflections about Roman culture became a quick classic. His writing style, which chronologically linked the past with present events, had a lasting influence on historiography into the eighteenth century (EPM, appendix 4.17n86; Essay 2.13n12; Essay 5.6n23; Essay 6.17n31; Essay 7.7n43).

Locke, John (1632–1704), English philosopher. Grounded in social contract theory, a support of religious toleration, and philosophical empiricism, Locke's works profoundly influenced the development of political liberalism. His political positions were widely adopted in England in the late seventeenth century and inspired the U.S. Declaration of Independence and, later, the Constitution. Contending that all knowledge is gained through experience, Locke is considered one of the first major empiricist philosophers of the Enlightenment (EPM, appendix 2.3; Essay 10.46n69).

Longinus [Gaius Cassius Longinus] (1st century BCE), Roman public official. He famously converted to Epicureanism, which some suggested helped justify his opposition to Julius Caesar's tyrannical rule. In 44 BCE Longinus inspired the plot to assassinate Caesar in an attempt to restore the republic along with Marcus Junius Brutus and other "Liberators." However, his immediate motives were more personal–he hated Caesar for appointing his younger brother-in-law to the position of senior magistrate. He was later defeated in the Battle of Philippi by Mark Anthony (EPM, 7.4–5).

Louis XIV (1638–1715), king of France (1643–1715). King Louis XIV was a symbol of absolute monarchy because of his belief in the divine right of monarchial rule and in centralized governance, seeking to root out the last of feudalism in France and breaking with tradition. This consolidated power of the monarch would continue until the French Revolution. During his rule from his palace in Versailles, he led a series of wars resulting in the eastern expansion of the French border, and clashed with French nobility (EPM, 3.34n16; Essay 8.8n49; Essay 10.45n68).

Lucian [Lucian of Samosata] (125–180), Assyrian satirist. Lucian's *Passing of Peregrinus* is one of the earliest references to Christianity and one that took a satirical stance. On Hume's deathbed, he read Lucian's *Downward Journey* (EPM, 6.21n40; Dialogue 24n93).

Lysias (445–380 BCE), Greek speechwriter. While only thirty-five of two hundred speeches written by Lysias have survived, his simplistic, modest style became the Attic Greek standard for his time, earning his place in the Alexandrian "Canon of Ten" Attic orators. His speeches were skillfully written and humorous, with careful attention to detail, covering a wide range of topics including politics and law (EPM, 7.25; Dialogue 44).

Machiavelli, Niccolò (1469–1527), Italian political philosopher, historian, statesman. As a political philosopher of the Italian Renaissance, Machiavelli was secretary to the Second Chancery of the Republic of Florence, and later in exile wrote his most famous works within political philosophy.

The Prince argues that a new political figure must first establish his power not by working toward an ideal leader but to follow the "effectual truth" to use moral knowledge prudently and according to necessity, which may justify otherwise immoral actions. Preferring instrumentalism and pragmatism over idealism, Machiavelli is known for founding modern political science (EPM, 6.9; Essay 2.10n8, 11, 12n9; Essay 12.5).

Malebranche, Nicolas (1638–1715), French philosopher, Roman Catholic priest. In his works, Malebranche sought to integrate his Cartesianism with Neoplatonism and St. Augustine's contributions to philosophy and theology. Foundational to his metaphysics was "Occasionalism," or his understanding that human knowledge through experience is only possible in relationship with God, and all change is due to God's causal agency. He also argued for Cartesian dualism between mind and body in orthodox Roman Catholicism (EPM, 3.34n16).

Mandeville [Bernard de Mandeville] (1670–1733), Dutch writer, philosopher. His notable work *The Fable of the Bees* argues for the utility of human vices, justified by his claim that all actions are principally motivated by self-interest and therefore equally immoral at the level of the individual. However, Mandeville concluded these actions usually improve society's well-being regardless of their selfish intentions (Essay 8.21n51).

Maurice [Maurice of Nassau] (1567–1625), prince of Orange (1618–1625). As sovereign prince or "stadtholder" of the Dutch Republic, Maurice succeeded his father, William I the Silent, and innovated military engineering and strategy, including reforms to ensure soldiers were well paid, equipped, and trained to prevent mutiny. These brought several calculated victories against Spanish conquests, which ultimately resulted in securing the borders of the Dutch Republic and a twelve-year truce with Spain. During his rule, he was known for his public defense of Calvinists (EPM, 8.9).

Mazarine, Jules Raymond (1602–1661), Italian cardinal, diplomat. Chief minister to King Louis XIV of France (1642–1661), Mazarine was mentored by Cardinal Richelieu, whom he succeeded as chief minister. Mazarine's unpopularity with the people manifested during the Fronde, in which the Paris mob harassed Mazarine and his associates (Essay 8.8).

Medea. In Greek mythology, granddaughter of the sun god Helios. Medea used her gifts of prophecy to assist her husband, Jason, leader of the Argonauts, collect the Golden Fleece from her father. In Euripides's play *Medea,* she slays her children to punish Jason for leaving her (EPM, 7.7).

Parisian culture and its social classes from the perspective of two Persian travelers to the city in *Persian Letters*. Initially published anonymously, Montesquieu was eventually identified as the author and became famous. He also promoted the separation of government into independent legislative, executive, and judicial bodies which inspired the U.S. Constitution (EPM, 3.34n16).

More, Sir Thomas (1478–1535), English statesman, lawyer, philosopher, humanist. Declared a saint by the Roman Catholic Church, Thomas More was a vocal opponent of the Protestant Reformation and Martin Luther. His work *Utopia* describes his conception of an ideal society on a small island, without private property and with relatively equal occupational status (with slaves as the exception) and a welfare state. He was tried, convicted, and beheaded for treason because he refused to acknowledge King Henry VIII's separation from the Catholic Church (Essay 12.4).

Nero [Nero Claudius Caesar Augustus Germanicus] (37–68 CE), Roman emperor (54–68 CE). Nero's rule was marked by controversy. As emperor, he implemented policies that benefited the poor, increased the Senate's autonomy, built theaters, and sought to increase trade. However, he ordered the murder of his mother, often turned to extravagant vices, and was allegedly connected to a fire in Rome (64 CE) that destroyed several districts (EPM, 5.34, 40; appendix 1.12, 17; Essay 9.6; Essay 11.2).

Newton, Isaac (1642–1727), English physicist, mathematician. One of the most influential scientists of all time, Newton was a natural philosopher. He founded classical mechanics of motion, developed infinitesimal calculus, and discovered that white light is composed of the colors of the visible spectrum. These findings contributed to the Scientific Revolution in the seventeenth century (EPM, 3.48n18).

Niger [Gaius Pescennius Niger Justus] (c. 140–194 CE), Roman emperor (193–194 CE). A former equestrian army officer, Niger became popular in Rome during the Commodus's rule. On the death of his successor, Pertinax, Niger became emperor of the Asiatic provinces. His rule was short-lived; the next year he was killed by Septimius Severus in battle (Essay 10.42).

Oedipus. King of Thebes in Greek mythology. Oedipus was prophesized to unwittingly kill his father and marry his mother. On his birth, his father, Laius, learned of this through an oracle at Delphi and left him on a mountaintop to die. He was then rescued by a shepherd and brought to Corinth, where he was raised by King Polybus and his wife. After learning about the prophecy, he attempted to avoid his fate by leaving Corinth.

Unfortunately, his father and mother met their fate when Oedipus returned to Thebes (EPM, appendix 1.12).

Ovid [Publius Ovidius Naso] (43 BCE–17 CE), Roman poet. Ovid is remembered for his mythological, epic narrative *Metamorphoses,* which has become the most comprehensive account of classic Greek mythology and has had a lasting influence on Western literature. *Metamorphoses* is written in chronological order, beginning with the origin of the universe and ending with the death of Julius Caesar (EPM, 5.30; Essay 8.6).

Palladio, Andrea (1508–1580), Italian architect. One of the most influential architects in history, Palladio designed palaces and villas near Vicenza. His work *The Four Books of Architecture* documenting his teachings earned him worldwide recognition (EPM, appendix 1.15).

Parmenio (400–330 BCE), Macedonian general. Parmenio served as a general during the reign of Philip II, leading the military victory against the Illyrians, and a delegate in a peace treaty with Athens. He defended Macedonian control of Euboea. Ultimately, he was accused on false charges of treason and executed by Alexander the Great (EPM, 7.5).

Pascal, Blaise (1623–1662), French mathematician, physicist, Christian philosopher. Pascal is one of the first inventors of the mechanical calculator. His largest philosophical contribution, known as Pascal's Wager, posited that a belief in God would be better than no belief due to the possibility of infinite gain while risking nothing (EPM, Dialogue 54–55).

Pericles (495–429 BCE), Greek statesman, orator, general. Pericles was instrumental in the development of the Athenian empire and its democratic governance. Regarded as "the first citizen of Athens" by the historian Thucydides, Pericles led the democratic party with his promotion of populist policies. In the aftermath of the Persian War, Pericles organized a conference to rebuild Greek temples and reinstitute tributes to the gods. With Athens taking the lead, construction began in 447 BCE on the Acropolis, the Parthenon, and its statue of Athena (EMP, 2.2n3).

Perrault, Charles (1628–1703), French poet, author. A member of the French Academy, Perrault is known for developing fairy tales as a literary genre. His most influential works include *Sleeping Beauty, Cinderella, Puss in Boots,* and *Little Red Riding Hood.* Perrault was also a leader of the Moderns in the Ancient and Moderns literary dispute during the seventeenth century. The Moderns, inspired by René Descartes and the Scientific Revolution, criticized the dominant classical tradition and advocated for progress in the arts (EPM, appendix 1.15).

Perseus. Hero in Greek mythology. Chronologically, Perseus was the first hero within Greek mythology, and his story became the foundation of the Twelve Olympian myths. He founded Mycenae, a citadel and town that was a center for Greek civilization. In expeditions he defeated monsters such as the Gorgon Medusa, which earned him his status as a hero (Essay 9.1).

Pertinax [Publius Helvius Pertinax Augustus] (126–193 BCE), Roman emperor (193 CE). Pertinax was a high-ranking military officer during the Parthian War (161–66 CE) and an influential senator. On the assassination of Commodus he was brought to the Praetorian Camp and proclaimed emperor. During his three-month reign, he attempted to reform policies subsidizing the grain market (Essay 10.41–42).

Petronius [Gaius Petronius Arbiter] (1st century CE), Roman author. Petronius was the governor of the province Bithynia and later held the office of the first magistrate of Rome. After his term ended, Nero chose him as his "director of elegance," which gave him legislative power on aesthetic matters. His major work, *Satyricon,* was an eclectic collection of stories on Roman society (Essay 8.6).

Phaedrus (15 BCE–50 CE), Roman author. As a freedman, Phaedrus joined Emperor Augustus's household and received an education in Greek and Latin authors. He is known for translating Greek fables to Latin under the name Aesop and distributing them for free, including *The Fox and the Sour Grapes* and *The Wolf and the Lamb,* which became popular during the Middle Ages (EPM, 4.5n19).

Philip II (382–336 BCE), king of Macedon (359–336 BCE). Father of, and succeeded by, Alexander the Great. Philip was assassinated at the wedding of his daughter and Alexander I of Epirus (EPM, 7.12; appendix 4.5; Essay 9.1; Essay 11.2).

Philip VI [Philip de Valois] (1293–1350), king of France (1328–1350). Philip came into the monarchy as the Hundred Years' War broke between England and France over the legitimate process of the succession of the French crown. While he continued past efforts to centralize administrative power in Paris, Philip VI struggled to maintain the power of the monarchy. He was pressured to concede power to the nobility, clergy, and other groups. During the last years of his life, France was not only preoccupied by war but also the spread of the Black Death plague (Essay 10.39).

Plato (427–347 BCE), Greek philosopher. One of the most influential philosophers of the Western tradition, Plato argued that reality could be understood by reference to immutable, abstract forms, or *eidos,* which would influence his positions on questions in metaphysics, art, and his approach to the moral virtues such as beauty, justice, and equality. In the *Republic,* Plato supported aristocratic forms of government ruled by a "philosopher king" and argued that it is better to be ruled by a bad tyrant than by bad democracy (EPM, 3.15n15, 4.5n19, 6.11n37, 7.25, appendix 4.20n89; Essay 9.1; Essay 1.47; Essay 12.4).

Plutarch (46–127 CE), Greek biographer, author. As an influential historian, biographer, and essayist, Plutarch is remembered for his collection of over seventy essays, *Moralia,* which explored ethical, political, religious, and literary topics important to Greek life. His most famous work, *Parallel Lives,* is a series of Greek and Roman biographies presented in pairs to emphasize shared virtues of famous soldiers, statesmen, and orators (EPM, 2.2n3, 4.5n19, 5.40n31, 7.8n50, appendix 4.16, Dialogue n96; Essay 6.12, 32n39; Essay 9.1n55).

Polybius (200–118 BCE), Greek historian, statesman. Polybius is noted for his detailed history of the rise of the Roman Republic during the Hellenistic period from 264 to 146 BCE. Advocating in *Histories* for the separation of the powers of the Roman government into the Roman Senate, consuls, and assemblies, his ideas would later influence the structure of the U.S. government (EPM, 5.6n24, 6.16n38, appendix 4.19n88; Essay 2.9n6, 10n8; Essay 7.8n44; Essay 10.17).

Polyphemus. Giant in Greek mythology. One of the Cyclopes in the *Odyssey,* Polyphemus is the son of Poseidon and a sea nymph. In Homer's account, he traps Odysseus in a cave with his men and devours several before the travelers get Polyphemus drunk and blind him, escaping the cave by hiding in his herd of sheep, which were let out to pasture (EPM, 6.8).

Pompey [Gnaeus Pompeius Magnus] (106–48 BCE), Roman statesman, general. Pompey's early success in the Sulla's Second Civil War as a general quickly earned his position as council of the Roman Republic. Soon after, he joined the First Triumvirate, a mutually beneficial political alliance with Marcus Licinius Crassus and Julius Caesar. Eventually the alliance dissolved as Pompey joined the conservative Roman Senate against Caesar. The conflict erupted into the Great Roman Civil War (49–45 BCE). Defeated at the Battle of Pharsalus, Pompey fled to Egypt where he was assassinated. The end of the civil war would mark the conversion of the Roman Republic to the Roman Empire (EPM, 6.26; appendix 4.10).

Pope, Alexander (1688–1744), English poet, satirist. Pope is noted in history for his poems *An Essay on Criticism* and *An Essay on Man,* as well as his English translations of Homer's *Iliad* and the *Odyssey*. His *Essay on Man* developed a system of ethics challenging anthropocentricism by arguing that humanity must seek salvation from sin and lead virtuous lives caught between the moral goodness of angels and the depravity of animals in the "Great Chain of Being" (Essay 2:1n2).

Pyrrhus (319/318–272 BCE), king of Epirus (306–302 and 297–272) and Macedonia (288–284 and 273–272), Greek general and statesman. He is the namesake of the term "Pyrrhic Victory" as some of his battles, although successful, suffered great losses. Pyrrhus was killed during the Siege of Sparta (Essay 8.11).

Quintilian [Marcus Fabius Quintilianus] (35–96 CE), Roman rhetorician, teacher. Quintilian was the first salaried teacher of Latin rhetoric and worked under the reign of Roman emperors Titus and Domitian. His greatest work, *Institutio oratoria,* critiqued contemporary educational theory with reference both to good judgment and practical experience. It placed particular emphasis on the importance of shaping moral character during a child's development and adjusting pedagogy to fit the particular strengths of the student (EPM, 5.38n29, 8.10n63; Essay 6.24).

Quintus [Quintus Curtius Rufus] (d. 53 CE), Roman historian. Little is known about the life of Quintus except that he was the author of *Histories of Alexander the Great,* a collection of 123 manuscripts that have only partially survived but included works from the Alexander Romance genre, which were popular in Italy until the Renaissance (Essay 6.32n38; Essay 9.1n55).

Rapin, Paul de (1661–1725), French historian. A military captain early in life, de Rapin fought in the Williamite War in Ireland and defended the future King William III. On retirement he wrote a work of English history for the British monarchy, spanning ancient Britain and in some detail the period 1724–27 (Essay 10.39).

Rochefoucauld [François VI, Duc de La Rochefoucauld, Prince de Marcillac] (1613–1680), French author. He wrote in maxims that largely concerned emotions, politics, and pride. His style was emulated by later philosophers, including Friedrich Nietzsche (EPM, appendix 4.3n77).

Rosaces. Persian commander under Artaxerxes I of Persia (Essay 2.10n8).

Sallust [Gaius Sallustius Crispus] (86–35 BCE), Roman historian, statesman. Although he was not born into the ruling class, Sallust served in the Roman Senate. Ousted likely because of his populist political positions, he found an ally in Julius Caesar and was placed in a position as commander of a military legion during the civil war against Pompey. Many of Sallust's writings explore themes of violence, political rivalry, and corruption. What remains of his *Histories* describe events in Rome between 78 and 67 BCE (EPM, 6.26n42, appendix 4.6; Essay 8.12).

Sannazarius, Jacopo [Jacopo Sannazaro] (1458–1530), Italian poet. Sannazarius's elegant, masterful poem *Arcadia* remained popular and influential in Italy until the Romantic movement. Alternating between prose and verse, it is a pastoral romance; the central character, Sincero, yearns to leave the city of Naples and join the shepherd-poets of Arcadia. He discovers the death of his lover on his journey home (EPM, 5.29).

Scipio [Publius Cornelius Scipio Africanus] (236–183 BC), Roman general, statesman. Scipio defeated Hannibal, ending the Second Punic War. Considered one of the greatest Roman generals, he was the first to expand outside of Italy (EPM, 6.9; Dialogue 36).

Seneca, Lucius Annaeus (4–65 CE), Roman philosopher, statesman, orator, tragedian. A tutor for the young soon-to-be emperor Nero, Seneca was a leading Roman intellectual. His first public speech, presented by Nero, defended the freedoms of the Senate and denounced what Seneca saw as the excessive political power of women and freedmen. With his political ally Brutus, however, he instituted some populist economic and judicial reforms to benefit Romans and supported humane treatment of slaves. During his lifetime, he studied natural science and philosophy and wrote a political skit and several tragedies. His works address themes ranging from scientific observations to reflections on mourning, anger, and morality (EPM, 5.40, appendix 2.13n73, appendix 4.20n89; Essay 8.6).

Servilia (1st century BCE), Roman aristocrat. Servilia is remembered both as Julius Caesar's mistress and as Marcus Brutus's mother, who would ultimately murder Caesar. Both powerful and clever, Servilia received from Caesar several estates won from the civil wars (Essay 8.6).

Severus [Lucius Septimius Severus Pertinax] (145–211 CE), Roman emperor (193–211 CE). On the murder of Publius Helvius Pertinax by the Praetorian Guards in 193 CE, Severus marched through Rome for vengeance. His own troops then proclaimed him emperor. During his time as emperor, he replaced the guard with his own, executed many senators that supported his political enemy, invaded and annexed Mesopotamia, and ruled the empire as a military monarch with absolute power (Essay 9.1; Essay 10.42).

Sextus Empiricus (3rd century CE), Greek philosopher, historian. In his major works *Outlines of Pyrrhonism* and *Against the Mathematicians* he articulated arguments for "suspended judgment" and history of thought in the Greek movement of Skepticism, doubting the reliability of induction. His *Outlines* had lasting influence on the debates within European philosophy from the seventeenth to eighteenth centuries (EPM, 2.15n9; 4.5n19).

Shaftesbury, Lord [Anthony Ashley Cooper, 3rd Earl of Shaftesbury] (1671–1713), English politician, philosopher. A pupil of John Locke, the 3rd Earl of Shaftesbury argued against the Christian doctrine of the Fall and the Lockean state of nature, defending instead humanity's natural moral conscience. He was an early English deist whose Neoplatonist views of religion and the arts articulated in his *Characteristics of Men, Manners, Opinions, Times* influenced thinkers like Alexander Pope and Immanuel Kant (EPM, 1.4).

Socrates (470–399 BCE), Greek philosopher. While it is difficult to separate out Plato's contributions to the dialogues, Socrates used a dialectical method to explore controversial moral and political positions. He believed that a life worth living was one that pursued moral virtue above all else, and some writers attribute Socrates to criticism of Athenian democracy (EPM, 7.17, 25; 8.10; Dialogue 17; Essay 10.47).

Solomon (d. 931 BCE), king of Israel (970–931 BCE). Referred to in both the Hebrew Bible and in the Qur'an, Solomon's succession to the throne of Israel came with conflict from his older brother Adonijah. Through his methods of resolving internal strife, he is remembered as Solomon the Wise (EPM, appendix 4.14).

Soranus [Quintus Marcius Barea Soranus] (1st century CE), Roman senator. Soranus came into conflict with Emperor Nero for failing to impose the imperial religion on a city after its sacking. This caused internal strife for Soranus that ultimately led to his suicide (EPM, 5.34).

Spenser, Edmund (1552/1553–1599), English poet. Spenser is the author of *The Faerie Queene,* which introduced a form of verse known as Spenserian Stanza. *The Faerie Queene* contained multiple levels of theme and allegory, focusing on virtue and contemporary society (EPM, 7.15n57).

Spinola, Ambrogio di Filippo (1569–1630), Spanish military officer. Appointed a Spanish commander after his impressive victory against a Dutch commander, Spinola mastered siege warfare and successfully negotiated a twelve-year truce during Spain's war against the Netherlands. His military skill is remembered best from his capture of the Dutch fortress of Breda, which became the subject of Velazquez's famous painting *The Surrender of Breda* (EPM, 8.9).

Spithridates (4th century BCE), Persian satrap, military officer. Spithridates was a Persian commander during the Battle of Granicus against Alexander the Great. Ultimately defeated in that battle and killed by another commander, Spithridates was able to stun Alexander with a blow from his axe. During his lifetime, he was also a satrap of Lydia and Ionia under King Darius III of Persia (Essay 2.10n8).

Strabo (63 BCE–24 CE), Greek geographer, historian, philosopher. Strabo's *Geography* covers the history of Greece and Rome during Augustus's reign, from 27 to 14 BCE. Throughout the work, he includes several references to contemporary Greek geography and relates those countries to their histories with his anthropological style. To inspire and inform his studies in geography and history Strabo traveled extensively throughout the Mediterranean and Near East (Essay 6.7n29; Essay 9.1n56).

Suetonius [Gaius Suetonius Tranquillus] (69–122 CE), Roman author. A highly capable, clear writer, Suetonius's works explore the development of civil service, Greek culture and life, and the history of Roman entertainment. His *Concerning Illustrious Men* contains biographies of famous Roman historians, poets, and orators, but he was most popular for his *Lives of the Caesars,* which includes gossip concerning the first eleven Roman emperors (EPM, 5.34, Dialogue 15n91; Essay 2.9n4; Essay 5.13n26).

Swift, Jonathan (1667–1745), Anglo-Irish author, clergyman. Swift is the author of the famous *Gulliver's Travels* (1726), which satirizes human pride in endeavors of war, politics, and the search for immortality, among others. Many of his works were first written under pseudonyms but his reputation as a master satirist and impressive poet means he was identified during his lifetime (EPM, 6.8).

Tacitus, Gaius Cornelius (56–120 CE), Roman senator, historian. Considered one of the greatest Latin historians and prose stylists, his works explore three approaches to Greek historiography: as a straightforward analysis of events, by developing historical characters to set a scene, and through dramatic interpretation. Tacitus learned this style of political interpretation from Sallust and demonstrated his mastery in his works, including *Germania,* which describes the history of Germanic tribes, and his histories of the Roman Empire, *Annals* and *Histories* (EPM, 5.34, 7.9n51, 13n54; Essay 1.3; Essay 2.9n3,4; Essay 6.24n34; Essay 9.31).

Temple, Sir William (1628–1699), English statesman, diplomat. Temple, as a diplomat during the reign of Charles II, was instrumental in negotiating the Triple Alliance among England, Sweden, and the Netherlands in 1666, though England would soon after declare war against the Netherlands. In 1674 he successfully instituted a treaty that ended the Dutch War. During this time he wrote several essays including *Observations upon the United Provinces,* which expresses his sympathy for the interests of those in foreign countries and would later influence his secretary Jonathan Swift (Essay 6.27n36).

Themistocles (524–459 BCE), Greek politician, general. A non-aristocratic politician, Themistocles worked to build the naval capabilities of Athens. He served as one of the Athenian generals at the Battle of Marathon (490 BCE) (EPM, Dialogue 16).

Thrasea [Publius Clodius Thrasea Paetus] (1st century CE), Roman senator, Stoic. Appointed consul in 56 CE, much of Thrasea's political life was preoccupied with his public opposition to the emperor Nero and his vices. In 66 CE Nero was persuaded to execute Thrasea because of his influence on the rival political party. Anticipating his fate, Thrasea committed suicide, leading some to draw parallels between his actions and Cato the Younger's similar suicide as described in Thrasea's biography (EPM, 5.34).

Thucydides (5th century BCE), Greek historian, political philosopher, general. Remembered as the greatest historian of ancient Greece, Thucydides authored the *History of the Peloponnesian War.* There he included an analysis of wartime policies, making it one of the first attempts at historical scholarship. He used remarkably high standards in gathering evidence, and his analysis did not include references to Greek mythology unlike works by his contemporaries. In other works he developed political realism as a theory to describe the way individuals make political decisions in response to self-interest and fear, and described other aspects of human nature through the lens of Sophism (EPM, 5.33; 7.15n56, 25; Essay 7.7n41).

Tiberius [Tiberius Caesar Augustus] (42 BCE–37 CE), Roman emperor (14–37 CE). The tyrannical second emperor of Rome, Tiberius was Augustus's adopted son and came to power at the age of fifty-four. A strong, skilled general, he led conquests to expand the northern border, though his personality was dark, brooding, and derisive (EPM, 5.34; Essay 2.9; Essay 5.13n26; Essay 9.1; Essay 10.25, 40).

Tigellinus, Ofonius (1st century CE), Roman official. Tigellinus was Emperor Nero's chief advisor (62–68 CE), rising from prefect of the

Praetorian Guard. Considered cruel and irresponsible, his relationship with the emperor negatively influenced Nero's behavior, which led to popular rebellions and ultimately the emperor's suicide (EPM, 5.40).

Timæus (350–264 BCE), Greek historian. Expelled from Sicily by Agathocles's conquest to impose a democratic constitution, Timæus traveled to Athens and studied rhetoric. His great work *Sicilian History* was the first Greek version of Roman history chronologically from its beginnings to the Punic War and Agathocles's death. Criticized during his lifetime by other historians, Timæus nonetheless researched records carefully and purposely integrated myths, which offered additional context for his readers (EPM, appendix 4.19).

Timon (b. 431 BCE), Athenian misanthrope who lived during the Peloponnesian War. Timon was made into a literary figure by Aristophanes and later William Shakespeare in a play that was once titled *The History of Timon of Athens, The Man-Hater* (EPM, 5.40; 6.21n40).

Titus Flamininus [Titus Quinctius Flamininus] (c. 229–c. 174 BCE), Roman politician, general. He defeated Philip V of Macedon in the Second Macedonian War in the Battle of the Auos. In 183 BCE, he attempted to secure the capture of Hannibal, who committed suicide to avoid it (Essay 10.3).

Trajan (53–117 CE), Roman emperor (98–117 CE). Emperor Trajan was known for his expansion of Roman territory to its zenith while also building infrastructure and social welfare policies. This gained him the reputation of one of the Five Good Emperors (Essay 10.3).

Turenne [Henri de La Tour d'Auvergne Vicomte de Turenne] (1611–1675), French military commander. Considered by Napoleon as history's greatest military leader, Turenne commanded the French royal armies during Louis XIV's reign including the Thirty Years' War, the civil war of the Fronde, the invasion of the Netherlands, and the third Dutch War. He achieved several strategic victories during his life that earned him enduring fame (EPM, 6.9).

Tygranes [Tigranes II] (140–55 BCE), king of Armenia (95–55 BCE). During Tygranes's rule, Armenia quickly grew in strength by the annexation of Sophene, northern Mesopotamia, and part of the Parthian Empire, dominating eastern Rome for a short period. Giving himself the title of "king of kings," Tygranes built the royal city of Tigranocerta with citizens from Cilcia and Syria. In 66 BCE he surrendered to the Roman general Pompey (Essay 2.10n8).

Vegetius [Publius Falvius Vegetius Renatus] (4th century CE), Roman military scholar, author. His treatise *De re militari* became the single most influential work in European military history and on European tactics at the end of the Middle Ages. His emphasis on sieges and the importance of a disciplined infantry were often referenced, though part of his readership was likely due to the fact he was the first Roman Christian to write about military tactics (EPM, 6.26n42).

Verres, Gaius (115–43 BCE), Roman magistrate. A notoriously corrupt Sicilian governor, among his misdeeds he accepted bribes, stole art, and executed citizens to build his political power. Pressured by public backlash, Cicero prosecuted Verres and gave a speech titled *Verrines,* which organized evidence for corruption within the Senate and informed later scholars about late Roman Republic administration (EPM, appendix 1.16; Essay 2.9).

Vespasian [Caesar Vespasianus Augustus] (9–79 CE), Roman emperor (69–79 CE), victor of the Year of Four Emperors. From a modest family, at first Vespasian was a successful military general during Nero's reign. He won campaigns across Judea and fought battles until Nero's death, when he turned his attention to his political rivals and became emperor. His rule was characterized by his goal to stabilize Rome through consolidating its territory, instituting tax reforms, and initiating construction projects (Essay 6.24; Essay 9.1).

Virgil [Publius Vergilius Maro] (70–19 BCE), Roman poet. Considered Rome's greatest poet, Virgil built his reputation for intricate, skilled verse from his national epic, the *Aeneid.* It describes the founding of Rome by a Trojan refugee, Aeneas, as he follows his divine fate to travel to Italy (EPM 6.24, 7.27, appendix 2.13n73; Essay 7.21n47).

Vitellius, Aulus (15–69 CE), third Roman emperor during the Year of Four Emperors (69 CE). Despite his army's opposition to emperor Galba, as imperial governor of Lower Germany Vitellius was able to win their allegiance and in 69 CE his men proclaimed him emperor. Months later he was defeated and executed at the Second Battle of Bedriacum by a rival legion (EPM, 7.9).

Voltaire (1694–1778), French philosopher, historian, author. Acknowledged as perhaps the greatest French writer in history, Voltaire's work demonstrates his wit and command of satire. As a freethinker and outspoken deist, he advocated for the separation of church and state and freedom of religion and expression, and criticized the Catholic Church (Essay 1.3n1).

Note on the Texts

Hume's *An Enquiry Concerning the Principles of Morals* (EPM) was first published in 1751. The last edition that was seen through press with Hume's supervision was published in 1772, and the last with his changes is the posthumous 1777 edition. The copytext of the *Enquiry Concerning the Principles of Morals* in this book is based on a photocopy of a 1912 reprint of the posthumous 1777 edition of Hume's *Essays and Treatises on Several Subjects*. To ensure accuracies in the text we consulted Project Gutenberg's version of the 1777 text (http://www.gutenberg.org/files/4320/4320-h/4320-h.htm) and the edition at davidhume.org (http://www.davidhume.org/texts/epm.html), which likewise reproduces the 1777 edition. A scanned copy of the original edition held at Eighteenth Century Collections Online (ECCO) has also been consulted.

All of the essays that appear in this edition grouped together as "Essays, Moral, Political and Literary" are from the 1777 edition of the *Essays and Treatises on Several Subjects.* To ensure accuracies we consulted Project Gutenberg's version of the text, the edition at davidhume.org (http://www.davidhume.org/texts/etv1.html), and Eugene Miller's Liberty Fund edition of the *Essays, Moral, Political and Literary* (1985). The scanned copy of the original edition held at ECCO has again been consulted.

The spelling and punctuation have not been modernized. The italics and original spellings of words have been preserved. A few adaptations from the original text have been made, and some of the original printer's conventions have been altered. For example, the eighteenth-century long "s" has been replaced with a regular "s." Ligatures that join letter combinations, such as "ct" and "fi," have been removed. The combinations "æ" and "œ," however, have been preserved. We also have changed the roman numerals associated with each section in the *Enquiry,* and with each essay, to Arabic numbers. In addition we have numbered each paragraph in Hume's *Enquiry* and the essays to facilitate referencing.

In the footnotes, all of the editorial annotations are marked by square brackets. These editorial notes fill out some of Hume's own textual citations, explain some of the more obscure words and events to which he refers, and provide translations of passages. The editorial notes are indebted to T. L. Beauchamp's Oxford critical edition of the *Enquiry Concerning the Principles of Morals* and Miller's edition of the *Essays, Moral, Political and Literary.* All translations in EPM are based on those in Beauchamp's critical edition.

Texts

An Enquiry Concerning the Principles of Morals

SECTION I

Of the General Principles of Morals

1.   DISPUTES with men, pertinaciously obstinate in their principles, are, of all others, the most irksome; except, perhaps, those with persons, entirely disingenuous, who really do not believe the opinions they defend, but engage in the controversy, from affectation, from a spirit of opposition, or from a desire of showing wit and ingenuity, superior to the rest of mankind. The same blind adherence to their own arguments is to be expected in both; the same contempt of their antagonists; and the same passionate vehemence, in enforcing sophistry and falsehood. And as reasoning is not the source, whence either disputant derives his tenets; it is in vain to expect, that any logic, which speaks not to the affections, will ever engage him to embrace sounder principles.

2.   Those who have denied the reality of moral distinctions, may be ranked among the disingenuous disputants; nor is it conceivable, that any human creature could ever seriously believe, that all characters and actions were alike entitled to the affection and regard of every one. The difference, which nature has placed between one man and another, is so wide, and this difference is still so much farther widened, by education, example, and habit, that, where the opposite extremes come at once under our apprehension, there is no scepticism so scrupulous, and scarce any assurance so determined, as absolutely to deny all distinction between them. Let a man's insensibility be ever so great, he must often be touched with the images of RIGHT and WRONG; and let his prejudices be ever so obstinate, he must observe, that others are susceptible of like impressions. The only way, therefore, of converting an antagonist of this kind, is to leave him to himself. For, finding that nobody keeps up the controversy with him, it is probable he will, at last, of himself, from mere weariness, come over to the side of common sense and reason.

3.   There has been a controversy started of late, much better worth examination, concerning the general foundation of MORALS; whether they be derived from REASON, or from SENTIMENT; whether we attain the knowledge of them by a chain of argument and induction, or by an immediate feeling and finer internal sense; whether, like all sound judgment of truth and falsehood, they should be the same to every rational intelligent being; or whether, like the perception of beauty and deformity, they be founded entirely on the particular fabric and constitution of the human species.

4.   The ancient philosophers, though they often affirm, that virtue is nothing but conformity to reason, yet, in general, seem to consider morals as deriving their existence from taste and sentiment. On the other hand, our modern enquirers, though they also talk much of the beauty of virtue, and deformity of vice, yet have commonly endeavoured to account for these distinctions by metaphysical reasonings, and by deductions from the most abstract principles of the understanding. Such confusion reigned in these subjects, that an opposition of the greatest consequence could prevail between one system and another, and even in the parts of almost each individual system; and yet nobody, till very lately, was ever sensible of it. The elegant Lord SHAFTESBURY, who first gave occasion to remark this distinction, and who, in general, adhered to the principles of the ancients, is not, himself, entirely free from the same confusion.

5.   It must be acknowledged, that both sides of the question are susceptible of specious arguments. Moral distinctions, it may be said, are discernible by pure *reason:* else, whence the many disputes that reign in common life, as well as in philosophy, with regard to this subject: the long chain of proofs often produced on both sides; the examples cited, the authorities appealed to, the analogies employed, the fallacies detected, the inferences drawn, and the several conclusions adjusted to their proper principles. Truth is disputable; not taste: what exists in the nature of things is the standard of our judgment; what each man feels within himself is the standard of sentiment. Propositions in geometry may be proved, systems in physics may be controverted; but the harmony of verse, the tenderness of passion, the brilliancy of wit, must give immediate pleasure. No man reasons concerning another's beauty; but frequently concerning the justice or injustice of his actions. In every criminal trial the first object of the prisoner is to disprove the facts alleged, and deny the actions imputed to him: the second to prove, that, even if these actions were real, they might be justified, as innocent and lawful. It is confessedly by deductions of the understanding, that the first point is ascertained: how can we suppose that a different faculty of the mind is employed in fixing the other?

6.   On the other hand, those who would resolve all moral determinations into *sentiment,* may endeavour to show, that it is impossible for reason ever to draw conclusions of this nature. To virtue, say they, it belongs to be *amiable,* and vice *odious.* This forms their very nature or essence. But can reason or argumentation distribute these different epithets to any subjects, and pronounce before-hand, that this must produce love, and that hatred? Or what other reason can we ever assign for these affections, but the original fabric and formation of the human mind, which is naturally adapted to receive them?

7.   The end of all moral speculations is to teach us our duty; and, by proper representations of the deformity of vice and beauty of virtue, beget correspondent habits, and engage us to avoid the one, and embrace the other. But is this ever to be expected from inferences and conclusions of the understanding, which of themselves have no hold of the affections or set in motion the active powers of men? They discover truths: But where the truths which they discover are indifferent, and beget no desire or aversion, they can have no influence on conduct and behaviour. What is honourable, what is fair, what is becoming, what is noble, what is generous, takes possession of the heart, and animates us to embrace and maintain it. What is intelligible, what is evident, what is probable, what is true, procures only the cool assent of the understanding; and gratifying a speculative curiosity, puts an end to our researches.

8.   Extinguish all the warm feelings and prepossessions in favour of virtue, and all disgust or aversion to vice: Render men totally indifferent towards these distinctions; and morality is no longer a practical study, nor has any tendency to regulate our lives and actions.

9.   These arguments on each side (and many more might be produced) are so plausible, that I am apt to suspect, they may, the one as well as the other, be solid and satisfactory, and that *reason* and *sentiment* concur in almost all moral determinations and conclusions. The final sentence, it is probable, which pronounces characters and actions amiable or odious, praise-worthy or blameable; that which stamps on them the mark of honour or infamy, approbation or censure; that which renders morality an active principle and constitutes virtue our happiness, and vice our misery; It is probable, I say, that this final sentence depends on some internal sense or feeling, which nature has made universal in the whole species. For what else can have an influence of this nature? But in order to pave the way for such a sentiment, and give a proper discernment of its object, it is often necessary, we find, that much reasoning should precede, that nice distinctions be made, just conclusions drawn, distant comparisons formed, complicated relations

examined, and general facts fixed and ascertained. Some species of beauty, especially the natural kinds, on their first appearance, command our affection and approbation; and where they fail of this effect, it is impossible for any reasoning to redress their influence, or adapt them better to our taste and sentiment. But in many orders of beauty, particularly those of the finer arts, it is requisite to employ much reasoning, in order to feel the proper sentiment; and a false relish may frequently be corrected by argument and reflection. There are just grounds to conclude, that moral beauty partakes much of this latter species, and demands the assistance of our intellectual faculties, in order to give it a suitable influence on the human mind.

10.   But though this question, concerning the general principles of morals, be curious and important, it is needless for us, at present, to employ farther care in our researches concerning it. For if we can be so happy, in the course of this enquiry, as to discover the true origin of morals, it will then easily appear how far either sentiment or reason enters into all determinations of this nature.[1] In order to attain this purpose, we shall endeavour to follow a very simple method: we shall analyze that complication of mental qualities, which form what, in common life, we call PERSONAL MERIT: we shall consider every attribute of the mind, which renders a man an object either of esteem and affection, or of hatred and contempt; every habit or sentiment or faculty, which, if ascribed to any person, implies either praise or blame, and may enter into any panegyric or satire[2] of his character and manners. The quick sensibility, which, on this head, is so universal among mankind, gives a philosopher sufficient assurance, that he can never be considerably mistaken in framing the catalogue, or incur any danger of misplacing the objects of his contemplation: he needs only enter into his own breast for a moment, and consider whether or not he should desire to have this or that quality ascribed to him, and whether such or such an imputation would proceed from a friend or an enemy. The very nature of language guides us almost infallibly in forming a judgment of this nature; and as every tongue possesses one set of words which are taken in a good sense, and another in the opposite, the least acquaintance with the idiom suffices, without any reasoning, to direct us in collecting and arranging the estimable or blameable qualities of men. The only object of reasoning is to discover the circumstances on both sides, which are common to these qualities; to observe that particular in which the estimable qualities agree on the one hand, and the blameable on the other; and thence to reach the

1. See Appendix 1.
2. [Commendation or scorn.]

foundation of ethics, and find those universal principles, from which all censure or approbation is ultimately derived. As this is a question of fact, not of abstract science, we can only expect success, by following the experimental method, and deducing general maxims from a comparison of particular instances. The other scientific method, where a general abstract principle is first established, and is afterwards branched out into a variety of inferences and conclusions, may be more perfect in itself, but suits less the imperfection of human nature, and is a common source of illusion and mistake in this as well as in other subjects. Men are now cured of their passion for hypotheses and systems in natural philosophy, and will hearken to no arguments but those which are derived from experience. It is full time they should attempt a like reformation in all moral disquisitions; and reject every system of ethics, however subtle or ingenious, which is not founded on fact and observation.

11. We shall begin our enquiry on this head by the consideration of the social virtues, benevolence and justice. The explication of them will probably give us an opening by which the others may be accounted for.

SECTION 2

Of Benevolence

Part I

1. IT may be esteemed, perhaps, a superfluous task to prove, that the benevolent or softer affections are ESTIMABLE; and wherever they appear, engage the approbation and good-will of mankind. The epithets *sociable, good-natured, humane, merciful, grateful, friendly, generous, beneficent,* or their equivalents, are known in all languages, and universally express the highest merit, which *human nature* is capable of attaining. Where these amiable qualities are attended with birth and power and eminent abilities, and display themselves in the good government or useful instruction of mankind, they seem even to raise the possessors of them above the rank of *human nature,* and make them approach in some measure to the divine. Exalted capacity, undaunted courage, prosperous success; these may only expose a hero or politician to the envy and ill-will of the public: but as soon as the praises are added of humane and beneficent; when instances are displayed of lenity, tenderness or friendship; envy itself is silent, or joins the general voice of approbation and applause.

2. When PERICLES, the great ATHENIAN statesman and general, was on his death-bed, his surrounding friends, deeming him now insensible, began to indulge their sorrow for their expiring patron, by enumerating his great qualities and successes, his conquests and victories, the unusual length of his administration, and his nine trophies erected over the enemies of the republic. *"You forget,"* cries the dying hero, who had heard all, *"you forget the most eminent of my praises, while you dwell so much on those vulgar advantages, in which fortune had a principal share. You have not observed, that no citizen has ever yet worne mourning on my account."*[3]

3. PLUTARCH in PERICLE. [Plutarch, *Lives,* "Pericles," chapter 38.]

3.   In men of more ordinary talents and capacity, the social virtues become, if possible, still more essentially requisite; there being nothing
eminent, in that case, to compensate for the want of them, or preserve the
person from our severest hatred, as well as contempt. A high ambition, an
elevated courage, is apt, says CICERO, in less perfect characters, to degenerate into a turbulent ferocity. The more social and softer virtues are there
chiefly to be regarded. These are always good and amiable.[4]

4.   The principal advantage, which JUVENAL discovers in the extensive
capacity of the human species, is that it renders our benevolence also more
extensive, and gives us larger opportunities of spreading our kindly influence than what are indulged to the inferior creation.[5] It must, indeed, be
confessed, that by doing good only, can a man truly enjoy the advantages
of being eminent. His exalted station, of itself but the more exposes him
to danger and tempest. His sole prerogative is to afford shelter to inferiors,
who repose themselves under his cover and protection.

5.   But I forget, that it is not my present business to recommend generosity and benevolence, or to paint, in their true colours, all the genuine charms
of the social virtues. These, indeed, sufficiently engage every heart, on the
first apprehension of them; and it is difficult to abstain from some sally of
panegyric,[6] as often as they occur in discourse or reasoning. But our object
here being more the speculative, than the practical part of morals, it will
suffice to remark, (what will readily, I believe, be allowed) that no qualities
are more entitled to the general good-will and approbation of mankind than
beneficence and humanity, friendship and gratitude, natural affection and
public spirit, or whatever proceeds from a tender sympathy with others,
and a generous concern for our kind and species. These wherever they appear seem to transfuse themselves, in a manner, into each beholder, and to
call forth, in their own behalf, the same favourable and affectionate sentiments, which they exert on all around.

Part 2

6.   We may observe that, in displaying the praises of any humane, beneficent man, there is one circumstance which never fails to be amply

---

4. CIC. de Officiis, lib. 1. [Cicero, *De officiis,* book 1, chapter 19.]
5. Sat. 15. 139 and seq. [Juvenal, *Satires* 15, lines 139–47.]
6. [An issuance of praise.]

insisted on, namely, the happiness and satisfaction, derived to society from his intercourse and good offices. To his parents, we are apt to say, he endears himself by his pious attachment and duteous care still more than by the connexions of nature. His children never feel his authority, but when employed for their advantage. With him, the ties of love are consolidated by beneficence and friendship. The ties of friendship approach, in a fond observance of each obliging office, to those of love and inclination. His domestics and dependents have in him a sure resource; and no longer dread the power of fortune, but so far as she exercises it over him. From him the hungry receive food, the naked clothing, the ignorant and slothful skill and industry. Like the sun, an inferior minister of providence he cheers, invigorates, and sustains the surrounding world.

7.   If confined to private life, the sphere of his activity is narrower; but his influence is all benign and gentle. If exalted into a higher station, mankind and posterity reap the fruit of his labours.

8.   As these topics of praise never fail to be employed, and with success, where we would inspire esteem for any one; may it not thence be concluded, that the UTILITY, resulting from the social virtues, forms, at least, a *part* of their merit, and is one source of that approbation and regard so universally paid to them?

9.   When we recommend even an animal or a plant as *useful* and *beneficial,* we give it an applause and recommendation suited to its nature. As, on the other hand, reflection on the baneful influence of any of these inferior beings always inspires us with the sentiment of aversion. The eye is pleased with the prospect of corn-fields and loaded vine-yards; horses grazing, and flocks pasturing: But flies the view of briars and brambles, affording shelter to wolves and serpents.

10.   A machine, a piece of furniture, a vestment, a house well contrived for use and conveniency, is so far beautiful, and is contemplated with pleasure and approbation. An experienced eye is here sensible to many excellencies, which escape persons ignorant and uninstructed.

11.   Can any thing stronger be said in praise of a profession, such as merchandize or manufacture, than to observe the advantages which it procures to society? And is not a monk and inquisitor[7] enraged when we treat his order as useless or pernicious to mankind?

---

7. [A monk who was also part of the tribunal of the Roman Catholic Inquisition.]

12. The historian exults in displaying the benefit arising from his labours. The writer of romance alleviates or denies the bad consequences ascribed to his manner of composition.

13. In general, what praise is implied in the simple epithet *useful!* What reproach in the contrary!

14. Your Gods, says CICERO,[8] in opposition to the EPICUREANS, cannot justly claim any worship or adoration, with whatever imaginary perfections you may suppose them endowed. They are totally useless and inactive. Even the EGYPTIANS, whom you so much ridicule, never consecrated any animal but on account of its utility.

15. The sceptics assert,[9] though absurdly, that the origin of all religious worship was derived from the utility of inanimate objects, as the sun and moon, to the support and well-being of mankind. This is also the common reason assigned by historians, for the deification of eminent heroes and legislators.[10]

16. To plant a tree, to cultivate a field, to beget children; meritorious acts, according to the religion of ZOROASTER.

17. In all determinations of morality, this circumstance of public utility is ever principally in view; and wherever disputes arise, either in philosophy or common life, concerning the bounds of duty, the question cannot, by any means, be decided with greater certainty, than by ascertaining, on any side, the true interests of mankind. If any false opinion, embraced from appearances, has been found to prevail; as soon as farther experience and sounder reasoning have given us juster notions of human affairs, we retract our first sentiment, and adjust anew the boundaries of moral good and evil.

18. Giving alms to common beggars is naturally praised; because it seems to carry relief to the distressed and indigent: but when we observe the encouragement thence arising to idleness and debauchery, we regard that species of charity rather as a weakness than a virtue.

19. *Tyrannicide,* or the assassination of usurpers and oppressive princes, was highly extolled in ancient times; because it both freed mankind from many of these monsters, and seemed to keep the others in awe, whom the sword or poinard could not reach. But history and experience having

---

8. De Nat. Deor. lib. 1. [Cicero, *De natura deorum,* book 1, chapter 36.]

9. SEXT. EMP. adversus mathem. lib. 9. [Sextus Empiricus, *Against the Physicists,* book 1 (*Adversus mathematicos,* book 9).]

10. DIOD. SIC. passim. [Diodorus Siculus, *Historical Library,* book 4, chapters 1–2.]

since convinced us, that this practice increases the jealousy and cruelty of princes, a TIMOLEON and a BRUTUS, though treated with indulgence on account of the prejudices of their times, are now considered as very improper models for imitation.

20. Liberality in princes is regarded as a mark of beneficence, but when it occurs, that the homely bread of the honest and industrious is often thereby converted into delicious cates for the idle and the prodigal, we soon retract our heedless praises. The regrets of a prince, for having lost a day, were noble and generous: but had he intended to have spent it in acts of generosity to his greedy courtiers, it was better lost than misemployed after that manner.

21. Luxury, or a refinement on the pleasures and conveniences of life, had not long been supposed the source of every corruption in government, and the immediate cause of faction, sedition, civil wars, and the total loss of liberty. It was, therefore, universally regarded as a vice, and was an object of declamation to all satirists, and severe moralists. Those, who prove, or attempt to prove, that such refinements rather tend to the increase of industry, civility, and arts regulate anew our *moral* as well as *political* sentiments, and represent, as laudable or innocent, what had formerly been regarded as pernicious and blameable.

22. Upon the whole, then, it seems undeniable, *that* nothing can bestow more merit on any human creature than the sentiment of benevolence in an eminent degree; and *that* a *part,* at least, of its merit arises from its tendency to promote the interests of our species, and bestow happiness on human society. We carry our view into the salutary consequences of such a character and disposition; and whatever has so benign an influence, and forwards so desirable an end, is beheld with complacency and pleasure. The social virtues are never regarded without their beneficial tendencies, nor viewed as barren and unfruitful. The happiness of mankind, the order of society, the harmony of families, the mutual support of friends, are always considered as the result of their gentle dominion over the breasts of men.

23. How considerable a *part* of their merit we ought to ascribe to their utility, will better appear from future disquisitions;[11] as well as the reason, why this circumstance has such a command over our esteem and approbation.[12]

11. Section 3d and 4th.
12. Section 5th.

SECTION 3
Of Justice

Part I

1. THAT justice is useful to society, and consequently that *part* of its merit, at least, must arise from that consideration, it would be a superfluous undertaking to prove. That public utility is the *sole* origin of justice, and that reflections on the beneficial consequences of this virtue are the *sole* foundation of its merit; this proposition, being more curious and important, will better deserve our examination and enquiry.

2. Let us suppose that nature has bestowed on the human race such profuse *abundance* of all *external* conveniencies, that, without any uncertainty in the event, without any care or industry on our part, every individual finds himself fully provided with whatever his most voracious appetites can want, or luxurious imagination wish or desire. His natural beauty, we shall suppose, surpasses all acquired ornaments: The perpetual clemency of the seasons renders useless all cloathes or covering: The raw herbage affords him the most delicious fare; the clear fountain, the richest beverage. No laborious occupation required: No tillage: No navigation. Music, poetry, and contemplation form his sole business: Conversation, mirth, and friendship his sole amusement.

3. It seems evident that, in such a happy state, every other social virtue would flourish, and receive tenfold increase; but the cautious, jealous virtue of justice would never once have been dreamed of. For what purpose make a partition of goods, where every one has already more than enough? Why give rise to property, where there cannot possibly be any injury? Why call this object *mine,* when upon the seizing of it by another, I need but stretch out my hand to possess myself to what is equally valuable? Justice, in that case, being totally USELESS, would be an idle ceremonial, and could never possibly have place in the catalogue of virtues.

4.   We see, even in the present necessitous condition of mankind, that, wherever any benefit is bestowed by nature in an unlimited abundance, we leave it always in common among the whole human race, and make no subdivisions of right and property. Water and air, though the most necessary of all objects, are not challenged as the property of individuals; nor can any man commit injustice by the most lavish use and enjoyment of these blessings. In fertile extensive countries, with few inhabitants, land is regarded on the same footing. And no topic is so much insisted on by those, who defend the liberty of the seas, as the unexhausted use of them in navigation. Were the advantages, procured by navigation, as inexhaustible, these reasoners had never had any adversaries to refute; nor had any claims ever been advanced of a separate, exclusive dominion over the ocean.

5.   It may happen, in some countries, at some periods, that there be established a property in water, none in land;[13] if the latter be in greater abundance than can be used by the inhabitants, and the former be found, with difficulty, and in very small quantities.

6.   Again; suppose, that, though the necessities of human race continue the same as at present, yet the mind is so enlarged, and so replete with friendship and generosity, that every man has the utmost tenderness for every man, and feels no more concern for his own interest than for that of his fellows; it seems evident, that the USE of justice would, in this case, be suspended by such an extensive benevolence, nor would the divisions and barriers of property and obligation have ever been thought of. Why should I bind another, by a deed or promise, to do me any good office, when I know that he is already prompted, by the strongest inclination, to seek my happiness, and would, of himself, perform the desired service; except the hurt, he thereby receives, be greater than the benefit accruing to me? In which case, he knows, that, from my innate humanity and friendship, I should be the first to oppose myself to his imprudent generosity. Why raise landmarks between my neighbour's field and mine, when my heart has made no division between our interests; but shares all his joys and sorrows with the same force and vivacity as if originally my own? Every man, upon this supposition, being a second self to another, would trust all his interests to the discretion of every man; without jealousy, without partition, without distinction. And the whole human race would form only one family; where all would lie in common, and be used freely, without regard to property; but cautiously too, with as entire regard to the necessities of each individual, as if our own interests were most intimately concerned.

13. Genesis, chaps. 13. and 21.

7.   In the present disposition of the human heart, it would, perhaps, be difficult to find complete instances of such enlarged affections; but still we may observe, that the case of families approaches towards it; and the stronger the mutual benevolence is among the individuals, the nearer it approaches; till all distinction of property be, in a great measure, lost and confounded among them. Between married persons, the cement of friendship is by the laws supposed so strong as to abolish all division of possessions; and has often, in reality, the force ascribed to it. And it is observable, that, during the ardour of new enthusiasms, when every principle is inflamed into extravagance, the community of goods has frequently been attempted; and nothing but experience of its inconveniencies, from the returning or disguised selfishness of men, could make the imprudent fanatics adopt anew the ideas of justice and of separate property. So true is it, that this virtue derives its existence entirely from its necessary *use* to the intercourse and social state of mankind.

8.   To make this truth more evident, let us reverse the foregoing suppositions; and carrying everything to the opposite extreme, consider what would be the effect of these new situations. Suppose a society to fall into such want of all common necessaries, that the utmost frugality and industry cannot preserve the greater number from perishing, and the whole from extreme misery; It will readily, I believe, be admitted, that the strict laws of justice are suspended, in such a pressing emergence, and give place to the stronger motives of necessity and self-preservation. Is it any crime, after a shipwreck, to seize whatever means or instrument of safety one can lay hold of, without regard to former limitations of property? Or if a city besieged were perishing with hunger; can we imagine, that men will see any means of preservation before them, and lose their lives, from a scrupulous regard to what, in other situations, would be the rules of equity and justice? The USE and TENDENCY of that virtue is to procure happiness and security, by preserving order in society: But where the society is ready to perish from extreme necessity, no greater evil can be dreaded from violence and injustice; and every man may now provide for himself by all the means, which prudence can dictate, or humanity permit. The public, even in less urgent necessities, opens granaries, without the consent of proprietors; as justly supposing, that the authority of magistracy may, consistent with equity, extend so far: But were any number of men to assemble, without the tie of laws or civil jurisdiction; would an equal partition of bread in a famine, though effected by power and even violence, be regarded as criminal or injurious?

9.   Suppose likewise, that it should be a virtuous man's fate to fall into the society of ruffians, remote from the protection of laws and government;

what conduct must he embrace in that melancholy situation? He sees such a desperate rapaciousness prevail; such a disregard to equity, such contempt of order, such stupid blindness to future consequences, as must immediately have the most tragical conclusion, and must terminate in destruction to the greater number, and in a total dissolution of society to the rest. He, mean while, can have no other expedient than to arm himself, to whomever the sword he seizes, or the buckler, may belong: To make provision of all means of defence and security: And his particular regard to justice being no longer of USE to his own safety or that of others, he must consult the dictates of self-preservation alone, without concern for those who no longer merit his care and attention.

10.   When any man, even in political society, renders himself by his crimes, obnoxious to the public, he is punished by the laws in his goods and person; that is, the ordinary rules of justice are, with regard to him, suspended for a moment, and it becomes equitable to inflict on him, for the *benefit* of society, what otherwise he could not suffer without wrong or injury.

11.   The rage and violence of public war; what is it but a suspension of justice among the warring parties, who perceive, that this virtue is now no longer of any *use* or advantage to them? The laws of war, which then succeed to those of equity and justice, are rules calculated for the *advantage* and *utility* of that particular state, in which men are now placed. And were a civilized nation engaged with barbarians, who observed no rules even of war, the former must also suspend their observance of them, where they no longer serve to any purpose; and must render every action or recounter as bloody and pernicious as possible to the first aggressors.

12.   Thus, the rules of equity or justice depend entirely on the particular state and condition in which men are placed, and owe their origin and existence to that UTILITY, which results to the public from their strict and regular observance. Reverse, in any considerable circumstance, the condition of men: Produce extreme abundance or extreme necessity: Implant in the human breast perfect moderation and humanity, or perfect rapaciousness and malice: By rendering justice totally *useless,* you thereby totally destroy its essence, and suspend its obligation upon mankind.

13.   The common situation of society is a medium amidst all these extremes. We are naturally partial to ourselves, and to our friends; but are capable of learning the advantage resulting from a more equitable conduct. Few enjoyments are given us from the open and liberal hand of nature; but by art, labour, and industry, we can extract them in great abundance. Hence the ideas of property become necessary in all civil society: Hence justice

derives its usefulness to the public: And hence alone arises its merit and moral obligation.

14. These conclusions are so natural and obvious, that they have not escaped even the poets, in their descriptions of the felicity attending the golden age or the reign of SATURN.[14] The seasons, in that first period of nature, were so temperate, if we credit these agreeable fictions, that there was no necessity for men to provide themselves with clothes and houses, as a security against the violence of heat and cold: The rivers flowed with wine and milk: The oaks yielded honey; and nature spontaneously produced her greatest delicacies. Nor were these the chief advantages of that happy age. Tempests were not alone removed from nature; but those more furious tempests were unknown to human breasts, which now cause such uproar, and engender such confusion. Avarice, ambition, cruelty, selfishness, were never heard of: Cordial affection, compassion, sympathy, were the only movements with which the mind was yet acquainted. Even the punctilious distinction of *mine* and *thine* was banished from among the happy race of mortals, and carried with it the very notion of property and obligation, justice and injustice.

15. This *poetical* fiction of the *golden age,* is in some respects, of a piece with the *philosophical* fiction of the *state of nature;* only that the former is represented as the most charming and most peaceable condition, which can possibly be imagined; whereas the latter is painted out as a state of mutual war and violence, attended with the most extreme necessity. On the first origin of mankind, we are told, their ignorance and savage nature were so prevalent, that they could give no mutual trust, but must each depend upon himself and his own force or cunning for protection and security. No law was heard of: No rule of justice known: No distinction of property regarded: Power was the only measure of right; and a perpetual war of all against all was the result of men's untamed selfishness and barbarity.[15]

14. [This is a reference to the ancient legend that an ideal period, a golden age, existed on earth during the reign of Saturn.]

15. This fiction of a state of nature, as a state of war, was not first started by Mr. HOBBES, as is commonly imagined. PLATO endeavours to refute an hypothesis very like it in the second, third, and fourth books de republica. CICERO, on the contrary, supposes it certain and universally acknowledged in the following passage. "Quis enim vestrum, judices, ignorat, ita naturam rerum tulisse, ut quodam tempore homines, nondum neque naturali neque civili jure descripto, fusi per agros ac dispersi vagarentur tantumque haberent quantum manu ac viribus, per caedem ac vulnera, aut eripere aut retinere potuissent? Qui igitur primi virtute & consilio

16. Whether such a condition of human nature could ever exist, or if it did, could continue so long as to merit the appellation of a *state,* may justly be doubted. Men are necessarily born in a family-society, at least; and are trained up by their parents to some rule of conduct and behaviour. But this must be admitted, that, if such a state of mutual war and violence was ever real, the suspension of all laws of justice, from their absolute inutility, is a necessary and infallible consequence.

17. The more we vary our views of human life, and the newer and more unusual the lights are in which we survey it, the more shall we be convinced, that the origin here assigned for the virtue of justice is real and satisfactory.

18. Were there a species of creatures intermingled with men, which, though rational, were possessed of such inferior strength, both of body and mind, that they were incapable of all resistance, and could never, upon the highest provocation, make us feel the effects of their resentment; the

---

praestanti extiterunt, ii perspecto genere humanae docilitatis atque ingenii, dissipatos unum in locum congregarunt, eosque ex feritate illa ad justitiam ac mansuetudinem transduxerunt. Tum res ad communem utilitatem, quas publicas appellamus, tum conventicula hominum, quae postea civitates nominatae sunt, tum domicilia conjuncta, quas urbes dicamus, invento & divino & humano jure, moenibus sepserunt. Atque inter hanc vitam, perpolitam humanitate, & llam immanem, nihil tam interest quam jus atque vis. Horum utro uti nolimus, altero est utendum. Vim volumus extingui? Jus valeat necesse est, idi est, judicia, quibus omne jus continetur. Judicia displicent, ant nulla sunt? Vis dominetur necesse est. Haec vident omnes." Pro SEXT. sec. 42. [Hobbes, *Leviathan;* Plato, *Republic,* books 2–4; Cicero, *Pro Sestio,* chapter 42. The passage from Cicero may be translated as follows: "Which judge among you is not aware of the natural course of events? There was once a time when neither natural nor civil law had yet been defined. Mankind led a wandering existence, scattered and dispersed across the land, and possessed no more than they could seize or retain by their own hand and strength, inflicting wounds and slaughter. Those therefore who first distinguished themselves by their merit and wisdom, having observed the distinctive learning skill and natural talent of human beings brought together the scattered population into a single place, and transformed their savagery into gentleness. They established what we call the public domain, serving the common good, and created communities of people which were afterwards called states. They then linked dwellings together and surrounded them with defensive walls, having introduced both divine and human law: These were what we call cities. Between this civilized life and the previous savagery there is no clear demarcation than that between law and violence. Whichever of these we reject, we must employ the other. Do we wish to eliminate violence? Then law must prevail that is, the legal institutions within which all law is sustained. Are legal institutions not to our taste, or do they not exist? Then violence will inevitably reign. Everyone knows these things."]

necessary consequence, I think, is that we should be bound by the laws of humanity to give gentle usage to these creatures, but should not, properly speaking, lie under any restraint of justice with regard to them, nor could they possess any right or property, exclusive of such arbitrary lords. Our intercourse with them could not be called society, which supposes a degree of equality; but absolute command on the one side, and servile obedience on the other. Whatever we covet, they must instantly resign: Our permission is the only tenure, by which they hold their possessions: Our compassion and kindness the only check, by which they curb our lawless will: And as no inconvenience ever results from the exercise of a power, so firmly established in nature, the restraints of justice and property, being totally *useless,* would never have place in so unequal a confederacy.

19.   This is plainly the situation of men, with regard to animals; and how far these may be said to possess reason, I leave it to others to determine. The great superiority of civilized EUROPEANS above barbarous INDIANS, tempted us to imagine ourselves on the same footing with regard to them, and made us throw off all restraints of justice, and even of humanity, in our treatment of them. In many nations, the female sex are reduced to like slavery, and are rendered incapable of all property, in opposition to their lordly masters. But though the males, when united, have in all countries bodily force sufficient to maintain this severe tyranny, yet such are the insinuation, address, and charms of their fair companions, that women are commonly able to break the confederacy, and share with the other sex in all the rights and privileges of society.

20.   Were the human species so framed by nature as that each individual possessed within himself every faculty, requisite both for his own preservation and for the propagation of his kind: Were all society and intercourse cut off between man and man, by the primary intention of the Supreme Creator: It seems evident, that so solitary a being would be as much incapable of justice, as of social discourse and conversation. Where mutual regards and forbearance serve to no manner of purpose, they would never direct the conduct of any reasonable man. The headlong course of the passions would be checked by no reflection on future consequences. And as each man is here supposed to love himself alone, and to depend only on himself and his own activity for safety and happiness, he would, on every occasion, to the utmost of his power, challenge the preference above every other being, to none of which he is bound by any ties, either of nature or of interest.

21.   But suppose the conjunction of the sexes to be established in nature, a family immediately arises; and particular rules being found requisite for its subsistence, these are immediately embraced; though without

comprehending the rest of mankind within their prescriptions. Suppose that several families unite together into one society, which is totally disjoined from all others, the rules, which preserve peace and order, enlarge themselves to the utmost extent of that society; but becoming then entirely useless, lose their force when carried one step farther. But again suppose, that several distinct societies maintain a kind of intercourse for mutual convenience and advantage, the boundaries of justice still grow larger, in proportion to the largeness of men's views, and the force of their mutual connexions. History, experience, reason sufficiently instruct us in this natural progress of human sentiments, and in the gradual enlargement of our regards to justice, in proportion as we become acquainted with the extensive utility of that virtue.

Part 2

22. If we examine the *particular* laws, by which justice is directed, and property determined; we shall still be presented with the same conclusion. The good of mankind is the only object of all these laws and regulations. Not only is it requisite, for the peace and interest of society, that men's possessions should be separated; but the rules, which we follow, in making the separation, are such as can best be contrived to serve farther the interests of society.

23. We shall suppose that a creature, possessed of reason, but unacquainted with human nature, deliberates with himself what RULES of justice or property would best promote public interest, and establish peace and security among mankind: His most obvious thought would be, to assign the largest possessions to the most extensive virtue, and give every one the power of doing good, proportioned to his inclination. In a perfect theocracy, where a being, infinitely intelligent, governs by particular volitions, this rule would certainly have place, and might serve to the wisest purposes: But were mankind to execute such a law; so great is the uncertainty of merit, both from its natural obscurity, and from the self-conceit of each individual, that no determinate rule of conduct would ever result from it; and the total dissolution of society must be the immediate consequence. Fanatics may suppose, *that dominion is founded on grace,* and *that saints alone inherit the earth;* but the civil magistrate very justly puts these sublime theorists on the same footing with common robbers, and teaches them by the severest discipline, that a rule, which, in speculation, may seem the most advantageous to society, may yet be found, in practice, totally pernicious and destructive.

24. That there were *religious* fanatics of this kind in ENGLAND, during the civil wars, we learn from history; though it is probable, that the obvious *tendency* of these principles excited such horror in mankind, as soon obliged the dangerous enthusiasts to renounce, or at least conceal their tenets. Perhaps the *levellers,* who claimed an equal distribution of property, were a kind of *political* fanatics, which arose from the religious species, and more openly avowed their pretensions; as carrying a more plausible appearance, of being practicable in themselves, as well as useful to human society. It must, indeed, be confessed, that nature is so liberal to mankind, that, were all her presents equally divided among the species, and improved by art and industry, every individual would enjoy all the necessaries, and even most of the comforts of life; nor would ever be liable to any ills but such as might accidentally arise from the sickly frame and constitution of his body.

25. It must, indeed, be confessed, that nature is so liberal to mankind, that, were all her presents equally divided among the species, and improved by art and industry, every individual would enjoy all the necessaries, and even most of the comforts of life; nor would ever be liable to any ills, but such as might accidentally arise from the sickly frame and constitution of his body. It must also be confessed, that, wherever we depart from this equality, we rob the poor of more satisfaction than we add to the rich, and that the slight gratification of a frivolous vanity, in one individual, frequently costs more than bread to many families, and even provinces. It may appear withal, that the rule of equality, as it would be highly *useful,* is not altogether *impracticable;* but has taken place, at least in an imperfect degree, in some republics; particularly that of SPARTA; where it was attended, it is said, with the most beneficial consequences. Not to mention, that the AGRARIAN laws, so frequently claimed in ROME, and carried into execution in many GREEK cities, proceeded, all of them, from a general idea of the utility of this principle.

26. But historians, and even common sense, may inform us, that, however specious these ideas of *perfect* equality may seem, they are really, at bottom, *impracticable;* and were they not so, would be extremely *pernicious* to human society. Render possessions ever so equal, men's different degrees of art, care, and industry will immediately break that equality. Or if you check these virtues, you reduce society to the most extreme indigence; and instead of preventing want and beggary in a few, render it unavoidable to the whole community. The most rigorous inquisition too is requisite to watch every inequality on its first appearance; and the most severe jurisdiction, to punish and redress it. But besides, that so much authority must soon

degenerate into tyranny, and be exerted with great partialities; who can possibly be possessed of it, in such a situation as is here supposed? Perfect equality of possessions, destroying all subordination, weakens extremely the authority of magistracy, and must reduce all power nearly to a level, as well as property.

27. We may conclude, therefore, that, in order to establish laws for the regulation of property, we must be acquainted with the nature and situation of man; must reject appearances, which may be false, though specious; and must search for those rules, which are, on the whole, most *useful* and *beneficial.* Vulgar sense and slight experience are sufficient for this purpose; where men give not way to too selfish avidity, or too extensive enthusiasm.

28. Who sees not, for instance, that whatever is produced or improved by a man's art or industry ought, for ever, to be secured to him, in order to give encouragement to such *useful* habits and accomplishments? That the property ought also to descend to children and relations, for the same *useful* purpose? That it may be alienated by consent, in order to beget that commerce and intercourse, which is so *beneficial* to human society? And that all contracts and promises ought carefully to be fulfilled, in order to secure mutual trust and confidence, by which the general *interest* of mankind is so much promoted?

29. Examine the writers on the laws of nature; and you will always find, that, whatever principles they set out with, they are sure to terminate here at last, and to assign, as the ultimate reason for every rule which they establish, the convenience and necessities of mankind. A concession thus extorted, in opposition to systems, has more authority than if it had been made in prosecution of them.

30. What other reason, indeed, could writers ever give, why this must be *mine* and that *yours;* since uninstructed nature surely never made any such distinction? The objects which receive those appellations are, of themselves, foreign to us; they are totally disjoined and separated from us; and nothing but the general interests of society can form the connexion.

31. Sometimes the interests of society may require a rule of justice in a particular case; but may not determine any particular rule, among several, which are all equally beneficial. In that case, the slightest analogies are laid hold of, in order to prevent that indifference and ambiguity, which would be the source of perpetual dissension. Thus possession alone, and first possession, is supposed to convey property, where no body else has any preceding claim and pretension. Many of the reasonings of lawyers are of this analogical nature, and depend on very slight connexions of the imagination.

32. Does any one scruple, in extraordinary cases, to violate all regard to
the private property of individuals, and sacrifice to public interest a distinction which had been established for the sake of that interest? The safety
of the people is the supreme law: All other particular laws are subordinate
to it, and dependent on it: And if, in the *common* course of things, they
be followed and regarded; it is only because the public safety and interest
commonly demand so equal and impartial an administration.

33. Sometimes both *utility* and *analogy* fail, and leave the laws of justice
in total uncertainty. Thus, it is highly requisite, that prescription or long
possession should convey property; but what number of days or months or
years should be sufficient for that purpose, it is impossible for reason alone
to determine. *Civil laws* here supply the place of the natural *code,* and assign different terms for prescription, according to the different *utilities,*
proposed by the legislator. Bills of exchange and promissory notes, by the
laws of most countries, prescribe sooner than bonds, and mortgages, and
contracts of a more formal nature.

34. In general we may observe that all questions of property are subordinate to the authority of civil laws, which extend, restrain, modify, and
alter the rules of natural justice, according to the particular *convenience* of
each community. The laws have, or ought to have, a constant reference to
the constitution of government, the manners, the climate, the religion, the
commerce, the situation of each society. A late author of genius, as well
as learning, has prosecuted this subject at large, and has established, from
these principles, a system of political knowledge, which abounds in ingenious and brilliant thoughts, and is not wanting in solidity.[16]

16. The author of *L'Esprit des Loix*. [Charles Louis de Secondat Montesquieu,
De l'esprit des lois (The Spirit of the Laws).] This illustrious writer, however, sets
out with a different theory, and supposes all right to be founded on certain *rap-
ports* or relations; which is a system, that, in my opinion, never will be reconciled
with true philosophy. Father MALEBRANCHE, as far as I can learn, was the first that
started this abstract theory of morals, which was afterwards adopted by CUDWORTH,
CLARKE, and others; and as it excludes all sentiment, and pretends to found everything on reason, it has not wanted followers in this philosophic age. See Section 1.
and Appendix 1. With regard to justice, the virtue here treated of, the inference
against this theory seems short and conclusive. Property is allowed to be dependent
on civil laws; civil laws are allowed to have no other object, but the interest of
society: This therefore must be allowed to be the sole foundation of property and
justice. Not to mention, that our obligation itself to obey the magistrate and his laws
is founded on nothing but the interests of society.

   If the ideas of justice, sometimes, do not follow the dispositions of civil law; we
shall find, that these cases, instead of objections, are confirmations of the theory
delivered above. Where a civil law is so perverse as to cross all the interests of

35. *What is a man's property?* Anything which it is lawful for him, and for him alone, to use. *But what rule have we, by which we can distinguish these objects?* Here we must have recourse to statutes, customs, precedents, analogies, and a hundred other circumstances; some of which are constant and inflexible, some variable and arbitrary. But the ultimate point, in which they all professedly terminate, is the interest and happiness of human society. Where this enters not into consideration, nothing can appear more whimsical, unnatural, and even superstitious, than all or most of the laws of justice and of property.

36. Those who ridicule vulgar superstitions, and expose the folly of particular regards to meats, days, places, postures, apparel, have an easy task; while they consider all the qualities and relations of the objects, and discover no adequate cause for that affection or antipathy, veneration or horror, which have so mighty an influence over a considerable part of mankind. A SYRIAN would have starved rather than taste pigeon; an EGYPTIAN would not have approached bacon: But if these species of food be examined by the senses of sight, smell, or taste, or scrutinized by the sciences of chemistry, medicine, or physics, no difference is ever found between them and any other species, nor can that precise circumstance be pitched on, which may afford a just foundation for the religious passion. A fowl on Thursday is lawful food; on Friday abominable: Eggs in this house and in this diocese, are permitted during Lent; a hundred paces farther, to eat them is a damnable sin. This earth or building, yesterday was profane; to-day, by the muttering of certain words, it has become holy and sacred. Such reflections as these, in the mouth of a philosopher, one may safely say, are too obvious to have any influence; because they must always, to every man, occur at first sight; and where they prevail not, of themselves, they are surely obstructed by education, prejudice, and passion, not by ignorance or mistake.

---

society, it loses all its authority, and men judge by the ideas of natural justice, which are conformable to those interests. Sometimes also civil laws, for useful purposes, require a ceremony or form to any deed; and where that is wanting, their decrees run contrary to the usual tenour of justice; but one who takes advantage of such chicanes, is not commonly regarded as an honest man. Thus, the interests of society require, that contracts be fulfilled; and there is not a more material article either of natural or civil justice: But the omission of a trifling circumstance will often, by law, invalidate a contract, *in foro humano,* but not *in foro conscientiae* [in a human court . . . before the bar (court) of conscience], as divines express themselves. In these cases, the magistrate is supposed only to withdraw his power of enforcing the right, not to have altered the right. Where his intention extends to the right, and is conformable to the interests of society; it never fails to alter the right; a clear proof of the origin of justice and of property, as assigned above.

37. It may appear to a careless view, or rather a too abstracted reflection, that there enters a like superstition into all the sentiments of justice; and that, if a man expose its object, or what we call property, to the same scrutiny of sense and science, he will not, by the most accurate enquiry, find any foundation for the difference made by moral sentiment. I may lawfully nourish myself from this tree; but the fruit of another of the same species, ten paces off, it is criminal for me to touch. Had I worn this apparel an hour ago, I had merited the severest punishment; but a man, by pronouncing a few magical syllables, has now rendered it fit for my use and service. Were this house placed in the neighbouring territory, it had been immoral for me to dwell in it; but being built on this side the river, it is subject to a different municipal law, and by its becoming mine I incur no blame or censure. The same species of reasoning it may be thought, which so successfully exposes superstition, is also applicable to justice; nor is it possible, in the one case more than in the other, to point out, in the object, that precise quality or circumstance, which is the foundation of the sentiment.

38. But there is this material difference between *superstition* and *justice,* that the former is frivolous, useless, and burdensome; the latter is absolutely requisite to the well-being of mankind and existence of society. When we abstract from this circumstance (for it is too apparent ever to be overlooked) it must be confessed, that all regards to right and property, seem entirely without foundation, as much as the grossest and most vulgar superstition. Were the interests of society nowise concerned, it is as unintelligible why another's articulating certain sounds implying consent, should change the nature of my actions with regard to a particular object, as why the reciting of a liturgy by a priest, in a certain habit and posture, should dedicate a heap of brick and timber, and render it, thenceforth and for ever, sacred.[17]

17. It is evident, that the will or consent alone never transfers property, nor causes the obligation of a promise (for the same reasoning extends to both), but the will must be expressed by words or signs, in order to impose a tie upon any man. The expression being once brought in as subservient to the will, soon becomes the principal part of the promise; nor will a man be less bound by his word, though he secretly give a different direction to his intention, and withhold the assent of his mind. But though the expression makes, on most occasions, the whole of the promise, yet it does not always so; and one who should make use of any expression, of which he knows not the meaning, and which he uses without any sense of the consequences, would not certainly be bound by it. Nay, though he know its meaning, yet if he use it in jest only, and with such signs as evidently show, that he has no serious intention of binding himself, he would not lie under any obligation of performance; but it is necessary, that the words be a perfect

39.   These reflections are far from weakening the obligations of justice, or diminishing anything from the most sacred attention to property. On the contrary, such sentiments must acquire new force from the present reasoning. For what stronger foundation can be desired or conceived for any duty, than to observe, that human society, or even human nature, could not subsist without the establishment of it; and will still arrive at greater degrees of happiness and perfection, the more inviolable the regard is, which is paid to that duty?

---

expression of the will, without any contrary signs. Nay, even this we must not carry so far as to imagine, that one, whom, by our quickness of understanding, we conjecture, from certain signs, to have an intention of deceiving us, is not bound by his expression or verbal promise, if we accept of it; but must limit this conclusion to those cases where the signs are of a different nature from those of deceit. All these contradictions are easily accounted for, if justice arise entirely from its usefulness to society; but will never be explained on any other hypothesis.

It is remarkable that the moral decisions of the JESUITS and other relaxed casuists, were commonly formed in prosecution of some such subtilties of reasoning as are here pointed out, and proceed as much from the habit of scholastic refinement as from any corruption of the heart, if we may follow the authority of Mons. BAYLE. See his *Dictionary,* article LOYOLA [Pierre Bayle, *Dictionnaire historique et critique* (*Historical and Critical Dictionary*), entry on "Loyola"]. And why has the indignation of mankind risen so high against these casuists; but because every one perceived, that human society could not subsist were such practices authorized, and that morals must always be handled with a view to public interest, more than philosophical regularity? If the secret direction of the intention, said every man of sense, could invalidate a contract; where is our security? And yet a metaphysical schoolman might think, that, where an intention was supposed to be requisite, if that intention really had not place, no consequence ought to follow, and no obligation be imposed. The casuistical subtilties may not be greater than the subtilties of lawyers, hinted at above; but as the former are *pernicious,* and the latter *innocent* and even *necessary,* this is the reason of the very different reception they meet with from the world.

It is a doctrine of the Church of ROME, that the priest, by a secret direction of his intention, can invalidate any sacrament. This position is derived from a strict and regular prosecution of the obvious truth, that empty words alone, without any meaning or intention in the speaker, can never be attended with any effect. If the same conclusion be not admitted in reasonings concerning civil contracts, where the affair is allowed to be of so much less consequence than the eternal salvation of thousands, it proceeds entirely from men's sense of the danger and inconvenience of the doctrine in the former case: And we may thence observe, that however positive, arrogant, and dogmatical any superstition may appear, it never can convey any thorough persuasion of the reality of its objects, or put them, in any degree, on a balance with the common incidents of life, which we learn from daily observation and experimental reasoning.

40. The dilemma seems obvious: As justice evidently tends to promote public utility and to support civil society, the sentiment of justice is either derived from our reflecting on that tendency, or like hunger, thirst, and other appetites, resentment, love of life, attachment to offspring, and other passions, arises from a simple original instinct in the human breast, which nature has implanted for like salutary purposes. If the latter be the case, it follows, that property, which is the object of justice, is also distinguished by a simple original instinct, and is not ascertained by any argument or reflection. But who is there that ever heard of such an instinct? Or is this a subject in which new discoveries can be made? We may as well expect to discover, in the body, new senses, which had before escaped the observation of all mankind.

41. But farther, though it seems a very simple proposition to say, that nature, by an instinctive sentiment, distinguishes property, yet in reality we shall find, that there are required for that purpose ten thousand different instincts, and these employed about objects of the greatest intricacy and nicest discernment. For when a definition of *property* is required, that relation is found to resolve itself into any possession acquired by occupation, by industry, by prescription, by inheritance, by contract, &c. Can we think that nature, by an original instinct, instructs us in all these methods of acquisition?

42. These words too, *inheritance* and *contract,* stand for ideas infinitely complicated; and to define them exactly, a hundred volumes of laws, and a thousand volumes of commentators, have not been found sufficient. Does nature, whose instincts in men are all simple, embrace such complicated and artificial objects, and create a rational creature, without trusting anything to the operation of his reason?

43. But even though all this were admitted, it would not be satisfactory. Positive laws can certainly transfer property. It is by another original instinct, that we recognize the authority of kings and senates, and mark all the boundaries of their jurisdiction? Judges too, even though their sentence be erroneous and illegal, must be allowed, for the sake of peace and order, to have decisive authority, and ultimately to determine property. Have we original innate ideas of praetors and chancellors and juries? Who sees not, that all these institutions arise merely from the necessities of human society?

44. All birds of the same species in every age and country, built their nests alike: In this we see the force of instinct. Men, in different times and places, frame their houses differently: Here we perceive the influence of

reason and custom. A like inference may be drawn from comparing the instinct of generation and the institution of property.

45. How great soever the variety of municipal laws, it must be confessed, that their chief outlines pretty regularly concur; because the purposes, to which they tend, are everywhere exactly similar. In like manner, all houses have a roof and walls, windows and chimneys; though diversified in their shape, figure, and materials. The purposes of the latter, directed to the conveniencies of human life, discover not more plainly their origin from reason and reflection, than do those of the former, which point all to a like end.

46. I need not mention the variations, which all the rules of property receive from the finer turns and connexions of the imagination, and from the subtilties and abstractions of law-topics and reasonings. There is no possibility of reconciling this observation to the notion of original instincts.

47. What alone will beget a doubt concerning the theory, on which I insist, is the influence of education and acquired habits, by which we are so accustomed to blame injustice, that we are not, in every instance, conscious of any immediate reflection on the pernicious consequences of it. The views the most familiar to us are apt, for that very reason, to escape us; and what we have very frequently performed from certain motives, we are apt likewise to continue mechanically, without recalling, on every occasion, the reflections, which first determined us. The convenience, or rather necessity, which leads to justice is so universal, and everywhere points so much to the same rules, that the habit takes place in all societies; and it is not without some scrutiny, that we are able to ascertain its true origin. The matter, however, is not so obscure, but that even in common life we have every moment recourse to the principle of public utility, and ask, *What must become of the world, if such practices prevail? How could society subsist under such disorders?* Were the distinction or separation of possessions entirely useless, can any one conceive, that it ever should have obtained in society?

48. Thus we seem, upon the whole, to have attained a knowledge of the force of that principle here insisted on, and can determine what degree of esteem or moral approbation may result from reflections on public interest and utility. The necessity of justice to the support of society is the SOLE foundation of that virtue; and since no moral excellence is more highly esteemed, we may conclude that this circumstance of usefulness has, in general, the strongest energy, and most entire command over our sentiments. It must, therefore, be the source of a considerable part of the merit ascribed to humanity, benevolence, friendship, public spirit, and other social virtues of that stamp; as it is the SOLE source of the moral approbation paid to fidelity,

justice, veracity, integrity, and those other estimable and useful qualities and principles. It is entirely agreeable to the rules of philosophy, and even of common reason; where any principle has been found to have a great force and energy in one instance, to ascribe to it a like energy in all similar instances. This indeed is NEWTON's chief rule of philosophizing.[18]

18. Principia. lib. 3. [Isaac Newton, *Philosophiæ naturalis principia mathematica* (*Mathematical Principles of Natural Philosophy*), book 3.]

Of Political Society

1.   HAD every man sufficient *sagacity* to perceive, at all times, the strong interest which binds him to the observance of justice and equity, and *strength of mind* sufficient to persevere in a steady adherence to a general and a distant interest, in opposition to the allurements of present pleasure and advantage; there had never, in that case, been any such thing as government or political society, but each man, following his natural liberty, had lived in entire peace and harmony with all others. What need of positive law where natural justice is, of itself, a sufficient restraint? Why create magistrates, where there never arises any disorder or iniquity? Why abridge our native freedom, when, in every instance, the utmost exertion of it is found innocent and beneficial? It is evident, that, if government were totally useless, it never could have place, and that the SOLE foundation of the duty of ALLEGIANCE is the *advantage,* which it procures to society, by preserving peace and order among mankind.

2.   When a number of political societies are erected, and maintain a great intercourse together, a new set of rules are immediately discovered to be *useful* in that particular situation; and accordingly take place under the title of LAWS OF NATIONS. Of this kind are, the sacredness of the person of ambassadors, abstaining from poisoned arms, quarter in war, with others of that kind, which are plainly calculated for the *advantage* of states and kingdoms in their intercourse with each other.

3.   The rules of justice, such as prevail among individuals, are not entirely suspended among political societies. All princes pretend a regard to the rights of other princes; and some, no doubt, without hypocrisy. Alliances and treaties are every day made between independent states, which would only be so much waste of parchment, if they were not found by experience to have *some* influence and authority. But here is the difference between kingdoms and individuals. Human nature cannot by any means subsist, without the association of individuals; and that association never could

have place, were no regard paid to the laws of equity and justice. Disorder, confusion, the war of all against all, are the necessary consequences of such a licentious conduct. But nations can subsist without intercourse. They may even subsist, in some degree, under a general war. The observance of justice, though useful among them, is not guarded by so strong a necessity as among individuals; and the moral obligation holds proportion with the *usefulness*. All politicians will allow, and most philosophers, that REASONS of STATE may, in particular emergencies, dispense with the rules of justice, and invalidate any treaty or alliance, where the strict observance of it would be prejudicial, in a considerable degree, to either of the contracting parties. But nothing less than the most extreme necessity, it is confessed, can justify individuals in a breach of promise, or an invasion of the properties of others.

4. In a confederated commonwealth, such as the ACHÆAN republic of old, or the SWISS Cantons and United Provinces in modern times; as the league has here a peculiar *utility*, the conditions of union have a peculiar sacredness and authority, and a violation of them would be regarded as no less, or even as more criminal, than any private injury or injustice.

5. The long and helpless infancy of man requires the combination of parents for the subsistence of their young; and that combination requires the virtue of CHASTITY or fidelity to the marriage bed. Without such a *utility*, it will readily be owned, that such a virtue would never have been thought of.[19]

---

19. The only solution, which PLATO gives to all the objections that might be raised against the community of women, established in his imaginary commonwealth, is, Καλλιϛα γαρ δη τουτο και λεγεται και λελεξεται, οτι το μεν ωφελιμον καλον, τὸ δε βλαβερον αισχρον. "Scite enim istud et dicitur et dicetur, Id quod utile sit honestum esse, quod autem inutile sit turpe esse." ["For it is an admirable saying and will remain so, that what is beneficial is beautiful and what is harmful is ugly."] De rep lib 5. p. 457 ex edit Serr. And this maxim will admit of no doubt, where public utility is concerned, which is PLATO's meaning. And indeed to what other purpose do all the ideas of chastity and modesty serve? "Nisi utile est quod facimus, frustra est gloria," says PHAEDRUS. ["Unless what we do is useful, the glory is in vain."] Καλον των βλαβερων ουδεν, says PLUTARCH, de vitioso pudore. "Nihil eorum quae damnosa sunt, pulchrum est." ["Nothing that is harmful is beautiful."] The same was the opinion of the STOICS. Φασιν ουν οι Στωικοι αγαθον ειναι ωφελειαν η ουκ ετεραν ωφελειας, ωφελειαν μεν λεγοντες την αρετην και την σπουδαιαν πραξιν. ["The Stoics, therefore, identify good with utility virtue and right action."] SEXT. EMP lib 3. cap. 20. [Plato, *Republic,* book 5; Phaedrus, *Aesopic Fables,* book 3; Plutarch, *Moralia,* chapter 3; Sextus Empiricus, *Outlines of Pyrrhonism,* book 3, chapter 22.]

6.   An infidelity of this nature is much more *pernicious* in *women* than in *men.* Hence the laws of chastity are much stricter over the one sex than over the other.

7.   These rules have all a reference to generation; and yet women past child-bearing are no more supposed to be exempted from them than those in the flower of their youth and beauty. *General rules* are often extended beyond the principle whence they first arise; and this in all matters of taste and sentiment. It is a vulgar story at PARIS, that, during the rage of the MIS-SISSIPPI,[20] a hump-backed fellow went every day into the RUE DE QUINCEM-POIX, where the stock-jobbers[21] met in great crowds, and was well paid for allowing them to make use of his hump as a desk, in order to sign their contracts upon it. Would the fortune, which he raised by this expedient, make him a handsome fellow; though it be confessed, that personal beauty arises very much from ideas of utility? The imagination is influenced by associations of ideas; which, though they arise at first from the judgment, are not easily altered by every particular exception that occurs to us. To which we may add, in the present case of chastity, that the example of the old would be pernicious to the young; and that women, continually foreseeing that a certain time would bring them the liberty of indulgence, would naturally advance that period, and think more lightly of this whole duty, so requisite to society.

8.   Those who live in the same family have such frequent opportunities of licence of this kind, that nothing could prevent purity of manners, were marriage allowed, among the nearest relations, or any intercourse of love between them ratified by law and custom. INCEST, therefore, being *pernicious* in a superior degree, has also a superior turpitude and moral deformity annexed to it.

9.   What is the reason, why, by the ATHENIAN laws, one might marry a half-sister by the father, but not by the mother? Plainly this: The manners

---

20. [This rage resulted from the Mississippi Scheme of the Mississippi Company, founded in France in 1684. The Mississippi Company (later called the "Compagnie des Indes") was granted a monopoly on the development of France's Mississippi Territory in North America. Based on the promise of a supposed immense bounty of resources in the Mississippi Territory, including gold and silver, the investors bid the Compagnie des Indes shares up to astronomical heights. The company's prospects were empty, and the shares crashed, taking down with it France's stock market and public finances.]

21. [A slang term for the buyers and sellers of stocks on the London Stock Exchange prior to October 1986.]

of the ATHENIANS were so reserved, that a man was never permitted to approach the women's apartment, even in the same family, unless where he visited his own mother. His step-mother and her children were as much shut up from him as the woman of any other family, and there was as little danger of any criminal correspondence between them. Uncles and nieces, for a like reason, might marry at ATHENS; but neither these, nor half-brothers and sisters, could contract that alliance at ROME, where the intercourse was more open between the sexes. Public utility is the cause of all these variations.

10. To repeat, to a man's prejudice, anything that escaped him in private conversation, or to make any such use of his private letters, is highly blamed. The free and social intercourse of minds must be extremely checked, where no such rules of fidelity are established.

11. Even in repeating stories, whence we can foresee no ill consequences to result, the giving of one's author is regarded as a piece of indiscretion, if not of immorality. These stories, in passing from hand to hand, and receiving all the usual variations, frequently come about to the persons concerned, and produce animosities and quarrels among people, whose intentions are the most innocent and inoffensive.

12. To pry into secrets, to open or even read the letters of others, to play the spy upon their words and looks and actions; what habits more inconvenient in society? What habits, of consequence, more blameable?

13. This principle is also the foundation of most of the laws of good manners; a kind of lesser morality, calculated for the ease of company and conversation. Too much or too little ceremony are both blamed, and everything, which promotes ease, without an indecent familiarity, is useful and laudable.

14. Constancy in friendships, attachments, and familiarities, is commendable, and is requisite to support trust and good correspondence in society. But in places of general, though casual concourse, where the pursuit of health and pleasure brings people promiscuously together, public conveniency has dispensed with this maxim; and custom there promotes an unreserved conversation for the time, by indulging the privilege of dropping afterwards every indifferent acquaintance, without breach of civility or good manners.

15. Even in societies, which are established on principles the most immoral, and the most destructive to the interests of the general society, there are required certain rules, which a species of false honour, as well as private interest, engages the members to observe. Robbers and pirates, it has

often been remarked, could not maintain their pernicious confederacy, did they not establish a new distributive justice among themselves, and recall those laws of equity, which they have violated with the rest of mankind.

16.   *I hate a drinking companion,* says the GREEK proverb, *who never forgets.* The follies of the last debauch should be buried in eternal oblivion, in order to give full scope to the follies of the next.

17.   Among nations, where an immoral gallantry, if covered with a thin veil of mystery, is, in some degree, authorized by custom, there immediately arise a set of rules, calculated for the conveniency of that attachment. The famous court or parliament of love in PROVENCE formerly decided all difficult cases of this nature.

18.   In societies for play, there are laws required for the conduct of the game; and these laws are different in each game. The foundation, I own, of such societies is frivolous; and the laws are, in a great measure, though not altogether, capricious and arbitrary. So far is there a material difference between them and the rules of justice, fidelity, and loyalty. The general societies of men are absolutely requisite for the subsistence of the species; and the public conveniency, which regulates morals, is inviolably established in the nature of man, and of the world, in which he lives. The comparison, therefore, in these respects, is very imperfect. We may only learn from it the necessity of rules, wherever men have any intercourse with each other.

19.   They cannot even pass each other on the road without rules. Waggoners, coachmen, and postilions have principles, by which they give the way; and these are chiefly founded on mutual ease and convenience. Sometimes also they are arbitrary, at least dependent on a kind of capricious analogy like many of the reasonings of lawyers.[22]

20.   To carry the matter farther, we may observe, that it is impossible for men so much as to murder each other without statutes, and maxims, and an idea of justice and honour. War has its laws as well as peace; and even that sportive kind of war, carried on among wrestlers, boxers, cudgel-players, gladiators, is regulated by fixed principles. Common interest and utility beget infallibly a standard of right and wrong among the parties concerned.

---

22. That the lighter machine yield to the heavier, and, in machines of the same kind, that the empty yield to the loaded; this rule is founded on convenience. That those who are going to the capital take place of those who are coming from it; this seems to be founded on some idea of dignity of the great city, and of the preference of the future to the past. From like reasons, among foot-walkers, the right-hand entitles a man to the wall, and prevents jostling, which peaceable people find very disagreeable and inconvenient.

SECTION 5

Why Utility Pleases

Part I

1. IT seems so natural a thought to ascribe to their utility the praise, which we bestow on the social virtues, that one would expect to meet with this principle everywhere in moral writers, as the chief foundation of their reasoning and enquiry. In common life, we may observe, that the circumstance of utility is always appealed to; nor is it supposed, that a greater eulogy can be given to any man, than to display his usefulness to the public, and enumerate the services, which he has performed to mankind and society. What praise, even of an inanimate form, if the regularity and elegance of its parts destroy not its fitness for any useful purpose! And how satisfactory an apology for any disproportion or seeming deformity, if we can show the necessity of that particular construction for the use intended! A ship appears more beautiful to an artist, or one moderately skilled in navigation, where its prow is wide and swelling beyond its poop, than if it were framed with a precise geometrical regularity, in contradiction to all the laws of mechanics. A building, whose doors and windows were exact squares, would hurt the eye by that very proportion; as ill adapted to the figure of a human creature, for whose service the fabric was intended. What wonder then, that a man, whose habits and conduct are hurtful to society, and dangerous or pernicious to every one who has an intercourse with him, should, on that account, be an object of disapprobation, and communicate to every spectator the strongest sentiment of disgust and hatred.[23]

23. We ought not to imagine, because an inanimate object may be useful as well as a man, that therefore it ought also, according to this system, to merit the appellation of *virtuous*. The sentiments, excited by utility, are, in the two cases, very different; and the one is mixed with affection, esteem, approbation, &c., and not the other. In like manner, an inanimate object may have good colour and proportions as well

2.   But perhaps the difficulty of accounting for these effects of usefulness, or its contrary, has kept philosophers from admitting them into their systems of ethics, and has induced them rather to employ any other principle, in explaining the origin of moral good and evil. But it is no just reason for rejecting any principle, confirmed by experience, that we cannot give a satisfactory account of its origin, nor are able to resolve it into other more general principles. And if we would employ a little thought on the present subject, we need be at no loss to account for the influence of utility, and to deduce it from principles, the most known and avowed in human nature.

3.   From the apparent usefulness of the social virtues, it has readily been inferred by sceptics, both ancient and modern, that all moral distinctions arise from education, and were, at first, invented, and afterwards encouraged, by the art of politicians, in order to render men tractable, and subdue their natural ferocity and selfishness, which incapacitated them for society. This principle, indeed, of precept and education, must so far be owned to have a powerful influence, that it may frequently increase or diminish, beyond their natural standard, the sentiments of approbation or dislike; and may even, in particular instances, create, without any natural principle, a new sentiment of this kind; as is evident in all superstitious practices and observances: But that *all* moral affection or dislike arises from this origin, will never surely be allowed by any judicious enquirer. Had nature made no such distinction, founded on the original constitution of the mind, the words, *honourable* and *shameful, lovely* and *odious, noble* and *despicable,* had never had place in any language; nor could politicians, had they invented these terms, ever have been able to render them intelligible, or make them convey any idea to the audience. So that nothing can be more superficial than this paradox of the sceptics; and it were well, if, in the abstruser studies of logic and metaphysics, we could as easily obviate the cavils of

---

as a human figure. But can we ever be in love with the former? There are a numerous set of passions and sentiments, of which thinking rational beings are, by the original constitution of nature, the only proper objects: and though the very same qualities be transferred to an insensible, inanimate being, they will not excite the same sentiments. The beneficial qualities of herbs and minerals are, indeed, sometimes called their *virtues;* but this is an effect of the caprice of language, which out not to be regarded in reasoning. For though there be a species of approbation attending even inanimate objects, when beneficial, yet this sentiment is so weak, and so different from that which is directed to beneficent magistrates or statesman; that they ought not to be ranked under the same class or appellation.

A very small variation of the object, even where the same qualities are preserved, will destroy a sentiment. Thus, the same beauty, transferred to a different sex, excites no amorous passion, where nature is not extremely perverted.

that sect, as in the practical and more intelligible sciences of politics and morals.

4.   The social virtues must, therefore, be allowed to have a natural beauty and amiableness, which, at first, antecedent to all precept or education, recommends them to the esteem of uninstructed mankind, and engages their affections. And as the public utility of these virtues is the chief circumstance, whence they derive their merit, it follows, that the end, which they have a tendency to promote, must be some way agreeable to us, and take hold of some natural affection. It must please, either from considerations of self-interest, or from more generous motives and regards.

5.   It has often been asserted, that, as every man has a strong connexion with society, and perceives the impossibility of his solitary subsistence, he becomes, on that account, favourable to all those habits or principles, which promote order in society, and insure to him the quiet possession of so inestimable a blessing, As much as we value our own happiness and welfare, as much must we applaud the practice of justice and humanity, by which alone the social confederacy can be maintained, and every man reap the fruits of mutual protection and assistance.

6.   This deduction of morals from self-love, or a regard to private interest, is an obvious thought, and has not arisen wholly from the wanton sallies and sportive assaults of the sceptics. To mention no others, POLYBIUS, one of the gravest and most judicious, as well as most moral writers of antiquity, has assigned this selfish origin to all our sentiments of virtue.[24] But though the solid practical sense of that author, and his aversion to all vain subtilties, render his authority on the present subject very considerable; yet is not this an affair to be decided by authority, and the voice of nature and experience seems plainly to oppose the selfish theory.

7.   We frequently bestow praise on virtuous actions, performed in very distant ages and remote countries; where the utmost subtilty of imagination

---

24. Undutifulness to parents is disapproved of by mankind, προορωμενους το ελλον, και συλλογιζομενους οτι το παραπλησιον εκαστοις αυτων συγκυρησει. Ingratitude for a like reason (though he seems there to mix a more generous regard) συναγανακτουντας μεν τω πελας, αναφεροντας δ' επ' αυτους το παραπλησιον εξ ων υπογιγνεται τις εννοια παρεκαστω του καθηκοντος δυναμεως και θεωριας. Lib. 6 cap. 4. [Polybius, *Histories,* book 6. This passage may be translated as follows: "Joining in their neighbours' resentment and attributing a similar feeling to themselves, from which each individual derives a sense of the function and principles of fit conduct."] Perhaps the historian only meant, that our sympathy and humanity was more enlivened, by our considering the similarity of our case with that of the person suffering; which is a just sentiment.

would not discover any appearance of self-interest, or find any connexion of our present happiness and security with events so widely separated from us.

8.　A generous, a brave, a noble deed, performed by an adversary, commands our approbation; while in its consequences it may be acknowledged prejudicial to our particular interest.

9.　Where private advantage concurs with general affection for virtue, we readily perceive and avow the mixture of these distinct sentiments, which have a very different feeling and influence on the mind. We praise, perhaps, with more alacrity, where the generous humane action contributes to our particular interest: But the topics of praise, which we insist on, are very wide of this circumstance. And we may attempt to bring over others to our sentiments, without endeavouring to convince them, that they reap any advantage from the actions which we recommend to their approbation and applause.

10.　Frame the model of a praiseworthy character, consisting of all the most amiable moral virtues: Give instances, in which these display themselves after an eminent and extraordinary manner: You readily engage the esteem and approbation of all your audience, who never so much as enquire in what age and country the person lived, who possessed these noble qualities: A circumstance, however, of all others, the most material to self-love, or a concern for our own individual happiness.

11.　Once on a time, a statesman, in the shock and contest of parties, prevailed so far as to procure, by his eloquence, the banishment of an able adversary; whom he secretly followed, offering him money for his support during his exile, and soothing him with topics of consolation in his misfortunes. "Alas"! cries the banished statesman, "with what regret must I leave my friends in this city, where even enemies are so generous!" Virtue, though in an enemy, here pleased him: And we also give it the just tribute of praise and approbation; nor do we retract these sentiments, when we hear, that the action passed at ATHENS, about two thousand years ago, and that the persons' names were ÆSCHINES and DEMOSTHENES.

12.　*What is that to me?* There are few occasions, when this question is not pertinent: And had it that universal, infallible influence supposed, it would turn into ridicule every composition, and almost every conversation, which contain any praise or censure of men and manners.

13.　It is but a weak subterfuge, when pressed by these facts and arguments, to say, that we transport ourselves, by the force of imagination, into distant ages and countries, and consider the advantage, which we should have reaped from these characters, had we been contemporaries, and had any commerce with the persons. It is not conceivable, how a *real* sentiment or passion can ever arise from a known *imaginary* interest; especially when our *real* interest is still kept in view, and is often acknowledged to be entirely distinct from the imaginary, and even sometimes opposite to it.

14. A man, brought to the brink of a precipice, cannot look down without trembling; and the sentiment of *imaginary* danger actuates him, in opposition to the opinion and belief of *real* safety. But the imagination is here assisted by the presence of a striking object; and yet prevails not, except it be also aided by novelty, and the unusual appearance of the object. Custom soon reconciles us to heights and precipices, and wears off these false and delusive terrors. The reverse is observable in the estimates which we form of characters and manners; and the more we habituate ourselves to an accurate scrutiny of morals, the more delicate feeling do we acquire of the most minute distinctions between vice and virtue. Such frequent occasion, indeed, have we, in common life, to pronounce all kinds of moral determinations, that no object of this kind can be new or unusual to us; nor could any *false* views or prepossessions maintain their ground against an experience, so common and familiar. Experience being chiefly what forms the associations of ideas, it is impossible that any association could establish and support itself, in direct opposition to that principle.

15. Usefulness is agreeable, and engages our approbation. This is a matter of fact, confirmed by daily observation. But, *useful?* For what? For somebody's interest, surely. Whose interest then? Not our own only: For our approbation frequently extends farther. It must, therefore, be the interest of those, who are served by the character or action approved of; and these we may conclude, however remote, are not totally indifferent to us. By opening up this principle, we shall discover one great source of moral distinctions.

Part 2

16. Self-love is a principle in human nature of such extensive energy, and the interest of each individual is, in general, so closely connected with that of the community, that those philosophers were excusable, who fancied that all our concern for the public might be resolved into a concern for our own happiness and preservation. They saw every moment, instances of approbation or blame, satisfaction or displeasure towards characters and actions; they denominated the objects of these sentiments, *virtues,* or *vices;* they observed, that the former had a tendency to increase the happiness,

and the latter the misery of mankind; they asked, whether it were possible that we could have any general concern for society, or any disinterested resentment of the welfare or injury of others; they found it simpler to consider all these sentiments as modifications of self-love; and they discovered a pretence, at least, for this unity of principle, in that close union of interest, which is so observable between the public and each individual.

17.   But notwithstanding this frequent confusion of interests, it is easy to attain what natural philosophers, after Lord BACON, have affected to call the *experimentum crucis,*[25] or that experiment which points out the right way in any doubt or ambiguity. We have found instances, in which private interest was separate from public; in which it was even contrary: And yet we observed the moral sentiment to continue, notwithstanding this disjunction of interests. And wherever these distinct interests sensibly concurred, we always found a sensible increase of the sentiment, and a more warm affection to virtue, and detestation of vice, or what we properly call, *gratitude* and *revenge.* Compelled by these instances, we must renounce the theory, which accounts for every moral sentiment by the principle of self-love. We must adopt a more public affection, and allow, that the interests of society are not, even on their own account, entirely indifferent to us. Usefulness is only a tendency to a certain end; and it is a contradiction in terms, that anything pleases as means to an end, where the end itself no wise affects us. If usefulness, therefore, be a source of moral sentiment, and if this usefulness be not always considered with a reference to self; it follows, that everything, which contributes to the happiness of society, recommends itself directly to our approbation and good-will. Here is a principle, which accounts, in great part, for the origin of morality: And what need we seek for abstruse and remote systems, when there occurs one so obvious and natural?[26]

25. [This may be translated as "crucial experiment" or "experiment of the crux."]

26. It is needless to push our researches so far as to ask, why we have humanity or a fellow-feeling with others. It is sufficient, that this is experienced to be a principle in human nature. We must stop somewhere in our examination of causes; and there are, in every science, some general principles, beyond which we cannot hope to find any principle more general. No man is absolutely indifferent to the happiness and misery of others. The first has a natural tendency to give pleasure; the second, pain. This every one may find in himself. It is not probable, that these principles can be resolved into principles more simple and universal, whatever attempts may have been made to that purpose. But if it were possible, it belongs not to the present subject; and we may here safely consider these principles as original; happy, if we can render all the consequences sufficiently plain and perspicuous!

18. Have we any difficulty to comprehend the force of humanity and benevolence? Or to conceive, that the very aspect of happiness, joy, prosperity, gives pleasure; that of pain, suffering, sorrow, communicates uneasiness? The human countenance, says HORACE,[27] borrows smiles or tears from the human countenance. Reduce a person to solitude, and he loses all enjoyment, except either of the sensual or speculative kind; and that because the movements of his heart are not forwarded by correspondent movements in his fellow-creatures. The signs of sorrow and mourning, though arbitrary, affect us with melancholy; but the natural symptoms, tears and cries and groans, never fail to infuse compassion and uneasiness. And if the effects of misery touch us in so lively a manner; can we be supposed altogether insensible or indifferent towards its causes; when a malicious or treacherous character and behaviour are presented to us?

19. We enter, I shall suppose, into a convenient, warm, well-contrived apartment: We necessarily receive a pleasure from its very survey; because it presents us with the pleasing ideas of ease, satisfaction, and enjoyment. The hospitable, good-humoured, humane landlord appears. This circumstance surely must embellish the whole; nor can we easily forbear reflecting, with pleasure, on the satisfaction which results to every one from his intercourse and good offices.

20. His whole family, by the freedom, ease, confidence, and calm enjoyment, diffused over their countenances, sufficiently express their happiness. I have a pleasing sympathy in the prospect of so much joy, and can never consider the source of it, without the most agreeable emotions.

21. He tells me, that an oppressive and powerful neighbour had attempted to dispossess him of his inheritance, and had long disturbed all his innocent and social pleasures. I feel an immediate indignation arise in me against such violence and injury.

22. But it is no wonder, he adds, that a private wrong should proceed from a man, who had enslaved provinces, depopulated cities, and made the field and scaffold stream with human blood. I am struck with horror at the prospect of so much misery, and am actuated by the strongest antipathy against its author.

23. In general, it is certain, that, wherever we go, whatever we reflect on or converse about, everything still presents us with the view of human happiness or misery, and excites in our breast a sympathetic movement of

27. "Uti ridentibus arrident, ita flentibus adflent Humani vultus,"—HOR. ["As human faces laugh with those who laugh so do they weep with those who weep." Horace, *Art of Poetry,* lines 101–2.]

pleasure or uneasiness. In our serious occupations, in our careless amusements, this principle still exerts its active energy.

24. A man who enters the theatre, is immediately struck with the view of so great a multitude, participating of one common amusement; and experiences, from their very aspect, a superior sensibility or disposition of being affected with every sentiment, which he shares with his fellow-creatures.

25. He observes the actors to be animated by the appearance of a full audience, and raised to a degree of enthusiasm, which they cannot command in any solitary or calm moment.

26. Every movement of the theatre, by a skilful poet, is communicated, as it were by magic, to the spectators; who weep, tremble, resent, rejoice, and are inflamed with all the variety of passions, which actuate the several personages of the drama.

27. Where any event crosses our wishes, and interrupts the happiness of the favourite characters, we feel a sensible anxiety and concern. But where their sufferings proceed from the treachery, cruelty, or tyranny of an enemy, our breasts are affected with the liveliest resentment against the author of these calamities.

28. It is here esteemed contrary to the rules of art to represent anything cool and indifferent. A distant friend, or a confident, who has no immediate interest in the catastrophe, ought, if possible, to be avoided by the poet; as communicating a like indifference to the audience, and checking the progress of the passions.

29. Few species of poetry are more entertaining than *pastoral;* and every one is sensible, that the chief source of its pleasure arises from those images of a gentle and tender tranquillity, which it represents in its personages, and of which it communicates a like sentiment to the reader. SANNAZARIUS, who transferred the scene to the sea-shore, though he presented the most magnificent object in nature, is confessed to have erred in his choice. The idea of toil, labour, and danger, suffered by the fishermen, is painful; by an unavoidable sympathy, which attends every conception of human happiness or misery.

30. When I was twenty, says a FRENCH poet,[28] OVID was my favourite: Now I am forty, I declare for HORACE. We enter, to be sure, more readily into sentiments, which resemble those we feel every day: But no passion, when well represented, can be entirely indifferent to us; because there is

---

28. [The French poet is Jean-Antoine du Cerceau.]

none, of which every man has not, within him, at least the seeds and first principles. It is the business of poetry to bring every affection near to us by lively imagery and representation, and make it look like truth and reality: A certain proof, that, wherever that reality is found, our minds are disposed to be strongly affected by it.

31. Any recent event or piece of news, by which the fate of states, provinces, or many individuals is affected, is extremely interesting even to those whose welfare is not immediately engaged. Such intelligence is propagated with celerity, heard with avidity, and enquired into with attention and concern. The interest of society appears, on this occasion, to be in some degree the interest of each individual. The imagination is sure to be affected; though the passions excited may not always be so strong and steady as to have great influence on the conduct and behaviour.

32. The perusal of a history seems a calm entertainment; but would be no entertainment at all, did not our hearts beat with correspondent movements to those which are described by the historian.

33. THUCYDIDES and GUICCIARDIN support with difficulty our attention; while the former describes the trivial encounters of the small cities of GREECE, and the latter the harmless wars of PISA. The few persons interested and the small interest fill not the imagination, and engage not the affections. The deep distress of the numerous ATHENIAN army before SYRACUSE; the danger which so nearly threatens VENICE; these excite compassion; these move terror and anxiety.

34. The indifferent, uninteresting style of SUETONIUS, equally with the masterly pencil of TACITUS, may convince us of the cruel depravity of NERO or TIBERIUS: But what a difference of sentiment! While the former coldly relates the facts; and the latter sets before our eyes the venerable figures of a SORANUS and a THRASEA, intrepid in their fate, and only moved by the melting sorrows of their friends and kindred. What sympathy then touches every human heart! What indignation against the tyrant, whose causeless fear or unprovoked malice gave rise to such detestable barbarity!

35. If we bring these subjects nearer: If we remove all suspicion of fiction and deceit: What powerful concern is excited, and how much superior, in many instances, to the narrow attachments of self-love and private interest! Popular sedition, party zeal, a devoted obedience to factious leaders; these are some of the most visible, though less laudable effects of this social sympathy in human nature.

36. The frivolousness of the subject too, we may observe, is not able to detach us entirely from what carries an image of human sentiment and affection.

37. When a person stutters, and pronounces with difficulty, we even sympathize with this trivial uneasiness, and suffer for him. And it is a rule in criticism, that every combination of syllables or letters, which gives pain to the organs of speech in the recital, appears also from a species of sympathy harsh and disagreeable to the ear. Nay, when we run over a book with our eye, we are sensible of such unharmonious composition; because we still imagine, that a person recites it to us, and suffers from the pronunciation of these jarring sounds. So delicate is our sympathy!

38. Easy and unconstrained postures and motions are always beautiful: An air of health and vigour is agreeable: Clothes which warm, without burthening the body; which cover, without imprisoning the limbs, are well-fashioned. In every judgment of beauty, the feelings of the person affected enter into consideration, and communicate to the spectator similar touches of pain or pleasure.[29] What wonder, then, if we can pronounce no judgment concerning the character and conduct of men, without considering the tendencies of their actions, and the happiness or misery which thence arises to society? What association of ideas would ever operate, were that principle here totally unactive.[30]

---

29. "Decentior equus cujus astricta suntilia; sed idem velocior. Pulcher aspectu sit athleta, cujus lacertos execitatio expressit; idem certamini paratior nunquam enim *species* ab *utilitate* dividitur. Sed hoc quidem discernere modici judicii est." QUINTILIAN, Inst. lib. 8. cap. 3. [Quintilian, *Institutes,* book 8, chapter 3. The passage may be translated as follows: "The horse whose flanks are spare is more becoming but also faster. The athlete whose arm muscles have been developed by exercise may please the eye but is also more equipped for contest. For outward appearance is never separate from usefulness. Any person of ordinary judgement can recognise this at least."]

30. In proportion to the station which a man possesses, according to the relations in which he is placed; we always expect from him a greater or less degree of good, and when disappointed, blame his inutility; and much more do we blame him, if any ill or prejudice arise from his conduct and behaviour. When the interests of one country interfere with those of another, we estimate the merits of a statesman by the good or ill, which results to his own country from his measures and councils, without regard to the prejudice which he brings on its enemies and rivals. His fellow-citizens are the objects, which lie nearest the eye, while we determine his character. And as nature has implanted in every one a superior affection to his own country, we never expect any regard to distant nations, where a competition arises. Not to mention, that, while every man consults the good of his own community, we are sensible, that the general interest of mankind is better promoted, than any loose indeterminate views to the good of a species, whence no beneficial action could ever result, for want of a duly limited object, on which they could exert themselves.

39. If any man from a cold insensibility, or narrow selfishness of temper, is unaffected with the images of human happiness or misery, he must be equally indifferent to the images of vice and virtue: As, on the other hand, it is always found, that a warm concern for the interests of our species is attended with a delicate feeling of all moral distinctions; a strong resentment of injury done to men; a lively approbation of their welfare. In this particular, though great superiority is observable of one man above another; yet none are so entirely indifferent to the interest of their fellow-creatures, as to perceive no distinctions of moral good and evil, in consequence of the different tendencies of actions and principles. How, indeed, can we suppose it possible in any one, who wears a human heart, that if there be subjected to his censure, one character or system of conduct, which is beneficial, and another which is pernicious to his species or community, he will not so much as give a cool preference to the former, or ascribe to it the smallest merit or regard? Let us suppose such a person ever so selfish; let private interest have ingrossed ever so much his attention; yet in instances, where that is not concerned, he must unavoidably feel *some* propensity to the good of mankind, and make it an object of choice, if everything else be equal. Would any man, who is walking along, tread as willingly on another's gouty toes, whom he has no quarrel with, as on the hard flint and pavement? There is here surely a difference in the case. We surely take into consideration the happiness and misery of others, in weighing the several motives of action, and incline to the former, where no private regards draw us to seek our own promotion or advantage by the injury of our fellow-creatures. And if the principles of humanity are capable, in many instances, of influencing our actions, they must, at all times, have some authority over our sentiments, and give us a general approbation of what is useful to society, and blame of what is dangerous or pernicious. The degrees of these sentiments may be the subject of controversy; but the reality of their existence, one should think, must be admitted in every theory or system.

40. A creature, absolutely malicious and spiteful, were there any such in nature, must be worse than indifferent to the images of vice and virtue. All his sentiments must be inverted, and directly opposite to those, which prevail in the human species. Whatever contributes to the good of mankind, as it crosses the constant bent of his wishes and desires, must produce uneasiness and disapprobation; and on the contrary, whatever is the source of disorder and misery in society, must, for the same reason, be regarded with pleasure and complacency. TIMON, who probably from his affected spleen more than an inveterate malice, was denominated the manhater, embraced

ALCIBIADES with great fondness. "Go on, my boy!" cried he, "acquire the confidence of the people: you will one day, I foresee, be the cause of great calamities to them:"[31] Could we admit the two principles of the MAN-ICHEANS, it is an infallible consequence, that their sentiments of human actions, as well as of everything else, must be totally opposite, and that every instance of justice and humanity, from its necessary tendency, must please the one deity and displease the other. All mankind so far resemble the good principle, that, where interest or revenge or envy perverts not our disposition, we are always inclined, from our natural philanthropy, to give the preference to the happiness of society, and consequently to virtue above its opposite. Absolute, unprovoked, disinterested malice has never perhaps place in any human breast; or if it had, must there pervert all the sentiments of morals, as well as the feelings of humanity. If the cruelty of NERO be allowed entirely voluntary, and not rather the effect of constant fear and resentment; it is evident that TIGELLINUS, preferably to SENECA or BURRHUS, must have possessed his steady and uniform approbation.

41. A statesman or patriot, who serves our own country in our own time, has always a more passionate regard paid to him, than one whose beneficial influence operated on distant ages or remote nations; where the good, resulting from his generous humanity, being less connected with us, seems more obscure, and affects us with a less lively sympathy. We may own the merit to be equally great, though our sentiments are not raised to an equal height, in both cases. The judgment here corrects the inequalities of our internal emotions and perceptions; in like manner, as it preserves us from error, in the several variations of images, presented to our external senses. The same object, at a double distance, really throws on the eye a picture of but half the bulk; yet we imagine that it appears of the same size in both situations; because we know that on our approach to it, its image would expand on the eye, and that the difference consists not in the object itself, but in our position with regard to it. And, indeed, without such a correction of appearances, both in internal and external sentiment, men could never think or talk steadily on any subject; while their fluctuating situations produce a continual variation on objects, and throw them into such different and contrary lights and positions.[32]

31. PLUTARCH in vita ALC. [Plutarch, *Lives,* "Alcibiades," chapter 16.]

32. For a little reason, the tendencies of actions and characters, not their real accidental consequences, are alone regarded in our more determinations or general judgments; though in our real feeling or sentiment, we cannot help paying greater

42. The more we converse with mankind, and the greater social intercourse we maintain, the more shall we be familiarized to these general preferences and distinctions, without which our conversation and discourse could scarcely be rendered intelligible to each other. Every man's interest is peculiar to himself, and the aversions and desires, which result from it, cannot be supposed to affect others in a like degree. General language, therefore, being formed for general use, must be moulded on some more general views, and must affix the epithets of praise or blame, in conformity to sentiments, which arise from the general interests of the community. And if these sentiments, in most men, be not so strong as those, which have a reference to private good; yet still they must make some distinction, even in persons the most depraved and selfish; and must attach the notion of good to a beneficent conduct, and of evil to the contrary. Sympathy, we shall allow, is much fainter than our concern for ourselves, and sympathy with persons remote from us much fainter than that with persons near and contiguous; but for this very reason it is necessary for us, in our calm judgments and discourse concerning the characters of men, to neglect all these differences, and render our sentiments more public and social. Besides, that we ourselves often change our situation in this particular, we every day meet with persons who are in a situation different from us, and who could never converse with us were we to remain constantly in that position and point of view, which is peculiar to ourselves. The intercourse of sentiments, therefore, in society and conversation, makes us form some general unalterable standard, by which we may approve or disapprove of characters and manners. And though the heart takes not part entirely with those general notions, nor regulates all its love and hatred by the universal abstract differences of vice and virtue, without regard to self, or the persons with whom we are more intimately connected; yet have these moral differences a considerable influence, and being sufficient, at least for discourse,

---

regard to one whose station, joined to virtue, renders him really useful to society, then to one, who exerts the social virtues only in good intentions and benevolent affections. Separating the character from the fortune, by an easy and necessary effort of thought, we pronounce these persons alike, and give them the appearance: But is not able entirely to prevail our sentiment.

Why is this peach-tree said to be better than that other; but because it produces more or better fruit? And would not the same praise be given it, though snails or vermin had destroyed the peaches, before they came to full maturity? In morals too, is not *the tree known by the fruit?* And cannot we easily distinguish between nature and accident, in the one case as well as in the other?

serve all our purposes in company, in the pulpit, on the theatre, and in the schools.[33]

43.   Thus, in whatever light we take this subject, the merit, ascribed to the social virtues, appears still uniform, and arises chiefly from that regard, which the natural sentiment of benevolence engages us to pay to the interests of mankind and society. If we consider the principles of the human make, such as they appear to daily experience and observation, we must, *a priori,* conclude it impossible for such a creature as man to be totally indifferent to the well or ill-being of his fellow-creatures, and not readily, of himself, to pronounce, where nothing gives him any particular bias, that what promotes their happiness is good, what tends to their misery is evil, without any farther regard or consideration. Here then are the faint rudiments, at least, or outlines, of a *general* distinction between actions; and in proportion as the humanity of the person is supposed to increase, his connexion with those who are injured or benefited, and his lively conception of their misery or happiness; his consequent censure or approbation acquires proportionable vigour. There is no necessity, that a generous action, barely mentioned in an old history or remote gazette, should communicate any strong feelings of applause and admiration. Virtue, placed at such a distance, is like a fixed star, which, though to the eye of reason it may appear as luminous as the sun in his meridian, is so infinitely removed as to affect the senses, neither with light nor heat. Bring this virtue nearer, by our acquaintance or connexion with the persons, or even by an eloquent recital of the case; our hearts are immediately caught, our sympathy enlivened, and our cool approbation converted into the warmest sentiments of friendship and regard. These seem necessary and infallible consequences of the general principles of human nature, as discovered in common life and practice.

44.   Again; reverse these views and reasonings: Consider the matter a posteriori; and weighing the consequences, enquire if the merit of social virtue be not, in a great measure, derived from the feelings of humanity, with which it affects the spectators. It appears to be matter of fact, that the circumstance of *utility,* in all subjects, is a source of praise and approbation:

33. It is wisely ordained by nature, that private connexions should commonly prevail over universal views and considerations; otherwise our affections and actions would be dissipated and lost, for want of a proper limited object. Thus a small benefit done to ourselves, or our near friends, excites more lively sentiments of love and approbation than a great benefit done to a distant commonwealth: But still we know here, as in all the senses, to correct these inequalities by reflection, and retain a general standard of vice and virtue, founded chiefly on a general usefulness.

That it is constantly appealed to in all moral decisions concerning the merit and demerit of actions: That it is the *sole* source of that high regard paid to justice, fidelity, honour, allegiance, and chastity: That it is inseparable from all the other social virtues, humanity, generosity, charity, affability, lenity, mercy, and moderation: And, in a word, that it is a foundation of the chief part of morals, which has a reference to mankind and our fellow-creatures.

45. It appears also, that, in our general approbation of characters and manners, the useful tendency of the social virtues moves us not by any regards to self-interest, but has an influence much more universal and extensive. It appears that a tendency to public good, and to the promoting of peace, harmony, and order in society, does always, by affecting the benevolent principles of our frame, engage us on the side of the social virtues. And it appears, as an additional confirmation, that these principles of humanity and sympathy enter so deeply into all our sentiments, and have so powerful an influence, as may enable them to excite the strongest censure and applause. The present theory is the simple result of all these inferences, each of which seems founded on uniform experience and observation.

46. Were it doubtful, whether there were any such principle in our nature as humanity or a concern for others, yet when we see, in numberless instances, that whatever has a tendency to promote the interests of society, is so highly approved of, we ought thence to learn the force of the benevolent principle; since it is impossible for anything to please as means to an end, where the end is totally indifferent. On the other hand, were it doubtful, whether there were, implanted in our nature, any general principle of moral blame and approbation, yet when we see, in numberless instances, the influence of humanity, we ought thence to conclude, that it is impossible, but that everything which promotes the interest of society must communicate pleasure, and what is pernicious give uneasiness. But when these different reflections and observations concur in establishing the same conclusion, must they not bestow an undisputed evidence upon it?

47. It is however hoped, that the progress of this argument will bring a farther confirmation of the present theory, by showing the rise of other sentiments of esteem and regard from the same or like principles.

SECTION 6
Of Qualities Useful to Ourselves

Part 1

1. It seems evident, that where a quality or habit is subjected to our examination, if it appear in any respect prejudicial to the person possessed of it, or such as incapacitates him for business and action, it is instantly blamed, and ranked among his faults and imperfections. Indolence, negligence, want of order and method, obstinacy, fickleness, rashness, credulity; these qualities were never esteemed by any one indifferent to a character; much less, extolled as accomplishments or virtues. The prejudice, resulting from them, immediately strikes our eye, and gives us the sentiment of pain and disapprobation.

2. No quality, it is allowed, is absolutely either blameable or praiseworthy. It is all according to its degree. A due medium, says the PERIPATET-ICS,[34] is the characteristic of virtue. But this medium is chiefly determined by utility. A proper celerity, for instance, and dispatch in business, is commendable. When defective, no progress is ever made in the execution of any purpose: When excessive, it engages us in precipitate and ill-concerted measures and enterprises: By such reasonings, we fix the proper and commendable mediocrity in all moral and prudential disquisitions; and never lose view of the advantages, which result from any character or habit.

3. Now as these advantages are enjoyed by the person possessed of the character, it can never be *self-love* which renders the prospect of them agreeable to us, the spectators, and prompts our esteem and approbation. No force of imagination can convert us into another person, and make us fancy, that we, being that person, reap benefit from those valuable quali-

---

34. ["Peripatetics" designates followers of the philosophy of Aristotle. The school derived its name, Peripatos, from the *peripatoi* of the Lyceum in Athens where the members met.]

ties, which belong to him. Or if it did, no celerity of imagination could immediately transport us back, into ourselves, and make us love and esteem the person, as different from us. Views and sentiments, so opposite to known truth and to each other, could never have place, at the same time, in the same person. All suspicion, therefore, of selfish regards, is here totally excluded. It is a quite different principle, which actuates our bosom, and interests us in the felicity of the person whom we contemplate. Where his natural talents and acquired abilities give us the prospect of elevation, advancement, a figure in life, prosperous success, a steady command over fortune, and the execution of great or advantageous undertakings; we are struck with such agreeable images, and feel a complacency and regard immediately arise towards him. The ideas of happiness, joy, triumph, prosperity, are connected with every circumstance of his character, and diffuse over our minds a pleasing sentiment of sympathy and humanity.[35]

4.   Let us suppose a person originally framed so as to have no manner of concern for his fellow-creatures, but to regard the happiness and misery of all sensible beings with greater indifference than even two contiguous shades of the same colour. Let us suppose, if the prosperity of nations were laid on the one hand, and their ruin on the other, and he were desired to choose; that he would stand like the schoolman's ass,[36] irresolute and undetermined, between equal motives; or rather, like the same ass between two pieces of wood or marble, without any inclination or propensity to either side. The consequence, I believe, must be allowed just, that such a person, being absolutely unconcerned, either for the public good of a community or the private utility of others, would look on every quality, however

---

35. One may venture to affirm, that there is no human nature, to whom the appearance of happiness (where envy or revenge has no place) does not give pleasure, that of misery, uneasiness. This seems inseparable from our make and constitution. But they are only more generous minds, that are thence prompted to seek zealously the good of others, and to have a real passion for their welfare. With men of narrow and ungenerous spirits, this sympathy goes not beyond a slight feeling of the imagination, which serves only to excite sentiments of complacency or ensure, and makes them apply to the object either honorable or dishonorable appellations. A griping miser, for instance, praises extremely *industry* and *frugality* even in others, and sets them, in his estimation, above all the other virtues. He knows the good that results from them, and feels that species of happiness with a more lively sympathy, than any other you could represent to him; though perhaps he would not part with a shilling to make the fortune of the industrious man, whom he praises so highly.

36. [This refers to a hypothetical situation often called "Buridan's ass" wherein an ass, when placed between two equally inviting stacks of hay, will starve since it cannot choose one over the other.]

pernicious, or however beneficial, to society, or to its possessor, with the same indifference as on the most common and uninteresting object.

5.   But if, instead of this fancied monster, we suppose a *man* to form a judgment or determination in the case, there is to him a plain foundation of preference, where everything else is equal; and however cool his choice may be, if his heart be selfish, or if the persons interested be remote from him; there must still be a choice or distinction between what is useful, and what is pernicious. Now this distinction is the same in all its parts, with the *moral distinction,* whose foundation has been so often, and so much in vain, enquired after. The same endowments of the mind, in every circumstance, are agreeable to the sentiment of morals and to that of humanity; the same temper is susceptible of high degrees of the one sentiment and of the other; and the same alteration in the objects, by their nearer approach or by connexions, enlivens the one and the other. By all the rules of philosophy, therefore, we must conclude, that these sentiments are originally the same; since, in each particular, even the most minute, they are governed by the same laws, and are moved by the same objects.

6.   Why do philosophers infer, with the greatest certainty, that the moon is kept in its orbit by the same force of gravity, that makes bodies fall near the surface of the earth, but because these effects are, upon computation, found similar and equal? And must not this argument bring as strong conviction, in moral as in natural disquisitions?

7.   To prove, by any long detail, that all the qualities, useful to the possessor, are approved of, and the contrary censured, would be superfluous. The least reflection on what is every day experienced in life, will be sufficient. We shall only mention a few instances, in order to remove, if possible, all doubt and hesitation.

8.   The quality, the most necessary for the execution of any useful enterprise, is DISCRETION; by which we carry on a safe intercourse with others, give due attention to our own and to their character, weigh each circumstance of the business which we undertake, and employ the surest and safest means for the attainment of any end or purpose. To a CROMWELL, perhaps, or a DE RETZ, discretion may appear an alderman-like virtue, as DR. SWIFT calls it; and being incompatible with those vast designs, to which their courage and ambition prompted them, it might really, in them, be a fault or imperfection. But in the conduct of ordinary life, no virtue is more requisite, not only to obtain success, but to avoid the most fatal miscarriages and disappointments. The greatest parts without it, as observed by an elegant writer, may be fatal to their owner; as POLYPHEMUS, deprived

of his eye, was only the more exposed, on account of his enormous strength and stature.

9. The best character, indeed, were it not rather too perfect for human nature, is that which is not swayed by temper of any kind; but alternately employs enterprise and caution, as each is useful to the particular purpose intended. Such is the excellence which St. Evremond ascribes to mareschal Turenne, who displayed every campaign, as he grew older, more temerity in his military enterprises; and being now, from long experience, perfectly acquainted with every incident in war, he advanced with greater firmness and security, in a road so well known to him. Fabius, says Machiavel, was cautious; Scipio enterprizing: And both succeeded, because the situation of the Roman affairs, during the command of each, was peculiarly adapted to his genius; but both would have failed, had these situations been reversed. He is happy, whose circumstances suit his temper; but he is more excellent, who can suit his temper to any circumstances.

10. What need is there to display the praises of industry, and to extol its advantages, in the acquisition of power and riches, or in raising what we call a *fortune* in the world? The tortoise, according to the fable, by his perseverance, gained the race of the hare, though possessed of much superior swiftness. A man's time, when well husbanded, is like a cultivated field, of which a few acres produce more of what is useful to life, than extensive provinces, even of the richest soil, when over-run with weeds and brambles.

11. But all prospect of success in life, or even of tolerable subsistence, must fail, where a reasonable frugality is wanting. The heap, instead of increasing, diminishes daily, and leaves its possessor so much more unhappy, as, not having been able to confine his expences to a large revenue, he will still less be able to live contentedly on a small one. The souls of men, according to Plato,[37] inflamed with impure appetites, and losing the body, which alone afforded means of satisfaction, hover about the earth, and haunt the places, where their bodies are deposited; possessed with a longing desire to recover the lost organs of sensation. So may we see worthless prodigals, having consumed their fortune in wild debauches, thrusting themselves into every plentiful table, and every party of pleasure, hated even by the vicious, and despised even by fools.

12. The one extreme of frugality is *avarice,* which, as it both deprives a man of all use of his riches, and checks hospitality and every social

37. Phædo. [Plato, *Phaedo,* 80c–81e.]

enjoyment, is justly censured on a double account. *Prodigality,* the other extreme, is commonly more hurtful to a man himself; and each of these extremes is blamed above the other, according to the temper of the person who censures, and according to his greater or less sensibility to pleasure, either social or sensual.

13. QUALITIES often derive their merit from complicated sources. Honesty, fidelity, truth, are praised for their immediate tendency to promote the interests of society; but after those virtues are once established upon this foundation, they are also considered as advantageous to the person himself, and as the source of that trust and confidence, which can alone give a man any consideration in life. One becomes contemptible, no less than odious, when he forgets the duty, which, in this particular, he owes to himself as well as to society.

14. Perhaps, this consideration is one *chief* source of the high blame, which is thrown on any instance of failure among women in point of *chastity.* The greatest regard, which can be acquired by that sex, is derived from their fidelity; and a woman becomes cheap and vulgar, loses her rank, and is exposed to every insult, who is deficient in this particular. The smallest failure is here sufficient to blast her character. A female has so many opportunities of secretly indulging these appetites, that nothing can give us security but her absolute modesty and reserve; and where a breach is once made, it can scarcely ever be fully repaired. If a man behave with cowardice on one occasion, a contrary conduct reinstates him in his character. But by what action can a woman, whose behaviour has once been dissolute, be able to assure us, that she has formed better resolutions, and has self-command enough to carry them into execution?

15. All men, it is allowed, are equally desirous of happiness; but few are successful in the pursuit: One considerable cause is the want of STRENGTH of MIND, which might enable them to resist the temptation of present ease or pleasure, and carry them forward in the search of more distant profit and enjoyment. Our affections, on a general prospect of their objects, form certain rules of conduct, and certain measures of preference of one above another: and these decisions, though really the result of our calm passions and propensities, (for what else can pronounce any object eligible or the contrary?) are yet said, by a natural abuse of terms, to be the determinations of pure *reason* and reflection. But when some of these objects approach nearer to us, or acquire the advantages of favourable lights and positions, which catch the heart or imagination; our general resolutions are frequently confounded, a small enjoyment preferred, and lasting shame and sorrow entailed upon us. And however poets may employ their wit and

eloquence, in celebrating present pleasure, and rejecting all distant views to fame, health, or fortune; it is obvious, that this practice is the source of all dissoluteness and disorder, repentance and misery. A man of a strong and determined temper adheres tenaciously to his general resolutions, and is neither seduced by the allurements of pleasure, nor terrified by the menaces of pain; but keeps still in view those distant pursuits, by which he, at once, ensures his happiness and his honour.

16. Self-satisfaction, at least in some degree, is an advantage, which equally attends the FOOL and the WISE MAN: But it is the only one; nor is there any other circumstance in the conduct of life, where they are upon an equal footing. Business, books, conversation; for all of these, a fool is totally incapacitated, and except condemned by his station to the coarsest drudgery, remains a useless burthen upon the earth. Accordingly, it is found, that men are extremely jealous of their character in this particular; and many instances are seen of profligacy and treachery, the most avowed and unreserved; none of bearing patiently the imputation of ignorance and stupidity. DICAEARCHUS, the MACEDONIAN general, who, as POLYBIUS tells us,[38] openly erected one altar to impiety, another to injustice, in order to bid defiance to mankind; even he, I am well assured, would have started at the epithet of *fool,* and have meditated revenge for so injurious an appellation. Except the affection of parents, the strongest and most indissoluble bond in nature, no connexion has strength sufficient to support the disgust arising from this character. Love itself, which can subsist under treachery, ingratitude, malice, and infidelity, is immediately extinguished by it, when perceived and acknowledged; nor are deformity and old age more fatal to the dominion of that passion. So dreadful are the ideas of an utter incapacity for any purpose or undertaking, and of continued error and misconduct in life!

17. When it is asked, Whether a quick or a slow apprehension be most valuable? Whether one, that, at first view, penetrates far into a subject, but can perform nothing upon study; or a contrary character, which must work out everything by dint of application? Whether a clear head or a copious invention? Whether a profound genius or a sure judgment? In short, what character, or peculiar turn of understanding, is more excellent than another? It is evident, that we can answer none of these questions, without considering which of those qualities capacitates a man best for the world, and carries him farthest in any undertaking.

38. Lib. 17. Cap. 35. [Polybius, *Histories,* book 18, chapter 54.]

18. If refined sense and exalted sense be not so *useful* as common sense, their rarity, their novelty, and the nobleness of their objects make some compensation, and render them the admiration of mankind: As gold, though less serviceable than iron, acquires from its scarcity a value which is much superior.

19. The defects of judgment can be supplied by no art or invention; but those of MEMORY frequently may, both in business and in study, by method and industry, and by diligence in committing everything to writing; and we scarcely ever hear a short memory given as a reason for a man's failure in any undertaking. But in ancient times, when no man could make a figure without the talent of speaking, and when the audience were too delicate to bear such crude, undigested harangues as our extemporary orators offer to public assemblies; the faculty of memory was then of the utmost consequence, and was accordingly much more valued than at present. Scarce any great genius is mentioned in antiquity, who is not celebrated for this talent; and CICERO enumerates it among the other sublime qualities of CÆSAR himself.[39]

20. Particular customs and manners alter the usefulness of qualities: they also alter their merit. Particular situations and accidents have, in some degree, the same influence. He will always be more esteemed, who possesses those talents and accomplishments, which suit his station and profession, than he whom fortune has misplaced in the part which she has assigned him. The private or selfish virtues are, in this respect, more arbitrary than the public and social. In other respects they are, perhaps, less liable to doubt and controversy.

21. In this kingdom, such continued ostentation, of late years, has prevailed among men in *active* life with regard to *public spirit,* and among those in *speculative* with regard to *benevolence;* and so many false pretensions to each have been, no doubt, detected, that men of the world are apt, without any bad intention, to discover a sullen incredulity on the head of those moral endowments, and even sometimes absolutely to deny their existence and reality. In like manner I find, that, of old, the perpetual cant of the STOICS and CYNICS concerning *virtue,* their magnificent professions and slender performances, bred a disgust in mankind; and LUCIAN, who, though licentious with regard to pleasure, is yet in other respects a very moral writer, cannot sometimes talk of virtue, so much boasted without

---

39. "Fuit in Illo Ingenium, ratio, memoria, literae, cura, cogitatio, diligentia," &c. PHILLIP. 2. ["In him was talent, intelligence, memory, writing skill, attentiveness, reflective judgement, diligence." Cicero, *Philippics* 2, chapter 45, §116.]

betraying symptoms of spleen and irony.[40] But surely this peevish delicacy, whence-ever it arises can never be carried so far as to make us deny the existence of every species of merit, and all distinction of manners and behaviour. Besides *discretion, caution, enterprise, industry, assiduity, frugality, economy, good-sense, prudence, discernment;* besides these endowments, I say, whose very names force an avowal of their merit, there are many others, to which the most determined scepticism cannot for a moment refuse the tribute of praise and approbation. *Temperance, sobriety, patience, constancy, perseverance, forethought, considerateness, secrecy, order, insinuation, address, presence of mind, quickness of conception, facility of expression;* these, and a thousand more of the same kind, no man will ever deny to be excellencies and perfections. As their merit consists in their tendency to serve the person, possessed of them, without any magnificent claim to public and social desert, we are the less jealous of their pretensions, and readily admit them into the catalogue of laudable qualities. We are not sensible that, by this concession, we have paved the way for all the other moral excellencies, and cannot consistently hesitate any longer, with regard to disinterested benevolence, patriotism, and humanity.

22. It seems, indeed, certain, that first appearances are here, as usual, extremely deceitful, and that it is more difficult, in a speculative way, to resolve into self-love the merit which we ascribe to the selfish virtues above mentioned, than that even of the social virtues, justice and beneficence. For this latter purpose, we need but say, that whatever conduct promotes the good of the community is loved, praised, and esteemed by the community, on account of that utility and interest, of which every one partakes; and though this affection and regard be, in reality, gratitude, not self-love, yet a distinction, even of this obvious nature, may not readily be made by superficial reasoners; and there is room, at least, to support the cavil and dispute for a moment. But as qualities, which tend only to the utility of their possessor, without any reference to us, or to the community, are yet

---

40. Αρετην τινα και ασωματα και ληρους μηγαλη τη φωνη ξυνειροντων. Luc. Timon. Again, Και συναγαγοντες (οι φιλοσοφοι) ενεξαπατητα μειρακια την τε πολυθρυλλητον αρετην τραγωδουσι. Icuro-men. In another place, Ηουπ γαρ εστιν η πολυθρυλλητος αρετη, και φυσις, και ιμαρμενη, και τυχη, ανυποστατα και κενα πραγματων ονοματα. Deor. Concil. [Lucian, *Timon; or, The Misanthrope,* §9; *Icaromenippus; or, The Sky Man,* §30; *The Parliament of the Gods,* §13. *Timon:* "people 'declaiming loudly on "virtue," "incorporeals," and [other] trumpery'"; *Icaromenippus:* "And collecting round them youths, they perform their 'vaunted virtue'"; and *Parliament:* "Where then are their vaunted 'virtue,' 'nature,' 'fate,' and 'fortune' – names without substance, empty of reality."]

esteemed and valued; by what theory or system can we account for this sentiment from self-love, or deduce it from that favourite origin? There seems here a necessity for confessing that the happiness and misery of others are not spectacles entirely indifferent to us; but that the view of the former, whether in its causes or effects, like sunshine or the prospect of well-cultivated plains (to carry our pretensions no higher), communicates a secret joy and satisfaction; the appearance of the latter, like a lowering cloud or barren landscape, throws a melancholy damp over the imagination. And this concession being once made, the difficulty is over; and a natural unforced interpretation of the phenomena of human life will afterwards, we may hope, prevail among all speculative enquirers.

Part 2

23. It may not be improper, in this place, to examine the influence of bodily endowments, and of the goods of fortune, over our sentiments of regard and esteem, and to consider whether these phænomena fortify or weaken the present theory. It will naturally be expected, that the beauty of the body, as is supposed by all ancient moralists, will be similar, in some respects, to that of the mind; and that every kind of esteem, which is paid to a man, will have something similar in its origin, whether it arise from his mental endowments, or from the situation of his exterior circumstances.

24. It is evident, that one considerable source of *beauty* in all animals is the advantage which they reap from the particular structure of their limbs and members, suitably to the particular manner of life, to which they are by nature destined. The just proportions of a horse, described by XENOPHON and VIRGIL, are the same that are received at this day by our modern jockeys; because the foundation of them is the same, namely, experience of what is detrimental or useful in the animal.

25. Broad shoulders, a lank belly, firm joints, taper legs; all these are beautiful in our species, because signs of force and vigour. Ideas of utility and its contrary, though they do not entirely determine what is handsome or deformed, are evidently the source of a considerable part of approbation or dislike.

26. In ancient times, bodily strength and dexterity, being of greater *use* and importance in war, was also much more esteemed and valued, than at present. Not to insist on HOMER and the poets, we may observe, that historians scruple not to mention *force of body* among the other accomplishments even of EPAMINONDAS, whom they acknowledge to be the greatest

hero, statesman, and general of all the GREEKS.[41] A like praise is given to POMPEY, one of the greatest of the ROMANS.[42] This instance is similar to what we observed above with regard to memory.

27. What derision and contempt, with both sexes, attend *impotence;* while the unhappy object is regarded as one deprived of so capital a pleasure in life, and at the same time, as disabled from communicating it to others. *Barrenness* in women, being also a species of *inutility,* is a reproach, but not in the same degree: of which the reason is very obvious, according to the present theory.

28. There is no rule in painting or statuary more indispensible than that of balancing the figures, and placing them with the greatest exactness on their proper center of gravity. A figure, which is not justly balanced, is ugly; because it conveys the disagreeable ideas of fall, harm, and pain.[43]

29. A disposition or turn of mind, which qualifies a man to rise in the world and advance his fortune, is entitled to esteem and regard, as has already been explained. It may, therefore, naturally be supposed, that the actual possession of riches and authority will have a considerable influence over these sentiments.

41. DIODORUS SICULUS, lib. 15. [Diodorus Siculus, *Historical Library,* book 15.] It may be improper to give the character of EPAMINONDAS, as drawn by the historian, in order to show the idea of perfect merit, which prevailed in those ages. In other illustrious men, say he, you will observe, that each possessed some one shining quality, which was the foundation of his fame: In EPAMINONDAS all the *virtues* are found united; force of body, eloquence of expression, vigour of mind, contempt of riches, gentleness of disposition, and *what is chiefly to be regarded,* courage and conduct of war.

42. "Cum alacribus, saltu; cumm velocibus, cursu; cum validis recte certabata." SALLUST. apud VEGET. ["He would contend appropriately with the fit, with the agile at jumping, with the swift at running." Vegetius, *De re militari,* book 1, chapter 8 (quoting Sallust).]

43. All men are equally liable to pain and disease and sickness; and may again recover health and ease. These circumstances, as they make no distinction between one man and another, are no source of pride or humility, regard or contempt. But comparing our own species to superior ones, it is a very mortifying consideration, that we should all be so liable to diseases and infirmities; and divines accordingly employ this topic, in order to depress self-conceit and vanity. They would have more success, if the common bent of our thoughts were not perpetually turned to compare ourselves with others.

The infirmities of old age are mortifying; because a comparison with the young may take place. The king's evil is industriously concealed, because it affects others, and is often transmitted to posterity. The case is nearly the same with such diseases as convey any nauseous or frightful images; the epilepsy, for instance, ulcers, sores, scabs, &c.

30. Let us examine any hypothesis by which we can account for the regard paid to the rich and powerful; we shall find none satisfactory, but that
which derives it from the enjoyment communicated to the spectator by
the images of prosperity, happiness, ease, plenty, authority, and the gratification of every appetite. Self-love, for instance, which some affect so
much to consider as the source of every sentiment, is plainly insufficient
for this purpose. Where no good-will or friendship appears, it is difficult to
conceive on what we can found our hope of advantage from the riches of
others; though we naturally respect the rich, even before they discover any
such favourable disposition towards us.

31. We are affected with the same sentiments, when we lie so much out
of the sphere of their activity, that they cannot even be supposed to possess the power of serving us. A prisoner of war, in all civilized nations, is
treated with a regard suited to his condition; and riches, it is evident, go far
towards fixing the condition of any person. If birth and quality enter for a
share, this still affords us an argument to our present purpose. For what is
it we call a man of birth, but one who is descended from a long succession
of rich and powerful ancestors, and who acquires our esteem by his connexion with persons whom we esteem? His ancestors, therefore, though
dead, are respected, in some measure, on account of their riches; and consequently, without any kind of expectation.

32. But not to go so far as prisoners of war or the dead, to find instances
of this disinterested regard for riches; we may only observe, with a little
attention, those phenomena which occur in common life and conversation.
A man, who is himself, we shall suppose, of a competent fortune, and of
no profession, being introduced to a company of strangers, naturally treats
them with different degrees of respect, as he is informed of their different
fortunes and conditions; though it is impossible that he can so suddenly
propose, and perhaps he would not accept of, any pecuniary advantage
from them. A traveller is always admitted into company, and meets with
civility, in proportion as his train and equipage speak him a man of great
or moderate fortune. In short, the different ranks of men are, in a great
measure, regulated by riches; and that with regard to superiors as well as
inferiors, strangers as well as acquaintance.

33. What remains, therefore, but to conclude, that, as riches are desired for
ourselves only as the means of gratifying our appetites, either at present or
in some imaginary future period, they beget esteem in others merely from
their having that influence. This indeed is their very nature or offence: they
have a direct reference to the commodities, conveniences, and pleasures of
life. The bill of a banker, who is broke, or gold in a desert island, would

otherwise be full as valuable. When we approach a man who is, as we say, at his ease, we are presented with the pleasing ideas of plenty, satisfaction, cleanliness, warmth; a cheerful house, elegant furniture, ready service, and whatever is desirable in meat, drink, or apparel. On the contrary, when a poor man appears, the disagreeable images of want, penury, hard labour, dirty furniture, coarse or ragged cloathes, nauseous meat and distasteful liquor, immediately strike our fancy. What else do we mean by saying that one is rich, the other poor? And as regard or contempt is the natural consequence of those different situations in life, it is easily seen what additional light and evidence this throws on our preceding theory, with regard to all moral distinctions.[44]

34. A man who has cured himself of all ridiculous prepossessions, and is fully, sincerely, and steadily convinced, from experience as well as philosophy, that the difference of fortune makes less difference in happiness than is vulgarly imagined; such a one does not measure out degrees of esteem according to the rent-rolls of his acquaintance. He may, indeed, externally pay a superior deference to the great lord above the vassal; because riches are the most convenient, being the most fixed and determinate, source of distinction. But his internal sentiments are more regulated by the personal characters of men, than by the accidental and capricious favours of fortune.

35. In most countries of EUROPE, family, that is, hereditary riches, marked with titles and symbols from the sovereign, is the chief source of distinction. In ENGLAND, more regard is paid to present opulence and plenty. Each practice has its advantages and disadvantages. Where birth is respected, unactive, spiritless minds remain in haughty indolence, and dream of nothing but pedigrees and genealogies: the generous and ambitious seek honour

---

44. There is something extraordinary, and seemingly unaccountable in the operation of our passions, when we consider the fortune and situation of others. Very often another's advancement and prosperity produces envy, which has a strong mixture of hatred, and arises chiefly from the comparison of ourselves with the person. At the very same time, or at least in very short intervals, we may feel the passion of respect, which is a species of affection or good-will, with a mixture of humility. On the other hand, the misfortunes of our fellows often cause pity, which has in it a strong mixture of good-will. This sentiment of pity is nearly allied to contempt, which is a species of dislike, with a mixture of pride. I only point out these phenomena, as a subject of speculation to such as are curious with regard to moral enquiries. It is sufficient for the present purpose to observe in general, that power and riches commonly cause respect, poverty and meanness contempt, though particular views and incidents may sometimes raise the passions of envy and of pity.

and authority, and reputation and favour. Where riches are the chief idol, corruption, venality, rapine prevail: arts, manufactures, commerce, agriculture flourish. The former prejudice, being favourable to military virtue, is more suited to monarchies. The latter, being the chief spur to industry, agrees better with a republican government. And we accordingly find that each of these forms of government, by varying the utility of those customs, has commonly a proportionable effect on the sentiments of mankind.

SECTION 7

Of Qualities Immediately Agreeable to Ourselves

1. WHOEVER has passed an evening with serious melancholy people, and has observed how suddenly the conversation was animated, and what sprightliness diffused itself over the countenance, discourse, and behaviour of every one, on the accession of a good-humoured, lively companion; such a one will easily allow that CHEERFULNESS carries great merit with it, and naturally conciliates the good-will of mankind. No quality, indeed, more readily communicates itself to all around; because no one has a greater propensity to display itself, in jovial talk and pleasant entertainment. The flame spreads through the whole circle; and the most sullen and morose are often caught by it. That the melancholy hate the merry, even though HORACE says it, I have some difficulty to allow; because I have always observed that, where the jollity is moderate and decent, serious people are so much the more delighted, as it dissipates the gloom with which they are commonly oppressed, and gives them an unusual enjoyment.

2. From this influence of cheerfulness, both to communicate itself and to engage approbation, we may perceive that there is another set of mental qualities, which, without any utility or any tendency to farther good, either of the community or of the possessor, diffuse a satisfaction on the beholders, and procure friendship and regard. Their immediate sensation, to the person possessed of them, is agreeable. Others enter into the same humour, and catch the sentiment, by a contagion or natural sympathy; and as we cannot forbear loving whatever pleases, a kindly emotion arises towards the person who communicates so much satisfaction. He is a more animating spectacle; his presence diffuses over us more serene complacency and enjoyment; our imagination, entering into his feelings and disposition, is affected in a more agreeable manner than if a melancholy, dejected, sullen, anxious temper were presented to us. Hence the affection and probation

which attend the former: the aversion and disgust with which we regard the latter.[45]

3.   Few men would envy the character which CAESAR gives of CASSIUS:

> He loves no play,
> As thou do'st, ANTHONY: he hears no music:
> Seldom he smiles; and smiles in such a sort,
> As if he mock'd himself, and scorn'd his spirit
> That could be mov'd to smile at any thing.

Not only such men, as CÆSAR adds, are commonly *dangerous,* but also, having little enjoyment within themselves, they can never become agreeable to others, or contribute to social entertainment. In all polite nations and ages, a relish for pleasure, if accompanied with temperance and decency, is esteemed a considerable merit, even in the greatest men; and becomes still more requisite in those of inferior rank and character. It is an agreeable representation, which a FRENCH writer gives of the situation of his own mind in this particular, "Virtue I love," says he, "without austerity: pleasure without effeminacy: and life, without fearing its end."[46]

4.   Who is not struck with any signal instance of GREATNESS of MIND or Dignity of Character; with elevation of sentiment, disdain of slavery, and with that noble pride and spirit, which arises from conscious virtue? The sublime, says LONGINUS, is often nothing but the echo or image of magnanimity; and where this quality appears in any one, even though a syllable be not uttered, it excites our applause and admiration; as may be observed of the famous silence of AJAX in the ODYSSEY, which expresses more noble disdain and resolute indignation than any language can convey.[47]

5.   "Were I ALEXANDER," said PARMENIO, "I would accept of these offers made by DARIUS." "So would I too," replied ALEXANDER, "were

---

45. There is no man, who, on particular occasions, is not affected with all the disagreeable passions, fear, anger, dejection, grief, melancholy, anxiety, &c. But these, so far as they are natural, and universal, make no difference between one man and another, and can never be the object of blame. It is only when the disposition gives a *propensity* to any of these disagreeable passions, that they disfigure the character, and by giving uneasiness, convey the sentiment of disapprobation to the spectator.

46. "J'aime la vertu, sans rudesse;
J'aime le plaisir, sans molesse;
J'aime la vie, et n'en crains point la fin." ST. EVREMOND.
[Seigneur de Saint Evremond, "Lettre à a M. le Comte Magalotti."]

47. Cap. 9. [Anon., *On the Sublime,* chapter 9.]

I Parmenio." This saying is admirable, says Longinus, from a like principle.[48]

6.   "Go!" cries the same hero to his soldiers, when they refused to follow him to the Indies, "go tell your countrymen, that you left Alexander completing the conquest of the world." "Alexander," said the Prince of Conde, who always admired this passage, "abandoned by his soldiers, among Barbarians, not yet fully subdued, felt in himself such a dignity and right of empire, that he could not believe it possible that any one would refuse to obey him. Whether in Europe or in Asia, among Greeks or Persians, all was indifferent to him: wherever he found men, he fancied he should find subjects."

7.   The confident of Medea in the tragedy recommends caution and submission; and enumerating all the distresses of that unfortunate heroine, asks her, what she has to support her against her numerous and implacable enemies. "Myself," replies she; "myself I say, and it is enough." Boileau justly recommends this passage as an instance of true sublime.[49]

8.   When Phocion, the modest, the gentle Phocion, was led to execution, he turned to one of his fellow-sufferers, who was lamenting his own hard fate. "Is it not glory enough for you," says he, "that you die with Phocion?"[50]

9.   Place in opposition the picture which Tacitus draws of Vitellius, fallen from empire, prolonging his ignominy from a wretched love of life, delivered over to the merciless rabble; tossed, buffeted, and kicked about; constrained, by their holding a poinard under his chin, to raise his head, and expose himself to every contumely. What abject infamy! What low humiliation! Yet even here, says the historian, he discovered some symptoms of a mind not wholly degenerate. To a tribune, who insulted him, he replied, "I am still your emperor."[51]

---

48. Idem.

49. Réflexion 10 sur Longin. [Nicolas Boileau-Despréaux, *Réflexions critiques sur quelques passages du longin,* réflexion 10.]

50. Plutarch in Phoc. [Plutarch, *Lives,* "Phocion," chapter 36.]

51. Tacit. hist. lib. 3. [Tacitus, *Histories,* chapter 3.] The author entering upon the narration, says, *laniata veste, foedum spectaculum ducebatur, multis increpantibus, nullo inlacrimante:* deformatitas exitus misericordiam abstulerat. ["He was led away, clothing in shreds, a pitiful sight. Many shouted at him; none wept. The ugliness of his exit had driven out compassion."] To enter thoroughly into this method of thinking, we must make allowance for the ancient maxims, that no one ought to prolong his life after it became dishonourable; but, as he had always a right to dispose of it, it then became a duty to part with it.

10. We never excuse the absolute want of spirit and dignity of character, or a proper sense of what is due to one's self, in society and the common intercourse of life. This vice constitutes what we properly call *meanness;* when a man can submit to the basest slavery, in order to gain his ends; fawn upon those who abuse him; and degrade himself by intimacies and familiarities with undeserving inferiors. A certain degree of generous pride or self-value is so requisite, that the absence of it in the mind displeases, after the same manner as the want of a nose, eye, or any of the most material feature of the face or member of the body.[52]

11. The utility of COURAGE, both to the public and to the person possessed of it, is an obvious foundation of merit. But to any one who duly considers of the matter, it will appear that this quality has a peculiar lustre, which it derives wholly from itself, and from that noble elevation inseparable from it. Its figure, drawn by painters and by poets, displays, in each feature, a sublimity and daring confidence; which catches the eye, engages the affections, and diffuses, by sympathy, a like sublimity of sentiment over every spectator.

12. Under what shining colours does DEMOSTHENES[53] represent PHILIP; where the orator apologizes for his own administration, and justifies that pertinacious love of liberty, with which he had inspired the ATHENIANS. "I beheld PHILIP," says he, "he with whom was your contest, resolutely, while in pursuit of empire and dominion, exposing himself to every wound; his eye gored, his neck wrested, his arm, his thigh pierced, what ever part of his body fortune should seize on, that cheerfully relinquishing; provided that, with what remained, he might live in honour and renown. And shall it be said that he, born in PELLA, a place heretofore mean and ignoble, should be inspired with so high an ambition and thirst of fame: while you, ATHENIANS, &c." These praises excite the most lively admiration; but the views presented by the orator, carry us not, we see, beyond the hero himself, nor ever regard the future advantageous consequences of his valour.

---

52. The absence of virtue may often be a vice; and that of the highest kind; as in the instance of ingratitude, as well as meanness. Where we expect a beauty, the disappointment gives an uneasy sensation, and produces a real deformity. An abjectness of character, likewise, is disgustful and contemptible in another view. Where a man has no sense of value in himself, we are not likely to have any higher esteem of him. And if the same person, who crouches to his superiors, is insolent to his inferiors (as often happens), this contrariety of behaviour, instead of correcting the former vice, aggravates it extremely by the addition of a vice still more odious. See Sect. VIII.

53. De corona. [Demosthenes, *On the Crown,* §§67–68.]

13. The martial temper of the ROMANS, inflamed by continual wars, had raised their esteem of courage so high, that, in their language, it was called *virtue,* by way of excellence and of distinction from all other moral qualities. "The SUEVI," in the opinion of TACITUS,[54] "dressed their hair with a laudible intent: not for the purpose of loving or being loves; they adorned themselves only for their enemies, and in order to appear more terrible." A sentiment of the historian, which would sound a little oddly in other nations and other ages.

14. The SCYTHIANS, according to HERODOTUS,[55] after scalping their enemies, dressed the skin like leather, and used it as a towel; and whoever had the most of those towels was most esteemed among them. So much had martial bravery, in that nation, as well as in many others, destroyed the sentiments of humanity; a virtue surely much more useful and engaging.

15. It is indeed observable, that, among all uncultivated nations, who have not as yet had full experience of the advantages attending beneficence, justice, and the social virtues, courage is the predominant excellence; what is most celebrated by poets, recommended by parents and instructors, and admired by the public in general. The ethics of HOMER are, in this particular, very different from those of FENELON, his elegant imitator; and such as were well suited to an age, when one hero, as remarked by THUCYDIDES,[56] could ask another, without offence, whether he were a robber or not. Such also very lately was the system of ethics which prevailed in many barbarous parts of IRELAND; if we may credit SPENCER, in his judicious account of the state of that kingdom.[57]

16. Of the same class of virtues with courage is that undisturbed philosophical TRANQUILLITY, superior to pain, sorrow, anxiety, and each assault of adverse fortune. Conscious of his own virtue, say the philosophers, the sage elevates himself above every accident of life; and securely placed in the temple of wisdom, looks down on inferior mortals engaged in pursuit of honours, riches, reputation, and every frivolous enjoyment.

---

54. De moribus GERM. [Tacitus, *Germania,* chapter 38.]

55. Lib. 4. [Herodotus, *Histories,* book 4.]

56. Lib. 1. [Thucydides, *History,* book 1.]

57. "It is a common use," says he, "amongst their gentlemen's sons, that, as soon as they are able to use their weapons, they strait gather to themselves three or four stragglers or kern, with whom wandering a while up and down idly the country, taking only meat, he at last falleth into some bad occasion, that shall be offered; which being once made known, he is thenceforth counted a man of worth, in whom there is courage." [Edmund Spenser, *A View of the (Present) State of Ireland.*]

These pretentious, no doubt, when stretched to the utmost, are by far too magnificent for human nature. They carry, however, a grandeur with them, which seizes the spectator, and strikes him with admiration. And the nearer we can approach in practice to this sublime tranquillity and indifference (for we must distinguish it from a stupid insensibility), the more secure enjoyment shall we attain within ourselves, and the more greatness of mind shall we discover to the world. The philosophical tranquillity may, indeed, be considered only as a branch of magnanimity.

17. Who admires not SOCRATES; his perpetual serenity and contentment, amidst the greatest poverty and domestic vexations; his resolute contempt of riches, and his magnanimous care of preserving liberty, while he refused all assistance from his friends and disciples, and avoided even the dependence of an obligation? EPICTETUS had not so much as a door to his little house or hovel; and therefore, soon lost his iron lamp, the only furniture which he had worth taking. But resolving to disappoint all robbers for the future, he supplied its place with an earthen lamp, of which he very peacefully kept possession ever after.

18. Among the ancients, the heroes in philosophy, as well as those in war and patriotism, have a grandeur and force of sentiment, which astonishes our narrow souls, and is rashly rejected as extravagant and supernatural. They, in their turn, I allow, would have had equal reason to consider as romantic and incredible, the degree of humanity, clemency, order, tranquillity, and other social virtues, to which, in the administration of government, we have attained in modern times, had any one been then able to have made a fair representation of them. Such is the compensation, which nature, or rather education, has made in the distribution of excellencies and virtues, in those different ages.

19. The merit of BENEVOLENCE, arising from its utility, and its tendency to promote the good of mankind has been already explained, and is, no doubt, the source of a *considerable* part of that esteem, which is so universally paid to it. But it will also be allowed, that the very softness and tenderness of the sentiment, its engaging endearments, its fond expressions, its delicate attentions, and all that flow of mutual confidence and regard, which enters into a warm attachment of love and friendship: it will be allowed, I say, that these feelings, being delightful in themselves, are necessarily communicated to the spectators, and melt them into the same fondness and delicacy. The tear naturally starts in our eye on the apprehension of a warm sentiment of this nature: our breast heaves, our heart is agitated, and every humane tender principle of our frame is set in motion, and gives us the purest and most satisfactory enjoyment.

20. When poets form descriptions of ELYSIAN fields, where the blessed inhabitants stand in no need of each other's assistance, they yet represent them as maintaining a constant intercourse of love and friendship, and sooth our fancy with the pleasing image of these soft and gentle passions. The idea of tender tranquillity in a pastoral ARCADIA is agreeable from a like principle, as has been observed above.[58]

21. Who would live amidst perpetual wrangling, and scolding, and mutual reproaches? The roughness and harshness of these emotions disturb and displease us: we suffer by contagion and sympathy; nor can we remain indifferent spectators, even though certain that no pernicious consequences would ever follow from such angry passions.

22. As a certain proof that the whole merit of benevolence is not derived from its usefulness, we may observe, that in a kind way of blame, we say, a person is *too good;* when he exceeds his part in society, and carries his attention for others beyond the proper bounds. In like manner, we say, a man is too *high-spirited, too intrepid, too indifferent about fortune:* Reproaches, which really, at bottom, imply more esteem than many panegyrics. Being accustomed to rate the merit and demerit of characters chiefly by their useful or pernicious tendencies, we cannot forbear applying the epithet of blame, when we discover a sentiment, which rises to a degree, that is hurtful; but it may happen, at the same time, that its noble elevation, or its engaging tenderness so seizes the heart, as rather to increase our friendship and concern for the person.[59]

23. The amours and attachments of HARRY the IVth of FRANCE, during the civil wars of the league, frequently hurt his interest and his cause; but all the young, at least, and amorous, who can sympathize with the tender passions, will allow that this very weakness (for they will readily call it such) chiefly endears that hero, and interests them in his fortunes.

24. The excessive bravery and resolute inflexibility of CHARLES the XIIth ruined his own country, and infested all his neighbours; but have such splendour and greatness in their appearance, as strikes us with admiration; and they might, in some degree, be even approved of, if they betrayed not sometimes too evident symptoms of madness and disorder.

25. The ATHENIANS pretended to the first invention of agriculture and of laws: and always valued themselves extremely on the benefit thereby

---

58. Sect. 5. Part 2.

59. Cheerfulness could scarce admit of blame from its excess, were it not that dissolute mirth, without a proper cause or subject, is a sure symptom and characteristic of folly, and on that account disgustful.

procured to the whole race of mankind. They also boasted, and with reason, of their war like enterprises; particularly against those innumerable fleets and armies of PERSIANS, which invaded GREECE during the reigns of DARIUS and XERXES. But though there be no comparison in point of utility, between these peaceful and military honours; yet we find, that the orators, who have writ such elaborate panegyrics on that famous city, have chiefly triumphed in displaying the warlike achievements. LYSIAS, THUCYDIDES, PLATO, and ISOCRATES discover, all of them, the same partiality; which, though condemned by calm reason and reflection, appears so natural in the mind of man.

26. It is observable, that the great charm of poetry consists in lively pictures of the sublime passions, magnanimity, courage, disdain of fortune; or those of the tender affections, love and friendship; which warm the heart, and diffuse over it similar sentiments and emotions. And though all kinds of passion, even the most disagreeable, such as grief and anger, are observed, when excited by poetry, to convey a satisfaction, from a mechanism of nature, not easy to be explained: Yet those more elevated or softer affections have a peculiar influence, and please from more than one cause or principle. Not to mention that they alone interest us in the fortune of the persons represented, or communicate any esteem and affection for their character.

27. And can it possibly be doubted, that this talent itself of poets, to move the passions, this PATHETIC and SUBLIME of sentiment, is a very considerable merit; and being enhanced by its extreme rarity, may exalt the person possessed of it, above every character of the age in which he lives? The prudence, address, steadiness, and benign government of AUGUSTUS, adorned with all the splendour of his noble birth and imperial crown, render him but an unequal competitor for fame with VIRGIL, who lays nothing into the opposite scale but the divine beauties of his poetical genius.

28. The very sensibility to these beauties, or a DELICACY of taste, is itself a beauty in any character; as conveying the purest, the most durable, and most innocent of all enjoyments.

29. These are some instances of the several species of merit, that are valued for the immediate pleasure which they communicate to the person possessed of them. No views of utility or of future beneficial consequences enter into this sentiment of approbation; yet is it of a kind similar to that other sentiment, which arises from views of a public or private utility. The same social sympathy, we may observe, or fellow-feeling with human happiness or misery, gives rise to both; and this analogy, in all the parts of the present theory, may justly be regarded as a confirmation of it.

SECTION 8

Of Qualities Immediately Agreeable to Others[60]

1.   As the mutual shocks, in *society*, and the oppositions of interest and self-love have constrained mankind to establish the laws of *justice*, in order to preserve the advantages of mutual assistance and protection: in like manner, the eternal contrarieties, in *company*, of men's pride and self-conceit, have introduced the rules of GOOD MANNERS or POLITENESS, in order to facilitate the intercourse of minds, and an undisturbed commerce and conversation. Among well-bred people, a mutual deference is affected; contempt of others disguised; authority concealed; attention given to each in his turn; and an easy stream of conversation maintained, without vehemence, without interruption, without eagerness for victory, and without any airs of superiority. These attentions and regards are immediately *agreeable* to others, abstracted from any consideration of utility or beneficial tendencies: they conciliate affection, promote esteem, and extremely enhance the merit of the person who regulates his behaviour by them.

2.   Many of the forms of breeding are arbitrary and casual; but the thing expressed by them is still the same. A SPANIARD goes out of his own house before his guest, to signify that he leaves him master of all. In other countries, the landlord walks out last, as a common mark of deference and regard.

3.   But, in order to render a man perfect *good company*, he must have WIT and INGENUITY as well as good manners. What wit is, it may not be easy

60. It is the nature and, indeed, the definition of virtue, that it *is a quality of the mind agreeable to or approved of by every one who considers or contemplates it.* But some qualities produce pleasure, because they are useful to society, or useful or agreeable to the person himself; others produce it more immediately, which is the case with the class of virtues here considered.

to define; but it is easy surely to determine that it is a quality immediately *agreeable* to others, and communicating, on its first appearance, a lively joy and satisfaction to every one who has any comprehension of it. The most profound metaphysics, indeed, might be employed in explaining the various kinds and species of wit; and many classes of it, which are now received on the sole testimony of taste and sentiment, might, perhaps, be resolved into more general principles. But this is sufficient for our present purpose, that it does affect taste and sentiment, and bestowing an immediate enjoyment, is a sure source of approbation and affection.

4.   In countries where men pass most of their time in conversation, and visits, and assemblies, these *companionable* qualities, so to speak, are of high estimation, and form a chief part of personal merit. In countries where men live a more domestic life, and either are employed in business, or amuse themselves in a narrower circle of acquaintance, the more solid qualities are chiefly regarded. Thus, I have often observed, that, among the FRENCH, the first questions with regard to a stranger are, *is he polite? Has he wit?* In our own country, the chief praise bestowed is always that of a *good-natured, sensible fellow.*

5.   In conversation, the lively spirit of dialogue is *agreeable,* even to those who desire not to have any share in the discourse: hence the teller of long stories, or the pompous declaimer, is very little approved of. But most men desire likewise their turn in the conversation, and regard, with a very evil eye, that *loquacity* which deprives them of a right they are naturally so jealous of.

6.   There is a sort of harmless *liars,* frequently to be met with in company, who deal much in the marvellous. Their usual intention is to please and entertain; but as men are most delighted with what they conceive to be truth, these people mistake extremely the means of pleasing, and incur universal blame. Some indulgence, however, to lying or fiction is given in *humorous* stories; because it is there really agreeable and entertaining, and truth is not of any importance.

7.   Eloquence, genius of all kinds, even good sense, and sound reasoning, when it rises to an eminent degree, and is employed upon subjects of any considerable dignity and nice discernment; all these endowments seem immediately agreeable, and have a merit distinct from their usefulness. Rarity, likewise, which so much enhances the price of every thing, must set an additional value on these noble talents of the human mind.

8.   Modesty may be understood in different senses, even abstracted from chastity, which has been already treated of. It sometimes means that tenderness and nicety of honour, that apprehension of blame, that dread of in-

trusion or injury towards others, that PUDOR,[61] which is the proper guardian of every kind of virtue, and a sure preservative against vice and corruption. But its most usual meaning is when it is opposed to *impudence* and *arrogance,* and expresses a diffidence of our own judgment, and a due attention and regard for others. In young men chiefly, this quality is a sure sign of good sense; and is also the certain means of augmenting that endowment, by preserving their ears open to instruction, and making them still grasp after new attainments. But it has a further charm to every spectator; by flattering every man's vanity, and presenting the appearance of a docile pupil, who receives, with proper attention and respect, every word they utter.

9.　　Men have, in general, a much greater propensity to overvalue than undervalue themselves; notwithstanding the opinion of ARISTOTLE.[62] This makes us more jealous of the excess on the former side, and causes us to regard, with a peculiar indulgence, all tendency to modesty and self-diffidence; as esteeming the danger less of falling into any vicious extreme of that nature. It is thus in countries where men's bodies are apt to exceed in corpulency, personal beauty is placed in a much greater degree of slenderness, than in countries where that is the most usual defect. Being so often struck with instances of one species of deformity, men think they can never keep at too great a distance from it, and wish always to have a leaning to the opposite side. In like manner, were the door opened to self-praise, and were MONTAIGNE's maxim observed, that one should say as frankly, *I have sense, I have learning, I have courage, beauty, or wit,* as it is sure we often think so; were this the case, I say, every one is sensible that such a flood of impertinence would break in upon us, as would render society wholly intolerable. For this reason custom has established it as a rule, in common societies, that men should not indulge themselves in self-praise, or even speak much of themselves; and it is only among intimate friends or people of very manly behaviour, that one is allowed to do himself justice. Nobody finds fault with MAURICE, Prince of ORANGE, for his reply to one who asked him, whom he esteemed the first general of the age, the Marquis of SPINOLA, said he, *is the second.* Though it is observable, that the self-praise implied is here better implied, than if it had been directly expressed, without any cover or disguise.

10.　　He must be a very superficial thinker, who imagines that all instances of mutual deference are to be understood in earnest, and that a man would be more esteemable for being ignorant of his own merits and accomplishments.

61. [A Latin term referring to the sense of shame one feels when one does something improper or bad.]

62. Ethic. ad Nicomachum. [Aristotle, *Nicomachean Ethics,* book 4, chapter 3.]

A small bias towards modesty, even in the internal sentiment, is favourably regarded, especially in young people; and a strong bias is required in the outward behaviour; but this excludes not a noble pride and spirit, which may openly display itself in its full extent, when one lies under calumny or oppression of any kind. The generous contumacy of SOCRATES, as CIC-ERO calls it, has been highly celebrated in all ages; and when joined to the usual modesty of his behaviour, forms a shining character. IPHICRATES, the ATHENIAN, being accused of betraying the interests of his country, asked his accuser, "Would you," says he, "have, on a like occasion, been guilty of that crime?" "By no means," replied the other. "And can you then imagine," cried the hero, "that IPHICRATES would be guilty?"[63] –In short, a generous spirit and self-value, well founded, decently disguised, and courageously supported under distress and calumny, is a great excellency, and seems to derive its merit from the noble elevation of its sentiment, or its immediate agreeableness to its possessor. In ordinary characters, we approve of a bias towards modesty, which is a quality immediately agreeable to others: the vicious excess of the former virtue, namely, insolence or haughtiness, is immediately disagreeable to others; the excess of the latter is so to the possessor. Thus are the boundaries of these duties adjusted.

11. A desire of fame, reputation, or a character with others, is so far from being blameable, that it seems inseparable from virtue, genius, capacity, and a generous or noble disposition. An attention even to trivial matters, in order to please, is also expected and demanded by society; and no one is surprised, if he find a man in company to observe a greater elegance of dress and more pleasant flow of conversation, than when he passes his time at home, and with his own family. Wherein, then, consists VANITY, which is so justly regarded as a fault or imperfection. It seems to consist chiefly in such an intemperate display of our advantages, honours, and accomplishments; in such an importunate and open demand of praise and admiration, as is offensive to others, and encroaches too far on their secret vanity and ambition. It is besides a sure symptom of the want of true dignity and elevation of mind, which is so great an ornament in any character. For why that impatient desire of applause; as if you were not justly entitled to it, and might not reasonably expect that it would for ever at tend you? Why so anxious to inform us of the great company which you have kept; the obliging things which were said to you; the honours, the distinctions which you met with; as if these were not things of course, and what we could readily, of ourselves, have imagined, without being told of them?

63. QUINTIL. lib. 5. cap. 12. [Quintilian, *Institutes,* book 5, chapter 12.]

12. DECENCY, or a proper regard to age, sex, character, and station in the world, may be ranked among the qualities which are immediately agreeable to others, and which, by that means, acquire praise and approbation. An effeminate behaviour in a man, a rough manner in a woman; these are ugly because unsuitable to each character, and different from the qualities which we expect in the sexes. It is as if a tragedy abounded in comic beauties, or a comedy in tragic. The disproportions hurt the eye, and convey a disagreeable sentiment to the spectators, the source of blame and disapprobation. This is that *indecorum,* which is explained so much at large by CICERO in his Offices.

13. Among the other virtues, we may also give CLEANLINESS a place; since it naturally renders us agreeable to others, and is no inconsiderable source of love and affection. No one will deny, that a negligence in this particular is a fault; and as faults are nothing but smaller vices, and this fault can have no other origin than the uneasy sensation which it excites in others; we may, in this instance, seemingly so trivial, clearly discover the origin of moral distinctions, about which the learned have involved themselves in such mazes of perplexity and error.

14. But besides all the *agreeable* qualities, the origin of whose beauty we can, in some degree, explain and account for, there still remains something mysterious and inexplicable, which conveys an immediate satisfaction to the spectator, but how, or why, or for what reason, he cannot pretend to determine. There is a MANNER, a grace, an ease, a genteelness, an I-know-not-what, which some men possess above others, which is very different from external beauty and comeliness, and which, however, catches our affection almost as suddenly and powerfully. And though this *manner* be chiefly talked of in the passion between the sexes, where the concealed magic is easily explained, yet surely much of it prevails in all our estimation of characters, and forms no inconsiderable part of personal merit. This class of accomplishments, therefore, must be trusted entirely to the blind, but sure testimony of taste and sentiment; and must be considered as a part of ethics, left by nature to baffle all the pride of philosophy, and make her sensible of her narrow boundaries and slender acquisitions.

15. We approve of another, because of his wit, politeness, modesty, decency, or any agreeable quality which he possesses; although he be not of our acquaintance, nor has ever given us any entertainment, by means of these accomplishments. The idea, which we form of their effect on his acquaintance, has an agreeable influence on our imagination, and gives us the sentiment of approbation. This principle enters into all the judgments which we form concerning manners and characters.

SECTION 9

Conclusion

Part I

1. IT may justly appear surprizing that any man in so late an age, should find it requisite to prove, by elaborate reasoning, that PERSONAL MERIT consists altogether in the possession of mental qualities, *useful* or *agreeable* to the *person himself* or to *others*. It might be expected that this principle would have occurred even to the first rude, unpracticed enquirers concerning morals, and been received from its own evidence, without any argument or disputation. Whatever is valuable in any kind, so naturally classes itself under the division of *useful* or *agreeable,* the *utile* or the *dulce,* that it is not easy to imagine why we should ever seek further, or consider the question as a matter of nice research or inquiry. And as every thing useful or agreeable must possess these qualities with regard either to the *person himself* or to *others,* the complete delineation or description of merit seems to be performed as naturally as a shadow is cast by the sun, or an image is reflected upon water. If the ground, on which the shadow is cast, be not broken and uneven; nor the surface from which the image is reflected, disturbed and confused; a just figure is immediately presented, without any art or attention. And it seems a reasonable presumption, that systems and hypotheses have perverted our natural understanding, when a theory, so simple and obvious, could so long have escaped the most elaborate examination.

2. But however the case may have fared with philosophy, in common life these principles are still implicitly maintained; nor is any other topic of praise or blame ever recurred to, when we employ any panegyric or satire, any applause or censure of human action and behaviour. If we observe men, in every intercourse of business or pleasure, in every discourse and conversation, we shall find them nowhere, except the schools, at any loss upon this subject. What so natural, for instance, as the following dialogue? You are very happy, we shall suppose one to say, addressing himself to

another, that you have given your daughter to CLEANTHES. He is a man of honour and humanity. Every one, who has any intercourse with him, is sure of *fair* and *kind* treatment.[64] I congratulate you too, says another, on the promising expectations of this son-in-law; whose assiduous application to the study of the laws, whose quick penetration and early knowledge both of men and business, prognosticate the greatest honours and advancement.[65] You surprize me, replies a third, when you talk of CLEANTHES as a man of business and application. I met him lately in a circle of the gayest company, and he was the very life and soul of our conversation: so much wit with good manners; so much gallantry without affectation; so much ingenious knowledge so genteelly delivered, I have never before observed in any one.[66] You would admire him still more, says a fourth, if you knew him more familiarly. That cheerfulness, which you might remark in him, is not a sudden flash struck out by company: It runs through the whole tenor of his life, and preserves a perpetual serenity on his countenance, and tranquillity in his soul. He has met with severe trials, misfortunes as well as dangers; and by his greatness of mind, was still superior to all of them.[67] The image, gentlemen, which you have here delineated of CLEANTHES, cried I, is that of accomplished merit. Each of you has given a stroke of the pencil to his figure; and you have unawares exceeded all the pictures drawn by GRATIAN or CASTIGLIONE. A philosopher might select this character as a model of perfect virtue.

3.   And as every quality which is useful or agreeable to ourselves or others is, in common life, allowed to be a part of personal merit; so no other will ever be received, where men judge of things by their natural, unprejudiced reason, without the delusive glosses of superstition and false religion. Celibacy, fasting, penance, mortification, self-denial, humility, silence, solitude, and the whole train of monkish virtues; for what reason are they everywhere rejected by men of sense, but because they serve to no manner of purpose; neither advance a man's fortune in the world, nor render him a more valuable member of society; neither qualify him for the entertainment of company, nor increase his power of self-enjoyment? We observe, on the contrary, that they cross all these desirable ends; stupify the understanding and harden the heart, obscure the fancy and sour the temper. We justly, therefore, transfer them to the opposite column, and place them

64. Qualities useful to others.
65. Qualities useful to the person himself.
66. Qualities immediately agreeable to others.
67. Qualities immediately agreeable to the person himself.

in the catalogue of vices; nor has any superstition force sufficient among men of the world, to pervert entirely these natural sentiments. A gloomy, hair-brained enthusiast, after his death, may have a place in the calendar; but will scarcely ever be admitted, when alive, into intimacy and society, except by those who are as delirious and dismal as himself.

4.   It seems a happiness in the present theory, that it enters not into that vulgar dispute concerning the *degrees* of benevolence or self-love, which prevail in human nature; a dispute which is never likely to have any is-sue, both because men, who have taken part, are not easily convinced, and because the phenomena, which can be produced on either side, are so dispersed, so uncertain, and subject to so many interpretations, that it is scarcely possible accurately to compare them, or draw from them any determinate inference or conclusion. It is sufficient for our present pur-pose, if it be allowed, what surely, without the greatest absurdity cannot be disputed, that there is some benevolence, however small, infused into our bosom; some spark of friendship for human kind; some particle of the dove kneaded into our frame, along with the elements of the wolf and serpent. Let these generous sentiments be supposed ever so weak; let them be insuf-ficient to move even a hand or finger of our body, they must still direct the determinations of our mind, and where everything else is equal, produce a cool preference of what is useful and serviceable to mankind, above what is pernicious and dangerous. A *moral distinction,* therefore, immediately arises; a general sentiment of blame and approbation; a tendency, however faint, to the objects of the one, and a proportionable aversion to those of the other. Nor will those reasoners, who so earnestly maintain the predomi-nant selfishness of human kind, be any wise scandalized at hearing of the weak sentiments of virtue implanted in our nature. On the contrary, they are found as ready to maintain the one tenet as the other; and their spirit of satire (for such it appears, rather than of corruption) naturally gives rise to both opinions; which have, indeed, a great and almost an indissoluble con-nexion together.

5.   Avarice, ambition, vanity, and all passions vulgarly, though improp-erly, comprised under the denomination of *self-love,* are here excluded from our theory concerning the origin of morals, not because they are too weak, but because they have not a proper direction for that purpose. The notion of morals implies some sentiment common to all mankind, which recommends the same object to general approbation, and makes every man, or most men, agree in the same opinion or decision concerning it. It also implies some sentiment, so universal and comprehensive as to extend to all mankind, and render the actions and conduct, even of the persons the

most remote, an object of applause or censure, according as they agree or disagree with that rule of right which is established. These two requisite circumstances belong alone to the sentiment of humanity here insisted on. The other passions produce in every breast, many strong sentiments of desire and aversion, affection and hatred; but these neither are felt so much in common, nor are so comprehensive, as to be the foundation of any general system and established theory of blame or approbation.

6.   When a man denominates another his *enemy,* his *rival,* his *antagonist,* his *adversary,* he is understood to speak the language of self-love, and to express sentiments, peculiar to himself, and arising from his particular circumstances and situation. But when he bestows on any man the epithets of *vicious* or *odious* or *depraved,* he then speaks another language, and expresses sentiments, in which he expects all his audience are to concur with him. He must here, therefore, depart from his private and particular situation, and must choose a point of view, common to him with others; he must move some universal principle of the human frame, and touch a string to which all mankind have an accord and symphony. If he mean, therefore, to express that this man possesses qualities, whose tendency is pernicious to society, he has chosen this common point of view, and has touched the principle of humanity, in which every man, in some degree, concurs. While the human heart is compounded of the same elements as at present, it will never be wholly indifferent to public good, nor entirely unaffected with the tendency of characters and manners. And though this affection of humanity may not generally be esteemed so strong as vanity or ambition, yet, being common to all men, it can alone be the foundation of morals, or of any-general system of blame or praise. One man's ambition is not another's ambition, nor will the same event or object satisfy both; but the humanity of one man is the humanity of every one, and the same object touches this passion in all human creatures.

7.   But the sentiments, which arise from humanity, are not only the same in all human creatures, and produce the same approbation or censure; but they also comprehend all human creatures; nor is there any one whose conduct or character is not, by their means, an object to every one of censure or approbation. On the contrary, those other passions, commonly denominated selfish, both produce different sentiments in each individual, according to his particular situation; and also contemplate the greater part of mankind with the utmost indifference and unconcern. Whoever has a high regard and esteem for me flatters my vanity; whoever expresses contempt mortifies and displeases me; but as my name is known but to a small part of mankind, there are few who come within the sphere of this passion, or

excite, on its account, either my affection or disgust. But if you represent a tyrannical, insolent, or barbarous behaviour, in any country or in any age of the world, I soon carry my eye to the pernicious tendency of such a conduct, and feel the sentiment of repugnance and displeasure towards it. No character can be so remote as to be, in this light, wholly indifferent to me. What is beneficial to society or to the person himself must still be preferred. And every quality or action, of every human being, must, by this means, be ranked under some class or denomination, expressive of general censure or applause.

8.   What more, therefore, can we ask to distinguish the sentiments, dependent on humanity, from those connected with any other passion, or to satisfy us, why the former are the origin of morals, not the latter? Whatever conduct gains my approbation, by touching my humanity, procures also the applause of all mankind, by affecting the same principle in them; but what serves my avarice or ambition pleases these passions in me alone, and affects not the avarice and ambition of the rest of mankind. There is no circumstance of conduct in any man, provided it have a beneficial tendency, that is not agreeable to my humanity, however remote the person; but every man, so far removed as neither to cross nor serve my avarice and ambition, is regarded as wholly indifferent by those passions. The distinction, therefore, between these species of sentiment being so great and evident, language must soon be moulded upon it, and must invent a peculiar set of terms, in order to express those universal sentiments of censure or approbation, which arise from humanity, or from views of general usefulness and its contrary. VIRTUE and VICE become then known; morals are recognized; certain general ideas are framed of human conduct and behaviour; such measures are expected from men in such situations. This action is determined to be conformable to our abstract rule; that other, contrary. And by such universal principles are the particular sentiments of self-love frequently controuled and limited.[68]

68. It seems certain, both from reason and experience, that a rude, untaught savage regulates chiefly his love and hatred by the ideas of private utility and injury, and has but faint conceptions of a general rule or system of behaviour. The man who stands opposite to him in battle, he hates heartedly, not only for the present moment, which is almost unavoidable, but for ever after; nor is he satisfied without the most extreme punishment and vengeance. But we, accustomed to society, and to more enlarged reflections, consider, that this man is serving his own country and community; that any man, in the same situation, would do the same; that we ourselves, in like circumstances, observe a like conduct; that, in general, human society is best supported on such maxims: and by these suppositions and views, we

9.   From instances of popular tumults, seditions, factions, panics, and of all passions, which are shared with a multitude, we may learn the influence of society in exciting and supporting any emotion; while the most ungovernable disorders are raised, we find, by that means, from the slightest and most frivolous occasions. SOLON was no very cruel, though, perhaps, an unjust legislator, who punished neuters in civil wars; and few, I believe, would, in such cases, incur the penalty, were their affection and discourse allowed sufficient to absolve them. No selfishness, and scarce any philosophy, have there force sufficient to support a total coolness and indifference; and he must be more or less than man, who kindles not in the common blaze. What wonder then, that moral sentiments are found of such influence in life; though springing from principles, which may appear, at first sight, somewhat small and delicate? But these principles, we must remark, are social and universal; they form, in a manner, the *party* of humankind against vice or disorder, its common enemy. And as the benevolent concern for others is diffused, in a greater or less degree, over all men, and is the same in all, it occurs more frequently in discourse, is cherished by society and conversation, and the blame and approbation, consequent on it, are thereby roused from that lethargy into which they are probably lulled, in solitary and uncultivated nature. Other passions, though perhaps originally stronger, yet being selfish and private, are often overpowered by its force, and yield the dominion of our breast to those social and public principles.

10.   Another spring of our constitution, that brings a great addition of force to moral sentiments, is the love of fame; which rules, with such uncontrolled authority, in all generous minds, and is often the grand object of all their designs and undertakings. By our continual and earnest pursuit of a character, a name, a reputation in the world, we bring our own deportment and conduct frequently in review, and consider how they appear in the eyes of those who approach and regard us. This constant habit of surveying ourselves, as it were, in reflection, keeps alive all the sentiments of right and wrong, and begets, in noble natures, a certain reverence for themselves

---

correct, in some measure, our ruder and narrower positions. And though much of our friendship and enmity be still regulated by private considerations of benefit and harm, we pay, at least, this homage to general rules, which we are accustomed to respect, that we commonly pervert our adversary's conduct, by imputing malice or injustice to him, in order to give vent to those passions, which arise from self-love and private interest. When the heart is full of rage, it never wants pretences of this nature; though sometimes as frivolous, as those from which HORACE, being almost crushed by the fall of a tree, effects to accuse of parricide the first planter of it. [Horace, *Odes,* book 2, ode 13.]

as well as others, which is the surest guardian of every virtue. The animal conveniencies and pleasures sink gradually in their value; while every inward beauty and moral grace is studiously acquired, and the mind is accomplished in every perfection, which can adorn or embellish a rational creature.

11. Here is the most perfect morality with which we are acquainted: Here is displayed the force of many sympathies. Our moral sentiment is itself a feeling chiefly of that nature, and our regard to a character with others seems to arise only from a care of preserving a character with ourselves; and in order to attain this end, we find it necessary to prop our tottering judgment on the correspondent approbation of mankind.

12. But, that we may accommodate matters, and remove if possible every difficulty, let us allow all these reasonings to be false. Let us allow that, when we resolve the pleasure, which arises from views of utility, into the sentiments of humanity and sympathy, we have embraced a wrong hypothesis. Let us confess it necessary to find some other explication of that applause, which is paid to objects, whether inanimate, animate, or rational, if they have a tendency to promote the welfare and advantage of mankind. However difficult it be to conceive that an object is approved of on account of its tendency to a certain end, while the end itself is totally indifferent: let us swallow this absurdity, and consider what are the consequences. The preceding delineation or definition of PERSONAL MERIT must still retain its evidence and authority: it must still be allowed that every quality of the mind, which is *useful* or *agreeable* to the *person himself* or to *others,* communicates a pleasure to the spectator, engages his esteem, and is admitted under the honourable denomination of virtue or merit. Are not justice, fidelity, honour, veracity, allegiance, chastity, esteemed solely on account of their tendency to promote the good of society? Is not that tendency inseparable from humanity, benevolence, lenity, generosity, gratitude, moderation, tenderness, friendship, and all the other social virtues? Can it possibly be doubted that industry, discretion, frugality, secrecy, order, perseverance, forethought, judgment, and this whole class of virtues and accomplishments, of which many pages would not contain the catalogue; can it be doubted, I say, that the tendency of these qualities to promote the interest and happiness of their possessor, is the sole foundation of their merit? Who can dispute that a mind, which supports a perpetual serenity and cheerfulness, a noble dignity and undaunted spirit, a tender affection and good-will to all around; as it has more enjoyment within itself, is also a more animating and rejoicing spectacle, than if dejected with melancholy, tormented with anxiety, irritated with rage, or sunk into the most abject baseness and

degeneracy? And as to the qualities, immediately *agreeable* to *others,* they speak sufficiently for themselves; and he must be unhappy, indeed, either in his own temper, or in his situation and company, who has never perceived the charms of a facetious wit or flowing affability, of a delicate modesty or decent genteelness of address and manner.

13. I am sensible, that nothing can be more unphilosophical than to be positive or dogmatical on any subject; and that, even if excessive scepticism could be maintained, it would not be more destructive to all just reasoning and inquiry. I am convinced that, where men are the most sure and arrogant, they are commonly the most mistaken, and have there given reins to passion, without that proper deliberation and suspense, which can alone secure them from the grossest absurdities. Yet, I must confess, that this enumeration puts the matter in so strong a light, that I cannot, at *present,* be more assured of any truth, which I learn from reasoning and argument, than that personal merit consists entirely in the usefulness or agreeableness of qualities to the person himself possessed of them, or to others, who have any intercourse with him. But when I reflect that, though the bulk and figure of the earth have been measured and delineated, though the motions of the tides have been accounted for, the order and economy of the heavenly bodies subjected to their proper laws, and INFINITE itself reduced to calculation; yet men still dispute concerning the foundation of their moral duties. When I reflect on this, I say, I fall back into diffidence and scepticism, and suspect that an hypothesis, so obvious, had it been a true one, would, long ere now, have been received by the unanimous suffrage and consent of mankind.

Part 2

14. Having explained the moral *approbation* attending merit or virtue, there remains nothing but briefly to consider our interested *obligation* to it, and to inquire whether every man, who has any regard to his own happiness and welfare, will not best find his account in the practice of every moral duty. If this can be clearly ascertained from the foregoing theory, we shall have the satisfaction to reflect, that we have advanced principles, which not only, it is hoped, will stand the test of reasoning and inquiry, but may contribute to the amendment of men's lives, and their improvement in morality and social virtue. And though the philosophical truth of any proposition by no means depends on its tendency to promote the interests of society; yet a man has but a bad grace, who delivers a theory, however true, which he must confess, leads to a practice dangerous and pernicious.

Why rake into those corners of nature which spread a nuisance all around? Why dig up the pestilence from the pit in which it is buried? The ingenuity of your researches may be admired, but your systems will be detested; and mankind will agree, if they cannot refute them, to sink them, at least, in eternal silence and oblivion. Truths which are *pernicious* to society, if any such there be, will yield to errors which are salutary and *advantageous*.

15. But what philosophical truths can be more advantageous to society, than those here delivered, which represent virtue in all her genuine and most engaging charms, and makes us approach her with ease, familiarity, and affection? The dismal dress falls off, with which many divines, and some philosophers, have covered her; and nothing appears but gentleness, humanity, beneficence, affability; nay, even at proper intervals, play, frolic, and gaiety. She talks not of useless austerities and rigours, suffering and self-denial. She declares that her sole purpose is to make her votaries and all mankind, during every instant of their existence, if possible, cheerful and happy; nor does she ever willingly part with any pleasure but in hopes of ample compensation in some other period of their lives. The sole trouble which she demands, is that of just calculation, and a steady preference of the greater happiness. And if any austere pretenders approach her, enemies to joy and pleasure, she either rejects them as hypocrites and deceivers; or, if she admit them in her train, they are ranked, however, among the least favoured of her votaries.

16. And, indeed, to drop all figurative expression, what hopes can we ever have of engaging mankind to a practice which we confess full of austerity and rigour? Or what theory of morals can ever serve any useful purpose, unless it can show, by a particular detail, that all the duties which it recommends, are also the true interest of each individual? The peculiar advantage of the foregoing system seems to be, that it furnishes proper mediums for that purpose.

17. That the virtues which are immediately *useful* or *agreeable* to the person possessed of them, are desirable in a view to self-interest, it would surely be superfluous to prove. Moralists, indeed, may spare themselves all the pains which they often take in recommending these duties. To what purpose collect arguments to evince that temperance is advantageous, and the excesses of pleasure hurtful, when it appears that these excesses are only denominated such, because they are hurtful; and that, if the unlimited use of strong liquors, for instance, no more impaired health or the faculties of mind and body than the use of air or water, it would not be a whit more vicious or blameable?

18. It seems equally superfluous to prove, that the *companionable* virtues of good manners and wit, decency and genteelness, are more desirable than the contrary qualities. Vanity alone, without any other consideration, is a sufficient motive to make us wish for the possession of these accomplishments. No man was ever willingly deficient in this particular. All our failures here proceed from bad education, want of capacity, or a perverse and unpliable disposition. Would you have your company coveted, admired, followed; rather than hated, despised, avoided? Can any one seriously deliberate in the case? As no enjoyment is sincere, without some reference to company and society; so no society can be agreeable, or even tolerable, where a man feels his presence unwelcome, and discovers all around him symptoms of disgust and aversion.

19. But why, in the greater society or confederacy of mankind, should not the case be the same as in particular clubs and companies? Why is it more doubtful, that the enlarged virtues of humanity, generosity, beneficence, are desirable with a view of happiness and self-interest, than the limited endowments of ingenuity and politeness? Are we apprehensive lest those social affections interfere, in a greater and more immediate degree than any other pursuits, with private utility, and cannot be gratified, without some important sacrifice of honour and advantage? If so, we are but ill-instructed in the nature of the human passions, and are more influenced by verbal distinctions than by real differences.

20. Whatever contradiction may vulgarly be supposed between the *selfish* and *social* sentiments or dispositions, they are really no more opposite than selfish and ambitious, selfish and revengeful, selfish and vain. It is requisite that there be an original propensity of some kind, in order to be a basis to self-love, by giving a relish to the objects of its pursuit; and none more fit for this purpose than benevolence or humanity. The goods of fortune are spent in one gratification or another: the miser who accumulates his annual income, and lends it out at interest, has really spent it in the gratification of his avarice. And it would be difficult to show why a man is more a loser by a generous action, than by any other method of expense; since the utmost which he can attain by the most elaborate selfishness, is the indulgence of some affection.

21. Now if life, without passion, must be altogether insipid and tiresome; let a man suppose that he has full power of modelling his own disposition, and let him deliberate what appetite or desire he would choose for the foundation of his happiness and enjoyment. Every affection, he would observe, when gratified by success, gives a satisfaction proportioned to its force and

violence; but besides this advantage, common to all, the immediate feeling of benevolence and friendship, humanity and kindness, is sweet, smooth, tender, and agreeable, independent of all fortune and accidents. These virtues are besides attended with a pleasing consciousness or remembrance, and keep us in humour with ourselves as well as others; while we retain the agreeable reflection of having done our part towards mankind and society. And though all men show a jealousy of our success in the pursuits of avarice and ambition; yet are we almost sure of their good-will and good wishes, so long as we persevere in the paths of virtue, and employ ourselves in the execution of generous plans and purposes. What other passion is there where we shall find so many advantages united; an agreeable sentiment, a pleasing consciousness, a good reputation? But of these truths, we may observe, men are, of themselves, pretty much convinced; nor are they deficient in their duty to society, because they would not wish to be generous, friendly, and humane; but because they do not feel themselves such.

22. Treating vice with the greatest candour, and making it all possible concessions, we must acknowledge that there is not, in any instance, the smallest pretext for giving it the preference above virtue, with a view of self-interest; except, perhaps, in the case of justice, where a man, taking things in a certain light, may often seem to be a loser by his integrity. And though it is allowed that, without a regard to property, no society could subsist; yet according to the imperfect way in which human affairs are conducted, a sensible knave, in particular incidents, may think that an act of iniquity or infidelity will make a considerable addition to his fortune, without causing any considerable breach in the social union and confederacy. That *honesty is the best policy,* may be a good general rule, but is liable to many exceptions; and he, it may perhaps be thought, conducts himself with most wisdom, who observes the general rule, and takes advantage of all the exceptions.

23. I must confess that, if a man think that this reasoning much requires an answer, it would be a little difficult to find any which will to him appear satisfactory and convincing. If his heart rebel not against such pernicious maxims, if he feel no reluctance to the thoughts of villainy or baseness, he has indeed lost a considerable motive to virtue; and we may expect that this practice will be answerable to his speculation. But in all ingenuous natures, the antipathy to treachery and roguery is too strong to be counterbalanced by any views of profit or pecuniary advantage. Inward peace of mind, consciousness of integrity, a satisfactory review of our own conduct; these are circumstances, very requisite to happiness, and will be cherished and cultivated by every honest man, who feels the importance of them.

24. Such a one has, besides, the frequent satisfaction of seeing knaves, with all their pretended cunning and abilities, betrayed by their own maxims; and while they purpose to cheat with moderation and secrecy, a tempting incident occurs, nature is frail, and they give into the snare; whence they can never extricate themselves, without a total loss of reputation, and the forfeiture of all future trust and confidence with mankind.

25. But were they ever so secret and successful, the honest man, if he has any tincture of philosophy, or even common observation and reflection, will discover that they themselves are, in the end, the greatest dupes, and have sacrificed the invaluable enjoyment of a character, with themselves at least, for the acquisition of worthless toys and gewgaws. How little is requisite to supply the *necessities* of nature? And in a view to *pleasure,* what comparison between the unbought satisfaction of conversation, society, study, even health and the common beauties of nature, but above all the peaceful reflection on one's own conduct; what comparison, I say, between these and the feverish, empty amusements of luxury and expense? These natural pleasures, indeed, are really without price; both because they are below all price in their attainment, and above it in their enjoyment.

Concerning Moral Sentiment

1.   IF the foregoing hypothesis be received, it will now be easy for us to determine the question first started,[69] concerning the general principles of morals; and though we postponed the decision of that question, lest it should then involve us in intricate speculations, which are unfit for moral discourses, we may resume it at present, and examine how far either *reason* or *sentiment* enters into all decisions of praise or censure.

2.   One principal foundation of moral praise being supposed to lie in the usefulness of any quality or action, it is evident that *reason* must enter for a considerable share in all decisions of this kind; since nothing but that faculty can instruct us in the tendency of qualities and actions, and point out their beneficial consequences to society and to their possessor. In many cases this is an affair liable to great controversy: doubts may arise; opposite interests may occur; and a preference must be given to one side, from very nice views, and a small overbalance of utility. This is particularly remarkable in questions with regard to justice; as is, indeed, natural to suppose, from that species of utility which attends this virtue.[70] Were every single instance of justice, like that of benevolence, useful to society; this would be a more simple state of the case, and seldom liable to great controversy. But as single instances of justice are often pernicious in their first and immediate tendency, and as the advantage to society results only from the observance of the general rule, and from the concurrence and combination of several persons in the same equitable conduct; the case here becomes more intricate and involved. The various circumstances of society; the various consequences of any practice; the various interests which may be proposed; these, on many occasions, are doubtful, and subject to great discussion and inquiry. The object of municipal laws is to fix all the questions

69. Sect. 1.
70. See App. 3.

with regard to justice: the debates of civilians; the reflections of politicians; the precedents of history and public records, are all directed to the same purpose. And a very accurate *reason* or *judgment* is often requisite, to give the true determination, amidst such intricate doubts arising from obscure or opposite utilities.

3. But though reason, when fully assisted and improved, be sufficient to instruct us in the pernicious or useful tendency of qualities and actions; it is not alone sufficient to produce any moral blame or approbation. Utility is only a tendency to a certain end; and were the end totally indifferent to us, we should feel the same indifference towards the means. It is requisite a *sentiment* should here display itself, in order to give a preference to the useful above the pernicious tendencies. This *sentiment* can be no other than a feeling for the happiness of mankind, and a resentment of their misery; since these are the different ends which virtue and vice have a tendency to promote. Here therefore *reason* instructs us in the several tendencies of actions, and *humanity* makes a distinction in favour of those which are useful and beneficial.

4. This partition between the faculties of understanding and sentiment, in all moral decisions, seems clear from the preceding hypothesis. But I shall suppose that hypothesis false: it will then be requisite to look out for some other theory that may be satisfactory; and I dare venture to affirm that none such will ever be found, so long as we suppose reason to be the sole source of morals. To prove this, it will be proper to weigh the five following considerations.

5. I. It is easy for a false hypothesis to maintain some appearance of truth, while it keeps wholly in generals, makes use of undefined terms, and employs comparisons, instead of instances. This is particularly remarkable in that philosophy, which ascribes the discernment of all moral distinctions to reason alone, without the concurrence of sentiment. It is impossible that, in any particular instance, this hypothesis can so much as be rendered intelligible, whatever specious figure it may make in general declamations and discourses. Examine the crime of *ingratitude,* for instance; which has place, wherever we observe good-will, expressed and known, together with good-offices performed, on the one side, and a return of ill-will or indifference, with ill-offices or neglect on the other: anatomize all these circumstances, and examine, by your reason alone, in what consists the demerit or blame. You never will come to any issue or conclusion.

6. Reason judges either of *matter of fact* or of *relations.* Enquire then, first, where is that matter of fact which we here call crime; point it out; determine the time of its existence; describe its essence or nature; explain

the sense or faculty to which it discovers itself. It resides in the mind of the person who is ungrateful. He must, therefore, feel it, and be conscious of it. But nothing is there, except the passion of ill-will or absolute indifference. You cannot say that these, of themselves, always, and in all circumstances, are crimes. No, They are only crimes when directed towards persons who have before expressed and displayed good-will towards us. Consequently, we may infer, that the crime of ingratitude is not any particular individual *fact;* but arises from a complication of circumstances, which, being presented to the spectator, excites the *sentiment* of blame, by the particular structure and fabric of his mind.

7.   This representation, you say, is false. Crime, indeed, consists not in a particular *fact,* of whose reality we are assured by *reason;* but it consists in certain *moral relations,* discovered by reason, in the same manner as we discover by reason the truths of geometry or algebra. But what are the relations, I ask, of which you here talk? In the case stated above, I see first good-will and good-offices in one person; then ill-will and ill-offices in the other. Between these, there is a relation of *contrariety.* Does the crime consist in that relation? But suppose a person bore me ill-will or did me ill-offices; and I, in return, were indifferent towards him, or did him good offices. Here is the same relation of *contrariety;* and yet my conduct is often highly laudable. Twist and turn this matter as much as you will, you can never rest the morality on relation; but must have recourse to the decisions of sentiment.

8.   When it is affirmed that two and three are equal to the half of ten, this relation of equality I understand perfectly. I conceive, that if ten be divided into two parts, of which one has as many units as the other; and if any of these parts be compared to two added to three, it will contain as many units as that compound number. But when you draw thence a comparison to moral relations, I own that I am altogether at a loss to understand you. A moral action, a crime, such as ingratitude, is a complicated object. Does the morality consist in the relation of its parts to each other? How? After what manner? Specify the relation: be more particular and explicit in your propositions, and you will easily see their falsehood.

9.   No, say you, the morality consists in the relation of actions to the rule of right; and they are denominated good or ill, according as they agree or disagree with it. What then is this rule of right? In what does it consist? How is it determined? By reason, you say, which examines the moral relations of actions. So that moral relations are determined by the comparison of action to a rule. And that rule is determined by considering the moral relations of objects. Is not this fine reasoning?

10. All this is metaphysics, you cry. That is enough; there needs nothing more to give a strong presumption of falsehood. Yes, reply I: Here are metaphysics surely: But they are all on your side, who advance an abstruse hypothesis, which can never be made intelligible, nor quadrate with any particular instance or illustration. The hypothesis which we embrace is plain. It maintains that morality is determined by sentiment. It defines virtue to be *whatever mental action or quality gives to a spectator the pleasing sentiment of approbation;* and vice the contrary. We then proceed to examine a plain matter of fact, to wit, what actions have this influence. We consider all the circumstances in which these actions agree, and thence endeavour to extract some general observations with regard to these sentiments. If you call this metaphysics, and find anything abstruse here, you need only conclude that your turn of mind is not suited to the moral sciences.

11. 2. When a man, at any time, deliberates concerning his own conduct (as, whether he had better, in a particular emergence, assist a brother or a benefactor), he must consider these separate relations, with all the circumstances and situations of the persons, in order to determine the superior duty and obligation; and in order to determine the proportion of lines in any triangle, it is necessary to examine the nature of that figure, and the relation which its several parts bear to each other. But notwithstanding this appearing similarity in the two cases, there is, at bottom, an extreme difference between them. A speculative reasoner concerning triangles or circles considers the several known and given relations of the parts of these figures; and thence infers some unknown relation, which is dependent on the former. But in moral deliberations we must be acquainted beforehand with all the objects, and all their relations to each other; and from a comparison of the whole, fix our choice or approbation. No new fact to be ascertained; no new relation to be discovered. All the circumstances of the case are supposed to be laid before us, ere we can fix any sentence of blame or approbation. If any material circumstance be yet unknown or doubtful, we must first employ our inquiry or intellectual faculties to assure us of it; and must suspend for a time all moral decision or sentiment. While we are ignorant whether a man were aggressor or not, how can we determine whether the person who killed him be criminal or innocent? But after every circumstance, every relation is known, the understanding has no further room to operate, nor any object on which it could employ itself. The approbation or blame which then ensues, cannot be the work of the judgment, but of the heart; and is not a speculative proposition or affirmation, but an active feeling or sentiment. In the disquisitions of the understanding, from

known circumstances and relations, we infer some new and unknown. In moral decisions, all the circumstances and relations must be previously known; and the mind, from the contemplation of the whole, feels some new impression of affection or disgust, esteem or contempt, approbation or blame.

12. Hence the great difference between a mistake of *fact* and one of *right;* and hence the reason why the one is commonly criminal and not the other. When OEDIPUS killed LAIUS, he was ignorant of the relation, and from circumstances, innocent and involuntary, formed erroneous opinions concerning the action which he committed. But when NERO killed AGRIPPINA, all the relations between himself and the person, and all the circumstances of the fact, were previously known to him; but the motive of revenge, or fear, or interest, prevailed in his savage heart over the sentiments of duty and humanity. And when we express that detestation against him to which he himself, in a little time, became insensible, it is not that we see any relations, of which he was ignorant; but that, for the rectitude of our disposition, we feel sentiments against which he was hardened from flattery and a long perseverance in the most enormous crimes. In these sentiments then, not in a discovery of relations of any kind, do all moral determinations consist. Before we can pretend to form any decision of this kind, everything must be known and ascertained on the side of the object or action. Nothing remains but to feel, on our part, some sentiment of blame or approbation; whence we pronounce the action criminal or virtuous.

13. 3. This doctrine will become still more evident, if we compare moral beauty with natural, to which in many particulars it bears so near a resemblance. It is on the proportion, relation, and position of parts, that all natural beauty depends; but it would be absurd thence to infer, that the perception of beauty, like that of truth in geometrical problems, consists wholly in the perception of relations, and was performed entirely by the understanding or intellectual faculties. In all the sciences, our mind from the known relations investigates the unknown. But in all decisions of taste or external beauty, all the relations are beforehand obvious to the eye; and we thence proceed to feel a sentiment of complacency or disgust, according to the nature of the object, and disposition of our organs.

14. EUCLID has fully explained all the qualities of the circle; but has not in any proposition said a word of its beauty. The reason is evident. The beauty is not a quality of the circle. It lies not in any part of the line, whose parts are equally distant from a common center. It is only the effect which that figure produces upon the mind, whose peculiar fabric of structure renders it susceptible of such sentiments. In vain would you look for it in the circle,

or seek it, either by your senses or by mathematical reasoning, in all the properties of that figure.

15. Attend to PALLADIO and PERRAULT, while they explain all the parts and proportions of a pillar. They talk of the cornice, and frieze, and base, and entablature, and shaft, and architrave; and give the description and position of each of these members. But should you ask the description and position of its beauty, they would readily reply, that the beauty is not in any of the parts or members of a pillar, but results from the whole, when that complicated figure is presented to an intelligent mind, susceptible to those finer sensations. Till such a spectator appear, there is nothing but a figure of such particular dimensions and proportions: from his sentiments alone arise its elegance and beauty.

16. Again; attend to CICERO, while he paints the crimes of a VERRES or a CATILINE. You must acknowledge that the moral turpitude results, in the same manner, from the contemplation of the whole, when presented to a being whose organs have such a particular structure and formation. The orator may paint rage, insolence, barbarity on the one side; meekness, suffering, sorrow, innocence on the other. But if you feel no indignation or compassion arise in you from this complication of circumstances, you would in vain ask him, in what consists the crime or villainy, which he so vehemently exclaims against? At what time, or on what subject it first began to exist? And what has a few months afterwards become of it, when every disposition and thought of all the actors is totally altered or annihilated? No satisfactory answer can be given to any of these questions, upon the abstract hypothesis of morals; and we must at last acknowledge, that the crime or immorality is no particular fact or relation, which can be the object of the understanding, but arises entirely from the sentiment of disapprobation, which, by the structure of human nature, we unavoidably feel on the apprehension of barbarity or treachery.

17. 4. Inanimate objects may bear to each other all the same relations which we observe in moral agents; though the former can never be the object of love or hatred, nor are consequently susceptible of merit or iniquity. A young tree, which over-tops and destroys its parent, stands in all the same relations with NERO, when he murdered AGRIPPINA; and if morality consisted merely in relations, would no doubt be equally criminal.

18. 5. It appears evident that--the ultimate ends of human actions can never, in any case, be accounted for by reason, but recommend themselves entirely to the sentiments and affections of mankind, without any dependence on the intellectual faculties. Ask a man *why he uses exercise;* he will answer, *because he desires to keep his health.* If you then enquire,

why he desires health, he will readily reply, *because sickness is painful.* If you push your enquiries farther, and desire a reason *why he hates pain,* it is impossible he can ever give any. This is an ultimate end, and is never referred to any other object.

19. Perhaps to your second question, why he desires health, he may also reply, that it is necessary for the exercise of his calling. If you ask, why he is anxious on that head, he will answer, because he desires to get money. If you demand Why? It is the instrument of pleasure, says he. And beyond this it is an absurdity to ask for a reason. It is impossible there can be a progress in infinitum; and that one thing can always be a reason why another is desired. Something must be desirable on its own account, and because of its immediate accord or agreement with human sentiment and affection.

20. Now as virtue is an end, and is desirable on its own account, without fee and reward, merely for the immediate satisfaction which it conveys; it is requisite that there should be some sentiment which it touches, some internal taste or feeling, or whatever you may please to call it, which distinguishes moral good and evil, and which embraces the one and rejects the other.

21. Thus the distinct boundaries and offices of *reason* and of *taste* are easily ascertained. The former conveys the knowledge of truth and falsehood: the latter gives the sentiment of beauty and deformity, vice and virtue. The one discovers objects as they really stand in nature, without addition and diminution: the other has a productive faculty, and gilding or staining all natural objects with the colours, borrowed from internal sentiment, raises in a manner a new creation. Reason being cool and disengaged, is no motive to action, and directs only the impulse received from appetite or inclination, by showing us the means of attaining happiness or avoiding misery: Taste, as it gives pleasure or pain, and thereby constitutes happiness or misery, becomes a motive to action, and is the first spring or impulse to desire and volition. From circumstances and relations, known or supposed, the former leads us to the discovery of the concealed and unknown: after all circumstances and relations are laid before us, the latter makes us feel from the whole a new sentiment of blame or approbation. The standard of the one, being founded on the nature of things, is eternal and inflexible, even by the will of the Supreme Being: the standard of the other arising from the eternal frame and constitution of animals, is ultimately derived from that Supreme Will, which bestowed on each being its peculiar nature, and arranged the several classes and orders of existence.

Of Self-Love

1.   THERE is a principle, supposed to prevail among many, which is utterly incompatible with all virtue or moral sentiment; and as it can proceed from nothing but the most depraved disposition, so in its turn it tends still further to encourage that depravity. This principle is, that all *benevolence* is mere hypocrisy, friendship a cheat, public spirit a farce, fidelity a snare to procure trust and confidence; and that while all of us, at bottom, pursue only our private interest, we wear these fair disguises, in order to put others off their guard, and expose them the more to our wiles and machinations. What heart one must be possessed of who possesses such principles, and who feels no internal sentiment that belies so pernicious a theory, it is easy to imagine: and also what degree of affection and benevolence he can bear to a species whom he represents under such odious colours, and supposes so little susceptible of gratitude or any return of affection. Or if we should not ascribe these principles wholly to a corrupted heart, we must at least account for them from the most careless and precipitate examination. Superficial reasoners, indeed, observing many false pretences among mankind, and feeling, perhaps, no very strong restraint in their own disposition, might draw a general and a hasty conclusion that all is equally corrupted, and that men, different from all other animals, and indeed from all other species of existence, admit of no degrees of good or bad, but are, in every instance, the same creatures under different disguises and appearances.

2.   There is another principle, somewhat resembling the former; which has been much insisted on by philosophers, and has been the foundation of many a system; that, whatever affection one may feel, or imagine he feels for others, no passion is, or can be disinterested; that the most generous friendship, however sincere, is a modification of self-love; and that, even unknown to ourselves, we seek only our own gratification, while we appear the most deeply engaged in schemes for the liberty and happiness of mankind. By a turn of imagination, by a refinement of reflection, by an

enthusiasm of passion, we seem to take part in the interests of others, and imagine ourselves divested of all selfish considerations: but, at bottom, the most generous patriot and most niggardly miser, the bravest hero and most abject coward, have, in every action, an equal regard to their own happiness and welfare.

3.   Whoever concludes from the seeming tendency of this opinion, that those, who make profession of it, cannot possibly feel the true sentiments of benevolence, or have any regard for genuine virtue, will often find himself, in practice, very much mistaken. Probity and honour were no strangers to EPICURUS and his sect. ATTICUS and HORACE seem to have enjoyed from nature, and cultivated by reflection, as generous and friendly dispositions as any disciple of the austerer schools. And among the modern, HOBBES and LOCKE, who maintained the selfish system of morals, lived irreproachable lives; though the former lay not under any restraint of religion which might supply the defects of his philosophy.

4.   An EPICUREAN or a HOBBIST readily allows, that there is such a thing as a friendship in the world, without hypocrisy or disguise; though he may attempt, by a philosophical chymistry, to resolve the elements of this passion, if I may so speak, into those of another, and explain every affection to be self-love, twisted and moulded, by a particular turn of imagination, into a variety of appearances. But as the same turn of imagination prevails not in every man, nor gives the same direction to the original passion; this is sufficient even according to the selfish system to make the widest difference in human characters, and denominate one man virtuous and humane, another vicious and meanly interested. I esteem the man whose self-love, by whatever means, is so directed as to give him a concern for others, and render him serviceable to society: as I hate or despise him, who has no regard to any thing beyond his own gratifications and enjoyments. In vain would you suggest that these characters, though seemingly opposite, are at bottom the same, and that a very inconsiderable turn of thought forms the whole difference between them. Each character, notwithstanding these inconsiderable differences, appears to me, in practice, pretty durable and untransmutable. And I find not in this more than in other subjects, that the natural sentiments arising from the general appearances of things are easily destroyed by subtile reflections concerning the minute origin of these appearances. Does not the lively, cheerful colour of a countenance inspire me with complacency and pleasure; even though I learn from philosophy that all difference of complexion arises from the most minute differences of thickness, in the most minute parts of the skin; by means of which a

superficies is qualified to reflect one of the original colours of light, and absorb the others?

5.   But though the question concerning the universal or partial selfishness of man be not so material as is usually imagined to morality and practice, it is certainly of consequence in the speculative science of human nature, and is a proper object of curiosity and enquiry. It may not, therefore, be unsuitable, in this place, to bestow a few reflections upon it.[71]

6.   The most obvious objection to the selfish hypothesis is, that, as it is contrary to common feeling and our most unprejudiced notions, there is required the highest stretch of philosophy to establish so extraordinary a paradox. To the most careless observer there appear to be such dispositions as benevolence and generosity; such affections as love, friendship, compassion, gratitude. These sentiments have their causes, effects, objects, and operations, marked by common language and observation, and plainly distinguished from those of the selfish passions. And as this is the obvious appearance of things, it must be admitted, till some hypothesis be discovered, which by penetrating deeper into human nature, may prove the former affections to be nothing but modifications of the latter. All attempts of this kind have hitherto proved fruitless, and seem to have proceeded entirely from that love of *simplicity* which has been the source of much false reasoning in philosophy. I shall not here enter into any detail on the present subject. Many able philosophers have shown the insufficiency of these systems. And I shall take for granted what, I believe, the smallest reflection will make evident to every impartial enquirer.

7.   But the nature of the subject furnishes the strongest presumption, that no better system will ever, for the future, be invented, in order to account for the origin of the benevolent from the selfish affections, and reduce all the various emotions of the human mind to a perfect simplicity. The case is not the same in this species of philosophy as in physics. Many an hypothesis

71. Benevolence naturally divides into two kinds, the *general* and the *particular*. The first is, where we have no friendship or connexion or esteem for the person, but feel only a general sympathy with him or a compassion for his pains, and a congratulation with his pleasures. The other species of benevolence is founded on an opinion of virtue, on services done us, or on some particular connexions. Both these sentiments must be allowed real in human nature: but whether they will resolve into some nice considerations of self-love, is a question more curious than important. The former sentiment, to wit, that of general benevolence, or humanity, or sympathy, we shall have occasion frequently to treat of in the course of this inquiry; and I assume it as real, from general experience, without any other proof.

in nature, contrary to first appearances, has been found, on more accurate scrutiny, solid and satisfactory. Instances of this kind are so frequent that a judicious, as well as witty philosopher,[72] has ventured to affirm, if there be more than one way in which any phenomenon may be produced, that there is general presumption for its arising from the causes which are the least obvious and familiar. But the presumption always lies on the other side, in all enquiries concerning the origin of our passions, and of the internal operations of the human mind. The simplest and most obvious cause which can there be assigned for any phenomenon, is probably the true one. When a philosopher, in the explication of his system, is obliged to have recourse to some very intricate and refined reflections, and to suppose them essential to the production of any passion or emotion, we have reason to be extremely on our guard against so fallacious an hypothesis. The affections are not susceptible of any impression from the refinements of reason or imagination; and it is always found that a vigorous exertion of the latter faculties, necessarily, from the narrow capacity of the human mind, destroys all activity in the former. Our predominant motive or intention is, indeed, frequently concealed from ourselves when it is mingled and confounded with other motives which the mind, from vanity or self-conceit, is desirous of supposing more prevalent: but there is no instance that a concealment of this nature has ever arisen from the abstruseness and intricacy of the motive. A man that has lost a friend and patron may flatter himself that all his grief arises from generous sentiments, without any mixture of narrow or interested considerations: but a man that grieves for a valuable friend, who needed his patronage and protection; how can we suppose, that his passionate tenderness arises from some metaphysical regards to a self-interest, which has no foundation or reality? We may as well imagine that minute wheels and springs, like those of a watch, give motion to a loaded waggon, as account for the origin of passion from such abstruse reflections.

8.   Animals are found susceptible of kindness, both to their own species and to ours; nor is there, in this case, the least suspicion of disguise or artifice. Shall we account for all *their* sentiments, too, from refined deductions of self-interest? Or if we admit a disinterested benevolence in the inferior species, by what rule of analogy can we refuse it in the superior?

9.   Love between the sexes begets a complacency and good-will, very distinct from the gratification of an appetite. Tenderness to their offspring, in all sensible beings, is commonly able alone to counter-balance the stron-

---

72. Mons. FONTENELLE. [Bernard Le Bovier de Fontenelle, *Entretiens sur la pluralité des mondes* (*Conversations on the Plurality of Worlds*).]

gest motives of self-love, and has no manner of dependence on that affection. What interest can a fond mother have in view, who loses her health by assiduous attendance on her sick child, and afterwards languishes and dies of grief, when freed, by its death, from the slavery of that attendance?

10. Is gratitude no affection of the human breast, or is that a word merely, without any meaning or reality? Have we no satisfaction in one man's company above another's, and no desire of the welfare of our friend, even though absence or death should prevent us from all participation in it? Or what is it commonly, that gives us any participation in it, even while alive and present, but our affection and regard to him?

11. These and a thousand other instances are marks of a general benevolence in human nature, where no *real* interest binds us to the object. And how an *imaginary* interest known and avowed for such, can be the origin of any passion or emotion, seems difficult to explain. No satisfactory hypothesis of this kind has yet been discovered; nor is there the smallest probability that the future industry of men will ever be attended with more favourable success.

12. But farther, if we consider rightly of the matter, we shall find that the hypothesis which allows of a disinterested benevolence, distinct from self-love, has really more *simplicity* in it, and is more conformable to the analogy of nature than that which pretends to resolve all friendship and humanity into this latter principle. There are bodily wants or appetites acknowledged by every one, which necessarily precede all sensual enjoyment, and carry us directly to seek possession of the object. Thus, hunger and thirst have eating and drinking for their end; and from the gratification of these primary appetites arises a pleasure, which may become the object of another species of desire or inclination that is secondary and interested. In the same manner there are mental passions by which we are impelled immediately to seek particular objects, such as fame or power, or vengeance without any regard to interest; and when these objects are attained a pleasing enjoyment ensues, as the consequence of our indulged affections. Nature must, by the internal frame and constitution of the mind, give an original propensity to fame, ere we can reap any pleasure from that acquisition, or pursue it from motives of self-love, and desire of happiness. If I have no vanity, I take no delight in praise: if I be void of ambition, power gives me no enjoyment: if I be not angry, the punishment of an adversary is totally indifferent to me. In all these cases there is a passion which points immediately to the object, and constitutes it our good or happiness; as there are other secondary passions which afterwards arise, and pursue it as a part of our happiness, when once it is constituted such by our original affections. Were there no appetite

of any kind antecedent to self-love, that propensity could scarcely ever exert itself; because we should, in that case, have felt few and slender pains or pleasures, and have little misery or happiness to avoid or to pursue.

13.   Now where is the difficulty in conceiving, that this may likewise be the case with benevolence and friendship, and that, from the original frame of our temper, we may feel a desire of another's happiness or good, which, by means of that affection, becomes our own good, and is afterwards pursued, from the combined motives of benevolence and self-enjoyments? Who sees not that vengeance, from the force alone of passion, may be so eagerly pursued, as to make us knowingly neglect every consideration of ease, interest, or safety; and, like some vindictive animals, infuse our very souls into the wounds we give an enemy?[73] And what a malignant philosophy must it be, that will not allow to humanity and friendship the same privileges which are undisputably granted to the darker passions of enmity and resentment? Such a philosophy is more like a satire than a true delineation or description of human nature; and may be a good foundation for paradoxical wit and raillery, but is a very bad one for any serious argument or reasoning.

---

73. Animasque in vulnere ponunt. VIRG Dum alteri noceat, sui negligens says SENECA of Anger. De Ira, 1.1. ["And they leave their lives in the wound." Virgil, *Georgics,* book 4. "Regardless of itself to hurt another." Seneca, *Moral Essays,* book 3, "De ira," chapter 1.1.]

Some Farther Considerations
with Regard to Justice

1.   THE intention of this Appendix is to give some more particular explication of the origin and nature of Justice, and to mark some differences between it and the other virtues.

2.   The social virtues of humanity and benevolence exert their influence immediately by a direct tendency or instinct, which chiefly keeps in view the simple object, moving the affections, and comprehends not any scheme or system, nor the consequences resulting from the concurrence, imitation, or example of others. A parent flies to the relief of his child; transported by that natural sympathy which actuates him, and which affords no leisure to reflect on the sentiments or conduct of the rest of mankind in like circumstances. A generous man cheerfully embraces an opportunity of serving his friend; because he then feels himself under the dominion of the beneficent affections, nor is he concerned whether any other person in the universe were ever before actuated by such noble motives, or will ever afterwards prove their influence. In all these cases the social passions have in view a single individual object, and pursue the safety or happiness alone of the person loved and esteemed. With this they are satisfied: in this they acquiesce. And as the good, resulting from their benign influence, is in itself complete and entire, it also excites the moral sentiment of approbation, without any reflection on farther consequences, and without any more enlarged views of the concurrence or imitation of the other members of society. On the contrary, were the generous friend or disinterested patriot to stand alone in the practice of beneficence, this would rather enhance his value in our eyes, and join the praise of rarity and novelty to his other more exalted merits.

3.   The case is not the same with the social virtues of justice and fidelity. They are highly useful, or indeed absolutely necessary to the well-being

of mankind: but the benefit resulting from them is not the consequence of every individual single act; but arises from the whole scheme or system concurred in by the whole, or the greater part of the society. General peace and order are the attendants of justice or a general abstinence from the possessions of others; but a particular regard to the particular right of one individual citizen may frequently, considered in itself, be productive of pernicious consequences. The result of the individual acts is here, in many instances, directly opposite to that of the whole system of actions; and the former may be extremely hurtful, while the latter is, to the highest degree, advantageous. Riches, inherited from a parent, are, in a bad man's hand, the instrument of mischief. The right of succession may, in one instance, be hurtful. Its benefit arises only from the observance of the general rule; and it is sufficient, if compensation be thereby made for all the ills and inconveniences which flow from particular characters and situations.

4.   CYRUS, young and unexperienced, considered only the individual case before him, and reflected on a limited fitness and convenience, when he assigned the long coat to the tall boy, and the short coat to the other of smaller size. His governor instructed him better, while he pointed out more enlarged views and consequences, and informed his pupil of the general, inflexible rules, necessary to support general peace and order in society.

5.   The happiness and prosperity of mankind, arising from the social virtue of benevolence and its subdivisions, may be compared to a wall, built by many hands, which still rises by each stone that is heaped upon it, and receives increase proportional to the diligence and care of each workman. The same happiness, raised by the social virtue of justice and its subdivisions, may be compared to the building of a vault, where each individual stone would, of itself, fall to the ground; nor is the whole fabric supported but by the mutual assistance and combination of its corresponding parts.

6.   All the laws of nature, which regulate property, as well as all civil laws, are general, and regard alone some essential circumstances of the case, without taking into consideration the characters, situations, and connexions of the person concerned, or any particular consequences which may result from the determination of these laws in any particular case which offers. They deprive, without scruple, a beneficent man of all his possessions, if acquired by mistake, without a good title; in order to bestow them on a selfish miser, who has already heaped up immense stores of superfluous riches. Public utility requires that property should be regulated by general inflexible rules; and though such rules are adopted as best serve the same end of public utility, it is impossible for them to prevent all particular hardships, or make beneficial consequences result from every individual case.

It is sufficient, if the whole plan or scheme be necessary to the support of civil society, and if the balance of good, in the main, do thereby preponderate much above that of evil. Even the general laws of the universe, though planned by infinite wisdom, cannot exclude all evil or inconvenience in every particular operation.

7.   It has been asserted by some, that justice arises from HUMAN CONVENTIONS, and proceeds from the voluntary choice, consent, or combination of mankind. If by convention be here meant a *promise* (which is the most usual sense of the word) nothing can be more absurd than this position. The observance of promises is itself one of the most considerable parts of justice, and we are not surely bound to keep our word because we have given our word to keep it. But if by convention be meant a sense of common interest, which sense each man feels in his own breast, which he remarks in his fellows, and which carries him, in concurrence with others, into a general plan or system of actions, which tends to public utility; it must be owned, that, in this sense, justice arises from human conventions. For if it be allowed (what is, indeed, evident) that the particular consequences of a particular act of justice may be hurtful to the public as well as to individuals; it follows that every man, in embracing that virtue, must have an eye to the whole plan or system, and must expect the concurrence of his fellows in the same conduct and behaviour. Did all his views terminate in the consequences of each act of his own, his benevolence and humanity, as well as his self-love, might often prescribe to him measures of conduct very different from those which are agreeable to the strict rules of right and justice.

8.   Thus two men pull the oars of a boat by common convention for common interest, without any promise or contract; thus gold and silver are made the measures of exchange; thus speech and words and language are fixed by human convention and agreement. Whatever is advantageous to two or more persons, if all perform their part; but what loses all advantage if only one perform, can arise from no other principle. There would otherwise be no motive for any one of them to enter into that scheme of conduct.[74]

74. This theory concerning the origin of property, and consequently of justice, is, in the main, the same with that hinted at and adopted by GROTIUS, "Hinc discimus, quae fuerit causa, ob quam a primaeva communione rerum primo mobilium, deinde et immobilinm discessum est: nimirum quod cum non contenti homines vesci sponte natis, antra habitare, corpore aut nudo agere, aut corticibus arborum ferarumve pellibus vestito, vitae genus exquisitius delegissent, industria opus fuit, quam singuli rebus singulls adhiberent: Quo minus autem fructus in commune conferrentur, primum obstitit locorum, in quae homines discesserunt, distantia, deinde

9.   The word *natural* is commonly taken in so many senses and is of so loose a signification, that it seems vain to dispute whether justice be natural or not. If self-love, if benevolence be natural to man; if reason and forethought be also natural; then may the same epithet be applied to justice, order, fidelity, property, society. Men's inclination, their necessities, lead them to combine; their understanding and experience tell them that this combination is impossible where each governs himself by no rule, and pays no regard to the possessions of others: and from these passions and reflections conjoined, as soon as we observe like passions and reflections in others, the sentiment of justice, throughout all ages, has infallibly and certainly had place to some degree or other in every individual of the human species. In so sagacious an animal, what necessarily arises from the exertion of his intellectual faculties may justly be esteemed natural.[75]

---

justitiae et amoris defectus, per quem fiebat, ut nee in labore, nee in consumtione fructuum, quae debebat, aequalitas servaretur. Simul discimus, quomodo res in proprietatem iverint; non animi actu solo, neque enim scire alii poterant, quid alil suum esse vellent, ut eo abstinerent, et idem velle plures poterant; sed pacto quodam aut expresso, ut per divisionem, aut tacito, ut per occupationem." De jure belli et pacis. Lib. 2. cap. 2. sec. 2. art. 4 and 5. [Hugo Grotius, *De jure belli ac pacis,* book 2, chapter 2. The passage may be translated as follows: "From them (several sources, some biblical) we learn why it was that the initial sharing, first of movable and later of immovable possessions, was abandoned: It was undoubtedly because people, not content to live on what grew naturally to hand, to live in caves, to go naked or clothed in the bark of trees or the hides of wild animals, opted for a choicer mode of life. That called for a life of application, each to his individual tasks. But too little produce was collected this way into the common store. The remoteness of the places people went to was the first obstacle, and then their deficiencies in justice and affection, which had the result that neither in the labour exerted nor in the produce consumed was fairness preserved. At the same time we learn how private property arose. It was not just by a mental act; because one party could not know what things another wished to have in order to abstain from them and there could be more who wanted the same thing. It was rather by a kind of agreement, either explicit, as when one divides between the parties, or tacit, as when one takes possession of something."]

75. Natural may be opposed, either to what is *unusual, miraculous* or *artificial.* In the two former senses, justice and property are undoubtedly natural. But as they suppose reason, forethought, design, and a social union and confederacy among men, perhaps that epithet cannot strictly, in the last sense, be applied to them. Had men lived without society, property had never been known, and neither justice nor injustice had ever existed. But society among human creatures had been impossible without reason and forethought. Inferior animals, that unite, are guided by instinct, which supplies the place for reason. But all these disputes are merely verbal.

10. Among all civilized nations it has been the constant endeavour to remove everything arbitrary and partial from the decision of property, and to fix the sentence of judges by such general views and considerations as may be equal to every member of society. For besides, that nothing could be more dangerous than to accustom the bench, even in the smallest instance, to regard private friendship or enmity; it is certain, that men, where they imagine that there was no other reason for the preference of their adversary but personal favour, are apt to entertain the strongest ill-will against the magistrates and judges. When natural reason, therefore, points out no fixed view of public utility by which a controversy of property can be decided, positive laws are often framed to supply its place, and direct the procedure of all courts of judicature. Where these too fail, as often happens, precedents are called for; and a former decision, though given itself without any sufficient reason, justly becomes a sufficient reason for a new decision. If direct laws and precedents be wanting, imperfect and indirect ones are brought in aid; and the controverted case is ranged under them by analogical reasonings and comparisons, and similitudes, and correspondencies, which are often more fanciful than real. In general, it may safely be affirmed that jurisprudence is, in this respect, different from all the sciences; and that in many of its nicer questions, there cannot properly be said to be truth or falsehood on either side. If one pleader bring the case under any former law or precedent, by a refined analogy or comparison; the opposite pleader is not at a loss to find an opposite analogy or comparison: and the preference given by the judge is often founded more on taste and imagination than on any solid argument. Public utility is the general object of all courts of judicature; and this utility too requires a stable rule in all controversies: but where several rules, nearly equal and indifferent, present themselves, it is a very slight turn of thought which fixes the decision in favour of either party.[76]

76. That there be a separation or distinction of possessions, and that this separation be steady and constant; this is absolutely required by the interests of society, and hence the origin of justice and property. What possessions are assigned to particular persons; this is, generally speaking, pretty indifferent; and is often determined by very frivolous views and considerations. We shall mention a few particulars.

Were a society formed among several independent members, the most obvious rule, which could be agreed on, would be to annex property to *present* possession, and leave every one a right to what he at present enjoys. The relation of possession, which takes place between the person and the object, naturally draws on the relation of property.

For a like reason, occupation or first possession becomes the foundation of property.

11. We may just observe, before we conclude this subject, that after the laws of justice are fixed by views of general utility, the injury, the hardship, the harm, which result to any individual from a violation of them, enter

---

Where a man bestows labour and industry upon any object, which before belonged to no body; as in cutting down and shaping a tree, in cultivating a field, &c., the alterations, which he produces, causes a relation between him and the object, and naturally engages us to annex it to him by the new relation of property. This cause here concurs with the public utility, which consists in the encouragement given to industry and labour.

Perhaps too, private humanity towards the possessor concurs, in this instance, with the other motives, and engages us to leave with him what he has acquired by his sweat and labour; and what he has flattered himself in the constant enjoyment of. For though private humanity can, by no means, be the origin of justice; since the latter virtue so often contradicts the former; yet when the rule of separate and constant possession is once formed by the indispensable necessities of society, private humanity, and an aversion to the doing a hardship to another, may, in a particular instance, give rise to a particular rule of property.

I am much inclined to think, that the right succession or inheritance much depends on those connexions of the imagination, and that the relation to a former proprietor begetting a relation to the object, is the cause why the property is transferred to a man after the death of his kinsman. It is true; industry is more encouraged by the transference of possession to children or near relations: but this consideration will only have place in a cultivated society; whereas the right of succession is regarded even among the greatest Barbarians.

Acquisition of property by accession can be explained no way but by having recourse to the relations and connexions of the imaginations.

The property of rivers, by the laws of most nations, and by the natural turn of our thoughts, is attributed to the proprietors of their banks, excepting such vast rivers as the Rhine or the Danube, which seem too large to follow as an accession to the property of the neighbouring fields. Yet even these rivers are considered as the property of that nation, through whose dominions they run; the idea of a nation being of a suitable bulk to correspond with them, and bear them such a relation in the fancy.

The accessions, which are made to land, bordering upon rivers, follow the land, say the civilians, provided it be made by what they call *alluvion* [the almost imperceptible increase of land on a shore or bank of a stream or sea as a result of the flow of water], that is, insensibly and imperceptibly; which are circumstances, that assist the imagination in the conjunction.

Where there is any considerable portion torn at once from one bank and added to another, it becomes not his property, whose land it falls on, till it unite with the land, and till the trees and plants have spread their roots into both. Before that, the thought does not sufficiently join them.

In short, we must ever distinguish between the necessity of a separation and constancy in men's possession, and the rules, which assign particular objects to particular persons. The first necessity is obvious, strong, and invincible: the latter may depend on a public utility more light and frivolous, on the sentiment of private

very much into consideration, and are a great source of that universal blame which attends every wrong or iniquity. By the laws of society, this coat, this horse is mine, and *ought* to remain perpetually in my possession: I reckon on the secure enjoyment of it: by depriving me of it, you disappoint my expectations, and doubly displease me, and offend every bystander. It is a public wrong, so far as the rules of equity are violated: it is a private harm, so far as an individual is injured. And though the second consideration could have no place, were not the former previously established: for otherwise the distinction of *mine* and *thine* would be unknown in society: yet there is no question but the regard to general good is much enforced by the respect to particular. What injures the community, without hurting any individual, is often more lightly thought of. But where the greatest public wrong is also conjoined with a considerable private one, no wonder the highest disapprobation attends so iniquitous a behaviour.

---

humanity and aversion to private hardship, on positive laws, on precedents, analogies, and very fine connexions and turns of the imagination.

Of Some Verbal Disputes

1. NOTHING is more usual than for philosophers to encroach upon the province of grammarians; and to engage in disputes of words, while they imagine that they are handling controversies of the deepest importance and concern. It was in order to avoid altercations, so frivolous and endless, that I endeavoured to state with the utmost caution the object of our present enquiry; and proposed simply to collect, on the one hand, a list of those mental qualities which are the object of love or esteem, and form a part of personal merit; and on the other hand, a catalogue of those qualities which are the object of censure or reproach, and which detract from the character of the person possessed of them; subjoining some reflections concerning the origin of these sentiments of praise or blame. On all occasions, where there might arise the least hesitation, I avoided the terms *virtue* and *vice;* because some of those qualities, which I classed among the objects of praise, receive, in the ENGLISH language, the appellation of *talents,* rather than of virtues; as some of the blameable or censurable qualities are often called *defects,* rather than vices. It may now, perhaps, be expected that before we conclude this moral enquiry, we should exactly separate the one from the other; should mark the precise boundaries of virtues and talents, vices and defects; and should explain the reason and origin of that distinction. But in order to excuse myself from this undertaking, which would, at last, prove only a grammatical enquiry, I shall subjoin the four following reflections, which shall contain all that I intend to say on the present subject.

2. *First,* I do not find that in the ENGLISH, or any other modern tongue, the boundaries are exactly fixed between virtues and talents, vices and defects, or that a precise definition can be given of the one as contradistinguished from the other. Were we to say, for instance, that the esteemable qualities alone, which are voluntary, are entitled to the appellations of virtues; we should soon recollect the qualities of courage, equanimity, patience, self-command; with many others, which almost every language

classes under this appellation, though they depend little or not at all on our choice. Should we affirm that the qualities alone, which prompt us to act our part in society, are entitled to that honourable distinction; it must immediately occur that these are indeed the most valuable qualities, and are commonly denominated the *social* virtues; but that this very epithet supposes that there are also virtues of another species. Should we lay hold of the distinction between *intellectual* and *moral* endowments, and affirm the last alone to be the real and genuine virtues, because they alone lead to action; we should find that many of those qualities, usually called intellectual virtues, such as prudence, penetration, discernment, discretion, had also a considerable influence on conduct. The distinction between the *heart* and the *head* may also be adopted: the qualities of the first may be defined such as in their immediate exertion are accompanied with a feeling of sentiment; and these alone may be called the genuine virtues: but industry, frugality, temperance, secrecy, perseverance, and many other laudable powers or habits, generally stilled virtues are exerted without any immediate sentiment in the person possessed of them, and are only known to him by their effects. It is fortunate, amidst all this seeming perplexity, that the question, being merely verbal, cannot possibly be of any importance. A moral, philosophical discourse needs not enter into all these caprices of language, which are so variable in different dialects, and in different ages of the same dialect. But on the whole, it seems to me, that though it is always allowed, that there are virtues of many different kinds, yet, when a man is called *virtuous,* or is denominated a man of virtue, we chiefly regard his social qualities, which are, indeed, the most valuable. It is, at the same time, certain, that any remarkable defect in courage, temperance, economy, industry, understanding, dignity of mind, would bereave even a very good-natured, honest man of this honourable appellation. Who did ever say, except by way of irony, that such a one was a man of great virtue, but an egregious blockhead?

3.   But, *secondly,* it is no wonder that languages should not be very precise in marking the boundaries between virtues and talents, vices and defects; since there is so little distinction made in our internal estimation of them. It seems indeed certain, that the *sentiment* of conscious worth, the self-satisfaction proceeding from a review of a man's own conduct and character; it seems certain, I say, that this sentiment, which, though the most common of all others, has no proper name in our language,[77] arises

---

77. The term, *pride,* is commonly taken in a bad sense; but this sentiment seems indifferent, and may be either good or bad, according as it is well or ill founded, and

from the endowments of courage and capacity, industry and ingenuity, as well as from any other mental excellencies. Who, on the other hand, is not deeply mortified with reflecting on his own folly and dissoluteness, and feels not a secret sting or compunction whenever his memory presents any past occurrence, where he behaved with stupidity of ill-manners? No time can efface the cruel ideas of a man's own foolish conduct, or of affronts, which cowardice or impudence has brought upon him. They still haunt his solitary hours, damp his most aspiring thoughts, and show him, even to himself, in the most contemptible and most odious colours imaginable.

4.   What is there too we are more anxious to conceal from others than such blunders, infirmities, and meannesses, or more dread to have exposed by raillery and satire? And is not the chief object of vanity, our bravery or learning, our wit or breeding, our eloquence or address, our taste or abilities? These we display with care, if not with ostentation; and we commonly show more ambition of excelling in them, than even in the social virtues themselves, which are, in reality, of such superior excellence. Good-nature and honesty, especially the latter, are so indispensably required, that, though the greatest censure attends any violation of these duties, no eminent praise follows such common instances of them, as seem essential to the support of human society. And hence the reason, in my opinion, why, though men often extol so liberally the qualities of their heart, they are shy in commending the endowments of their head: because the latter virtues, being supposed more rare and extraordinary, are observed to be the more usual objects of pride and self-conceit; and when boasted of, beget a strong suspicion of these sentiments.

5.   It is hard to tell, whether you hurt a man's character most by calling him a knave or a coward, and whether a beastly glutton or drunkard be not as odious and contemptible, as a selfish, ungenerous miser. Give me my choice, and I would rather, for my own happiness and self-enjoyment, have a friendly, humane heart, than possess all the other virtues of DEMOS-THENES and PHILIP united: but I would rather pass with the world for one endowed with extensive genius and intrepid courage, and should thence expect stronger instances of general applause and admiration. The figure which a man makes in life, the reception which he meets with in company, the esteem paid him by his acquaintance; all these advantages depend as

---

according to the other circumstances which accompany it. The FRENCH express this sentiment by the term, *amour propre,* but as they also express self-love as well as vanity by the same term, there arises thence a great confusion in ROCHEFOUCAULT, and many of their moral writers. [François de La Rochefoucault, *Maximes.*]

much upon his good sense and judgment, as upon any other part of his character. Had a man the best intentions in the world, and were the farthest removed from all injustice and violence, he would never be able to make himself be much regarded, without a moderate share, at least, of parts and understanding.

6.   What is it then we can here dispute about? If sense and courage, temperance and industry, wisdom and knowledge confessedly form a considerable part of *personal merit:* if a man, possessed of these qualities, is both better satisfied with himself, and better entitled to the good-will, esteem, and services of others, than one entirely destitute of them; if, in short, the *sentiments* are similar which arise from these endowments and from the social virtues; is there any reason for being so extremely scrupulous about a *word,* or disputing whether they be entitled to the denomination of virtues? It may, indeed, be pretended, that the sentiment of approbation, which those accomplishments produce, besides its being *inferior,* is also somewhat *different* from that which attends the virtues of justice and humanity. But this seems not a sufficient reason for ranking them entirely under different classes and appellations. The character of CÆSAR and that of CATO, as drawn by SALLUST, are both of them virtuous, in the strictest and most limited sense of the word; but in a different way: nor are the sentiments entirely the same which arise from them. The one produces love, the other esteem: The one is amiable, the other awful: we should wish to meet the one character in a friend; the other we should be ambitious of in ourselves. In like manner the approbation, which attends temperance or industry or frugality, may be somewhat different from that which is paid to the social virtues, without making them entirely of a different species. And, indeed, we may observe, that these endowments, more than the other virtues, produce not, all of them, the same kind of approbation. Good sense and genius beget esteem and regard: Wit and humour excite love and affection.[78]

---

78. Love and esteem are nearly the same passion, and arise from similar causes. The qualities, which produce both, are such as communicate pleasures. But where this pleasure is severe and serious; or where its object is great, and makes a strong impression, or where it produces any degree of humility and awe; in all these cases, the passion, which arises from the pleasure, is more properly denominated esteem than love. Benevolence attends both; but is connected with love in a more eminent degree. There seems to be still a stronger mixture of pride in contempt than of humility in esteem; and the reason would not be difficulty to one, who studied accurately the passions. All these various mixtures and compositions and appearances of sentiment from a very curious subject of speculation, but are wide for our present purpose. Throughout this enquiry, we always consider in general, what qualities are

7.   Most people, I believe, will naturally, without premeditation, assent to the definition of the elegant and judicious poet:

> Virtue (for mere good-nature is a fool)
> Is sense and spirit with humanity.[79]

8.   What pretensions has a man to our generous assistance or good offices, who has dissipated his wealth in profuse expenses, idle vanities, chimerical projects, dissolute pleasures or extravagant gaming? These vices (for we scruple not to call them such) bring misery unpitied, and contempt on every one addicted to them.

9.   ACHÆUS, a wise and prudent prince, fell into a fatal snare, which cost him his crown and life, after having used every reasonable precaution to guard himself against it. On that account, says the historian, he is a just object of regard and compassion: his betrayers alone of hatred and contempt.[80]

10.   The precipitate flight and improvident negligence of POMPEY, at the beginning of the civil wars, appeared such notorious blunders to CICERO, as quite palled his friendship towards that great man. "In the same manner," says he, "as want of cleanliness, decency, or discretion in a mistress are found to alienate our affections." For so he expresses himself, where he talks, not in the character of a philosopher, but in that of a statesman and man of the world, to his friend ATTICUS.[81]

11.   But the same CICERO, in imitation of all the ancient moralists, when he reasons as a philosopher, enlarges very much his ideas of virtue, and comprehends every laudable quality or endowment of the mind, under that honourable appellation. This leads to the *third* reflection, which we proposed to make, to wit, that the ancient moralists, the best models, made no material distinction among the different species of mental endowments and defects, but treated all alike under the appellation of virtues and vices,

---

a subject of praise or of censure, without entering into all the minute differences of sentiment, which they excite. It is evident, that whatever is contemned, is also disliked, as well as what is hated; and we here endeavour to take objects, according to their most simple views and appearances. These sciences are but too apt to appear abstract to common readers, even with all the precautions which we can take to clear them from superfluous speculations, and bring them down to every capacity.

79. *The Art of preserving Health.* Book 4. [John Armstrong, *The Art of Preserving Health,* book 4.]

80. POLYBIUS, lib. 3. cap. 2. [Polybius, *Histories,* book 8, chapters 20–21.]

81. Lib. 9. epist. 10. [Cicero, *Letters to Atticus,* book 9, letter 10.]

and made them indiscriminately the object of their moral reasonings. The *prudence* explained in CICERO's *Offices*[82] is that sagacity, which leads to the discovery of truth, and preserves us from error and mistake. *Magnanimity, temperance, decency,* are there also at large discoursed of. And as that eloquent moralist followed the common received division of the four cardinal virtues, our social duties form but one head, in the general distribution of his subject.[83]

82. Lib. i. cap. 6. [Cicero, *De officiis,* book 1, chapter 6.]

83. The following passage of CICERO is worth quoting, as being the most clear and express to our purpose, that any thing can be imagined, and, in a dispute, which is chiefly verbal, must, on account of the author, carry an authority, from which there can be no appeal.

"Virtus autem, quae est per se ipsa laudabilis, et sine qua nihil laudari potest, tamen habet plures partes, quarum alia est alia ad laudationem aptior. Sunt enim aliae virtutes, quae videntur in moribus hominum, et quadam comitate ac beneficentia positae: aliae quae in ingenii aliqua facultate, aut animi magnitudine ac robore. Nam clementia, justitia, benignitas, fides, fortitudo in periculis communibus, jucunda est auditu in laudationibus. Omnes enim hae virtutes non tam ipsis, qui eas in se habent, quam generi hominum fructuosae putantur. Sapientia et magnitude animi, qua omnes res humanae tenues et pro nihilo putantur, et in cogitando vis quaedam ingenii, et ipsa eloquentia admirationis habet non minus, jucunditatis minus. Ipsos enim magis videntur, quos laudamus, quam illos, apud quos laudamus ornare ac tueri: sed tamen in laudenda jungenda sunt eliam haec genera virtutum. Ferunt enim aures bominum, cum ilia quae jucunda et grata, tum etiam ilia, quae mirabilia sunt in virtute, laudari." De orat. lib. 2. cap. 84. [Cicero, *De oratore,* book 2, chapter 84. The passage may be translated as follows: "Virtue merits praise in itself and is essential to anything else that can be praised; it has, however, several sides to it, some of which are more appropriately praised than others. For there are some virtues that are exhibited in people's conduct and with a certain courtesy and humanity, and others that appear in some faculty of mind, or in magnanimity and strength. Clemency, justice, friendliness, honesty, fortitude in common dangers--these are the virtues we enjoy hearing extolled in eulogies, because they are all considered advantageous not so much to those who possess them as to the whole human race; whereas wisdom, magnanimity (which regards all human affairs as slight and nugatory), strength and invention of intellect, and even eloquence, though they elicit no less admiration, give less pleasure, because they seem to adorn and protect those on whom we bestow the praise rather than those in whose presence it is bestowed. Nevertheless these kinds of virtues should be included in our praises, because mankind likes to hear praised both what gives joy and pleasure, and whatever there is in virtue that is a cause for admiration."]

I suppose, if CICERO were now alive, it would be found difficult to fetter his moral sentiments by narrow systems; or persuade him, that no qualities were to be admitted as *virtues,* or acknowledged to be a part of *personal merit,* but what were recommended by The Whole Duty of Man. [Anon., *The Whole Duty of Man.*]

12. We need only peruse the titles of chapters in ARISTOTLE's Ethics to be convinced that he ranks courage, temperance, magnificence, magnanimity, modesty, prudence, and a manly openness, among the virtues, as well as justice and friendship.

13. To *sustain* and to *abstain,* that is, to be patient and continent, appeared to some of the ancients a summary comprehension of all morals.

14. EPICTETUS has scarcely ever mentioned the sentiment of humanity and compassion, but in order to put his disciples on their guard against it. The virtue of the STOICS seems to consist chiefly in a firm temper and a sound understanding. With them, as with SOLOMON and the eastern moralists, folly and wisdom are equivalent to vice and virtue.

15. Men will praise thee, says DAVID,[84] when thou dost well unto thyself. I hate a wise man, says the GREEK poet, who is not wise to himself.[85]

16. PLUTARCH is no more cramped by systems in his philosophy than in his history. Where he compares the great men of GREECE and ROME, he fairly sets in opposition all their blemishes and accomplishments of whatever kind, and omits nothing considerable, which can either depress or exalt their characters. His moral discourses contain the same free and natural censure of men and manners.

17. The character of HANNIBAL, as drawn by LIVY,[86] is esteemed partial, but allows him many eminent virtues. Never was there a genius, says the historian, more equally fitted for those opposite offices of commanding and obeying; and it were, therefore, difficult to determine whether he rendered himself *dearer* to the general or to the army. To none would HASDRUBAL entrust more willingly the conduct of any dangerous enterprize; under none did the soldiers discover more courage and confidence. Great boldness in facing danger; great prudence in the midst of it. No labour could fatigue his body or subdue his mind. Cold and heat were indifferent to him: Meat and drink he sought as supplies to the necessities of nature, not as gratifications of his voluptuous appetites. Waking or rest he used indiscriminately, by night or by day.--These great VIRTUES were balanced by great VICES; inhuman cruelty; perfidy more than *punic;* no truth, no faith, no regard to oaths, promises, or religion.

18. The character of ALEXANDER the Sixth, to be found in GUICCIARDIN,[87] is pretty similar, but juster; and is a proof that even the moderns, where

84. Psalm 49th. [Ps. 49:18.]

85. Μισω σοφιςην οσις ουκ αυτω σοφος EURIPIDES. [Euripides, *Fragments.*]

86. Lib. 21. cap. 4. [Livy, *History,* book 21, chapter 4.]

87. Lib. 1. [Francesco Guicciardini, *Della historia d'Italia* (*The History of Italy*), book 1, chapter 2.]

they speak naturally, hold the same language with the ancients. In this pope, says he, there was a singular capacity and judgment: admirable prudence; a wonderful talent of persuasion; and in all momentous enterprizes a diligence and dexterity incredible. But these *virtues* were infinitely overbalanced by his *vices;* no faith, no religion, insatiable avarice, exorbitant ambition, and a more than barbarous cruelty.

19. POLYBIUS,[88] reprehending TIMÆUS for his partiality against AGATHOCLES, whom he himself allows to be the most cruel and impious of all tyrants, says: if he took refuge in SYRACUSE, as asserted by that historian, flying the dirt and smoke and toil of his former profession of a potter; and if proceeding from such slender beginnings, he became master, in a little time, of all SICILY; brought the CARTHAGINIAN state into the utmost danger; and at last died in old age, and in possession of sovereign dignity: must he not be allowed something prodigious and extraordinary, and to have possessed great talents and capacity for business and action? His historian, therefore, ought not to have alone related what tended to his reproach and infamy; but also what might redound to his PRAISE and HONOUR.

20. In general, we may observe, that the distinction of voluntary or involuntary was little regarded by the ancients in their moral reasonings; where they frequently treated the question as very doubtful, *whether virtue could be taught or not?*[89] They justly considered that cowardice, meanness, levity, anxiety, impatience, folly, and many other qualities of the mind, might appear ridiculous and deformed, contemptible and odious, though independent of the will. Nor could it be supposed, at all times, in every man's power to attain every kind of mental more than of exterior beauty.

21. And here there occurs the *fourth* reflection which I purposed to make, in suggesting the reason why modern philosophers have often followed a course in their moral enquiries so different from that of the ancients. In later times, philosophy of all kinds, especially ethics, have been more closely united with theology than ever they were observed to be among the heathens; and as this latter science admits of no terms of composition, but bends every branch of knowledge to its own purpose, without much regard to the phænomena of nature, or to the unbiassed sentiments of the mind,

---

88. Lib. 12. [Polybius, *Histories,* book 12.]

89. Vid. PLATO in MENONE, SENECA de otio sap. cap. 31. So also HORACE, Virtutem doctrina paret, naturane donet, Epist. lib. I. ep. 18. AESCHINES SOCRATICUS, Dial. I. [Plato, *Meno;* Seneca, *Moral Essays,* book 8, "De otio," chapter 4 (31 in older citations); Horace, *Epistles,* book 1, epistle 18; Aeschines Socraticus, *Dialogues* 1.]

hence reasoning, and even language, have been warped from their natural course, and distinctions have been endeavoured to be established where the difference of the objects was, in a manner, imperceptible. Philosophers, or rather divines under that disguise, treating all morals as on a like footing with civil laws, guarded by the sanctions of reward and punishment, were necessarily led to render this circumstance, of *voluntary* or *involuntary,* the foundation of their whole theory. Every one may employ *terms* in what sense he pleases: but this, in the mean time, must be allowed, that *sentiments* are every day experienced of blame and praise, which have objects beyond the dominion of the will or choice, and of which it behoves us, if not as moralists, as speculative philosophers at least, to give some satisfactory theory and explication.

22.   A blemish, a fault, a vice, a crime; these expressions seem to denote different degrees of censure and disapprobation; which are, however, all of them, at the bottom, pretty nearly all the same kind of species. The explication of one will easily lead us into a just conception of the others; and it is of greater consequence to attend to things than to verbal appellations. That we owe a duty to ourselves is confessed even in the most vulgar system of morals; and it must be of consequence to examine that duty, in order to see whether it bears any affinity to that which we owe to society. It is probable that the approbation attending the observance of both is of a similar nature, and arises from similar principles, whatever appellation we may give to either of these excellencies.

A Dialogue

1.   MY friend, PALAMEDES, who is as great a rambler in his principles as in his person, and who has run over, by study and travel, almost every region of the intellectual and material world, surprized me lately with an account of a nation, with whom, he told me, he had passed a considerable part of his life, and whom, he found, in the main, a people extremely civilized and intelligent.

2.   There is a country, said he, in the world, called FOURLI, no matter for its longitude or latitude, whose inhabitants have ways of thinking, in many things, particularly in morals, diametrically opposite to ours. When I came among them, I found that I must submit to double pains; first to learn the meaning of the terms in their language, and then to know the import of those terms, and the praise or blame attached to them. After a word had been explained to me, and the character, which it expressed, had been described, I concluded, that such an epithet must necessarily be the greatest reproach in the world; and was extremely surprized to find one in a public company, apply it to a person, with whom he lived in the strictest intimacy and friendship. *"You fancy,"* said I, one day, to an acquaintance, *"that* CHANGUIS *is your mortal enemy: I love to extinguish quarrels; and I must, therefore, tell you, that I heard him talk of you in the most obliging manner."* But to my great astonishment, when I repeated CHANGUIS's words, though I had both remembered and understood them perfectly, I found, that they were taken for the most mortal affront, and that I had very innocently rendered the breach between these persons altogether irreparable.

3.   As it was my fortune to come among this people on a very advantageous footing, I was immediately introduced to the best company; and being desired by ALCHEIC to live with him, I readily accepted of his invitation; as I found him universally esteemed for his personal merit, and indeed regarded by every one in FOURLI, as a perfect character.

4.   One evening he invited me, as an amusement, to bear him company in a serenade, which he intended to give to GULKI, with whom, he told me, he was extremely enamoured; and I soon found that his taste was not

singular: For we met many of his rivals, who had come on the same errand. I very naturally concluded, that this mistress of his must be one of the finest women in town; and I already felt a secret inclination to see her, and be acquainted with her. But as the moon began to rise, I was much surprized to find, that we were in the midst of the university, where GULKI studied: And I was somewhat ashamed for having attended my friend, on such an errand.

5.   I was afterwards told, that ALCHEIC's choice of GULKI was very much approved of by all the good company in town; and that it was expected, while he gratified his own passion, he would perform to that young man the same good office, which he had himself owed to ELCOUF. If seems ALCHEIC had been very handsome in his youth, and been courted by many lovers; but had bestowed his favours chiefly on the sage ELCOUF; to whom he was supposed to owe, in a great measure, the astonishing progress which he had made in philosophy and virtue.

6.   It gave me some surprize, that ALCHEIC's wife (who by-the-bye happened also to be his sister) was no wise scandalized at this species of infidelity.

7.   Much about the same time I discovered (for it was not attempted to be kept a secret from me or any body) that ALCHEIC was a murderer and a parricide, and had put to death an innocent person, the most nearly connected with him, and whom he was bound to protect and defend by all the ties of nature and humanity. When I asked, with all the caution and deference imaginable, what was his motive for this action; he replied coolly, that he was not then so much at ease in his circumstances as he is at present, and that he had acted, in that particular, by the advice of all his friends.

8.   Having heard ALCHEIC's virtue so extremely celebrated, I pretended to join in the general voice of acclamation, and only asked, by way of curiosity, as a stranger, which of all his noble actions was most highly applauded; and I soon found, that all sentiments were united in giving preference to the assassination of USBEK. This USBEK has been to the last moment ALCHEIC's intimate friend, had laid many high obligations upon him, had even saved his life on a certain occasion, and had, by his will, which was found after the murder, made him heir to a considerable part of his fortune. ALCHEIC, it seems, conspired with about twenty or thirty more, most of them also USBEK's friends; and falling all together on that unhappy man, when he was not aware, they had torn him with a hundred wounds; and given him that reward for all his past favours and obligations. USBEK, said the general voice of the people, had many great and good qualities: His very vices were shining, magnificent, and generous: But this action of

ALCHEIC's sets him far above USBEK in the eyes of all judges of merit; and is one of the noblest that ever perhaps the sun shone upon.

9.   Another part of ALCHEIC's conduct, which I also found highly applauded, was his behaviour towards CALISH, with whom he was joined in a project or undertaking of some importance. CALISH, being a passionate man, gave ALCHEIC, one day, a sound drubbing; which he took very patiently, waited the return of CALISH's good-humour, kept still a fair correspondence with him; and by that means brought the affair, in which they were joined, to a happy issue, and gained to himself immortal honour by his remarkable temper and moderation.

10. I have lately received a letter from a correspondent in FOURLI, by which I learn, that, since my departure, ALCHEIC, falling into a bad state of health, has fairly hanged himself; and has died universally regretted and applauded in that country. So virtuous and noble a life, says each FOUR-LIAN, could not be better crowned than by so noble an end; and ALCHEIC has proved by this, as well as by all his other actions, what was his constant principle during his life, and what be boasted of near his last moments, that a wise man is scarcely inferior to the great god, VITZLI. This is the name of the supreme deity among the FOURLIANS.

11. The notions of this people, continued PALAMEDES, are as extraordinary with regard to good-manners and sociableness, as with regard to morals. My friend ALCHEIC formed once a party for my entertainment, composed of all the prime wits and philosophers of Fourli; and each of us brought his mess along with him to the place where we assembled. I observed one of them to be worse provided than the rest, and offered him a share of my mess, which happened to be a roasted pullet: And I could not but remark, that he and all the rest of the company smiled at my simplicity. I was told, that ALCHEIC had once so much interest with his club as to prevail with them to eat in common, and that he had made use of an artifice for that purpose. He persuaded those, whom he observed to be *worst* provided, to offer their mess to the company; after which, the others who had brought more delicate fare, were ashamed not to make the same offer. This is regarded as so extraordinary an event, that it has since, as I learn, been recorded in the history of ALCHEIC's life, composed by one of the greatest geniuses of FOURLI.

12. Pray, said I, PALAMEDES, when you were at FOURLI, did you also learn the art of turning your friends into ridicule, by telling them such strange stories, and then laughing at them, if they believed you. I assure you, replied he, had I been disposed to learn such a lesson, there was no place in the world more proper. My friend, so often mentioned, did nothing, from

morning to night, but sneer, and banter, and rally; and you could scarcely ever distinguish, whether he were in jest or earnest. But you think then, that my story is improbable; and that I have used, or rather abused the privilege of a traveller. To be sure, said I, you were but in jest. Such barbarous and savage manners are not only incompatible with a civilized, intelligent people, such as you said these were; but are scarcely compatible with human nature. They exceed all we ever read of, among the MINGRELIANS, and TOPINAMBOUES.

13. Have a care, cried he, have a care! You are not aware that you are speaking blasphemy, and are abusing your favourites, the GREEKS, especially the ATHENIANS, whom I have couched, all along, under these bizzare names I employed. If you consider aright, there is not one stroke of the foregoing character, which might not be found in the man of highest merit at ATHENS, without diminishing in the least from the brightness of his character. The amours of the GREEKS, their marriages,[90] and the exposing of their children cannot but strike you immediately. The death of USBEK is an exact counter-part to that of CÆSAR.

14. All to a trifle, said I, interrupting him: You did not mention that USBEK was an usurper.

15. I did not, replied he; lest you should discover the parallel I aimed at. But even adding this circumstance, we should make no scruple, according to our sentiments or morals, to denominate BRUTUS, and CASSIUS, ungrateful traitors and assassins: Though you know, that they are, perhaps, the highest characters of all antiquity; and the ATHENIANS erected statues to them; which they placed near those of HARMODIUS and ARISTOGITON, their own deliverers. And if you think this circumstance, which you mention, so material to absolve these patriots, I shall compensate it by another, not mentioned, which will equally aggravate their crime. A few days before the execution of their fatal purpose, they all swore fealty to CAESAR; and protesting to hold his person ever sacred, they touched the altar with those hands, which they had already armed for his destruction.[91]

16. I need not remind you of the famous and applauded story of THEMISTOCLES, and of his patience towards EURYBIADES, the SPARTAN, his com-

90. The laws of ATHENS allowed a man to marry his sister by the father. SOLON's law forbid pæderasty to slaves, as being an act of too great dignity for such mean persons.

91. APPIAN. Bell. Civ. lib. iii. SUETONIUS in vita CAESARIS. [Appian, *Roman History,* book 2, chapter 16, §111–17; Suetonius, *Lives of the Caesers,* book 2, chapters 78–84.]

manding officer, who, heated by debate, lifted his cane to him in a council of war (the same thing as if he had cudgelled him), *"Strike!"* cries the ATHENIAN, *"strike! but hear me."*

17. You are too good a scholar not to discover the ironical SOCRATES and his ATHENIAN club in my last story; and you will certainly observe, that it is exactly copied from XENOPHON, with a variation only of the names.[92] And I think I have fairly made it appear, that an ATHENIAN man of merit might be such a one as with us would pass for incestuous, a parricide, an assassin, an ungrateful, perjured traitor, and something else too abominable to be named; not to mention his rusticity and ill-manners. And having lived in this manner, his death might be entirely suitable: He might conclude the scene by a desperate act of self-murder, and die with the most absurd blasphemies in his mouth. And notwithstanding all this, he shall have statues, if not altars, erected to his praise; great sects shall be proud of calling themselves by his name; and the most distant posterity shall blindly continue their admiration: Though were such a one to arise among ourselves, they would justly regard him with horror and execration.

18. I might have been aware, replied I, of your artifice. You seem to take pleasure in this topic: and are indeed the only man I ever knew, who was well acquainted with the ancients, and did not extremely admire them. But instead of attacking their philosophy, their eloquence, or poetry, the usual subjects of controversy between us, you now seem to impeach their morals, and accuse them of ignorance in a science, which is the only one, in my opinion, in which they are not surpassed by the moderns. Geometry, physics, astronomy, anatomy, botany, geography, navigation; in these we justly claim the superiority: But what have we to oppose in their moralists? Your representation of things is fallacious. You have no indulgence for the manners and customs of different ages. Would you try a GREEK or ROMAN by the common law of ENGLAND? Hear him defend himself by his own maxims; and then pronounce.

19. There are no manners so innocent or reasonable, but may be rendered odious or ridiculous, if measured by a standard, unknown to the persons; especially, if you employ a little art or eloquence, in aggravating some circumstances, and extenuating others, as best suits the purpose of your discourse. All these artifices may easily be retorted on you. Could I inform the ATHENIANS, for instance, that there was a nation, in which adultery, both active and passive, so to speak, was in the highest vogue and esteem: In

92. Mem. Soc. lib. iii. sub fine. [Xenophon, *Memorabilia,* book 3, chapter 14, §1.]

which every man of education chose for his mistress a married woman, the wife, perhaps, of his friend and companion; and valued himself upon these infamous conquests, as much as if he had been several times a conqueror in boxing or wrestling at the *Olympic* games: In which every man also took a pride in his tameness and facility with regard to his own wife, and was glad to make friends or gain interest by allowing her to prostitute her charms; and even, without any such motive, gave her full liberty and indulgence: I ask, what sentiments the ATHENIANS would entertain of such a people; they who never mentioned the crime of adultery but in conjunction with robbery and poisoning? Which would they admire most, the villany or the meanness of such a conduct?

20. Should I add, that the same people were as proud of their slavery and dependence as the ATHENIANS of their liberty; and though a man among them were oppressed, disgraced, impoverished, insulted, or imprisoned by the tyrant, he would still regard it as the highest merit to love, serve, and obey him; and even to die for his smallest glory or satisfaction: These noble GREEKS would probably ask me, whether I spoke of a human society, or some inferior, servile species?

21. It was then that I might inform my ATHENIAN audience, that these people, however, wanted not spirit and bravery. If a man, say I, though their intimate friend, should throw out, in a private company, a raillery against them, nearly approaching any of those, with which your generals and dema-gogues every day regale each other, in the face of the whole city, they never can forgive him; but in order to revenge themselves, they oblige him im-mediately to run them through the body, or be himself murdered. And if a man, who is an absolute stranger to them, should desire them, at the peril of their own life, to cut the throat of their bosom-companion, they immediately obey, and think themselves highly obliged and honoured by the commis-sion. These are their maxims of honour: This is their favourite morality.

22. But though so ready to draw their sword against their friends and coun-trymen; no disgrace, no infamy, no pain, no poverty will ever engage these people to turn the point against their own breast. A man of rank would row in the gallies, would beg his bread, would languish in prison, would suffer any tortures; and still preserve his wretched life. Rather than escape his enemies by a generous contempt of death, he would infamously receive the same death from his enemies, aggravated by their triumphant insults, and by the most exquisite sufferings.

23. It is very usual too, continue I, among this people to erect jails, where every art of plaguing and tormenting the unhappy prisoners is carefully studied and practiced: And in these jails it is usual for a parent voluntarily

to shut up several of his children; in order, that another child, whom he owns to have no greater or rather less merit than the rest, may enjoy his whole fortune, and wallow in every kind of voluptuousness and pleasure. Nothing so virtuous in their opinion as this barbarous partiality.

24. But what is more singular in this whimsical nation, say I to the ATHE-NIANS, is, that a frolic of yours during the SATURNALIA,[93] when the slaves are served by their masters, is seriously continued by them throughout the whole year, and throughout the whole course of their lives; accompanied too with some circumstances, which still farther augment the absurdity and ridicule. Your sport only elevates for a few days those whom fortune has thrown down, and whom she too, in sport, may really elevate for ever above you: But this nation gravely exalts those, whom nature has subjected to them, and whose inferiority and infirmities are absolutely incurable. The women, though without virtue, are their masters and sovereigns: These they reverence, praise, and magnify: To these, they pay the highest deference and respect: And in all places and all times, the superiority of the females is readily acknowledged and submitted to by every one, who has the least pretensions to education and politeness. Scarce any crime would be so universally detested as an infraction of this rule.

25. You need go no farther, replied PALAMEDES; I can easily conjecture the people whom you aim at. The strokes, with which you have painted them, are pretty just; and yet you must acknowledge, that scarce any people are to be found, either in ancient or modern times, whose national character is, upon the whole, less liable to exception. But I give you thanks for helping me out with my argument. I had no intention of exalting the moderns at the expence of the ancients. I only meant to represent the uncertainty of all these judgments concerning characters; and to convince you, that fashion, vogue, custom, and law, were the chief foundation of all moral determinations. The ATHENIANS surely, were a civilized, intelligent people, if ever there were one; and yet their man of merit might, in this age, be held in horror and execration. The FRENCH are also, without doubt, a very civilized, intelligent people; and yet their man of merit might, with the ATHENIANS, be an object of the highest contempt and ridicule, and even hatred. And what renders the matter more extraordinary: These two people are supposed to be the most similar in their national character of any in ancient and modern times; and while the ENGLISH flatter themselves that they resemble the ROMANS, their neighbours on the continent draw the parallel between

93. The GREEKS kept the feast of SATURN or CHRONUS, as well as the ROMANS. See LUCIAN. Epist. SATURN. [Lucian, *Saturnalia,* §10–39.]

themselves and those polite GREEKS. What wide difference, therefore, in the sentiments of morals, must be found between civilized nations and Barbarians, or between nations whose characters have little in common? How shall we pretend to fix a standard for judgments of this nature?

26. By tracing matters, replied I, a little higher, and examining the first principles, which each nation establishes, of blame or censure. The RHINE flows north, the RHONE south; yet both spring from the *same* mountain, and are also actuated, in their opposite directions, by the *same* principle of gravity. The different inclinations of the ground, on which they run, cause all the difference in their courses.

27. In how many circumstances would an ATHENIAN and a FRENCH man of merit resemble each other? Good sense, knowledge, wit, eloquence, humanity, fidelity, truth, justice, courage, temperance, constancy, dignity of mind: These you have all omitted; in order to insist only on the points, in which they may, by accident, differ. Very well: I am willing to comply with you; and shall endeavour to account for these differences from the most universal, established principles of morals.

28. The GREEK loves, I care not to examine more particularly. I shall only observe, that, however blameable, they arose from a very innocent cause, the frequency of the gymnastic exercises among that people; and were recommended, though absurdly, as the source of friendship, sympathy, mutual attachment, and fidelity;[94] qualities esteemed in all nations and ages.

29. The marriage of half-brothers and sisters seems no great difficulty. Love between nearer relations is contrary to reason and public utility; but the precise point, where we are to stop, can scarcely be determined by natural reason; and is therefore a very proper subject for a municipal law or custom. If the ATHENIANS went a little too far on the one side, the canon law has surely pushed matters a great way into the other extreme.[95]

30. Had you asked a parent at ATHENS, why he bereaved his child of that life, which he had so lately given it. It is because I love it, he would reply; and regard the poverty which it must inherit from me, as a greater evil than death, which it is not capable of dreading, feeling, or resenting.[96]

31. How is public liberty, the most valuable of all blessings, to be recovered from the hands of an usurper or tyrant, if his power shields him from

94. PLAT. symp. p. 182. Ex edit. SERR. [Plato, *Symposium,* 182A–85c.]

95. See *Enquiry,* Sect. IV. [*An Enquiry Concerning the Principles of Morals,* 4.9.]

96. PLUTARCH. de amore prolis, sub fine. [Plutarch *Moralia,* chapter 5, 497.]

public rebellion, and our scruples from private vengeance? That his crime is capital by law, you acknowledge: And must the highest aggravation of his crime, the putting of himself above law, form his full security? You can reply nothing, but by showing the great inconveniences of assassination; which could any one have proved clearly to the ancients, he had reformed their sentiments in this particular.

32. Again, to cast your eye on the picture which I have drawn of modern manners; there is almost as great a difficulty, I acknowledge, to justify FRENCH as GREEK gallantry; except only, that the former is much more natural and agreeable than the latter. But our neighbours, it seems, have resolved to sacrifice some of the domestic to the sociable pleasures; and to prefer ease, freedom, and an open commerce, to a strict fidelity and constancy. These ends are both good, and are somewhat difficult to reconcile; nor need we be surprised, if the customs of nations incline too much, sometimes to the one side, sometimes to the other.

33. The most inviolable attachment to the laws of our country is every where acknowledged a capital virtue; and where the people are not so happy, as to have any legislature but a single person, the strictest loyalty is, in that case, the truest patriotism.

34. Nothing surely can be more absurd and barbarous than the practice of duelling; but those, who justify it, say, that it begets civility and good-manners. And a duellist, you may observe, always values himself upon his courage, his sense of honour, his fidelity and friendship; qualities, which are here indeed very oddly directed, but which have been esteemed universally, since the foundation of the world.

35. Have the gods forbid self-murder? An ATHENIAN allows, that it ought to be forborn. Has the Deity permitted it? A FRENCHMAN allows, that death is preferable to pain and infamy.

36. You see then, continued I, that the principles upon which men reason in morals are always the same; though the conclusions which they draw are often very different. That they all reason aright with regard to this subject, more than with regard to any other, it is not incumbent on any moralist to show. It is sufficient, that the original principles of censure or blame are uniform, and that erroneous conclusions can be corrected by sounder reasoning and a larger experience. Though many ages have elapsed since the fall of GREECE and ROME; though many changes have arrived in religion, language, laws, and customs; none of these revolutions has ever produced any considerable innovation in the primary sentiments of morals, more than in those of external beauty. Some minute differences, perhaps, may

be observed in both. HORACE[97] celebrates a low forehead, and ANACREON joined eye-brows:[98] But the APOLLO and the VENUS of antiquity are still our models for male and female beauty; in like manner as the character of SCIPIO continues our standard for the glory of heroes, and that of CORNELIA for the honour of matrons.

37. It appears, that there never was any quality recommended by any one, as a virtue or moral excellence, but on account of its being *useful,* or *agreeable* to a man *himself,* or to *others.* For what other reason can ever be assigned for praise or approbation? Or where would be the sense of extolling a *good* character or action, which, at the same time, is allowed to be *good for nothing?* All the differences, therefore, in morals, may be reduced to this one general foundation, and may be accounted for by the different views, which people take of these circumstances.

38. Sometimes men differ in their judgment about the usefulness of any habit or action: Sometimes also the peculiar circumstances of things render one moral quality more useful than others, and give it a peculiar preference.

39. It is not surprising, that, during a period of war and disorder, the military virtues should be more celebrated than the pacific, and attract more the admiration and attention of mankind. "How useful is it," says TULLY,[99] "to find CIMBRIANS, CELTIBERIANS, and other Barbarians, who bear, with inflexible constancy, all the fatigues and dangers of the field; but are immediately dispirited under the pain and hazard of a languishing distemper: While, on the other hand, the GREEKS patiently endure the slow approaches of death, when armed with sickness and disease; but timorously fly his presence, when he attacks them violently with swords and falchions!" So different is even the same virtue of courage among warlike or peaceful nations! And indeed, we may observe, that, as the difference between war and peace is the greatest that arises among nations and public societies, it produces also the greatest variations in moral sentiment, and diversifies the most our ideas of virtue and personal merit.

40. Sometimes too, magnanimity, greatness of mind, disdain of slavery, inflexible rigour and integrity, may better suit the circumstances of one age than those of another, and have a more kindly influence, both on public

---

97. Epist. lib. i. epist. 7. Also lib. i. ode 3. [Horace, *Epistles,* book 1, epistle 7, lines 26–28; also *Odes,* book 1, ode 33, lines 5–6.]

98. Ode 28. PETRONIUS (cap. 86.) joins both these circumstances as beauties. [Petronius, *Satyricon,* chapter 126.]

99. Tusc. Quæst. lib. ii. [Cicero, *Tusculan Disputations,* book 2, chapter 27, §65.]

affairs, and on a man's own safety and advancement. Our idea of merit, therefore, will also vary a little with these variations; and LABEO, perhaps, be censured for the same qualities, which procured CATO the highest approbation.

41. A degree of luxury may be ruinous and pernicious in a native of SWITZERLAND, which only fosters the arts, and encourages industry in a FRENCHMAN or ENGLISHMAN. We are not, therefore, to expect, either the same sentiments, or the same laws in BERNE, which prevail in LONDON or PARIS.

42. Different customs have also some influence as well as different utilities; and by giving an early biass to the mind, may produce a superior propensity, either to the useful or the agreeable qualities; to those which regard self, or those which extend to society. These four sources of moral sentiment still subsist; but particular accidents may, at one time, make any one of them flow with greater abundance than at another.

43. The customs of some nations shut up the women from all social commerce: Those of others make them so essential a part of society and conversation, that, except where business is transacted, the male-sex alone are supposed almost wholly incapable of mutual discourse and entertainment. As this difference is the most material that can happen in private life, it must also produce the greatest variation in our moral sentiments.

44. Of the nations in the world, where polygamy was not allowed, the GREEKS seem to have been the most reserved in their commerce with the fair sex, and to have imposed on them the strictest laws of modesty and decency. We have a strong instance of this in an oration of LYSIAS.[100] A widow injured, ruined, undone, calls a meeting of a few of her nearest friends and relations; and though never before accustomed, says the orator, to speak in the presence of men, the distress of her circumstances constrained her to lay the case before them. The very opening of her mouth in such company required, it seems, an apology.

45. When DEMOSTHENES prosecuted his tutors, to make them refund his patrimony, it became necessary for him, in the course of the law-suit, to prove that the marriage of APHOBUS's sister with ONETER was entirely fraudulent, and that, notwithstanding her sham marriage, she had lived with her brother at ATHENS for two years past, ever since her divorce from her former husband. And it is remarkable, that though these were people of the first fortune and distinction in the city, the orator could prove this fact no way, but by calling for her female slaves to be put to the question, and

100. Orat. 33. [Lysias, *Orations,* oration 32.]

by the evidence of one physician, who had seen her in her brother's house during her illness.[101] So reserved were GREEK manners.

46.   We may be assured, that an extreme purity of manners was the consequence of this reserve. Accordingly we find, that, except the fabulous stories of HELEN and CLYTEMNESTRA, there scarcely is an instance of any event in the GREEK history, which proceeded from the intrigues of women. On the other hand, in modern times, particularly in a neighbouring nation, the females enter into all transactions and all management of church and state: And no man can expect success, who takes not care to obtain their good graces. HARRY the third, by incurring the displeasure of the fair, endangered his crown, and lost his life, as much as by his indulgence to heresy.

47.   It is needless to dissemble: The consequence of a very free commerce between the sexes, and of their living much together, will often terminate in intrigues of gallantry. We must sacrifice somewhat of the *useful,* if we be very anxious to obtain all the *agreeable* qualities; and cannot pretend to reach alike every kind of advantage. Instances of licence, daily multiplying, will weaken the scandal with the one sex, and teach the other, by degrees, to adopt the famous maxim of LA FONTAINE, with regard to female infidelity, *that if one knows it, it is but a small matter; if one knows it not, it is nothing.*[102]

48.   Some people are inclined to think, that the best way of adjusting all the differences, and of keeping the proper medium between the *agreeable* and the *useful* qualities of the sex, is to live with them after the manner of the ROMANS and the ENGLISH (for the customs of these two nations seem similar in this respect[103]); that is, without gallantry,[104] and without jealousy. By a parity of reason, the customs of the SPANIARDS and of the ITALIANS

---

101. In ONETOREM. [Demosthenes, *Against Oneter,* 1, §33–36.]

102. "Quand on le sçait c'est peu de chose;
   Quand on l'ignore, ce n'est rien."
   [Jean de La Fontaine, *Contes et nouvelles en vers,* "La coupe enchantée."]

103. During the time of the emperors, the ROMANS seem to have been more given to intrigues and gallantry than the ENGLISH are at present: And the women of condition, in order to retain their lovers, endeavoured to fix a name of reproach on those who were addicted to wenching and low amours. They were called *Ancillarioli.* See SENECA de beneficiis. Lib. i. cap. 9. See also MARTIAL, lib. xii. epig. 58.

104. The gallantry here meant is that of amours and attachments, not that of complaisance, which is as much paid to the fair-sex in ENGLAND as in any other country.

of an age ago (for the present are very different) must be the worst of any; because they favour both gallantry and jealousy.

49. Nor will these different customs of nations affect the one sex only: Their idea of personal merit in the males must also be somewhat different with regard, at least, to conversation, address, and humour. The one nation, where the men live much apart, will naturally more approve of prudence; the other of gaiety. With the one simplicity of manners will be in the highest esteem; with the other, politeness. The one will distinguish themselves by good-sense and judgment; the other, by taste and delicacy. The eloquence of the former will shine most in the senate; that of the other, on the theatre.

50. These, I say, are the *natural* effects of such customs. For it must be confessed, that chance has a great influence on national manners; and many events happen in society, which are not to be accounted for by general rules. Who could imagine, for instance, that the ROMANS, who lived freely with their women, should be very indifferent about music, and esteem dancing infamous: While the GREEKS, who never almost saw a woman but in their own houses, were continually piping, singing, and dancing?

51. The differences of moral sentiment, which naturally arise from a republican or monarchical government, are also very obvious; as well as those which proceed from general riches or poverty, union or faction, ignorance or learning. I shall conclude this long discourse with observing, that different customs and situations vary not the original ideas of merit (however they may, some consequences) in any very essential point, and prevail chiefly with regard to young men, who can aspire to the agreeable qualities, and may attempt to please. The MANNER, the ORNAMENTS, the GRACES, which succeed in this shape, are more arbitrary and casual: But the merit of riper years is almost every where the same; and consists chiefly in integrity, humanity, ability, knowledge, and the other more solid and useful qualities of the human mind.

52. What you insist on, replied PALAMEDES, may have some foundation, when you adhere to the maxims of common life and ordinary conduct. Experience and the practice of the world readily correct any great extravagance on either side. But what say you to *artificial* lives and manners? How do you reconcile the maxims, on which, in different ages and nations, these are founded?

53. What do you understand by *artificial* lives and manners? said I. I explain myself, replied he. You know, that religion had, in ancient times, very little influence on common life, and that, after men had performed their duty in sacrifices and prayers at the temple, they thought, that the gods left

the rest of their conduct to themselves, and were little pleased or offended with those virtues or vices, which only affected the peace and happiness of human society. In those ages, it was the business of philosophy alone to regulate men's ordinary behaviour and deportment; and accordingly, we may observe, that this being the sole principle, by which a man could elevate himself above his fellows, it acquired a mighty ascendant over many, and produced great singularities of maxims and of conduct. At present, when philosophy has lost the allurement of novelty, it has no such extensive influence; but seems to confine itself mostly to speculations in the closet; in the same manner, as the ancient religion was limited to sacrifices in the temple. Its place is now supplied by the modern religion, which inspects our whole conduct, and prescribes an universal rule to our actions, to our words, to our very thoughts and inclinations; a rule so much the more austere, as it is guarded by infinite, though distant, rewards and punishments; and no infaction of it can ever be concealed or disguised.

54. DIOGENES is the most celebrated model of extravagant philosophy. Let us seek a parallel to him in modern times. We shall not disgrace any philosphic name by a comparison with the DOMINICS or LOYOLAS, or any canonized monk or friar. Let us compare him to PASCAL, a man of parts and genius as well as DIOGENES himself; and perhaps too, a man or virtue, had he allowed his virtuous inclinations to have exerted and displayed themselves.

55. The foundation of DIOGENES's conduct was an endeavour to render himself an indpendent being as much as possible, and to confine all his wants and desires and pleasures within himself and his own mind: The aim of PASCAL was to keep a perpetual sense of his dependence before his eyes, and never to forget his numberless wants and infirmites. The ancient supported himself by magnanimity, ostentation, pride, and the idea of his own superiority above his fellow-creatures. The modern made constant profession of humility and abasement, of the contempt and hatred of himself; and endeavoured to attain these supposed virtues, as far as they are attainable. The austerities of the GREEK were in order to inure himself to hardships, and prevent his ever suffering: Those of the FRENCHMAN were embraced merely for their own sake, and in order to suffer as much as possible. The philosopher indulged himself in the most beastly pleasures, even in public: The saint refused himself the most innocent, even in private. The former thought it his duty to love his friends, and to rail at them, and reprove them, and scold them: The latter endeavoured to be absolutely indifferent towards his nearest relations, and to love and speak well of his enemies. The great object of DIOGENES's wit was every kind of superstition, that is every kind

of religion known in his time. The mortality of the soul was his standard principle; and even his sentiments of a divine providence seem to have been licentious. The most ridiculous superstitions directed PASCAL's faith and practice; and an extreme contempt of this life, in comparison of the future, was the chief foundation of his conduct.

56. In such a remarkable contrast do these two men stand: Yet both of them have met with general admiration in their different ages, and have been proposed as models of imitation. Where then is the universal standard of morals, which you talk of? And what rule shall we establish for the many different, nay contrary sentiments of mankind?

57. An experiment, said I, which succeeds in the air, will not always succeed in a vacuum. When men depart from the maxims of common reason, and affect these *artificial* lives, as you call them, no one can answer to what will please or displease them. They are in a different element from the rest of mankind; and the natural principles of their mind play not with the same regularity, as if left to themselves, free from the illusions of religious superstition or philosophical enthusiasm.

Essays, Moral, Political and Literary

I.

Of the Liberty of the Press

1. NOTHING is more apt to surprize a foreigner, than the extreme liberty, which we enjoy in this country, of communicating whatever we please to the public, and of openly censuring every measure, entered into by the king or his ministers. If the administration resolve upon war, it is affirmed, that, either wilfully or ignorantly, they mistake the interests of the nation, and that peace, in the present situation of affairs, is infinitely preferable. If the passion of the ministers lie towards peace, our political writers breathe nothing but war and devastation, and represent the pacific conduct of the government as mean and pusillanimous. As this liberty is not indulged in any other government, either republican or monarchical; in HOLLAND and VENICE, more than in FRANCE or SPAIN; it may very naturally give occasion to a question, *How it happens that* GREAT BRITAIN *alone enjoys this peculiar privilege?*

2. The reason, why the laws indulge us in such a liberty seems to be derived from our mixed form of government, which is neither wholly monarchical, nor wholly republican. It will be found, if I mistake not, a true observation in politics, that the two extremes in government, liberty and slavery, commonly approach nearest to each other; and that, as you depart from the extremes, and mix a little of monarchy with liberty, the government becomes always the more free; and on the other hand, when you mix a little of liberty with monarchy, the yoke becomes always the more grievous and intolerable. In a government, such as that of FRANCE, which is absolute, and where law, custom, and religion concur, all of them, to make the people fully satisfied with their condition, the monarch cannot entertain any *jealousy* against his subjects, and therefore is apt to indulge them in great *liberties* both of speech and action. In a government altogether republican, such as that of HOLLAND, where there is no magistrate so eminent as to give *jealousy* to the state, there is no danger in intrusting the magistrates with large discretionary powers; and though many advantages result from

such powers, in preserving peace and order, yet they lay a considerable restraint on men's actions, and make every private citizen pay a great respect
to the government. Thus it seems evident, that the two extremes of absolute
monarchy and of a republic, approach near to each other in some material
circumstances. In the *first,* the magistrate has no jealousy of the people: in
the *second,* the people have none of the magistrate: Which want of jealousy
begets a mutual confidence and trust in both cases, and produces a species
of liberty in monarchies, and of arbitrary power in republics.

3.   To justify the other part of the foregoing observation, that, in every
government, the means are most wide of each other, and that the mixtures
of monarchy and liberty render the yoke either more easy or more grievous; I must take notice of a remark in TACITUS with regard to the ROMANS
under the emperors, that they neither could bear total slavery nor total liberty, *Nec totam servitutem, nec totam libertatem pati possunt.* This remark
a celebrated poet has translated and applied to the ENGLISH, in his lively
description of queen ELIZABETH's policy and government,

> *Et fit aimer son joug a l'Anglois indompté,*
> *Qui ne peut ni servir, ni vivre en liberté,*
> HENRIADE, *liv.* I.[1]

4.   According to these remarks, we are to consider the ROMAN government
under the emperors as a mixture of despotism and liberty, where the despotism prevailed; and the ENGLISH government as a mixture of the same kind,
where the liberty predominates. The consequences are conformable to the
foregoing observation; and such as may be expected from those mixed
forms of government, which beget a mutual watchfulness and jealousy.
The ROMAN emperors were, many of them, the most frightful tyrants that
ever disgraced human nature; and it is evident, that their cruelty was chiefly
excited by their *jealousy,* and by their observing that all the great men of
ROME bore with impatience the dominion of a family, which, but a little
before, was no wise superior to their own. On the other hand, as the republican part of the government prevails in ENGLAND, though with a great
mixture of monarchy, it is obliged, for its own preservation, to maintain a
watchful *jealousy* over the magistrates, to remove all discretionary powers,
and to secure every one's life and fortune by general and inflexible laws.
No action must be deemed a crime but what the law has plainly determined

---

1. ["And she made her yoke dear to the unconquered English, who can neither
serve nor live in liberty." Voltaire, *La Henriade.*]

to be such: No crime must be imputed to a man but from a legal proof before his judges; and even these judges must be his fellow-subjects, who are obliged, by their own interest, to have a watchful eye over the encroachments and violence of the ministers. From these causes it proceeds, that there is as much liberty, and even, perhaps, licentiousness in GREAT BRITAIN, as there were formerly slavery and tyranny in ROME.

5.   These principles account for the great liberty of the press in these kingdoms, beyond what is indulged in any other government. It is apprehended, that arbitrary power would steal in upon us, were we not careful to prevent its progress, and were there not an easy method of conveying the alarm from one end of the kingdom to the other. The spirit of the people must frequently be rouzed, in order to curb the ambition of the court; and the dread of rouzing this spirit must be employed to prevent that ambition. Nothing so effectual to this purpose as the liberty of the press, by which all the learning, wit, and genius of the nation may be employed on the side of freedom, and every one be animated to its defence. As long, therefore, as the republican part of our government can maintain itself against the monarchical, it will naturally be careful to keep the press open, as of importance to its own preservation.

6.   It must however be allowed, that the unbounded liberty of the press, though it be difficult, perhaps impossible, to propose a suitable remedy for it, is one of the evils, attending those mixt forms of government.

2.

That Politics May Be
Reduced to a Science

1.   IT is a question with several, whether there be any essential difference between one form of government and another? and, whether every form may not become good or bad, according as it is well or ill administered?[2] Were it once admitted, that all governments are alike, and that the only difference consists in the character and conduct of the governors, most political disputes would be at an end, and all *Zeal* for one constitution above another, must be esteemed mere bigotry and folly. But, though a friend to moderation, I cannot forbear condemning this sentiment, and should be sorry to think, that human affairs admit of no greater stability, than what they receive from the casual humours and characters of particular men.

2.   It is true; those who maintain, that the goodness of all government consists in the goodness of the administration, may cite many particular instances in history, where the very same government, in different hands, has varied suddenly into the two opposite extremes of good and bad. Compare the FRENCH government under HENRY III. and under HENRY IV. Oppression, levity, artifice on the part of the rulers; faction, sedition, treachery, rebellion, disloyalty on the part of the subjects: These compose the character of the former miserable aera. But when the patriot and heroic prince, who succeeded, was once firmly seated on the throne, the government, the people, every thing seemed to be totally changed; and all from the difference of the temper and conduct of these two sovereigns. Instances of this kind may be multiplied, almost without number, from ancient as well as modern history, foreign as well as domestic.

---

2. For forms of government let fools contest,
Whate'er is best administer'd is best.
ESSAY on Man, Book 3 [Alexander Pope, *Essay on Man,* published 1732–34.]

3.   But here it may be proper to make a distinction. All absolute governments must very much depend on the administration; and this is one of the great inconveniences attending that form of government. But a republican and free government would be an obvious absurdity, if the particular checks and controuls, provided by the constitution, had really no influence, and made it not the interest, even of bad men, to act for the public good. Such is the intention of these forms of government, and such is their real effect, where they are wisely constituted: As on the other hand, they are the source of all disorder, and of the blackest crimes, where either skill or honesty has been wanting in their original frame and institution.

4   So great is the force of laws, and of particular forms of government, and so little dependence have they on the humours and tempers of men, that consequences almost as general and certain may sometimes be deduced from them, as any which the mathematical sciences afford us.

5.   The constitution of the ROMAN republic gave the whole legislative power to the people, without allowing a negative voice either to the nobility or consuls. This unbounded power they possessed in a collective, not in a representative body. The consequences were: When the people, by success and conquest, had become very numerous, and had spread themselves to a great distance from the capital, the city-tribes, though the most contemptible, carried almost every vote: They were, therefore, most cajoled by every one that affected popularity: They were supported in idleness by the general distribution of corn, and by particular bribes, which they received from almost every candidate: By this means, they became every day more licentious, and the CAMPUS MARTIUS was a perpetual scene of tumult and sedition: Armed slaves were introduced among these rascally citizens; so that the whole government fell into anarchy, and the greatest happiness, which the ROMANS could look for, was the despotic power of the CÆSARS. Such are the effects of democracy without a representative.

6.   A Nobility may possess the whole, or any part of the legislative power of a state, in two different ways. Either every nobleman shares the power as part of the whole body, or the whole body enjoys the power as composed of parts, which have each a distinct power and authority. The VENETIAN aristocracy is an instance of the first kind of government: The POLISH of the second. In the VENETIAN government the whole body of nobility possesses the whole power, and no nobleman has any authority which he receives not from the whole. In the POLISH government every nobleman, by means of his fiefs, has a distinct hereditary authority over his vassals, and the whole body has no authority but what it receives from the concurrence of its parts. The different operations and tendencies of these two species of government

might be made apparent even *a priori*. A VENETIAN nobility is preferable to a POLISH, let the humours and education of men be ever so much varied. A nobility, who possess their power in common, will preserve peace and order, both among themselves, and their subjects; and no member can have authority enough to controul the laws for a moment. The nobles will preserve their authority over the people, but without any grievous tyranny, or any breach of private property; because such a tyrannical government promotes not the interests of the whole body, however it may that of some individuals. There will be a distinction of rank between the nobility and people, but this will be the only distinction in the state. The whole nobility will form one body, and the whole people another, without any of those private feuds and animosities, which spread ruin and desolation every where. It is easy to see the disadvantages of a POLISH nobility in every one of these particulars.

7.   It is possible so to constitute a free government, as that a single person, call him doge, prince, or king, shall possess a large share of power, and shall form a proper balance or counterpoise to the other parts of the legislature. This chief magistrate may be either *elective* or *hereditary;* and though the former institution may, to a superficial view, appear the most advantageous; yet a more accurate inspection will discover in it greater inconveniencies than in the latter, and such as are founded on causes and principles eternal and immutable. The filling of the throne, in such a government, is a point of too great and too general interest, not to divide the whole people into factions: Whence a civil war, the greatest of ills, may be apprehended, almost with certainty, upon every vacancy. The prince elected must be either a *Foreigner* or a *Native:* The former will be ignorant of the people whom he is to govern; suspicious of his new subjects, and suspected by them; giving his confidence entirely to strangers, who will have no other care but of enriching themselves in the quickest manner, while their master's favour and authority are able to support them. A native will carry into the throne all his private animosities and friendships, and will never be viewed in his elevation, without exciting the sentiment of envy in those, who formerly considered him as their equal. Not to mention that a crown is too high a reward ever to be given to merit alone, and will always induce the candidates to employ force, or money, or intrigue, to procure the votes of the electors: So that such an election will give no better chance for superior merit in the prince, than if the state had trusted to birth alone for determining their sovereign.

8.   It may therefore be pronounced as an universal axiom in politics, *That an hereditary prince, a nobility without vassals, and a people voting by*

their representatives, form the best MONARCHY, ARISTOCRACY, *and* DE-
MOCRACY. But in order to prove more fully, that politics admit of general
truths, which are invariable by the humour or education either of subject
or sovereign, it may not be amiss to observe some other principles of this
science, which may seem to deserve that character.

9.   It may easily be observed, that, though free governments have been
commonly the most happy for those who partake of their freedom; yet are
they the most ruinous and oppressive to their provinces: And this observation may, I believe, be fixed as a maxim of the kind we are here speaking
of. When a monarch extends his dominions by conquest, he soon learns
to consider his old and his new subjects as on the same footing; because,
in reality, all his subjects are to him the same, except the few friends and
favourites, with whom he is personally acquainted. He does not, therefore,
make any distinction between them in his *general* laws; and, at the same
time, is careful to prevent all *particular* acts of oppression on the one as
well as on the other. But a free state necessarily makes a great distinction,
and must always do so, till men learn to love their neighbours as well as
themselves. The conquerors, in such a government, are all legislators, and
will be sure to contrive matters, by restrictions on trade, and by taxes, so
as to draw some private, as well as public, advantage from their conquests.
Provincial governors have also a better chance, in a republic, to escape with
their plunder, by means of bribery or intrigue; and their fellow-citizens,
who find their own state to be enriched by the spoils of the subject provinces, will be the more inclined to tolerate such abuses. Not to mention,
that it is a necessary precaution in a free state to change the governors
frequently; which obliges these temporary tyrants to be more expeditious
and rapacious, that they may accumulate sufficient wealth before they give
place to their successors. What cruel tyrants were the ROMANS over the
world during the time of their commonwealth! It is true, they had laws to
prevent oppression in their provincial magistrates; but CICERO informs us,
that the ROMANS could not better consult the interests of the provinces than
by repealing these very laws. For, in that case, says he, our magistrates,
having entire impunity, would plunder no more than would satisfy their
own rapaciousness; whereas, at present, they must also satisfy that of their
judges, and of all the great men in ROME, of whose protection they stand
in need. Who can read of the cruelties and oppressions of VERRES without
horror and astonishment? And who is not touched with indignation to hear,
that, after CICERO had exhausted on that abandoned criminal all the thun-
ders of his eloquence, and had prevailed so far as to get him condemned
to the utmost extent of the laws; yet that cruel tyrant lived peaceably to

old age, in opulence and ease, and, thirty years afterwards, was put into the proscription by MARK ANTHONY, on account of his exorbitant wealth, where he fell with CICERO himself, and all the most virtuous men of ROME? After the dissolution of the commonwealth, the ROMAN yoke became easier upon the provinces, as TACITUS informs us;[3] and it may be observed, that many of the worst emperors, DOMITIAN,[4] for instance, were careful to prevent all oppression on the provinces. In[5] TIBERIUS's time, GAUL was esteemed richer than ITALY itself: Nor, do I find, during the whole time of the ROMAN monarchy, that the empire became less rich or populous in any of its provinces; though indeed its valour and military discipline were always upon the decline. The oppression and tyranny of the CARTHAGINIANS over their subject states in AFRICA went so far, as we learn from POLYBIUS,[6] that, not content with exacting the half of all the produce of the land, which of itself was a very high rent, they also loaded them with many other taxes. If we pass from ancient to modern times, we shall still find the observation to hold. The provinces of absolute monarchies are always better treated than those of free states. Compare the *Païs conquis*[7] of FRANCE with IRELAND, and you will be convinced of this truth; though this latter kingdom, being, in a good measure, peopled from ENGLAND, possesses so many rights and privileges as should naturally make it challenge better treatment than that of a conquered province. CORSICA is also an obvious instance to the same purpose.

10.   There is an observation in MACHIAVEL, with regard to the conquests of ALEXANDER the Great, which I think, may be regarded as one of those eternal political truths, which no time nor accidents can vary. It may seem strange, says that politician, that such sudden conquests, as those of ALEXANDER, should be possessed so peaceably by his successors, and that the PERSIANS, during all the confusions and civil wars among the GREEKS, never made the smallest effort towards the recovery of their former independent government. To satisfy us concerning the cause of this remarkable

---

3. Ann. Lib. I. cap. 2. [Tacitus, *Annals.*]

4. SUET. in vita DOMIT. [Suetonius, *Lives of the Caesars.*]

5. *Egregium resumendae libertati tempus, si ipsi florentes, quam inops* Italia, *quam imbellis urbana plebs, nihil validum in exercitibus, nisi quod externum cogitarent.* TACIT. Ann. lib. 3. ["It was an unequalled opportunity for regaining their independence: they had only to look from their own resources to the poverty of Italy, the unwarlike city population, the feebleness of the armies except for the leavening of foreigners." Tacitus, *Annals,* translated by John Jackson.]

6. Lib. I. cap. 72. [Polybius, *Histories.*]

7. [Conquered lands.]

event, we may consider, that a monarch may govern his subjects in two different ways. He may either follow the maxims of the eastern princes, and stretch his authority so far as to leave no distinction of rank among his subjects, but what proceeds immediately from himself; no advantages of birth; no hereditary honours and possessions; and, in a word, no credit among the people, except from his commission alone. Or a monarch may exert his power after a milder manner, like other EUROPEAN princes; and leave other sources of honour, beside his smile and favour: Birth, titles, possessions, valour, integrity, knowledge, or great and fortunate achievements. In the former species of government, after a conquest, it is impossible ever to shake off the yoke; since no one possesses, among the people, so much personal credit and authority as to begin such an enterprize: Whereas, in the latter, the least misfortune, or discord among the victors, will encourage the vanquished to take arms, who have leaders ready to prompt and conduct them in every undertaking.[8]

8. I have taken it for granted, according to the supposition of MACHIAVEL, that the ancient PERSIANS had no nobility; though there is reason to suspect, that the FLORENTINE secretary, who seems to have been better acquainted with the ROMAN than the GREEK authors, was mistaken in this particular. The more ancient PERSIANS, whose manners are described by XENOPHON, were a free people, and had nobility. Their ομοτιμοι were preserved even after the extending of their conquests and the consequent change of their government. ARRIAN mentions them in DARIUS's time, *De exped.* ALEX. lib. ii. Historians also speak often of the persons in command as men of family. TYGRANES, who was general of the MEDES under XERXES, was of the race of ACHMÆNES, HEROD. lib. vii. cap. 62. ARTACHÆAS, who directed the cutting of the canal about mount ATHOS, was of the same family. Id. cap. 117. MEGABYZUS was one of the seven eminent PERSIANS who conspired against the MAGI. His son, ZOPYRUS, was in the highest command under DARIUS, and delivered BABYLON to him. His grandson, MEGABYZUS, commanded the army, defeated at MARATHON. His great-grandson, ZOPYRUS, was also eminent, and was banished from PERSIA. HEROD. lib. iii. THUC. lib. i. ROSACES, who commanded an army in EGYPT under ARTAXERXES, was also descended from one of the seven conspirators, DIOD. SIC. lib. xvi. AGESILAUS, in XENOPHON, Hist. GRÆC. lib. iv. being desirous of making a marriage betwixt king COTYS his ally, and the daughter of SPITHRIDATES, a PERSIAN of rank, who had deserted to him, first asks COTYS what family SPITHRIDATES is of. One of the most considerable in PERSIA, says COTYS. ARIÆUS, when offered the sovereignty by CLEARCHUS and the ten thousand GREEKS, refused it as of too low a rank, and said, that so many eminent PERSIANS would never endure his rule. *Id. de exped.* lib. ii. Some of the families descended from the seven PERSIANS abovementioned remained during all ALEXANDER's successors; and MITHRIDATES, in ANTIOCHUS's time, is said by POLYBIUS to be descended from one of them, lib. v. cap. 43. ARTABAZUS was esteemed, as ARRIAN says, εν τοις πρωτοις Περσων lib. iii. And when ALEXANDER married in one day 80 of his captains to PERSIAN women, his intention

11. Such is the reasoning of MACHIAVEL, which seems solid and conclusive; though I wish he had not mixed falsehood with truth, in asserting, that monarchies, governed according to eastern policy, though more easily kept when once subdued, yet are the most difficult to subdue; since they cannot contain any powerful subject, whose discontent and faction may facilitate the enterprizes of an enemy. For besides, that such a tyrannical government enervates the courage of men, and renders them indifferent towards the fortunes of their sovereign; besides this, I say, we find by experience, that even the temporary and delegated authority of the generals and magistrates; being always, in such governments, as absolute within its sphere, as that of the prince himself; is able, with barbarians, accustomed to a blind submission, to produce the most dangerous and fatal revolutions. So that, in every respect, a gentle government is preferable, and gives the greatest security to the sovereign as well as to the subject.

12. Legislators, therefore, ought not to trust the future government of a state entirely to chance, but ought to provide a system of laws to regulate the administration of public affairs to the latest posterity. Effects will always correspond to causes; and wise regulations in any commonwealth are the most valuable legacy that can be left to future ages. In the smallest court or office, the stated forms and methods, by which business must be conducted, are found to be a considerable check on the natural depravity of mankind. Why should not the case be the same in public affairs? Can we ascribe the stability and wisdom of the VENETIAN government, through so many ages, to any thing but the form of government? And is it not easy to point out those defects in the original constitution, which produced the tumultuous governments of ATHENS and ROME, and ended at last in the ruin of these two famous republics? And so little dependance has this affair on the humours and education of particular men, that one part of the same republic may be wisely conducted, and another weakly, by the very same

---

plainly was to ally the MACEDONIANS with the most eminent PERSIAN families. Id. lib. vii. DIODORUS SICULUS says they were of the most noble birth in PERSIA, lib. xvii. The government of PERSIA was despotic, and conducted in many respects, after the eastern manner, but was not carried so far as to extirpate all nobility, and confound all ranks and orders. It left men who were still great, by themselves and their family, independent of their office and commission. And the reason why the MACEDONIANS kept so easily dominion over them was owing to other causes easy to be found in the historians; though it must be owned that MACHIAVEL's reasoning is, in itself, just, however doubtful its application to the present case.

men, merely on account of the difference of the forms and institutions, by which these parts are regulated. Historians inform us that this was actually the case with GENOA. For while the state was always full of sedition, and tumult, and disorder, the bank of St. GEORGE, which had become a considerable part of the people, was conducted, for several ages, with the utmost integrity and wisdom.[9]

13. The ages of greatest public spirit are not always most eminent for private virtue. Good laws may beget order and moderation in the government, where the manners and customs have instilled little humanity or justice into the tempers of men. The most illustrious period of the ROMAN history, considered in a political view, is that between the beginning of the first and end of the last PUNIC war;[10] the due balance between the nobility and the people being then fixed by the contests of the tribunes, and not being yet lost by the extent of conquests. Yet at this very time, the horrid practice of poisoning was so common, that, during part of a season, a *Prætor*[11] punished capitally for this crime above three thousand[12] persons in a part of ITALY; and found informations of this nature still multiplying upon him. There is a similar, or rather a worse instance,[13] in the more early times of the commonwealth. So depraved in private life were that people, whom in their histories we so much admire. I doubt not but they were really more virtuous during the time of the two *Triumvirates;* when they were tearing

---

9. *Essempio veramente raro, & da Filosofi intante loro imaginate & vedute Republiche mai non trovato, vedere dentro ad un medesimo cerchio, fra medesimi cittadini, la liberta, & la tirannide, la vita civile & la corotta, la giustitia & la licenza; perche quello ordine solo mantiere quella citta piena di costumi antichi & venerabili. E s'egli auvenisse (che col tempo in ogni modo auverrà) que* SAN GIORGIO *tutta quel la città occupasse, sarrebbe quella una Republica piu dalla* VENETIANA *memorabile.* Della Hist. Florentinè, lib. [Machiavelli, *History of Florence,* 8.29. The passage may be translated as follows: "A truly rare example, and one never found by the philosophers in all their imagined or dreamed republics, to see in the same circle, among the same citizens, liberty and tyranny, the civil and the corrupt life, justice and license; because that order alone keeps that city full of ancient and venerable customs. And should it happen which in time will happen anyway, that St. George will occupy all that city, it would be a republic more memorable than the Venetian one."]

10. [The Punic Wars include three separate wars fought between Rome and Carthage.]

11. [A high judicial officer or a governor of a province.]

12. T. Livii, lib. 40. cap. 43. [Livy, *History of Rome.*]

13. *Id.* lib. 8. cap. 18.

their common country to pieces, and spreading slaughter and desolation over the face of the earth, merely for the choice of tyrants.[14]

14. Here, then, is a sufficient inducement to maintain, with the utmost ZEAL, in every free state, those forms and institutions, by which liberty is secured, the public good consulted, and the avarice or ambition of particular men restrained and punished. Nothing does more honour to human nature, than to see it susceptible of so noble a passion; as nothing can be a greater indication of meanness of heart in any man, than to see him destitute of it. A man who loves only himself, without regard to friendship and desert, merits the severest blame; and a man, who is only susceptible of friendship, without public spirit, or a regard to the community, is deficient in the most material part of virtue.

15. But this is a subject which needs not be longer insisted on at present. There are enow[15] of zealots on both sides who kindle up the passions of their partizans, and under pretence of public good, pursue the interests and ends of their particular faction. For my part, I shall always be more fond of promoting moderation than zeal; though perhaps the surest way of producing moderation in every party is to increase our zeal for the public. Let us therefore try, if it be possible, from the foregoing doctrine, to draw a lesson of moderation with regard to the parties, into which our country is at present divided; at the same time, that we allow not this moderation to abate the industry and passion, with which every individual is bound to pursue the good of his country.

16. Those who either attack or defend a minister in such a government as ours, where the utmost liberty is allowed, always carry matters to an extreme, and exaggerate his merit or demerit with regard to the public. His enemies are sure to charge him with the greatest enormities, both in domestic and foreign management; and there is no meanness or crime, of which, in their account, he is not capable. Unnecessary wars, scandalous treaties, profusion of public treasure, oppressive taxes, every kind of maladministration is ascribed to him. To aggravate the charge, his pernicious

---

14. *L'Aigle contre L'Aigle*, ROMAINS *contre* ROMAINS,
Combatans seulement pour le choix de tyrans.
CORNEILLE.
[Corneille, *Cinna*. These lines are adapted loosely from the tragedy *Cinna*, act 1, scene 3, which was produced by Pierre Corneille in late 1640 or early 1641. The quote may be translated as follows: "Eagle against Eagle, Romans against Romans, / Fighting only for the choice of tyrants."]
15. [The plural of "enough."]

conduct, it is said, will extend its baleful influence even to posterity, by undermining the best constitution in the world, and disordering that wise system of laws, institutions, and customs, by which our ancestors, during so many centuries, have been so happily governed. He is not only a wicked minister in himself, but has removed every security provided against wicked ministers for the future.

17. On the other hand, the partizans of the minister make his panegyric run as high as the accusation against him, and celebrate his wise, steady, and moderate conduct in every part of his administration. The honour and interest of the nation supported abroad, public credit maintained at home, persecution restrained, faction subdued; the merit of all these blessings is ascribed solely to the minister. At the same time, he crowns all his other merits by a religious care of the best constitution in the world, which he has preserved in all its parts, and has transmitted entire, to be the happiness and security of the latest posterity.

18. When this accusation and panegyric are received by the partizans of each party, no wonder they beget an extraordinary ferment on both sides, and fill the nation with violent animosities. But I would fain persuade these party-zealots, that there is a flat contradiction both in the accusation and panegyric, and that it were impossible for either of them to run so high, were it not for this contradiction. If our constitution be really *that noble fabric, the pride of* BRITAIN, *the envy of our neighbours, raised by the labour of so many centuries, repaired at the expence of so many millions, and cemented by such a profusion of blood;*[16] I say, if our constitution does in any degree deserve these eulogies, it would never have suffered a wicked and weak minister to govern triumphantly for a course of twenty years, when opposed by the greatest geniuses in the nation, who exercised the utmost liberty of tongue and pen, in parliament, and in their frequent appeals to the people. But, if the minister be wicked and weak, to the degree so strenuously insisted on, the constitution must be faulty in its original principles, and he cannot consistently be charged with undermining the best form of government in the world. A constitution is only so far good, as it provides a remedy against mal-administration; and if the BRITISH, when in its greatest vigour, and repaired by two such remarkable events, as the *Revolution* and *Accession,* by which our ancient royal family was sacrificed to it; if our constitution, I say, with so great advantages, does not,

---

16. *Dissertation on parties,* Letter 10 [Henry St. John, later Lord Bolingbroke, *Dissertation on Parties.*]

in fact, provide any such remedy, we are rather beholden to any minister who undermines it, and affords us an opportunity of erecting a better in its place.

19. I would employ the same topics to moderate the zeal of those who defend the minister. *Is our constitution so excellent?* Then a change of ministry can be no such dreadful event; since it is essential to such a constitution, in every ministry, both to preserve itself from violation, and to prevent all enormities in the administration. *Is our constitution very bad?* Then so extraordinary a jealousy and apprehension, on account of changes, is ill placed; and a man should no more be anxious in this case, than a husband, who had married a woman from the stews, should be watchful to prevent her infidelity. Public affairs, in such a government, must necessarily go to confusion, by whatever hands they are conducted; and the zeal of *patriots* is in that case much less requisite than the patience and submission of *philosophers.* The virtue and good intentions of CATO and BRUTUS are highly laudable; but, to what purpose did their zeal serve? Only to hasten the fatal period of the ROMAN government, and render its convulsions and dying agonies more violent and painful.

20. I would not be understood to mean, that public affairs deserve no care and attention at all. Would men be moderate and consistent, their claims might be admitted; at least might be examined. The *country-party* might still assert, that our constitution, though excellent, will admit of maladministration to a certain degree; and therefore, if the minister be bad, it is proper to oppose him with a *suitable* degree of zeal. And, on the other hand, the *court-party* may be allowed, upon the supposition that the minister were good, to defend, and with *some* zeal too, his administration. I would only persuade men not to contend, as if they were fighting *pro aris & focis,*[17] and change a good constitution into a bad one, by the violence of their factions.

21. I have not here considered any thing that is personal in the present controversy. In the best civil constitution, where every man is restrained by the most rigid laws, it is easy to discover either the good or bad intentions of a minister, and to judge, whether his personal character deserve love or hatred. But such questions are of little importance to the public, and lay those, who employ their pens upon them, under a just suspicion either of malevolence or of flattery.

17. ["For God and country."]

3.

Of the First Principles
of Government

1.   NOTHING appears more surprizing to those, who consider human affairs with a philosophical eye, than the easiness with which the many are governed by the few; and the implicit submission, with which men resign their own sentiments and passions to those of their rulers. When we enquire by what means this wonder is effected, we shall find, that, as FORCE is always on the side of the governed, the governors have nothing to support them but opinion. It is therefore, on opinion only that government is founded; and this maxim extends to the most despotic and most military governments, as well as to the most free and most popular. The soldan[18] of EGYPT, or the emperor of ROME, might drive his harmless subjects, like brute beasts, against their sentiments and inclination: But he must, at least, have led his *mamalukes,*[19] or *praetorian bands,*[20] like men, by their opinion.

2.   Opinion is of two kinds, to wit, opinion of INTEREST, and opinion of RIGHT. By opinion of interest, I chiefly understand the sense of the general advantage which is reaped from government; together with the persuasion, that the particular government, which is established, is equally advantageous with any other that could easily be settled. When this opinion prevails among the generality of a state, or among those who have the force in their hands, it gives great security to any government.

3.   Right is of two kinds, right to POWER and right to PROPERTY. What prevalence opinion of the first kind has over mankind, may easily be

---

18. [Sultan.]

19. [Mamalukes were members of the military body that seized the throne of Egypt in 1254 and continued to form the ruling class in that country in the eighteenth century.]

20. [Praetorian bands were the bodyguards of the emperors of ancient Rome.]

understood, by observing the attachment which all nations have to their ancient government, and even to those names, which have had the sanction of antiquity. Antiquity always begets the opinion of right; and whatever disadvantageous sentiments we may entertain of mankind, they are always found to be prodigal both of blood and treasure in the maintenance of public justice. There is, indeed, no particular, in which, at first sight, there may appear a greater contradiction in the frame of the human mind than the present. When men act in a faction, they are apt, without shame or remorse, to neglect all the ties of honour and morality, in order to serve their party; and yet, when a faction is formed upon a point of right or principle, there is no occasion, where men discover a greater obstinacy, and a more determined sense of justice and equity. The same social disposition of mankind is the cause of these contradictory appearances.

4.   It is sufficiently understood, that the opinion of right to property is of moment in all matters of government. A noted author[21] has made property the foundation of all government; and most of our political writers seem inclined to follow him in that particular. This is carrying the matter too far; but still it must be owned, that the opinion of right to property has a great influence in this subject.

5.   Upon these three opinions, therefore, of public *interest,* of *right to power,* and of *right to property,* are all governments founded, and all authority of the few over the many. There are indeed other principles, which add force to these, and determine, limit, or alter their operation; such as *self-interest, fear,* and *affection:* But still we may assert, that these other principles can have no influence alone, but suppose the antecedent influence of those opinions above-mentioned. They are, therefore, to be esteemed the secondary, not the original principles of government.

6.   For, *first,* as to *self-interest,* by which I mean the expectation of particular rewards, distinct from the general protection which we receive from government, it is evident that the magistrate's authority must be antecedently established, at least be hoped for, in order to produce this expectation. The prospect of reward may augment his authority with regard to some particular persons; but can never give birth to it, with regard to the public. Men naturally look for the greatest favours from their friends and acquaintance; and therefore, the hopes of any considerable number of the state would never center in any particular set of men, if these men had no other title to magistracy, and had no separate influence over the opinions

21. [The reference here is most likely to James Harrington, author of the *Commonwealth of Oceana* (1656).]

of mankind. The same observation may be extended to the other two principles of *fear* and *affection.* No man would have any reason to *fear* the fury of a tyrant, if he had no authority over any but from fear; since, as a single man, his bodily force can reach but a small way, and all the farther power he possesses must be founded either on our own opinion, or on the presumed opinion of others. And though *affection* to wisdom and virtue in a *sovereign* extends very far, and has great influence; yet he must antecedently be supposed invested with a public character, otherwise the public esteem will serve him in no stead, nor will his virtue have any influence beyond a narrow sphere.

7.   A Government may endure for several ages, though the balance of power, and the balance of property do not coincide. This chiefly happens, where any rank or order of the state has acquired a large share in the property; but from the original constitution of the government, has no share in the power. Under what pretence would any individual of that order assume authority in public affairs? As men are commonly much attached to their ancient government, it is not to be expected, that the public would ever favour such usurpations. But where the original constitution allows any share of power, though small, to an order of men, who possess a large share of the property, it is easy for them gradually to stretch their authority, and bring the balance of power to coincide with that of property. This has been the case with the house of commons in ENGLAND.

8.   Most writers, that have treated of the BRITISH government, have supposed, that, as the lower house represents all the commons of GREAT BRITAIN, its weight in the scale is proportioned to the property and power of all whom it represents. But this principle must not be received as absolutely true. For though the people are apt to attach themselves more to the house of commons, than to any other member of the constitution; that house being chosen by them as their representatives, and as the public guardians of their liberty; yet are there instances where the house, even when in opposition to the crown, has not been followed by the people; as we may particularly observe of the *tory* house of commons in the reign of king WILLIAM.[22] Were the members obliged to receive instructions from their constituents, like the DUTCH deputies, this would entirely alter the case; and if such immense power and riches, as those of all the commons of GREAT BRITAIN, were brought into the scale, it is not easy to conceive, that the crown could either influence that multitude of people, or withstand that overbalance of property. It is true, the crown has great influence over the collective body in

22. [This marks the period from 1698 to 1701.]

the elections of members; but were this influence, which at present is only exerted once in seven years, to be employed in bringing over the people to every vote, it would soon be wasted; and no skill, popularity, or revenue, could support it. I must, therefore, be of opinion, that an alteration in this particular would introduce a total alteration in our government, and would soon reduce it to a pure republic; and, perhaps, to a republic of no inconvenient form. For though the people, collected in a body like the ROMAN tribes, be quite unfit for government, yet when dispersed in small bodies, they are more susceptible both of reason and order; the force of popular currents and tides is, in a great measure, broken; and the public interest may be pursued with some method and constancy. But it is needless to reason any farther concerning a form of government, which is never likely to have place in GREAT BRITAINS, and which seems not to be the aim of any party amongst us. Let us cherish and improve our ancient government as much as possible, without encouraging a passion for such dangerous novelties.

4.

Of the Origin of Government

1. MAN, born in a family, is compelled to maintain society, from necessity, from natural inclination, and from habit. The same creature, in his farther progress, is engaged to establish political society, in order to administer justice; without which there can be no peace among them, nor safety, nor mutual intercourse. We are, therefore, to look upon all the vast apparatus of our government, as having ultimately no other object or purpose but the distribution of justice, or, in other words, the support of the twelve judges. Kings and parliaments, fleets and armies, officers of the court and revenue, ambassadors, ministers, and privy-counsellors, are all subordinate in their end to this part of administration. Even the clergy, as their duty leads them to inculcate morality, may justly be thought, so far as regards this world, to have no other useful object of their institution.

2. All men are sensible of the necessity of justice to maintain peace and order; and all men are sensible of the necessity of peace and order for the maintenance of society. Yet, notwithstanding this strong and obvious necessity, such is the frailty or perverseness of our nature! it is impossible to keep men, faithfully and unerringly, in the paths of justice. Some extraordinary circumstances may happen, in which a man finds his interests to be more promoted by fraud or rapine, than hurt by the breach which his injustice makes in the social union. But much more frequently, he is seduced from his great and important, but distant interests, by the allurement of present, though often very frivolous temptations. This great weakness is incurable in human nature.

3. Men must, therefore, endeavour to palliate what they cannot cure. They must institute some persons, under the appellation of magistrates, whose peculiar office it is, to point out the decrees of equity, to punish transgressors, to correct fraud and violence, and to oblige men, however reluctant, to consult their own real and permanent interests. In a word, OBEDIENCE is

a new duty which must be invented to support that of JUSTICE; and the tyes of equity must be corroborated by those of allegiance.

4.   But still, viewing matters in an abstract light, it may be thought, that nothing is gained by this alliance, and that the factitious duty of obedience, from its very nature, lays as feeble a hold of the human mind, as the primitive and natural duty of justice. Peculiar interests and present temptations may overcome the one as well as the other. They are equally exposed to the same inconvenience. And the man, who is inclined to be a bad neighbour, must be led by the same motives, well or ill understood, to be a bad citizen and subject. Not to mention, that the magistrate himself may often be negligent, or partial, or unjust in his administration.

5.   Experience, however, proves, that there is a great difference between the cases. Order in society, we find, is much better maintained by means of government; and our duty to the magistrate is more strictly guarded by the principles of human nature, than our duty to our fellow-citizens. The love of dominion is so strong in the breast of man, that many, not only submit to, but court all the dangers, and fatigues, and cares of government; and men, once raised to that station, though often led astray by private passions, find, in ordinary cases, a visible interest in the impartial administration of justice. The persons, who first attain this distinction by the consent, tacit or express, of the people, must be endowed with superior personal qualities of valour, force, integrity, or prudence, which command respect and confidence: and after government is established, a regard to birth, rank, and station has a mighty influence over men, and enforces the decrees of the magistrate. The prince or leader exclaims against every disorder, which disturbs his society. He summons all his partizans and all men of probity to aid him in correcting and redressing it: and he is readily followed by all indifferent persons in the execution of his office. He soon acquires the power of rewarding these services; and in the progress of society, he establishes subordinate ministers and often a military force, who find an immediate and a visible interest, in supporting his authority. Habit soon consolidates what other principles of human nature had imperfectly founded; and men, once accustomed to obedience, never think of departing from that path, in which they and their ancestors have constantly trod, and to which they are confined by so many urgent and visible motives.

6.   But though this progress of human affairs may appear certain and inevitable, and though the support which allegiance brings to justice, be founded on obvious principles of human nature, it cannot be expected that men should beforehand be able to discover them, or foresee their operation. Government commences more casually and more imperfectly. It is

probable, that the first ascendant of one man over multitudes begun during a state of war; where the superiority of courage and of genius discovers itself most visibly, where unanimity and concert are most requisite, and where the pernicious effects of disorder are most sensibly felt. The long continuance of that state, an incident common among savage tribes, enured the people to submission; and if the chieftain possessed as much equity as prudence and valour, he became, even during peace, the arbiter of all differences, and could gradually, by a mixture of force and consent, establish his authority. The benefit sensibly felt from his influence, made it be cherished by the people, at least by the peaceable and well disposed among them; and if his son enjoyed the same good qualities, government advanced the sooner to maturity and perfection; but was still in a feeble state, till the farther progress of improvement procured the magistrate a revenue, and enabled him to bestow rewards on the several instruments of his administration, and to inflict punishments on the refractory and disobedient. Before that period, each exertion of his influence must have been particular, and founded on the peculiar circumstances of the case. After it, submission was no longer a matter of choice in the bulk of the community, but was rigorously exacted by the authority of the supreme magistrate.

7.   In all governments, there is a perpetual intestine struggle, open or secret, between AUTHORITY and LIBERTY; and neither of them can ever absolutely prevail in the contest. A great sacrifice of liberty must necessarily be made in every government; yet even the authority, which confines liberty, can never, and perhaps ought never, in any constitution, to become quite entire and uncontroulable. The sultan is master of the life and fortune of any individual; but will not be permitted to impose new taxes on his subjects: a French monarch can impose taxes at pleasure; but would find it dangerous to attempt the lives and fortunes of individuals. Religion also, in most countries, is commonly found to be a very intractable principle; and other principles or prejudices frequently resist all the authority of the civil magistrate; whose power, being founded on opinion, can never subvert other opinions, equally rooted with that of his title to dominion. The government, which, in common appellation, receives the appellation of free, is that which admits of a partition of power among several members, whose united authority is no less, or is commonly greater than that of any monarch; but who, in the usual course of administration, must act by general and equal laws, that are previously known to all the members and to all their subjects. In this sense, it must be owned, that liberty is the perfection of civil society; but still authority must be acknowledged essential to its very existence: and in those contests, which so often take place between the

one and the other, the latter may, on that account, challenge the preference. Unless perhaps one may say (and it may be said with some reason) that a circumstance, which is essential to the existence of civil society, must always support itself, and needs be guarded with less jealousy, than one that contributes only to its perfection, which the indolence of men is so apt to neglect, or their ignorance to overlook.

5.

Of Parties in General

1.   OF all men, that distinguish themselves by memorable achievements, the first place of honour seems due to LEGISLATORS and founders of states, who transmit a system of laws and institutions to secure the peace, happiness, and liberty of future generations. The influence of useful inventions in the arts and sciences may, perhaps, extend farther than that of wise laws, whose effects are limited both in time and place; but the benefit arising from the former, is not so sensible as that which results from the latter. Speculative sciences do, indeed, improve the mind; but this advantage reaches only to a few persons, who have leisure to apply themselves to them. And as to practical arts, which encrease the commodities and enjoyments of life, it is well known, that men's happiness consists not so much in an abundance of these, as in the peace and security with which they possess them; and those blessings can only be derived from good government. Not to mention, that general virtue and good morals in a state, which are so requisite to happiness, can never arise from the most refined precepts of philosophy, or even the severest injunctions of religion; but must proceed entirely from the virtuous education of youth, the effect of wise laws and institutions. I must, therefore, presume to differ from Lord BACON in this particular, and must regard antiquity as somewhat unjust in its distribution of honours, when it made gods of all the inventors of useful arts, such as CERES, BACCHUS, ÆSCULAPIUS; and dignify legislators, such as ROMULUS and THESEUS, only with the appellation of demigods and heroes.

2.   As much as legislators and founders of states ought to be honoured and respected among men, as much ought the founders of sects and factions to be detested and hated; because the influence of faction is directly contrary to that of laws. Factions subvert government, render laws impotent, and beget the fiercest animosities among men of the same nation, who ought to give mutual assistance and protection to each other. And what should render the founders of parties more odious is, the difficulty of extirpating

these weeds, when once they have taken root in any state. They naturally propagate themselves for many centuries, and seldom end but by the total dissolution of that government, in which they are sown. They are, besides, plants which grow most plentifully in the richest soil; and though absolute governments be not wholly free from them, it must be confessed, that they rise more easily, and propagate themselves faster in free governments, where they always infect the legislature itself, which alone could be able, by the steady application of rewards and punishments, to eradicate them.

3.   Factions may be divided into PERSONAL and REAL; that is, into factions, founded on personal friendship or animosity among such as compose the contending parties, and into those founded on some real difference of sentiment or interest. The reason of this distinction is obvious; though I must acknowledge, that parties are seldom found pure and unmixed, either of the one kind or the other. It is not often seen, that a government divides into factions, where there is no difference in the views of the constituent members, either real or apparent, trivial or material: And in those factions, which are founded on the most real and most material difference, there is always observed a great deal of personal animosity or affection. But notwithstanding this mixture, a party may be denominated either personal or real, according to that principle which is predominant, and is found to have the greatest influence.

4.   Personal factions arise most easily in small republics. Every domestic quarrel, there, becomes an affair of state. Love, vanity, emulation, any passion, as well as ambition and resentment, begets public division. The NERI and BIANCHI of FLORENCE, the FREGOSI and ADORNI of GENOA, the COLONESI and ORSINI of modern ROME, were parties of this kind.

5.   Men have such a propensity to divide into personal factions, that the smallest appearance of real difference will produce them. What can be imagined more trivial than the difference between one colour of livery and another in horse races? Yet this difference begat two most inveterate factions in the GREEK empire, the PRASINI and VENETI, who never suspended their animosities, till they ruined that unhappy government.

6.   We find in the ROMAN history a remarkable dissension between two tribes, the POLLIA and PAPIRIA, which continued for the space of near three hundred years, and discovered itself in their suffrages at every election of magistrates.[23] This faction was the more remarkable, as it could continue

---

23. As this fact has not been much observed by antiquaries or politicians, I shall deliver it in the words of the ROMAN historian. *Populus* TUSCULANUS *cum conjugibus ac liberis* ROMAM *venit: Ea multitudo, veste mutata, & specie reorum*

for so long a tract of time; even though it did not spread itself, nor draw any of the other tribes into a share of the quarrel. If mankind had not a strong propensity to such divisions, the indifference of the rest of the community must have suppressed this foolish animosity, that had not any aliment of new benefits and injuries, of general sympathy and antipathy, which never fail to take place, when the whole state is rent into two equal factions.

7.   Nothing is more usual than to see parties, which have begun upon a real difference, continue even after that difference is lost. When men are once inlisted on opposite sides, they contract an affection to the persons with whom they are united, and an animosity against their antagonists: And these passions they often transmit to their posterity. The real difference between GUELF and GHIBBELLINE was long lost in ITALY, before these factions were extinguished. The GUELFS adhered to the pope, the GHIB-BELLINES to the emperor; yet the family of SFORZA, who were in alliance with the emperor, though they were GUELFS, being expelled MILAN by the king[24] of FRANCE, assisted by JACOMO TRIVULZIO and the GHIBBELLINES, the pope concurred with the latter, and they formed leagues with the pope against the emperor.

8.   The civil wars which arose some few years ago in MOROCCO, between the *blacks* and *whites,* merely on account of their complexion, are founded on a pleasant difference. We laugh at them; but I believe, were things rightly examined, we afford much more occasion of ridicule to the MOORS. For, what are all the wars of religion, which have prevailed in this polite

---

tribus circuit, genibus se omnium advolvens. Plus itaque misericordia ad poenae veniam impetrandam, quam causa ad crimen purgandum valuit. Tribus omnes praeter POLLIAM, *antiquarunt legem.* POLLIÆ *sententia fuit, puberes verberatos necari, liberos conjugesque sub corona lege belli venire: Memoriamque ejus irae* TUSCULANIS *in poenae tam atrocis auctores mansisse ad patris aetatem constat; nec quemquam fere ex* POLLIA *tribu candidatum* PAPIRAM *ferre solitam,* T. Livii, lib. 8. The CASTELANI and NICOLLOTI are two mobbish factions in Venice, who frequently box together, and then lay aside their quarrels presently. ["The citizens of Tusculum, with their wives and children, came to Rome; and the great throng, putting on the sordid raiment of defendants, went about amongst the tribes and classed the knees of the citizens in supplication. And it so happened that pity was more effective in gaining them remission of their punishment than were their arguments in clearing away the charges. All the tribes rejected the proposal, save only the Pollian, which voted that the grown men should be scourged and put to death, and their wives and children sold at auction under the laws of war. It seems that the resentment engendered in the Tusculuns by so cruel a proposal lasted down to our fathers' time, and that a candidate of the Pollian tribe almost never got the vote of the Papirian." Livy, *History of Rome,* translated by B. O. Foster, 8.37.]

24. LEWIS XII.

and knowing part of the world? They are certainly more absurd than the MOORISH civil wars. The difference of complexion is a sensible and a real difference: But the controversy about an article of faith, which is utterly absurd and unintelligible, is not a difference in sentiment, but in a few phrases and expressions, which one party accepts of, without understanding them; and the other refuses in the same manner.

9.   *Real* factions may be divided into those from *interest*, from *principle*, and from *affection*. Of all factions, the first are the most reasonable, and the most excusable. Where two orders of men, such as the nobles and people, have a distinct authority in a government, not very accurately balanced and modelled, they naturally follow a distinct interest; nor can we reasonably expect a different conduct, considering that degree of selfishness implanted in human nature. It requires great skill in a legislator to prevent such parties; and many philosophers are of opinion, that this secret, like the *grand elixir,* or *perpetual motion,*[25] may amuse men in theory, but can never possibly be reduced to practice. In despotic governments, indeed, factions often do not appear; but they are not the less real; or rather, they are more real and more pernicious, upon that very account. The distinct orders of men, nobles and people, soldiers and merchants, have all a distinct interest; but the more powerful oppresses the weaker with impunity, and without resistance; which begets a seeming tranquillity in such governments.

10.   There has been an attempt in ENGLAND to divide the *landed* and *trading* part of the nation; but without success. The interests of these two bodies are not really distinct, and never will be so, till our public debts encrease to such a degree, as to become altogether oppressive and intolerable.

11.   Parties from *principle,* especially abstract speculative principle, are known only to modern times, and are, perhaps, the most extraordinary and unaccountable *phænomenon,* that has yet appeared in human affairs. Where different principles beget a contrariety of conduct, which is the case with all different political principles, the matter may be more easily explained. A man, who esteems the true right of government to lie in one man, or one family, cannot easily agree with his fellow-citizen, who thinks that another man or family is possessed of this right. Each naturally wishes that right may take place, according to his own notions of it. But where the difference of principle is attended with no contrariety of action, but every one may follow his own way, without interfering with his neighbour, as happens in

---

25. [The "grand elixir" is a universal medicine that could supposedly cure all disease. Theories of perpetual motion envision a machine that once set in motion will go on forever.]

all religious controversies; what madness, what fury can beget such unhappy and such fatal divisions?

12. Two men travelling on the highway, the one east, the other west, can
easily pass each other, if the way be broad enough: But two men, reasoning upon opposite principles of religion, cannot so easily pass, without
shocking; though one should think, that the way were also, in that case,
sufficiently broad, and that each might proceed, without interruption, in
his own course. But such is the nature of the human mind, that it always
lays hold on every mind that approaches it; and as it is wonderfully fortified by an unanimity of sentiments, so is it shocked and disturbed by any
contrariety. Hence the eagerness, which most people discover in a dispute;
and hence their impatience of opposition, even in the most speculative and
indifferent opinions.

13. This principle, however frivolous it may appear, seems to have been
the origin of all religious wars and divisions. But as this principle is universal in human nature, its effects would not have been confined to one age,
and to one sect of religion, did it not there concur with other more accidental causes, which raise it to such a height, as to produce the greatest misery
and devastation. Most religions of the ancient world arose in the unknown
ages of government, when men were as yet barbarous and uninstructed,
and the prince, as well as peasant, was disposed to receive, with implicit
faith, every pious tale or fiction, which was offered him. The magistrate
embraced the religion of the people, and entering cordially into the care
of sacred matters, naturally acquired an authority in them, and united the
ecclesiastical with the civil power. But the *Christian* religion arising, while
principles directly opposite to it were firmly established in the polite part
of the world, who despised the nation that first broached this novelty; no
wonder, that, in such circumstances, it was but little countenanced by the
civil magistrate, and that the priesthood was allowed to engross all the authority in the new sect. So bad a use did they make of this power, even in
those early times, that the primitive persecutions may, perhaps, *in part*,[26] be

---

26. I say, *in part;* For it is a vulgar error to imagine, that the ancients were
as great friends to toleration as the ENGLISH or DUTCH are at present. The laws
against external superstition, amongst the ROMANS, were as ancient as the time of
the twelve tables; and the JEWS as well as CHRISTIANS were sometimes punished
by them; though, in general, these laws were not rigorously executed. Immediately
after the conquest of GAUL, they forbad all but the natives to be initiated into the religion of the DRUIDS; and this was a kind of persecution. In about a century after this
conquest, the emperor, CLAUDIUS, quite abolished that superstition by penal laws;
which would have been a very grievous persecution, if the imitation of the ROMAN

ascribed to the violence instilled by them into their followers. And the same principles of priestly government continuing, after Christianity became the established religion, they have engendered a spirit of persecution, which has ever since been the poison of human society, and the source of the most inveterate factions in every government. Such divisions, therefore, on the part of the people, may justly be esteemed factions of *principle;* but, on the part of the priests, who are the prime movers, they are really factions of *interest.*

14. There is another cause (beside the authority of the priests, and the separation of the ecclesiastical and civil powers) which has contributed to render CHRISTENDOM the scene of religious wars and divisions. Religions, that arise in ages totally ignorant and barbarous, consist mostly of traditional tales and fictions, which may be different in every sect, without being contrary to each other; and even when they are contrary, every one adheres to the tradition of his own sect, without much reasoning or disputation. But as philosophy was widely spread over the world, at the time when Christianity arose, the teachers of the new sect were obliged to form a system of speculative opinions; to divide, with some accuracy, their articles of faith; and to explain, comment, confute, and defend with all the subtilty of argument and science. Hence naturally arose keenness in dispute, when the Christian religion came to be split into new divisions and heresies: And this keenness assisted the priests in their policy, of begetting a mutual hatred and antipathy among their deluded followers. Sects of philosophy, in the ancient world, were more zealous than parties of religion; but in modern times, parties of religion are more furious and enraged than the most cruel factions that ever arose from interest and ambition.

15. I have mentioned parties from *affection* as a kind of *real* parties, beside those from *interest* and *principle.* By parties from affection, I understand those which are founded on the different attachments of men towards particular families and persons, whom they desire to rule over them. These factions are often very violent; though, I must own, it may seem

---

manners had not, before-hand, weaned the GAULS from their ancient prejudices. SUETONIUS *in vita* CLAUDII. PLINY ascribes the abolition of the Druidical superstitions to TIBERIUS, probably because that emperor had taken some steps towards restraining them (lib. xxx. cap. i.). This is an instance of the usual caution and moderation of the ROMANS in such cases; and very different from their violent and sanguinary method of treating the *Christians.* Hence we may entertain a suspicion, that those furious persecutions of *Christianity* were in some measure owing to the imprudent zeal and bigotry of the first propagators of that sect; and Ecclesiastical history affords us many reasons to confirm this suspicion.

unaccountable, that men should attach themselves so strongly to persons, with whom they are no wise acquainted, whom perhaps they never saw, and from whom they never received, nor can ever hope for any favour. Yet this we often find to be the case, and even with men, who, on other occasions, discover no great generosity of spirit, nor are found to be easily transported by friendship beyond their own interest. We are apt to think the relation between us and our sovereign very close and intimate. The splendour of majesty and power bestows an importance on the fortunes even of a single person. And when a man's good-nature does not give him this imaginary interest, his ill-nature will, from spite and opposition to persons whose sentiments are different from his own.

6.

Of National Characters

1.   THE vulgar are apt to carry all *national characters* to extremes; and having once established it as a principle, that any people are knavish, or cowardly, or ignorant, they will admit of no exception, but comprehend every individual under the same censure. Men of sense condemn these undistinguishing judgments: Though at the same time, they allow, that each nation has a peculiar set of manners, and that some particular qualities are more frequently to be met with among one people than among their neighbours. The common people in SWITZERLAND have probably more honesty than those of the same rank in IRELAND; and every prudent man will, from that circumstance alone, make a difference in the trust which he reposes in each. We have reason to expect greater wit and gaiety in a FRENCHMAN than in a SPANIARD; though CERVANTES was born in SPAIN. An ENGLISH-MAN will naturally be supposed to have more knowledge than a DANE; though TYCHO BRAHE was a native of DENMARK.

2.   Different reasons are assigned for these *national characters;* while some account for them from *moral,* others from *physical* causes. By *moral* causes, I mean all circumstances, which are fitted to work on the mind as motives or reasons, and which render a peculiar set of manners habitual to us. Of this kind are, the nature of the government, the revolutions of public affairs, the plenty or penury in which the people live, the situation of the nation with regard to its neighbours, and such like circumstances. By *physical* causes I mean those qualities of the air and climate, which are supposed to work insensibly on the temper, by altering the tone and habit of the body, and giving a particular complexion, which, though reflection and reason may sometimes overcome it, will yet prevail among the generality of mankind, and have an influence on their manners.

3.   That the character of a nation will much depend on *moral* causes, must be evident to the most superficial observer; since a nation is nothing but a collection of individuals, and the manners of individuals are frequently

determined by these causes. As poverty and hard labour debase the minds of the common people, and render them unfit for any science and ingenious profession; so where any government becomes very oppressive to all its subjects, it must have a proportional effect on their temper and genius, and must banish all the liberal arts from among them.

4.   The same principle of moral causes fixes the character of different professions, and alters even that disposition, which the particular members receive from the hand of nature. A *soldier* and a *priest* are different characters, in all nations, and all ages; and this difference is founded on circumstances, whose operation is eternal and unalterable.

5.   The uncertainty of their life makes soldiers lavish and generous, as well as brave: Their idleness, together with the large societies, which they form in camps or garrisons, inclines them to pleasure and gallantry: By their frequent change of company, they acquire good breeding and an openness of behaviour: Being employed only against a public and an open enemy, they become candid, honest, and undesigning: And as they use more the labour of the body than that of the mind, they are commonly thoughtless and ignorant.[27]

6.   It is a trite, but not altogether a false maxim, that *priests of all religions are the same;* and though the character of the profession will not, in every instance, prevail over the personal character, yet is it sure always to predominate with the greater number. For as chymists observe, that spirits, when raised to a certain height, are all the same, from whatever materials they be extracted; so these men, being elevated above humanity, acquire a uniform character, which is entirely their own, and which, in my opinion, is, generally speaking, not the most amiable that is to be met with in human society. It is, in most points, opposite to that of a soldier; as is the way of life, from which it is derived.[28]

27. It is a saying of MENANDER, Κομψος σρατιωτης, ονδ' αν ει πλαττει θεος Ονθεις γενοιτ' αν. MEN. Apud STOBÆUM. *It is not in the power even of God to make a polite soldier.* The contrary observation with regard to the manners of soldiers takes place in our days. This seems to me a presumption, that the ancients owed all their refinement and civility to books and study; for which, indeed, a soldier's life is not so well calculated. Company and the world is their sphere. And if there be any politeness to be learned from company, they will certainly have a considerable share of it.

28. Though all mankind have a strong propensity to religion at certain times and in certain dispositions; yet are there few or none, who have it to that degree, and with that constancy, which is requisite to support the character of this profession.

It must, therefore, happen, that clergymen, being drawn from the common mass of mankind, as people are to other employments, by the views of profit, the greater

7.   As to *physical causes,* I am inclined to doubt altogether of their operation in this particular; nor do I think, that men owe any thing of their
temper or genius to the air, food, or climate. I confess, that the contrary

---

part, though no atheists or free-thinkers, will find it necessary, on particular occasions, to feign more devotion than they are, at that time, possessed of, and to maintain the appearance of fervor and seriousness, even when jaded with the exercises
of their religion, or when they have their minds engaged in the common occupations
of life. They must not, like the rest of the world, give scope to their natural movements and sentiments: They must set a guard over their looks and words and actions: And in order to support the veneration paid them by the multitude, they must
not only keep a remarkable reserve, but must promote the spirit of superstition, by
a continued grimace and hypocrisy. This dissimulation often destroys the candor
and ingenuity of their temper, and makes an irreparable breach in their character. If
by chance any of them be possessed of a temper more susceptible of devotion than
usual, so that he has but little occasion for hypocrisy to support the character of his
profession; it is so natural for him to over-rate this advantage, and to think that it
atones for every violation of morality, that frequently he is not more virtuous than
the hypocrite. And though few dare openly avow those exploded opinions, *that
every thing is lawful to the saints,* and *that they alone have property in their goods;*
yet may we observe, that these principles lurk in every bosom, and represent a zeal
for religious observances as so great a merit, that it may compensate for many vices
and enormities. This observation is so common, that all prudent men are on their
guard, when they meet with any extraordinary appearance of religion; though at the
same time, they confess, that there are many exceptions to this general rule, and that
probity and superstition, or even probity and fanaticism, are not altogether and in
every instance incompatible.

Most men are ambitious; but the ambition of other men may commonly be satisfied, by excelling in their particular profession, and thereby promoting the interests
of society. The ambition of the clergy can often be satisfied only by promoting
ignorance and superstition and implicit faith and pious frauds. And having got what
ARCHIMEDES only wanted, (namely, another world, on which he could fix his en-
gines) no wonder they move this world at their pleasure.

Most men have an overweaning conceit of themselves; but *these* have a peculiar temptation to that vice, who are regarded with such veneration, and are even
deemed sacred, by the ignorant multitude.

Most men are apt to bear a particular regard for members of their own profession; but as a lawyer, or physician, or merchant, does, each of them, follow out his
business apart, the interests of men of these professions are not so closely united
as the interests of clergymen of the same religion; where the whole body gains by
the veneration, paid to their common tenets, and by the suppression of antagonists.

Few men can bear contradiction with patience; but the clergy too often proceed
even to a degree of fury on this head: Because all their credit and livelihood depend
upon the belief, which their opinions meet with; and they alone pretend to a divine
and supernatural authority, or have any colour for representing their antagonists as
impious and prophane. The *Odium Theologicum,* or Theological Hatred, is noted

opinion may justly, at first sight, seem probable; since we find, that these circumstances have an influence over every other animal, and that even those creatures, which are fitted to live in all climates, such as dogs, horses, &c. do not attain the same perfection in all. The courage of bull-dogs and game-cocks seems peculiar to ENGLAND. FLANDERS is remarkable for large and heavy horses: SPAIN for horses light, and of good mettle. And any breed of these creatures, transplanted from one country to another, will soon lose the qualities, which they derived from their native climate. It may be asked, why not the same with men?[29]

---

even to a proverb, and means that degree of rancour, which is the most furious and implacable.

Revenge is a natural passion to mankind; but seems to reign with the greatest force in priests and women: Because, being deprived of the immediate exertion of anger, in violence and combat, they are apt to fancy themselves despised on that account; and their pride supports their vindictive disposition.

Thus many of the vices of human nature are, by fixed moral causes, inflamed in that profession; and though several individuals escape the contagion, yet all wise governments will be on their guard against the attempts of a society, who will for ever combine into one faction, and while it acts as a society, will for ever be actuated by ambition, pride, revenge, and a persecuting spirit.

The temper of religion is grave and serious; and this is the character required of priests, which confines them to strict rules of decency, and commonly prevents irregularity and intemperance amongst them. The gaiety, much less the excesses of pleasure, is not permitted in that body; and this virtue is, perhaps, the only one which they owe to their profession. In religions, indeed, founded on speculative principles, and where public discourses make a part of religious service, it may also be supposed that the clergy will have a considerable share in the learning of the times; though it is certain that their taste in eloquence will always be greater than their proficiency in reasoning and philosophy. But whoever possesses the other noble virtues of humanity, meekness, and moderation, as very many of them, no doubt, do, is beholden for them to nature or reflection, not to the genius of his calling.

It was no bad expedient in the old ROMANS, for preventing the strong effect of the priestly character, to make it a law that no one should be received into the sacerdotal office, till he was past fifty years of age, DION. *Hal.* lib. i. The living a layman till that age, it is presumed, would be able to fix the character.

29. CÆSAR (*de Bello* GALLICO, lib. I. [*The Gallic War,* Loeb edition, 4.2]) says, that the GALLIC horses were very good; the GERMAN very bad. We find in lib. vii. [7.65] that he was obliged to remount some GERMAN cavalry with GALLIC horses. At present, no part of EUROPE has so bad horses of all kinds as FRANCE: But GERMANY abounds with excellent war horses. This may beget a little suspicion, that even animals depend not on the climate; but on the different breeds, and on the skill and care in rearing them. The north of ENGLAND abounds in the best horses of all kinds which are perhaps in the world. In the neighbouring counties, north side

8.   There are few questions more curious than this, or which will oftener occur in our enquiries concerning human affairs; and therefore it may be proper to give it a full examination.

9.   The human mind is of a very imitative nature; nor is it possible for any set of men to converse often together, without acquiring a similitude of manners, and communicating to each other their vices as well as virtues. The propensity to company and society is strong in all rational creatures; and the same disposition, which gives us this propensity, makes us enter deeply into each other's sentiments, and causes like passions and inclinations to run, as it were, by contagion, through the whole club or knot of companions. Where a number of men are united into one political body, the occasions of their intercourse must be so frequent, for defence, commerce, and government, that, together with the same speech or language, they must acquire a resemblance in their manners, and have a common or national character, as well as a personal one, peculiar to each individual. Now though nature produces all kinds of temper and understanding in great abundance, it does not follow, that she always produces them in like proportions, and that in every society the ingredients of industry and indolence, valour and cowardice, humanity and brutality, wisdom and folly, will be mixed after the same manner. In the infancy of society, if any of these dispositions be found in greater abundance than the rest, it will naturally prevail in the composition, and give a tincture to the national character. Or should it be asserted, that no species of temper can reasonably be presumed to predominate, even in those contracted societies, and that the same proportions will always be preserved in the mixture; yet surely the persons in credit and authority, being still a more contracted body, cannot always be presumed to be of the same character; and their influence on the manners of the people, must, at all times, be very considerable. If on the first establishment of a republic, a BRUTUS should be placed in authority, and be transported with such an enthusiasm for liberty and public good, as to overlook all the ties of nature, as well as private interest, such an illustrious example will naturally have an effect on the whole society, and kindle the same passion in every bosom. Whatever it be that forms the manners of one

---

of the TWEED, no good horses of any kind are to be met with. STRABO [64 or 63 BCE–CE 21], lib. ii [*Geography,* 2.3.7]. Rejects, in a great measure, the influence of climates upon men. All is custom and education, says he. It is not from nature, that the ATHENIANS are learned, the LACEDEMONIANS ignorant, and the THEBANS too, who are still nearer neighbours to the former. Even the difference of animals, he adds, depends not on climate.

generation, the next must imbibe a deeper tincture of the same dye; men being more susceptible of all impressions during infancy, and retaining these impressions as long as they remain in the world. I assert, then, that all national characters, where they depend not on fixed *moral* causes, proceed from such accidents as these, and that physical causes have no discernible operation on the human mind. It is a maxim in all philosophy, that causes, which do not appear, are to be considered as not existing.

10. If we run over the globe, or revolve the annals of history, we shall discover every where signs of a sympathy or contagion of manners, none of the influence of air or climate.

11. *First.* We may observe, that, where a very extensive government has been established for many centuries, it spreads a national character over the whole empire, and communicates to every part a similarity of manners. Thus the CHINESE have the greatest uniformity of character imaginable: though the air and climate, in different parts of those vast dominions, admit of very considerable variations.

12. *Secondly.* In small governments, which are contiguous, the people have notwithstanding a different character, and are often as distinguishable in their manners as the most distant nations. ATHENS and THEBES were but a short day's journey from each other; though the ATHENIANS were as re-markable for ingenuity, politeness, and gaiety, as the THEBANS for dulness, rusticity, and a phlegmatic temper. PLUTARCH, discoursing of the effects of air on the minds of men, observes, that the inhabitants of the PIRÆUM possessed very different tempers from those of the higher town in ATHENS, which was distant about four miles from the former: But I believe no one attributes the difference of manners in WAPPING and St. JAMES's, to a dif-ference of air or climate.

13. *Thirdly.* The same national character commonly follows the authority of government to a precise boundary; and upon crossing a river or pass-ing a mountain, one finds a new set of manners, with a new government. The LANGUEDOCIANS and GASCONS are the gayest people in FRANCE; but whenever you pass the PYRENEES, you are among SPANIARDS. Is it conceiv-able, that the qualities of the air should change exactly with the limits of an empire, which depend so much on the accidents of battles, negociations, and marriages?

14. *Fourthly.* Where any set of men, scattered over distant nations, main-tain a close society or communication together, they acquire a similitude of manners, and have but little in common with the nations amongst whom they live. Thus the JEWS in EUROPE, and the ARMENIANS in the east, have a peculiar character; and the former are as much noted for fraud, as the

latter for probity.[30] The *Jesuits,* in all *Roman-catholic* countries, are also observed to have a character peculiar to themselves.

15. *Fifthly.* Where any accident, as a difference in language or religion, keeps two nations, inhabiting the same country, from mixing with each other, they will preserve, during several centuries, a distinct and even opposite set of manners. The integrity, gravity, and bravery of the TURKS, form an exact contrast to the deceit, levity, and cowardice of the modern GREEKS.

16. *Sixthly.* The same set of manners will follow a nation, and adhere to them over the whole globe, as well as the same laws and language. The SPANISH, ENGLISH, FRENCH and DUTCH colonies are all distinguishable even between the tropics.

17. *Seventhly.* The manners of a people change very considerably from one age to another; either by great alterations in their government, by the mixtures of new people, or by that inconstancy, to which all human affairs are subject. The ingenuity, industry, and activity of the ancient GREEKS have nothing in common with the stupidity and indolence of the present inhabitants of those regions. Candour, bravery, and love of liberty formed the character of the ancient ROMANS; as subtilty, cowardice, and a slavish disposition do that of the modern. The old SPANIARDS were restless, turbulent, and so addicted to war, that many of them killed themselves, when deprived of their arms by the ROMANS.[31] One would find an equal difficulty at present, (at least one would have found it fifty years ago) to rouze up the modern SPANIARDS to arms. The BATAVIANS were all soldiers of fortune, and hired themselves into the ROMAN armies. Their posterity make use of foreigners for the same purpose that the ROMANS did their ancestors. Though some few strokes of the FRENCH character be the same with that which CÆSAR has ascribed to the GAULS; yet what comparison between the civility, humanity, and knowledge of the modern inhabitants of that country, and the ignorance, barbarity, and grossness of the ancient? Not to insist upon the great difference between the present possessors of BRITAIN, and those before the ROMAN conquest; we may observe that our ancestors, a few centuries ago, were sunk into the most abject superstition, last century

30. A small sect or society amidst a greater are commonly most regular in their morals; because they are more remarked, and the faults of individuals draw dishonour on the whole. The only exception to this rule is, when the superstition and prejudices of the large society are so strong as to throw an infamy on the smaller society, independent of their morals. For in that case, having no character either to save or gain, they become careless of their behaviour, except among themselves.

31. TIT. LIVII, lib. xxxiv. cap. 17. [Livy, *History of Rome,* 34.17.]

they were inflamed with the most furious enthusiasm, and are now settled into the most cool indifference with regard to religious matters, that is to be found in any nation of the world.

18. *Eighthly.* Where several neighbouring nations have a very close communication together, either by policy, commerce, or travelling, they acquire a similitude of manners, proportioned to the communication. Thus all the FRANKS appear to have a uniform character to the eastern nations. The differences among them are like the peculiar accents of different provinces, which are not distinguishable, except by an ear accustomed to them, and which commonly escape a foreigner.

19. *Ninthly.* We may often remark a wonderful mixture of manners and characters in the same nation, speaking the same language, and subject to the same government: And in this particular the ENGLISH are the most remarkable of any people, that perhaps ever were in the world. Nor is this to be ascribed to the mutability and uncertainty of their climate, or to any other *physical* causes; since all these causes take place in the neighbouring country of SCOTLAND, without having the same effect. Where the government of a nation is altogether republican, it is apt to beget a peculiar set of manners. Where it is altogether monarchical, it is more apt to have the same effect; the imitation of superiors spreading the national manners faster among the people. If the governing part of a state consist altogether of merchants, as in HOLLAND, their uniform way of life will fix their character. If it consists chiefly of nobles and landed gentry, like GERMANY, FRANCE, and SPAIN, the same effect follows. The genius of a particular sect or religion is also apt to mould the manners of a people. But the ENGLISH government is a mixture of monarchy, aristocracy, and democracy. The people in authority are composed of gentry and merchants. All sects of religion are to be found among them. And the great liberty and independency, which every man enjoys, allows him to display the manners peculiar to him. Hence the ENGLISH, of any people in the universe, have the least of a national character; unless this very singularity may pass for such.

20. If the characters of men depended on the air and climate, the degrees of heat and cold should naturally be expected to have a mighty influence; since nothing has a greater effect on all plants and irrational animals. And indeed there is some reason to think, that all the nations, which live beyond the polar circles or between the tropics, are inferior to the rest of the species, and are incapable of all the higher attainments of the human mind. The poverty and misery of the northern inhabitants of the globe, and the indolence of the southern, from their few necessities, may, perhaps, account for this remarkable difference, without our having recourse to *physical* causes.

This however is certain, that the characters of nations are very promiscuous in the temperate climates, and that almost all the general observations, which have been formed of the more southern or more northern people in these climates, are found to be uncertain and fallacious.[32]

21. Shall we say, that the neighbourhood of the sun inflames the imagination of men, and gives it a peculiar spirit and vivacity. The FRENCH, GREEKS, EGYPTIANS, and PERSIANS are remarkable for gaiety. The SPANIARDS, TURKS, and CHINESE are noted for gravity and a serious deportment, without any such difference of climate as to produce this difference of temper.

22. The GREEKS and ROMANS, who called all other nations barbarians, confined genius and a fine understanding to the more southern climates, and pronounced the northern nations incapable of all knowledge and civility. But our island has produced as great men, either for action or learning, as GREECE or ITALY has to boast of.

23. It is pretended, that the sentiments of men become more delicate as the country approaches nearer to the sun; and that the taste of beauty and elegance receives proportional improvements in every latitude; as we may particularly observe of the languages, of which the more southern are smooth and melodious, the northern harsh and untuneable. But this observation holds not universally. The ARABIC is uncouth and disagreeable: The MUSCOVITE soft and musical. Energy, strength, and harshness form the character of the LATIN tongue: The ITALIAN is the most liquid, smooth, and effeminate language that can possibly be imagined. Every language will depend somewhat on the manners of the people; but much more on that original stock of words and sounds, which they received from their ancestors, and which remain unchangeable, even while their manners admit of

---

32. I am apt to suspect the negroes to be naturally inferior to the whites. There scarcely ever was a civilized nation of that complexion, nor even any individual eminent either in action or speculation. No ingenious manufactures amongst them, no arts, no sciences. On the other hand, the most rude and barbarous of the whites, such as the ancient GERMANS, the present TARTARS, have still something eminent about them, in their valour, form of government, or some other particular. Such a uniform and constant difference could not happen, in so many countries and ages, if nature had not made an original distinction between these breeds of men. Not to mention our colonies, there are NEGROE slaves dispersed all over EUROPE, of whom none ever discovered any symptoms of ingenuity; though low people, without education, will start up amongst us, and distinguish themselves in every profession. In JAMAICA, indeed, they talk of one negroe as a man of parts and learning; but it is likely he is admired for slender accomplishments, like a parrot, who speaks a few words plainly.

the greatest alterations. Who can doubt, but the ENGLISH are at present a more polite and knowing people than the GREEKS were for several ages after the siege of TROY? Yet is there no comparison between the language of MILTON and that of HOMER. Nay, the greater are the alterations and improvements, which happen in the manners of a people, the less can be expected in their language. A few eminent and refined geniuses will communicate their taste and knowledge to a whole people, and produce the greatest improvements; but they fix the tongue by their writings, and prevent, in some degree, its farther changes.

24. Lord BACON has observed, that the inhabitants of the south are, in general, more ingenious than those of the north; but that, where the native of a cold climate has genius, he rises to a higher pitch than can be reached by the southern wits. This observation a late[33] writer confirms, by comparing the southern wits to cucumbers, which are commonly all good in their kind; but at best are an insipid fruit: While the northern geniuses are like melons, of which not one in fifty is good; but when it is so, it has an exquisite relish. I believe this remark may be allowed just, when confined to the EUROPEAN nations, and to the present age, or rather to the preceding one: But I think it may be accounted for from moral causes. All the sciences and liberal arts have been imported to us from the south; and it is easy to imagine, that, in the first ardor of application, when excited by emulation and by glory, the few, who were addicted to them, would carry them to the greatest height, and stretch every nerve, and every faculty, to reach the pinnacle of perfection. Such illustrious examples spread knowledge every where, and begot an universal esteem for the sciences: After which, it is no wonder, that industry relaxes; while men meet not with suitable encouragement, nor arrive at such distinction by their attainments. The universal diffusion of learning among a people, and the entire banishment of gross ignorance and rusticity, is, therefore, seldom attended with any remarkable perfection in particular persons. It seems to be taken for granted in the dialogue *de Oratoribus,*[34] that knowledge was much more common in VESPASIAN'S age than in that of CICERO and AUGUSTUS. QUINTILIAN also complains of the profanation of learning, by its becoming too common. "Formerly," says JUVENAL, "science was confined to GREECE and ITALY. Now the whole world emulates ATHENS and ROME. Eloquent GAUL has taught BRITAIN, knowing in the laws. Even THULE entertains thoughts of hiring rhetoricians for its

---

33. Dr. Berkeley: Minute Philosopher. [George Berkeley, *Alciphron; or, The Minute Philosopher,* 5.26.]

34. [Tacitus, *Dialogue on Oratory.*]

instruction."[35] This state of learning is remarkable; because JUVENAL is himself the last of the ROMAN writers, that possessed any degree of genius. Those, who succeeded, are valued for nothing but the matters of fact, of which they give us information. I hope the late conversion of MUSCOVY to the study of the sciences will not prove a like prognostic to the present period of learning.

25. Cardinal BENTIVOGLIO gives the preference to the northern nations above the southern with regard to candour and sincerity; and mentions, on the one hand, the SPANIARDS and ITALIANS, and on the other, the FLEMINGS and GERMANS. But I am apt to think, that this has happened by accident. The ancient ROMANS seem to have been a candid sincere people, as are the modern TURKS. But if we must needs suppose, that this event has arisen from fixed causes, we may only conclude from it, that all extremes are apt to concur, and are commonly attended with the same consequences. Treachery is the usual concomitant of ignorance and barbarism; and if civilized nations ever embrace subtle and crooked politics, it is from an excess of refinement, which makes them disdain the plain direct path to power and glory.

26. Most conquests have gone from north to south; and it has hence been inferred, that the northern nations possess a superior degree of courage and ferocity. But it would have been juster to have said, that most conquests are made by poverty and want upon plenty and riches. The SARACENS, leaving the deserts of ARABIA, carried their conquests northwards upon all the fertile provinces of the ROMAN empire; and met the TURKS half way, who were coming southwards from the deserts of TARTARY.

27. An eminent writer[36] has remarked, that all courageous animals are also carnivorous, and that greater courage is to be expected in a people, such as the ENGLISH, whose food is strong and hearty, than in the half-

---

35. "Sed Cantaber unde
    Stoicus? antiqui præsertim ætate Merelli.
    Nunc totus GRAIAS, nostrasque habet orbis ATHENAS.
    GALLIA causidicos docuit facunda BRITANNOS:
    De conducendo loquitur jam rhetore THULE."
    Sat. 15.

["But how could a Cantabrian be a Stoic, and that too in the days of the old Metellus? Today the whole world has its Greek and its Roman Athens; eloquent Gaul has trained the pleaders of Britain, and distant Thule talks of hiring a rhetorician." Juvenal, *Satires,* 15, translated by G. G. Ramsay.]

36. Sir WILLIAM TEMPLE's account of the Netherlands. [William Temple, *Observations upon the United Provinces of the Netherlands* (1673), chapter 4.]

starved commonalty of other countries. But the SWEDES, notwithstanding their disadvantages in this particular, are not inferior, in martial courage, to any nation that ever was in the world.

28. In general, we may observe, that courage, of all national qualities, is the most precarious; because it is exerted only at intervals, and by a few in every nation; whereas industry, knowledge, civility, may be of constant and universal use, and for several ages, may become habitual to the whole people. If courage be preserved, it must be by discipline, example, and opinion. The tenth legion of CÆSAR, and the regiment of PICARDY in FRANCE were formed promiscuously from among the citizens; but having once entertained a notion, that they were the best troops in the service, this very opinion really made them such.

29. As a proof how much courage depends on opinion, we may observe, that, of the two chief tribes of the GREEKS, the DORIANS, and IONIANS, the former were always esteemed, and always appeared more brave and manly than the latter; though the colonies of both the tribes were interspersed and intermingled throughout all the extent of GREECE, the Lesser ASIA, SICILY, ITALY, and the islands of the ÆGEAN sea. The ATHENIANS were the only IONIANS that ever had any reputation for valour or military atchievements; though even these were deemed inferior to the LACEDEMONIANS, the bravest of the DORIANS.

30. The only observation, with regard to the difference of men in different climates, on which we can rest any weight, is the vulgar one, that people in the northern regions have a greater inclination to strong liquors, and those in the southern to love and women. One can assign a very probable *physical* cause for this difference. Wine and distilled waters warm the frozen blood in the colder climates, and fortify men against the injuries of the weather: As the genial heat of the sun, in the countries exposed to his beams, inflames the blood, and exalts the passion between the sexes.

31. Perhaps too, the matter may be accounted for by *moral* causes. All strong liquors are rarer in the north, and consequently are more coveted. DIODORUS SICULUS[37] tells us, that the GAULS in his time were great drunkards, and much addicted to wine; chiefly, I suppose, from its rarity and novelty. On the other hand, the heat in the southern climates, obliging men and women to go half naked, thereby renders their frequent commerce more

---

37. *Lib.* v [*Library of History,* 5.26]. The same author ascribes taciturnity to that people; a new proof that national characters may alter very much. Taciturnity, as a national character, implies unsociableness. ARISTOTLE in his Politics, book ii. cap. 9. says, that the GAULS are the only warlike nation, who are negligent of women.

dangerous, and inflames their mutual passion. This makes parents and husbands more jealous and reserved; which still farther inflames the passion. Not to mention, that, as women ripen sooner in the southern regions, it is necessary to observe greater jealousy and care in their education; it being evident, that a girl of twelve cannot possess equal discretion to govern this passion, with one who feels not its violence till she be seventeen or eighteen. Nothing so much encourages the passion of love as ease and leisure, or is more destructive to it than industry and hard labour; and as the necessities of men are evidently fewer in the warm climates than in the cold ones, this circumstance alone may make a considerable difference between them.

32. But perhaps the fact is doubtful, that nature has, either from moral or physical causes, distributed these respective inclinations to the different climates. The ancient Greeks, though born in a warm climate, seem to have been much addicted to the bottle; nor were their parties of pleasure any thing but matches of drinking among men, who passed their time altogether apart from the fair. Yet when Alexander led the Greeks into Persia, a still more southern climate, they multiplied their debauches of this kind, in imitation of the Persians manners.[38] So honourable was the character of a drunkard among the Persians, that Cyrus the younger, soliciting the sober Lacedemonians for succour against his brother Artaxerxes, claims it chiefly on account of his superior endowments, as more valorous, more bountiful, and a better drinker.[39] Darius Hystaspes made it be inscribed on his tomb-stone, among his other virtues and princely qualities, that no one could bear a greater quantity of liquor. You may obtain any thing of the Negroes by offering them strong drink; and may easily prevail with them to sell, not only their children, but their wives and mistresses, for a cask of brandy. In France and Italy few drink pure wine, except in the greatest heats of summer; and indeed, it is then almost as necessary, in order to recruit the spirits, evaporated by heat, as it is in Sweden, during the winter, in order to warm the bodies congealed by the rigour of the season.

---

38. Babylonii *maxime in vinum, & quæ ebrietatem sequuntur, effusi sunt.* Quint. Cur. lib. v. cap. I. ["The Babylonians in particular are lavishly devoted to wine and the concomitants of drunkenness." Quintus Curtius Rufus, *Historiæ Alexandri magni Macedonis* (*History of Alexander the Great of Macedonia*), 5.1.37–38.]

39. Plut. Symp. lib. i. quæst. 4. ["What manner of man should a steward of a feast be?" Plutarch, *Symposiaca Problemata* (*Symposiacs*), book 1, question 4.]

33. If jealousy be regarded as a proof of an amorous disposition, no peo-ple were more jealous than the MUSCOVITES, before their communication with EUROPE had somewhat altered their manners in this particular.

34. But supposing the fact true, that nature, by physical principles, has regularly distributed these two passions, the one to the northern, the other to the southern regions; we can only infer, that the climate may affect the grosser and more bodily organs of our frame; not that it can work upon those finer organs, on which the operations of the mind and understanding depend. And this is agreeable to the analogy of nature. The races of animals never degenerate when carefully tended; and horses, in particular, always show their blood in their shape, spirit, and swiftness: But a coxcomb may beget a philosopher; as a man of virtue may leave a worthless progeny.

35. I shall conclude this subject with observing, that though the passion for liquor be more brutal and debasing than love, which, when properly managed, is the source of all politeness and refinement; yet this gives not so great an advantage to the southern climates, as we may be apt, at first sight, to imagine. When love goes beyond a certain pitch, it renders men jealous, and cuts off the free intercourse between the sexes, on which the politeness of a nation will commonly much depend. And if we would sub-tilize and refine upon this point, we might observe, that the people, in very temperate climates, are the most likely to attain all sorts of improvement; their blood not being so inflamed as to render them jealous, and yet being warm enough to make them set a due value on the charms and endowments of the fair sex.

7.

Of Commerce

1. THE greater part of mankind may be divided into two classes; that of *shallow* thinkers, who fall short of the truth; and that of *abstruse* thinkers, who go beyond it. The latter class are by far the most rare: and I may add, by far the most useful and valuable. They suggest hints, at least, and start difficulties, which they want, perhaps, skill to pursue; but which may produce fine discoveries, when handled by men who have a more just way of thinking. At worst, what they say is uncommon; and if it should cost some pains to comprehend it, one has, however, the pleasure of hearing something that is new. An author is little to be valued, who tells us nothing but what we can learn from every coffee-house conversation.

2. All people of *shallow* thought are apt to decry even those of *solid* understanding, as *abstruse* thinkers, and metaphysicians, and refiners; and never will allow any thing to be just which is beyond their own weak conceptions. There are some cases, I own, where an extraordinary refinement affords a strong presumption of falsehood, and where no reasoning is to be trusted but what is natural and easy. When a man deliberates concerning his conduct in any *particular* affair, and forms schemes in politics, trade, œconomy, or any business in life, he never ought to draw his arguments too fine, or connect too long a chain of consequences together. Something is sure to happen, that will disconcert his reasoning, and produce an event different from what he expected. But when we reason upon *general* subjects, one may justly affirm, that our speculations can scarcely ever be too fine, provided they be just; and that the difference between a common man and a man of genius is chiefly seen in the shallowness or depth of the principles upon which they proceed. General reasonings seem intricate, merely because they are general; nor is it easy for the bulk of mankind to distinguish, in a great number of particulars, that common circumstance in which they all agree, or to extract it, pure and unmixed, from the other superfluous circumstances. Every judgment or conclusion, with them, is particular. They

cannot enlarge their view to those universal propositions, which comprehend under them an infinite number of individuals, and include a whole science in a single theorem. Their eye is confounded with such an extensive prospect; and the conclusions, derived from it, even though clearly expressed, seem intricate and obscure. But however intricate they may seem, it is certain, that general principles, if just and sound, must always prevail in the general course of things, though they may fail in particular cases; and it is the chief business of philosophers to regard the general course of things. I may add, that it is also the chief business of politicians; especially in the domestic government of the state, where the public good, which is, or ought to be their object, depends on the concurrence of a multitude of causes; not, as in foreign politics, on accidents and chances, and the caprices of a few persons. This therefore makes the difference between *particular* deliberations and *general* reasonings, and renders subtilty and refinement much more suitable to the latter than to the former.

3.   I thought this introduction necessary before the following discourses on *commerce, money, interest, balance of trade, &c.* where, perhaps, there will occur some principles which are uncommon, and which may seem too refined and subtile for such vulgar subjects. If false, let them be rejected: But no one ought to entertain a prejudice against them, merely because they are out of the common road.

4.   The greatness of a state, and the happiness of its subjects, how independent soever they may be supposed in some respects, are commonly allowed to be inseparable with regard to commerce; and as private men receive greater security, in the possession of their trade and riches, from the power of the public, so the public becomes powerful in proportion to the opulence and extensive commerce of private men. This maxim is true in general; though I cannot forbear thinking, that it may possibly admit of exceptions, and that we often establish it with too little reserve and limitation. There may be some circumstances, where the commerce and riches and luxury of individuals, instead of adding strength to the public, will serve only to thin its armies, and diminish its authority among the neighbouring nations. Man is a very variable being, and susceptible of many different opinions, principles, and rules of conduct. What may be true, while he adheres to one way of thinking, will be found false, when he has embraced an opposite set of manners and opinions.

5.   The bulk of every state may be divided into *husbandmen* and *manufacturers.* The former are employed in the culture of the land; the latter work up the materials furnished by the former, into all the commodities which are necessary or ornamental to human life. As soon as men quit

their savage state, where they live chiefly by hunting and fishing, they must fall into these two classes; though the arts of agriculture employ *at first* the most numerous part of the society.[40] Time and experience improve so much these arts, that the land may easily maintain a much greater number of men, than those who are immediately employed in its culture, or who furnish the more necessary manufactures to such as are so employed.

6.   If these superfluous hands apply themselves to the finer arts, which are commonly denominated the arts of *luxury,* they add to the happiness of the state; since they afford to many the opportunity of receiving enjoyments, with which they would otherwise have been unacquainted. But may not another scheme be proposed for the employment of these superfluous hands? May not the sovereign lay claim to them, and employ them in fleets and armies, to encrease the dominions of the state abroad, and spread its fame over distant nations? It is certain that the fewer desires and wants are found in the proprietors and labourers of land, the fewer hands do they employ; and consequently the superfluities of the land, instead of maintaining tradesmen and manufacturers, may support fleets and armies to a much greater extent, than where a great many arts are required to minister to the luxury of particular persons. Here therefore seems to be a kind of opposition between the greatness of the state and the happiness of the subject. A state is never greater than when all its superfluous hands are employed in the service of the public. The ease and convenience of private persons require, that these hands should be employed in their service. The one can never be satisfied, but at the expence of the other. As the ambition of the sovereign must entrench on the luxury of individuals; so the luxury of individuals must diminish the force, and check the ambition of the sovereign.

7.   Nor is this reasoning merely chimerical; but is founded on history and experience. The republic of SPARTA was certainly more powerful than any state now in the world, consisting of an equal number of people; and this was owing entirely to the want of commerce and luxury. The HELOTES were the labourers: The SPARTANS were the soldiers or gentlemen. It is evident, that the labour of the HELOTES could not have maintained so great a

---

40. Mons. MELON, in his political essay on commerce, asserts, that even at present, if you divide FRANCE into 20 parts, 16 are labourers or peasants; two only artizans; one belonging to the law, church, and military; and one merchants, financiers, and bourgeois. This calculation is certainly very erroneous. In FRANCE, ENGLAND, and indeed most parts of EUROPE, half of the inhabitants live in cities; and even of those who live in the country, a great number are artizans, perhaps above a third. [Jean-François Melon, *Essai politique sur le commerce* (1734; expanded 2nd ed., 1736; translated ed., *A Political Essay upon Commerce,* 1738).]

number of SPARTANS, had these latter lived in ease and delicacy, and given employment to a great variety of trades and manufactures. The like policy may be remarked in ROME. And indeed, throughout all ancient history, it is observable, that the smallest republics raised and maintained greater armies, than states consisting of triple the number of inhabitants, are able to support at present. It is computed, that, in all EUROPEAN nations, the proportion between soldiers and people does not exceed one to a hundred. But we read, that the city of ROME alone, with its small territory, raised and maintained, in early times, ten legions against the LATINS. ATHENS, the whole of whose dominions was not larger than YORKSHIRE, sent to the expedition against SICILY near forty thousand men.[41] DIONYSIUS the elder, it is said, maintained a standing army of a hundred thousand foot and ten thousand horse, besides a large fleet of four hundred sail;[42] though his territories extended no farther than the city of SYRACUSE, about a third of the island of SICILY, and some sea-port towns and garrisons on the coast of ITALY and ILLYRICUM. It is true, the ancient armies, in time of war, subsisted much upon plunder: But did not the enemy plunder in their turn? which was a more ruinous way of levying a tax, than any other that could be devised. In short, no probable reason can be assigned for the great power of the more ancient states above the modern, but their want of commerce and luxury. Few artizans were maintained by the labour of the farmers, and therefore more soldiers might live upon it. LIVY says, that ROME, in his time, would find it difficult to raise as large an army as that which, in her early days, she sent out against the GAULS and LATINS.[43] Instead of those soldiers who fought for liberty and empire in CAMILLUS's time, there were, in AUGUSTUS's days, musicians, painters, cooks, players, and tailors; and if the land was equally cultivated at both periods, it could certainly maintain equal numbers in the one profession as in the other. They added nothing to the mere necessaries of life, in the latter period more than in the former.

8.   It is natural on this occasion to ask, whether sovereigns may not return to the maxims of ancient policy, and consult their own interest in this respect, more than the happiness of their subjects? I answer, that it appears

41. THUCYDIDES, lib. vii.

42. DIOD. SIC. lib. vii. This account, I own, is somewhat suspicious, not to say worse; chiefly because this army was not composed of citizens, but of mercenary forces.

43. TITI LIVII, lib. vii. cap. 24. "Adeo in quæ laboramus," says he, "sola crevimus, divitias luxuriemque." ["So strictly has our growth been limited to the only things for which we strive,--wealth and luxury." Livy, *History of Rome,* translated by B. O. Foster, 7.25.]

to me, almost impossible; and that because ancient policy was violent, and contrary to the more natural and usual course of things. It is well known with what peculiar laws SPARTA was governed, and what a prodigy that republic is justly esteemed by every one, who has considered human nature as it has displayed itself in other nations, and other ages. Were the testimony of history less positive and circumstantial, such a government would appear a mere philosophical whim or fiction, and impossible ever to be reduced to practice. And though the ROMAN and other ancient republics were supported on principles somewhat more natural, yet was there an extraordinary concurrence of circumstances to make them submit to such grievous burthens. They were free states; they were small ones; and the age being martial, all their neighbours were continually in arms. Freedom naturally begets public spirit, especially in small states; and this public spirit, this *amor patriæ,* must encrease, when the public is almost in continual alarm, and men are obliged, every moment, to expose themselves to the greatest dangers for its defence. A continual succession of wars makes every citizen a soldier: He takes the field in his turn: And during his service he is chiefly maintained by himself. This service is indeed equivalent to a heavy tax; yet is it less felt by a people addicted to arms, who fight for honour and revenge more than pay, and are unacquainted with gain and industry as well as pleasure.[44] Not to mention the great equality of fortunes among the inhabitants of the ancient republics, where every field, belonging to a different proprietor, was able to maintain a family, and rendered the numbers of citizens very considerable, even without trade and manufactures.

9.   But though the want of trade and manufactures, among a free and very martial people, may *sometimes* have no other effect than to render the public more powerful, it is certain, that, in the common course of human

44. The more ancient ROMANS lived in perpetual war with all their neighbours: And in old LATIN, the term *hostis,* expressed both a stranger and an enemy. This is remarked by CICERO; but by him is ascribed to the humanity of his ancestors, who softened, as much as possible, the denomination of an enemy, by calling him by the same appellation which signified a stranger. *De Off.* lib. ii. It is however much more probable, from the manners of the times, that the ferocity of those people was so great as to make them regard all strangers as enemies, and call them by the same name. It is not, besides, consistent with the most common maxims of policy or of nature, that any state should regard its public enemies with a friendly eye, or preserve any such sentiments for them as the ROMAN orator would ascribe to his ancestors. Not to mention, that the early ROMANS really exercised piracy, as we learn from their first treaties with CARTHAGE, preserved by POLYBIUS, lib. iii. and consequently, like the SALLEE and ALGERINE rovers, were actually at war with most nations, and a stranger and an enemy were with them almost synonymous.

affairs, it will have a quite contrary tendency. Sovereigns must take mankind as they find them, and cannot pretend to introduce any violent change in their principles and ways of thinking. A long course of time, with a variety of accidents and circumstances, are requisite to produce those great revolutions, which so much diversify the face of human affairs. And the less natural any set of principles are, which support a particular society, the more difficulty will a legislator meet with in raising and cultivating them. It is his best policy to comply with the common bent of mankind, and give it all the improvements of which it is susceptible. Now, according to the most natural course of things, industry and arts and trade encrease the power of the sovereign as well as the happiness of the subjects; and that policy is violent, which aggrandizes the public by the poverty of individuals. This will easily appear from a few considerations, which will present to us the consequences of sloth and barbarity.

10. Where manufactures and mechanic arts are not cultivated, the bulk of the people must apply themselves to agriculture; and if their skill and industry encrease, there must arise a great superfluity from their labour beyond what suffices to maintain them. They have no temptation, therefore, to encrease their skill and industry; since they cannot exchange that superfluity for any commodities, which may serve either to their pleasure or vanity. A habit of indolence naturally prevails. The greater part of the land lies uncultivated. What is cultivated, yields not its utmost for want of skill and assiduity in the farmers. If at any time the public exigencies require, that great numbers should be employed in the public service, the labour of the people furnishes now no superfluities, by which these numbers can be maintained. The labourers cannot encrease their skill and industry on a sudden. Lands uncultivated cannot be brought into tillage for some years. The armies, mean while, must either make sudden and violent conquests, or disband for want of subsistence. A regular attack or defence, therefore, is not to be expected from such a people, and their soldiers must be as ignorant and unskilful as their farmers and manufacturers.

11. Every thing in the world is purchased by labour; and our passions are the only causes of labour. When a nation abounds in manufactures and mechanic arts, the proprietors of land, as well as the farmers, study agriculture as a science, and redouble their industry and attention. The superfluity, which arises from their labour, is not lost; but is exchanged with manufactures for those commodities, which men's luxury now makes them covet. By this means, land furnishes a great deal more of the necessaries of life, than what suffices for those who cultivate it. In times of peace and tranquillity, this superfluity goes to the maintenance of manufacturers, and

the improvers of liberal arts. But it is easy for the public to convert many of these manufacturers into soldiers, and maintain them by that superfluity, which arises from the labour of the farmers. Accordingly we find, that this is the case in all civilized governments. When the sovereign raises an army, what is the consequence? He imposes a tax. This tax obliges all the people to retrench what is least necessary to their subsistence. Those, who labour in such commodities, must either enlist in the troops, or turn themselves to agriculture, and thereby oblige some labourers to enlist for want of business. And to consider the matter abstractedly, manufactures encrease the power of the state only as they store up so much labour, and that of a kind to which the public may lay claim, without depriving any one of the necessaries of life. The more labour, therefore, is employed beyond mere necessaries, the more powerful is any state; since the persons engaged in that labour may easily be converted to the public service. In a state without manufactures, there may be the same number of hands; but there is not the same quantity of labour, nor of the same kind. All the labour is there bestowed upon necessaries, which can admit of little or no abatement.

12.   Thus the greatness of the sovereign and the happiness of the state are, in a great measure, united with regard to trade and manufactures. It is a violent method, and in most cases impracticable, to oblige the labourer to toil, in order to raise from the land more than what subsists himself and family. Furnish him with manufactures and commodities, and he will do it of himself. Afterwards you will find it easy to seize some part of his superfluous labour, and employ it in the public service, without giving him his wonted return. Being accustomed to industry, he will think this less grievous, than if, at once, you obliged him to an augmentation of labour without any reward. The case is the same with regard to the other members of the state. The greater is the stock of labour of all kinds, the greater quantity may be taken from the heap, without making any sensible alteration in it.

13.   A public granary of corn, a storehouse of cloth, a magazine of arms; all these must be allowed real riches and strength in any state. Trade and industry are really nothing but a stock of labour, which, in times of peace and tranquillity, is employed for the ease and satisfaction of individuals; but in the exigencies of state, may, in part, be turned to public advantage. Could we convert a city into a kind of fortified camp, and infuse into each breast so martial a genius, and such a passion for public good, as to make every one willing to undergo the greatest hardships for the sake of the public; these affections might now, as in ancient times, prove alone a sufficient spur to industry, and support the community. It would then be advantageous, as in camps, to banish all arts and luxury; and, by restrictions

on equipage and tables, make the provisions and forage last longer than if the army were loaded with a number of superfluous retainers. But as these principles are too disinterested and too difficult to support, it is requisite to govern men by other passions, and animate them with a spirit of avarice and industry, art and luxury. The camp is, in this case, loaded with a superfluous retinue; but the provisions flow in proportionably larger. The harmony of the whole is still supported; and the natural bent of the mind being more complied with, individuals, as well as the public, find their account in the observance of those maxims.

14.   The same method of reasoning will let us see the advantage of *foreign* commerce, in augmenting the power of the state, as well as the riches and happiness of the subject. It encreases the stock of labour in the nation; and the sovereign may convert what share of it he finds necessary to the service of the public. Foreign trade, by its imports, furnishes materials for new manufactures; and by its exports, it produces labour in particular commodities, which could not be consumed at home. In short, a kingdom, that has a large import and export, must abound more with industry, and that employed upon delicacies and luxuries, than a kingdom which rests contented with its native commodities. It is, therefore, more powerful, as well as richer and happier. The individuals reap the benefit of these commodities, so far as they gratify the senses and appetites. And the public is also a gainer, while a greater stock of labour is, by this means, stored up against any public exigency; that is, a greater number of laborious men are maintained, who may be diverted to the public service, without robbing any one of the necessaries, or even the chief conveniencies of life.

15.   If we consult history, we shall find, that, in most nations, foreign trade has preceded any refinement in home manufactures, and given birth to domestic luxury. The temptation is stronger to make use of foreign commodities, which are ready for use, and which are entirely new to us, than to make improvements on any domestic commodity, which always advance by slow degrees, and never affect us by their novelty. The profit is also very great, in exporting what is superfluous at home, and what bears no price, to foreign nations, whose soil or climate is not favourable to that commodity. Thus men become acquainted with the *pleasures* of luxury and the *profits* of commerce; and their *delicacy* and *industry*, being once awakened, carry them on to farther improvements, in every branch of domestic as well as foreign trade. And this perhaps is the chief advantage which arises from a commerce with strangers. It rouses men from their indolence; and presenting the gayer and more opulent part of the nation with objects of luxury, which they never before dreamed of, raises in them a desire of a more

splendid way of life than what their ancestors enjoyed. And at the same time, the few merchants, who possess the secret of this importation and exportation, make great profits; and becoming rivals in wealth to the ancient nobility, tempt other adventurers to become their rivals in commerce. Imitation soon diffuses all those arts; while domestic manufactures emulate the foreign in their improvements, and work up every home commodity to the utmost perfection of which it is susceptible. Their own steel and iron, in such laborious hands, become equal to the gold and rubies of the INDIES.

16. When the affairs of the society are once brought to this situation, a nation may lose most of its foreign trade, and yet continue a great and powerful people. If strangers will not take any particular commodity of ours, we must cease to labour in it. The same hands will turn themselves towards some refinement in other commodities, which may be wanted at home. And there must always be materials for them to work upon; till every person in the state, who possesses riches, enjoys as great plenty of home commodities, and those in as great perfection, as he desires; which can never possibly happen. CHINA is represented as one of the most flourishing empires in the world; though it has very little commerce beyond its own territories.

17. It will not, I hope, be considered as a superfluous digression, if I here observe, that, as the multitude of mechanical arts is advantageous, so is the great number of persons to whose share the productions of these arts fall. A too great disproportion among the citizens weakens any state. Every person, if possible, ought to enjoy the fruits of his labour, in a full possession of all the necessaries, and many of the conveniencies of life. No one can doubt, but such an equality is most suitable to human nature, and diminishes much less from the *happiness* of the rich than it adds to that of the poor. It also augments the *power of the state,* and makes any extraordinary taxes or impositions be paid with more chearfulness. Where the riches are engrossed by a few, these must contribute very largely to the supplying of the public necessities. But when the riches are dispersed among multitudes, the burthen feels light on every shoulder, and the taxes make not a very sensible difference on any one's way of living.

18. Add to this, that, where the riches are in few hands, these must enjoy all the power, and will readily conspire to lay the whole burthen on the poor, and oppress them still farther, to the discouragement of all industry.

19. In this circumstance consists the great advantage of ENGLAND above any nation at present in the world, or that appears in the records of any story. It is true, the ENGLISH feel some disadvantages in foreign trade by the high price of labour, which is in part the effect of the riches of their

artisans, as well as of the plenty of money: But as foreign trade is not the most material circumstance, it is not to be put in competition with the happiness of so many millions. And if there were no more to endear to them that free government under which they live, this alone were sufficient. The poverty of the common people is a natural, if not an infallible effect of absolute monarchy; though I doubt, whether it be always true, on the other hand, that their riches are an infallible result of liberty. Liberty must be attended with particular accidents, and a certain turn of thinking, in order to produce that effect. Lord BACON, accounting for the great advantages obtained by the ENGLISH in their wars with FRANCE, ascribes them chiefly to the superior ease and plenty of the common people amongst the former; yet the government of the two kingdoms was, at that time, pretty much alike.[45] Where the labourers and artisans are accustomed to work for low wages, and to retain but a small part of the fruits of their labour, it is difficult for them, even in a free government, to better their condition, or conspire among themselves to heighten their wages. But even where they are accustomed to a more plentiful way of life, it is easy for the rich, in an arbitrary government, to conspire against *them,* and throw the whole burthen of the taxes on their shoulders.

20. It may seem an odd position, that the poverty of the common people in FRANCE, ITALY, and SPAIN, is, in some measure, owing to the superior riches of the soil and happiness of the climate; yet there want not reasons to justify this paradox. In such a fine mould or soil as that of those more southern regions, agriculture is an easy art; and one man, with a couple of sorry horses, will be able, in a season, to cultivate as much land as will pay a pretty considerable rent to the proprietor. All the art, which the farmer knows, is to leave his ground fallow for a year, as soon as it is exhausted; and the warmth of the sun alone and temperature of the climate enrich it, and restore its fertility. Such poor peasants, therefore, require only a simple maintenance for their labour. They have no stock or riches, which claim more; and at the same time, they are for ever dependant on their landlord, who gives no leases, nor fears that his land will be spoiled by the ill methods of cultivation. In ENGLAND, the land is rich, but coarse; must be cultivated at a great expence; and produces slender crops, when not carefully managed, and by a method which gives not the full profit but in a course of several years. A farmer, therefore, in ENGLAND must have a considerable stock, and a long lease; which beget proportional profits. The fine vineyards of CHAMPAGNE and BURGUNDY, that often yield to the

45. [Bacon, *Essays,* 29.]

landlord above five pounds *per* acre, are cultivated by peasants, who have scarcely bread: The reason is, that such peasants need no stock but their own limbs, with instruments of husbandry, which they can buy for twenty shillings. The farmers are commonly in some better circumstances in those countries. But the grasiers[46] are most at their ease of all those who cultivate the land. The reason is still the same. Men must have profits proportionable to their expence and hazard. Where so considerable a number of the labouring poor as the peasants and farmers are in very low circumstances, all the rest must partake of their poverty, whether the government of that nation be monarchical or republican.

21. We may form a similar remark with regard to the general history of mankind. What is the reason, why no people, living between the tropics, could ever yet attain to any art or civility, or reach even any police in their government, and any military discipline; while few nations in the temperate climates have been altogether deprived of these advantages? It is probable that one cause of this phænomenon is the warmth and equality of weather in the torrid zone, which render clothes and houses less requisite for the inhabitants, and thereby remove, in part, that necessity, which is the great spur to industry and invention. *Curis acuens mortalia corda.*[47] Not to mention, that the fewer goods or possessions of this kind any people enjoy, the fewer quarrels are likely to arise amongst them, and the less necessity will there be for a settled police or regular authority to protect and defend them from foreign enemies, or from each other.

46. [Those who feed cattle.]

47. ["Sharpening men's wits by care." Virgil, *Georgics,* translated by H. Rushton Fairclough, 1.123.]

8.

Of Refinement in the Arts

1. LUXURY is a word of an uncertain signification, and may be taken in a good as well as in a bad sense. In general, it means great refinement in the gratification of the senses; and any degree of it may be innocent or blameable, according to the age, or country, or condition of the person. The bounds between the virtue and the vice cannot here be exactly fixed, more than in other moral subjects. To imagine, that the gratifying of any sense, or the indulging of any delicacy in meat, drink, or apparel, is of itself a vice, can never enter into a head, that is not disordered by the frenzies of enthusiasm. I have, indeed, heard of a monk abroad, who, because the windows of his cell opened upon a noble prospect, made a *covenant with his eyes* never to turn that way, or receive so sensual a gratification. And such is the crime of drinking CHAMPAGNE or BURGUNDY, preferably to small beer or porter. These indulgences are only vices, when they are pursued at the expence of some virtue, as liberality or charity; in like manner as they are follies, when for them a man ruins his fortune, and reduces himself to want and beggary. Where they entrench upon no virtue, but leave ample subject whence to provide for friends, family, and every proper object of generosity or compassion, they are entirely innocent, and have in every age been acknowledged such by almost all moralists. To be entirely occupied with the luxury of the table, for instance, without any relish for the pleasures of ambition, study, or conversation, is a mark of stupidity, and is incompatible with any vigour of temper or genius. To confine one's expence entirely to such a gratification, without regard to friends or family, is an indication of a heart destitute of humanity or benevolence. But if a man reserve time sufficient for all laudable pursuits, and money sufficient for all generous purposes, he is free from every shadow of blame or reproach.

2. Since luxury may be considered either as innocent or blameable, one may be surprized at those preposterous opinions, which have been

entertained concerning it; while men of libertine principles bestow praises even on vicious luxury, and represent it as highly advantageous to society; and on the other hand, men of severe morals blame even the most innocent luxury, and represent it as the source of all the corruptions, disorders, and factions, incident to civil government. We shall here endeavour to correct both these extremes, by proving, *first,* that the ages of refinement are both the happiest and most virtuous; *secondly,* that wherever luxury ceases to be innocent, it also ceases to be beneficial; and when carried a degree too far, is a quality pernicious, though perhaps not the most pernicious, to political society.

3.   To prove the first point, we need but consider the effects of refinement both on *private* and on *public* life. Human happiness, according to the most received notions, seems to consist in three ingredients; action, pleasure, and indolence: And though these ingredients ought to be mixed in different proportions, according to the particular disposition of the person; yet no one ingredient can be entirely wanting, without destroying, in some measure, the relish of the whole composition. Indolence or repose, indeed, seems not of itself to contribute much to our enjoyment; but, like sleep, is requisite as an indulgence to the weakness of human nature, which cannot support an uninterrupted course of business or pleasure. That quick march of the spirits, which takes a man from himself, and chiefly gives satisfaction, does in the end exhaust the mind, and requires some intervals of repose, which, though agreeable for a moment, yet, if prolonged, beget a languor and lethargy, that destroys all enjoyment. Education, custom, and example, have a mighty influence in turning the mind to any of these pursuits; and it must be owned, that, where they promote a relish for action and pleasure, they are so far favourable to human happiness. In times when industry and the arts flourish, men are kept in perpetual occupation, and enjoy, as their reward, the occupation itself, as well as those pleasures which are the fruit of their labour. The mind acquires new vigour; enlarges its powers and faculties; and by an assiduity in honest industry, both satisfies its natural appetites, and prevents the growth of unnatural ones, which commonly spring up, when nourished by ease and idleness. Banish those arts from society, you deprive men both of action and of pleasure; and leaving nothing but indolence in their place, you even destroy the relish of indolence, which never is agreeable, but when it succeeds to labour, and recruits the spirits, exhausted by too much application and fatigue.

4.   Another advantage of industry and of refinements in the mechanical arts, is, that they commonly produce some refinements in the liberal;

nor can one be carried to perfection, without being accompanied, in some degree, with the other. The same age, which produces great philosophers and politicians, renowned generals and poets, usually abounds with skilful weavers, and ship-carpenters. We cannot reasonably expect, that a piece of woollen cloth will be wrought to perfection in a nation, which is ignorant of astronomy, or where ethics are neglected. The spirit of the age affects all the arts; and the minds of men, being once roused from their lethargy, and put into a fermentation, turn themselves on all sides, and carry improvements into every art and science. Profound ignorance is totally banished, and men enjoy the privilege of rational creatures, to think as well as to act, to cultivate the pleasures of the mind as well as those of the body.

5.   The more these refined arts advance, the more sociable men become: nor is it possible, that, when enriched with science, and possessed of a fund of conversation, they should be contented to remain in solitude, or live with their fellow-citizens in that distant manner, which is peculiar to ignorant and barbarous nations. They flock into cities; love to receive and communicate knowledge; to show their wit or their breeding; their taste in conversation or living, in clothes or furniture. Curiosity allures the wise; vanity the foolish; and pleasure both. Particular clubs and societies are every where formed: Both sexes meet in an easy and sociable manner; and the tempers of men, as well as their behaviour, refine apace. So that, beside the improvements which they receive from knowledge and the liberal arts, it is impossible but they must feel an encrease of humanity, from the very habit of conversing together, and contributing to each other's pleasure and entertainment. Thus *industry, knowledge,* and *humanity,* are linked together by an indissoluble chain, and are found, from experience as well as reason, to be peculiar to the more polished, and, what are commonly denominated, the more luxurious ages.

6.   Nor are these advantages attended with disadvantages, that bear any proportion to them. The more men refine upon pleasure, the less will they indulge in excesses of any kind; because nothing is more destructive to true pleasure than such excesses. One may safely affirm, that the TARTARS are oftener guilty of beastly gluttony, when they feast on their dead horses, than EUROPEAN courtiers with all their refinements of cookery. And if libertine love, or even infidelity to the marriage-bed, be more frequent in polite ages, when it is often regarded only as a piece of gallantry; drunkenness, on the other hand, is much less common: A vice more odious, and more pernicious both to mind and body. And in this matter I would appeal, not only to an OVID or a PETRONIUS, but to a SENECA or a CATO. We know, that CÆSAR, during CATILINE's conspiracy, being necessitated to put into

CATO's hands a *billet-doux,*[48] which discovered an intrigue with SERVILIA, CATO's own sister, that stern philosopher threw it back to him with indignation; and in the bitterness of his wrath, gave him the appellation of drunkard, as a term more opprobrious than that with which he could more justly have reproached him.

7.   But industry, knowledge, and humanity, are not advantageous in private life alone: They diffuse their beneficial influence on the *public,* and render the government as great and flourishing as they make individuals happy and prosperous. The encrease and consumption of all the commodities, which serve to the ornament and pleasure of life, are advantageous to society; because, at the same time that they multiply those innocent gratifications to individuals, they are a kind of *storehouse* of labour, which, in the exigencies of state, may be turned to the public service. In a nation, where there is no demand for such superfluities, men sink into indolence, lose all enjoyment of life, and are useless to the public, which cannot maintain or support its fleets and armies, from the industry of such slothful members.

8.   The bounds of all the EUROPEAN kingdoms are, at present, nearly the same they were two hundred years ago: But what a difference is there in the power and grandeur of those kingdoms? Which can be ascribed to nothing but the encrease of art and industry. When CHARLES VIII. of FRANCE invaded ITALY, he carried with him about 20,000 men: Yet this armament so exhausted the nation, as we learn from GUICCIARDIN, that for some years it was not able to make so great an effort. The late king of FRANCE, in time of war, kept in pay above 400,000 men;[49] though from MAZARINE's death to his own, he was engaged in a course of wars that lasted near thirty years.

9.   This industry is much promoted by the knowledge inseparable from ages of art and refinement; as, on the other hand, this knowledge enables the public to make the best advantage of the industry of its subjects. Laws, order, police, discipline; these can never be carried to any degree of perfection, before human reason has refined itself by exercise, and by an application to the more vulgar arts, at least, of commerce and manufacture. Can we expect, that a government will be well modelled by a people, who know not how to make a spinning-wheel, or to employ a loom to advantage? Not to mention, that all ignorant ages are infested with superstition, which throws the government off its bias, and disturbs men in the pursuit of their interest and happiness.

48. [A love letter.]

49. The inscription on the PLACE-DE-VENDOME says 440,000. [Hume refers in the text to Louis XIV, who died in 1715.]

10. Knowledge in the arts of government naturally begets mildness and moderation, by instructing men in the advantages of humane maxims above rigour and severity, which drive subjects into rebellion, and make the return to submission impracticable, by cutting off all hopes of pardon. When the tempers of men are softened as well as their knowledge improved, this humanity appears still more conspicuous, and is the chief characteristic which distinguishes a civilized age from times of barbarity and ignorance. Factions are then less inveterate, revolutions less tragical, authority less severe, and seditions less frequent. Even foreign wars abate of their cruelty; and after the field of battle, where honour and interest steel men against compassion as well as fear, the combatants divest themselves of the brute, and resume the man.

11. Nor need we fear, that men, by losing their ferocity, will lose their martial spirit, or become less undaunted and vigorous in defence of their country or their liberty. The arts have no such effect in enervating either the mind or body. On the contrary, industry, their inseparable attendant, adds new force to both. And if anger, which is said to be the whetstone of courage, loses somewhat of its asperity, by politeness and refinement; a sense of honour, which is a stronger, more constant, and more governable principle, acquires fresh vigour by that elevation of genius which arises from knowledge and a good education. Add to this, that courage can neither have any duration, nor be of any use, when not accompanied with discipline and martial skill, which are seldom found among a barbarous people. The ancients remarked, that DATAMES was the only barbarian that ever knew the art of war. And PYRRHUS, seeing the ROMANS marshal their army with some art and skill, said with surprize, *These barbarians have nothing barbarous in their discipline!* It is observable, that, as the old ROMANS, by applying themselves solely to war, were almost the only uncivilized people that ever possessed military discipline; so the modern ITALIANS are the only civilized people, among EUROPEANS, that ever wanted courage and a martial spirit. Those who would ascribe this effeminacy of the ITALIANS to their luxury, or politeness, or application to the arts, need but consider the FRENCH and ENGLISH, whose bravery is as uncontestable, as their love for the arts, and their assiduity in commerce. The ITALIAN historians give us a more satisfactory reason for this degeneracy of their countrymen. They shew us how the sword was dropped at once by all the ITALIAN sovereigns; while the VENETIAN aristocracy was jealous of its subjects, the FLORENTINE democracy applied itself entirely to commerce; ROME was governed by priests, and NAPLES by women. War then became the business of soldiers of fortune, who spared one

another, and to the astonishment of the world, could engage a whole day in what they called a battle, and return at night to their camp, without the least bloodshed.

12.   What has chiefly induced severe moralists to declaim against refinement in the arts, is the example of ancient ROME, which, joining, to its poverty and rusticity, virtue and public spirit, rose to such a surprizing height of grandeur and liberty; but having learned from its conquered provinces the ASIATIC luxury, fell into every kind of corruption; whence arose sedition and civil wars, attended at last with the total loss of liberty. All the LATIN classics, whom we peruse in our infancy, are full of these sentiments, and universally ascribe the ruin of their state to the arts and riches imported from the East: Insomuch that SALLUST represents a taste for painting as a vice, no less than lewdness and drinking. And so popular were these sentiments, during the later ages of the republic, that this author abounds in praises of the old rigid ROMAN virtue, though himself the most egregious instance of modern luxury and corruption; speaks contemptuously of the GRECIAN eloquence, though the most elegant writer in the world; nay, employs preposterous digressions and declamations to this purpose, though a model of taste and correctness.

13.   But it would be easy to prove, that these writers mistook the cause of the disorders in the ROMAN state, and ascribed to luxury and the arts, what really proceeded from an ill modelled government, and the unlimited extent of conquests. Refinement on the pleasures and conveniencies of life has no natural tendency to beget venality and corruption. The value, which all men put upon any particular pleasure, depends on comparison and experience; nor is a porter less greedy of money, which he spends on bacon and brandy, than a courtier, who purchases champagne and orto-lans.[50] Riches are valuable at all times, and to all men; because they always purchase pleasures, such as men are accustomed to, and desire: Nor can any thing restrain or regulate the love of money, but a sense of honour and virtue; which, if it be not nearly equal at all times, will naturally abound most in ages of knowledge and refinement.

14.   Of all EUROPEAN kingdoms, POLAND seems the most defective in the arts of war as well as peace, mechanical as well as liberal; yet it is there that venality and corruption do most prevail. The nobles seem to have preserved their crown elective for no other purpose, than regularly to sell it to the highest bidder. This is almost the only species of commerce, with which that people are acquainted.

50. [Small birds.]

15. The liberties of ENGLAND, so far from decaying since the improvements in the arts, have never flourished so much as during that period. And though corruption may seem to encrease of late years; this is chiefly to be ascribed to our established liberty, when our princes have found the impossibility of governing without parliaments, or of terrifying parliaments by the phantom of prerogative. Not to mention, that this corruption or venality prevails much more among the electors than the elected; and therefore cannot justly be ascribed to any refinements in luxury.

16. If we consider the matter in a proper light, we shall find, that a progress in the arts is rather favourable to liberty, and has a natural tendency to preserve, if not produce a free government. In rude unpolished nations, where the arts are neglected, all labour is bestowed on the cultivation of the ground; and the whole society is divided into two classes, proprietors of land, and their vassals or tenants. The latter are necessarily dependent, and fitted for slavery and subjection; especially where they possess no riches, and are not valued for their knowledge in agriculture; as must always be the case where the arts are neglected. The former naturally erect themselves into petty tyrants; and must either submit to an absolute master, for the sake of peace and order; or if they will preserve their independency, like the ancient barons, they must fall into feuds and contests among themselves, and throw the whole society into such confusion, as is perhaps worse than the most despotic government. But where luxury nourishes commerce and industry, the peasants, by a proper cultivation of the land, become rich and independent; while the tradesmen and merchants acquire a share of the property, and draw authority and consideration to that middling rank of men, who are the best and firmest basis of public liberty. These submit not to slavery, like the peasants, from poverty and meanness of spirit; and having no hopes of tyrannizing over others, like the barons, they are not tempted, for the sake of that gratification, to submit to the tyranny of their sovereign. They covet equal laws, which may secure their property, and preserve them from monarchical, as well as aristocratical tyranny.

17. The lower house is the support of our popular government; and all the world acknowledges, that it owed its chief influence and consideration to the encrease of commerce, which threw such a balance of property into the hands of the commons. How inconsistent then is it to blame so violently a refinement in the arts, and to represent it as the bane of liberty and public spirit!

18. To declaim against present times, and magnify the virtue of remote ancestors, is a propensity almost inherent in human nature: And as the sentiments and opinions of civilized ages alone are transmitted to posterity,

hence it is that we meet with so many severe judgments pronounced against luxury, and even science; and hence it is that at present we give so ready an assent to them. But the fallacy is easily perceived, by comparing different nations that are contemporaries; where we both judge more impartially, and can better set in opposition those manners, with which we are sufficiently acquainted. Treachery and cruelty, the most pernicious and most odious of all vices, seem peculiar to uncivilized ages; and by the refined GREEKS and ROMANS were ascribed to all the barbarous nations, which surrounded them. They might justly, therefore, have presumed, that their own ancestors, so highly celebrated, possessed no greater virtue, and were as much inferior to their posterity in honour and humanity, as in taste and science. An ancient FRANK or SAXON may be highly extolled: But I believe every man would think his life or fortune much less secure in the hands of a MOOR or TARTAR, than in those of a FRENCH or ENGLISH gentleman, the rank of men the most civilized in the most civilized nations.

19.   We come now to the *second* position which we proposed to illustrate, to wit, that, as innocent luxury, or a refinement in the arts and conveniencies of life, is advantageous to the public; so wherever luxury ceases to be innocent, it also ceases to be beneficial; and when carried a degree farther, begins to be a quality pernicious, though, perhaps, not the most pernicious, to political society.

20.   Let us consider what we call vicious luxury. No gratification, however sensual, can of itself be esteemed vicious. A gratification is only vicious, when it engrosses all a man's expence, and leaves no ability for such acts of duty and generosity as are required by his situation and fortune. Suppose, that he correct the vice, and employ part of his expence in the education of his children, in the support of his friends, and in relieving the poor; would any prejudice result to society? On the contrary, the same consumption would arise; and that labour, which, at present, is employed only in producing a slender gratification to one man, would relieve the necessitous, and bestow satisfaction on hundreds. The same care and toil that raise a dish of peas at CHRISTMAS, would give bread to a whole family during six months. To say, that, without a vicious luxury, the labour would not have been employed at all, is only to say, that there is some other defect in human nature, such as indolence, selfishness, inattention to others, for which luxury, in some measure, provides a remedy; as one poison may be an antidote to another. But virtue, like wholesome food, is better than poisons, however corrected.

21.   Suppose the same number of men, that are at present in GREAT BRITAIN, with the same soil and climate; I ask, is it not possible for them to be

happier, by the most perfect way of life that can be imagined, and by the greatest reformation that Omnipotence itself could work in their temper and disposition? To assert, that they cannot, appears evidently ridiculous. As the land is able to maintain more than all its present inhabitants, they could never, in such a UTOPIAN state, feel any other ills than those which arise from bodily sickness; and these are not the half of human miseries. All other ills spring from some vice, either in ourselves or others; and even many of our diseases proceed from the same origin. Remove the vices, and the ills follow. You must only take care to remove all the vices. If you remove part, you may render the matter worse. By banishing *vicious* luxury, without curing sloth and an indifference to others, you only diminish industry in the state, and add nothing to men's charity or their generosity. Let us, therefore, rest contented with asserting, that two opposite vices in a state may be more advantageous than either of them alone; but let us never pronounce vice in itself advantageous. Is it not very inconsistent for an author to assert in one page, that moral distinctions are inventions of politicians for public interest; and in the next page maintain, that vice is advantageous to the public?[51] And indeed it seems upon any system of morality, little less than a contradiction in terms, to talk of a vice, which is in general beneficial to society.

22. I thought this reasoning necessary, in order to give some light to a philosophical question, which has been much disputed in ENGLAND. I call it a *philosophical* question, not a *political* one. For whatever may be the consequence of such a miraculous transformation of mankind, as would endow them with every species of virtue, and free them from every species of vice; this concerns not the magistrate, who aims only at possibilities. He cannot cure every vice by substituting a virtue in its place. Very often he can only cure one vice by another; and in that case, he ought to prefer what is least pernicious to society. Luxury, when excessive, is the source of many ills; but is in general preferable to sloth and idleness, which would commonly succeed in its place, and are more hurtful both to private persons and to the public. When sloth reigns, a mean uncultivated way of life prevails amongst individuals, without society, without enjoyment. And if the sovereign, in such a situation, demands the service of his subjects, the labour of the state suffices only to furnish the necessaries of life to the labourers, and can afford nothing to those who are employed in the public service.

51. Fable of the Bees. [Bernard de Mandeville, *The Fable of the Bees; or, Private Vices, Publick Benefits* (1714; enlarged eds. in 1723 and 1728–29).]

9.

Of Public Credit

1. IT appears to have been the common practice of antiquity, to make provision, during peace, for the necessities of war, and to hoard up treasures before-hand, as the instruments either of conquest or defence; without trusting to extraordinary impositions, much less to borrowing, in times of disorder and confusion. Besides the immense sums above mentioned,[52] which were amassed by ATHENS, and by the PTOLEMIES, and other successors of ALEXANDER; we learn from PLATO,[53] that the frugal LACEDEMONIANS had also collected a great treasure; and ARRIAN[54] and PLUTARCH[55] take notice of the riches which ALEXANDER got possession of on the conquest of SUSA and ECBATANA, and which were reserved, some of them, from the time of CYRUS. If I remember right, the scripture also mentions the treasure of HEZEKIAH and the JEWISH princes; as profane history does that of PHILIP and PERSEUS, kings of MACEDON. The ancient republics of GAUL had commonly large sums in reserve.[56] Every one knows the treasure seized in ROME by JULIUS CÆSAR, during the civil wars: and we find afterwards, that the wiser emperors, AUGUSTUS, TIBERIUS, VESPASIAN, SEVERUS, &c. always discovered the prudent foresight, of saving great sums against any public exigency.

2. On the contrary, our modern expedient, which has become very general, is to mortgage the public revenues, and to trust that posterity will pay off the incumbrances contracted by their ancestors: And they, having before their eyes, so good an example of their wise fathers, have the same

52. Essay V. ["Of the Balance of Trade."]
53. ALCIB. I. [1.122d–123b.]
54. Lib. iii. [*Expedition of Alexander,* 3.16, 19.]
55. PLUT. *in vita* ALEX. He makes these treasures amount to 80,000 talents, or about 15 millions sterl. QUINTUS CURTIUS (lib. v. cap. 2.) says, that ALEXANDER found in SUSA above 50,000 talents.
56. STRABO, lib. iv.

prudent reliance on *their* posterity; who, at last, from necessity more than choice, are obliged to place the same confidence in a new posterity. But not to waste time in declaiming against a practice which appears ruinous, beyond all controversy; it seems pretty apparent, that the ancient maxims are, in this respect, more prudent than the modern; even though the latter had been confined within some reasonable bounds, and had ever, in any instance, been attended with such frugality, in time of peace, as to discharge the debts incurred by an expensive war. For why should the case be so different between the public and an individual, as to make us establish different maxims of conduct for each? If the funds of the former be greater, its necessary expences are proportionably larger; if its resources be more numerous, they are not infinite; and as its frame should be calculated for a much longer duration than the date of a single life, or even of a family, it should embrace maxims, large, durable, and generous, agreeably to the supposed extent of its existence. To trust to chances and temporary expedients, is, indeed, what the necessity of human affairs frequently renders unavoidable; but whoever voluntarily depend on such resources, have not necessity, but their own folly, to accuse for their misfortunes, when any such befal them.

3.   If the abuses of treasures be dangerous, either by engaging the state in rash enterprizes, or making it neglect military discipline, in confidence of its riches; the abuses of mortgaging are more certain and inevitable; poverty, impotence, and subjection to foreign powers. According to modern policy war is attended with every destructive circumstance; loss of men, encrease of taxes, decay of commerce, dissipation of money, devastation by sea and land.

4.   According to ancient maxims, the opening of the public treasure, as it produced an uncommon affluence of gold and silver, served as a temporary encouragement to industry, and atoned, in some degree, for the inevitable calamities of war.

5.   It is very tempting to a minister to employ such an expedient, as enables him to make a great figure during his administration, without over-burthening the people with taxes, or exciting any immediate clamours against himself. The practice, therefore, of contracting debt will almost infallibly be abused, in every government. It would scarcely be more imprudent to give a prodigal son a credit in every banker's shop in London, than to impower a statesman to draw bills, in this manner, upon posterity.

6.   What then shall we say to the new paradox, that public incumbrances, are, of themselves, advantageous, independent of the necessity of contracting them; and that any state, even though it were not pressed by a foreign

enemy, could not possibly have embraced a wiser expedient for promoting commerce and riches, than to create funds, and debts, and taxes, without limitation? Reasonings, such as these, might naturally have passed for trials of wit among rhetoricians, like the panegyrics on folly and a fever, on BUSIRIS and NERO, had we not seen such absurd maxims patronized by great ministers, and by a whole party among us.

7.   Let us examine the consequences of public debts, both in our domestic management, by their influence on commerce and industry; and in our foreign transactions, by their effect on wars and negociations.

8.   Public securities are with us become a kind of money, and pass as readily at the current price as gold or silver. Wherever any profitable undertaking offers itself, how expensive soever, there are never wanting hands enow to embrace it; nor need a trader, who has sums in the public stocks, fear to launch out into the most extensive trade; since he is possessed of funds, which will answer the most sudden demand that can be made upon him. No merchant thinks it necessary to keep by him any considerable cash. Bank-stock, or India-bonds, especially the latter, serve all the same purposes; because he can dispose of them, or pledge them to a banker, in a quarter of an hour; and at the same time they are not idle, even when in his scritoire,[57] but bring him in a constant revenue. In short, our national debts furnish merchants with a species of money, that is continually multiplying in their hands, and produces sure gain, besides the profits of their commerce. This must enable them to trade upon less profit. The small profit of the merchant renders the commodity cheaper, causes a greater consumption, quickens the labour of the common people, and helps to spread arts and industry throughout the whole society.

9.   There are also, we may observe, in ENGLAND and in all states, which have both commerce and public debts, a set of men, who are half merchants, half stock-holders, and may be supposed willing to trade for small profits; because commerce is not their principal or sole support, and their revenues in the funds are a sure resource for themselves and their families. Were there no funds, great merchants would have no expedient for realizing or securing any part of their profit, but by making purchases of land; and land has many disadvantages in comparison of funds. Requiring more care and inspection, it divides the time and attention of the merchant; upon any tempting offer or extraordinary accident in trade, it is not so easily converted into money; and as it attracts too much, both by the many natural pleasures it affords, and the authority it gives, it soon converts the

57. [A large cabinet with drawers and a writing table.]

citizen into the country gentleman. More men, therefore, with large stocks and incomes, may naturally be supposed to continue in trade, where there are public debts; and this, it must be owned, is of some advantage to commerce, by diminishing its profits, promoting circulation, and encouraging industry.

10. But, in opposition to these two favourable circumstances, perhaps of no very great importance, weigh the many disadvantages which attend our public debts, in the whole *interior* œconomy of the state: You will find no comparison between the ill and the good which result from them.

11. *First,* It is certain, that national debts cause a mighty confluence of people and riches to the capital, by the great sums, levied in the provinces to pay the interest; and perhaps, too, by the advantages in trade above mentioned, which they give the merchants in the capital above the rest of the kingdom. The question is, whether, in our case, it be for the public interest, that so many privileges should be conferred on LONDON, which has already arrived at such an enormous size, and seems still encreasing? Some men are apprehensive of the consequences. For my own part, I cannot forbear thinking, that, though the head is undoubtedly too large for the body, yet that great city is so happily situated, that its excessive bulk causes less inconvenience than even a smaller capital to a greater kingdom. There is more difference between the prices of all provisions in PARIS and LANGUE-DOC, than between those in LONDON and YORKSHIRE. The immense greatness, indeed, of LONDON, under a government which admits not of discretionary power, renders the people factious, mutinous, seditious, and even perhaps rebellious. But to this evil the national debts themselves tend to provide a remedy. The first visible eruption, or even immediate danger, of public disorders must alarm all the stockholders, whose property is the most precarious of any; and will make them fly to the support of government, whether menaced by Jacobitish violence or democratical frenzy.

12. *Secondly,* Public stocks, being a kind of paper-credit, have all the disadvantages attending that species of money. They banish gold and silver from the most considerable commerce of the state, reduce them to common circulation, and by that means render all provisions and labour dearer than otherwise they would be.

13. *Thirdly,* The taxes, which are levied to pay the interests of these debts, are apt either to heighten the price of labour, or be an oppression on the poorer sort.

14. *Fourthly,* As foreigners possess a great share of our national funds, they render the public, in a manner, tributary to them, and may in time occasion the transport of our people and our industry.

15. *Fifthly,* The greater part of the public stock being always in the hands of idle people, who live on their revenue, our funds, in that view, give great encouragement to an useless and unactive life.

16. But though the injury, that arises to commerce and industry from our public funds, will appear, upon balancing the whole, not inconsiderable, it is trivial, in comparison of the prejudice that results to the state considered as a body politic, which must support itself in the society of nations, and have various transactions with other states in wars and negociations. The ill, there, is pure and unmixed, without any favourable circumstance to atone for it; and it is an ill too of a nature the highest and most important.

17. We have, indeed, been told, that the public is no weaker upon account of its debts; since they are mostly due among ourselves, and bring as much property to one as they take from another. It is like transferring money from the right hand to the left; which leaves the person neither richer nor poorer than before. Such loose reasonings and specious comparisons will always pass, where we judge not upon principles. I ask, Is it possible, in the nature of things, to overburthen a nation with taxes, even where the sovereign resides among them? The very doubt seems extravagant; since it is requisite, in every community, that there be a certain proportion observed between the laborious and the idle part of it. But if all our present taxes be mortgaged, must we not invent new ones? And may not this matter be carried to a length that is ruinous and destructive?

18. In every nation, there are always some methods of levying money more easy than others, agreeably to the way of living of the people, and the commodities they make use of. In GREAT BRITAIN, the excises upon malt and beer afford a large revenue; because the operations of malting and brewing are tedious, and are impossible to be concealed; and at the same time, these commodities are not so absolutely necessary to life, as that the raising of their price would very much affect the poorer sort. These taxes being all mortgaged, what difficulty to find new ones! what vexation and ruin of the poor!

19. Duties upon consumptions are more equal and easy than those upon possessions. What a loss to the public, that the former are all exhausted, and that we must have recourse to the more grievous method of levying taxes!

20. Were all the proprietors of land only stewards to the public, must not necessity force them to practise all the arts of oppression used by stewards; where the absence or negligence of the proprietor render them secure against enquiry?

21. It will scarcely be asserted, that no bounds ought ever to be set to national debts; and that the public would be no weaker, were twelve or

fifteen shillings in the pound, land-tax, mortgaged, with all the present customs and excises. There is something, therefore, in the case, beside the mere transferring of property from the one hand to another. In 500 years, the posterity of those now in the coaches, and of those upon the boxes, will probably have changed places, without affecting the public by these revolutions.

22. Suppose the public once fairly brought to that condition, to which it is hastening with such amazing rapidity; suppose the land to be taxed eighteen or nineteen shillings in the pound; for it can never bear the whole twenty; suppose all the excises and customs to be screwed up to the utmost which the nation can bear, without entirely losing its commerce and industry; and suppose that all those funds are mortgaged to perpetuity, and that the invention and wit of all our projectors can find no new imposition, which may serve as the foundation of a new loan; and let us consider the necessary consequences of this situation. Though the imperfect state of our political knowledge, and the narrow capacities of men, make it difficult to fortel the effects which will result from any untried measure, the seeds of ruin are here scattered with such profusion as not to escape the eye of the most careless observer.

23. In this unnatural state of society, the only persons, who possess any revenue beyond the immediate effects of their industry, are the stock-holders, who draw almost all the rent of the land and houses, besides the produce of all the customs and excises. These are men, who have no connexions with the state, who can enjoy their revenue in any part of the globe in which they chuse to reside, who will naturally bury themselves in the capital or in great cities, and who will sink into the lethargy of a stupid and pampered luxury, without spirit, ambition, or enjoyment. Adieu to all ideas of nobility, gentry, and family. The stocks can be transferred in an instant, and being in such a fluctuating state, will seldom be transmitted during three generations from father to son. Or were they to remain ever so long in one family, they convey no hereditary authority or credit to the possessor; and by this means, the several ranks of men, which form a kind of independent magistracy in a state, instituted by the hand of nature, are entirely lost; and every man in authority derives his influence from the commission alone of the sovereign. No expedient remains for preventing or suppressing insurrections, but mercenary armies: No expedient at all remains for resisting tyranny: Elections are swayed by bribery and corruption alone: And the middle power between king and people being totally removed, a grievous despotism must infallibly prevail. The landholders, despised for their poverty, and hated for their oppressions, will be utterly unable to make any opposition to it.

24. Though a resolution should be formed by the legislature never to impose any tax which hurts commerce and discourages industry, it will be impossible for men, in subjects of such extreme delicacy, to reason so justly as never to be mistaken, or amidst difficulties so urgent, never to be seduced from their resolution. The continual fluctuations in commerce require continual alterations in the nature of the taxes; which exposes the legislature every moment to the danger both of wilful and involuntary error. And any great blow given to trade, whether by injudicious taxes or by other accidents, throws the whole system of government into confusion.

25. But what expedient can the public now employ, even supposing trade to continue in the most flourishing condition, in order to support its foreign wars and enterprizes, and to defend its own honour and interests, or those of its allies? I do not ask how the public is to exert such a prodigious power as it has maintained during our late wars; where we have so much exceeded, not only our own natural strength, but even that of the greatest empires. This extravagance is the abuse complained of, as the source of all the dangers, to which we are at present exposed. But since we must still suppose great commerce and opulence to remain, even after every fund is mortgaged; these riches must be defended by proportional power; and whence is the public to derive the revenue which supports it? It must plainly be from a continual taxation of the annuitants, or, which is the same thing, from mortgaging anew, on every exigency, a certain part of their annuities; and thus making them contribute to their own defence, and to that of the nation. But the difficulties, attending this system of policy, will easily appear, whether we suppose the king to have become absolute master, or to be still controuled by national councils, in which the annuitants themselves must necessarily bear the principal sway.

26. If the prince has become absolute, as may naturally be expected from this situation of affairs, it is so easy for him to encrease his exactions upon the annuitants, which amount only to the retaining money in his own hands, that this species of property would soon lose all its credit, and the whole income of every individual in the state must lie entirely at the mercy of the sovereign: A degree of despotism, which no oriental monarchy has ever yet attained. If, on the contrary, the consent of the annuitants be requisite for every taxation, they will never be persuaded to contribute sufficiently even to the support of government; as the diminution of their revenue must in that case be very sensible, would not be disguised under the appearance of a branch of excise or customs, and would not be shared by any other order of the state, who are already supposed to be taxed to the utmost. There are instances, in some republics, of a hundredth penny, and sometimes of

the fiftieth, being given to the support of the state; but this is always an extraordinary exertion of power, and can never become the foundation of a constant national defence. We have always found, where a government has mortgaged all its revenues, that it necessarily sinks into a state of languor, inactivity, and impotence.

27.   Such are the inconveniencies, which may reasonably be foreseen, of this situation, to which GREAT BRITAIN is visibly tending. Not to mention, the numberless inconveniencies, which cannot be foreseen, and which must result from so monstrous a situation as that of making the public the chief or sole proprietor of land, besides investing it with every branch of customs and excise, which the fertile imagination of ministers and projectors have been able to invent.

28.   I must confess, that there is a strange supineness, from long custom, creeped into all ranks of men, with regard to public debts, not unlike what divines so vehemently complain of with regard to their religious doctrines. We all own, that the most sanguine imagination cannot hope, either that this or any future ministry will be possessed of such rigid and steady frugality, as to make a considerable progress in the payment of our debts; or that the situation of foreign affairs will, for any long time, allow them leisure and tranquillity for such an undertaking. *What then is to become of us?* Were we ever so good Christians, and ever so resigned to Providence; this, methinks, were a curious question, even considered as a speculative one, and what it might not be altogether impossible to form some conjectural solution of. The events here will depend little upon the contingencies of battles, negociations, intrigues, and factions. There seems to be a natural progress of things, which may guide our reasoning. As it would have required but a moderate share of prudence, when we first began this practice of mortgaging, to have foretold, from the nature of men and of ministers, that things would necessarily be carried to the length we see; so now, that they have at last happily reached it, it may not be difficult to guess at the consequences. It must, indeed, be one of these two events; either the nation must destroy public credit, or public credit will destroy the nation. It is impossible that they can both subsist, after the manner they have been hitherto managed, in this, as well as in some other countries.

29.   There was, indeed, a scheme for the payment of our debts, which was proposed by an excellent citizen, Mr. HUTCHINSON, above thirty years ago, and which was much approved of by some men of sense, but never was likely to take effect. He asserted, that there was a fallacy in imagining that the public owed this debt; for that really every individual owed a proportional share of it, and paid, in his taxes, a proportional share of the

interest, beside the expence of levying these taxes. Had we not better, then, says he, make a distribution of the debt among ourselves, and each of us contribute a sum suitable to his property, and by that means discharge at once all our funds and public mortgages? He seems not to have considered, that the laborious poor pay a considerable part of the taxes by their annual consumptions, though they could not advance, at once, a proportional part of the sum required. Not to mention, that property in money and stock in trade might easily be concealed or disguised; and that visible property in lands and houses would really at last answer for the whole: An inequality and oppression, which never would be submitted to. But though this project is not likely to take place; it is not altogether improbable, that, when the nation becomes heartily sick of their debts, and is cruelly oppressed by them, some daring projector may arise with visionary schemes for their discharge. And as public credit will begin, by that time, to be a little frail, the least touch will destroy it, as happened in FRANCE during the regency; and in this manner it will *die of the doctor*.

30.   But it is more probable, that the breach of national faith will be the necessary effect of wars, defeats, misfortunes, and public calamities, or even perhaps of victories and conquests. I must confess, when I see princes and states fighting and quarrelling, amidst their debts, funds, and public mortgages, it always brings to my mind a match of cudgel-playing[58] fought in a *China* shop. How can it be expected, that sovereigns will spare a species of property, which is pernicious to themselves and to the public, when they have so little compassion on lives and properties, that are useful to both? Let the time come (and surely it will come) when the new funds, created for the exigencies of the year, are not subscribed to, and raise not the money projected. Suppose, either that the cash of the nation is exhausted; or that our faith, which has hitherto been so ample, begins to fail us. Suppose, that, in this distress, the nation is threatened with an invasion; a rebellion is suspected or broken out at home; a squadron cannot be equipped for want of pay, victuals, or repairs; or even a foreign subsidy cannot be advanced. What must a prince or minister do in such an emergence? The right of self-preservation is unalienable in every individual, much more in every community. And the folly of our statesmen must then be greater than the folly of those who first contracted debt, or, what is more, than that of those who trusted, or continue to trust this security, if these statesmen have the means of safety in their hands, and do not employ them. The funds, created and mortgaged, will, by that time, bring in a large yearly revenue,

58. [Fighting with short heavy sticks or clubs.]

sufficient for the defence and security of the nation: Money is perhaps lying in the exchequer,[59] ready for the discharge of the quarterly interest: Necessity calls, fear urges, reason exhorts, compassion alone exclaims: The money will immediately be seized for the current service, under the most solemn protestations, perhaps, of being immediately replaced. But no more is requisite. The whole fabric, already tottering, falls to the ground, and buries thousands in its ruins. And this, I think, may be called the *natural death* of public credit: For to this period it tends as naturally as an animal body to its dissolution and destruction.

31. So great dupes are the generality of mankind, that, notwithstanding such a violent shock to public credit, as a voluntary bankruptcy in ENGLAND would occasion, it would not probably be long ere credit would again revive in as flourishing a condition as before. The present king of FRANCE, during the late war, borrowed money at lower interest than ever his grandfather did; and as low as the BRITISH parliament, comparing the natural rate of interest in both kingdoms. And though men are commonly more governed by what they have seen, than by what they foresee, with whatever certainty; yet promises, protestations, fair appearances, with the allurements of present interest, have such powerful influence as few are able to resist. Mankind are, in all ages, caught by the same baits: The same tricks, played over and over again, still trepan them. The heights of popularity and patriotism are still the beaten road to power and tyranny; flattery to treachery; standing armies to arbitrary government; and the glory of God to the temporal interest of the clergy. The fear of an everlasting destruction of credit, allowing it to be an evil, is a needless bugbear. A prudent man, in reality, would rather lend to the public immediately after we had taken a spunge to our debts, than at present; as much as an opulent knave, even though one could not force him to pay, is a preferable debtor to an honest bankrupt: For the former, in order to carry on business, may find it his interest to discharge his debts, where they are not exorbitant: The latter has it not in his power. The reasoning of TACITUS,[60] as it is eternally true, is very applicable to our present case. *Sed vulgus ad magnitudinem beneficiorum aderat: Stultissimus quisque pecuniis mercabatur: Apud sapientes cassa habebantur, quæ neque dari neque accipi, salva*

59. [The court to which are brought all the revenue belonging to the Crown.]

60. *Hist. lib.* iii. ["But the mob attended in delight on the great indulgences that he bestowed; the most foolish citizens bought them, while the wise regarded as worthless privileges which could neither be granted nor accepted if the state was to stand." Tacitus, *Histories,* translated by Clifford H. Moore, 55.]

republica, poterant. The public is a debtor, whom no man can oblige to pay. The only check which the creditors have upon her, is the interest of preserving credit; an interest, which may easily be overbalanced by a great debt, and by a difficult and extraordinary emergence, even supposing that credit irrecoverable. Not to mention, that a present necessity often forces states into measures, which are, strictly speaking, against their interest.

32.   These two events, supposed above, are calamitous, but not the most calamitous. Thousands are thereby sacrificed to the safety of millions. But we are not without danger, that the contrary event may take place, and that millions may be sacrificed for ever to the temporary safety of thousands.[61] Our popular government, perhaps, will render it difficult or dangerous for a minister to venture on so desperate an expedient, as that of a voluntary bankruptcy. And though the house of Lords be altogether composed of proprietors of land, and the house of Commons chiefly; and consequently neither of them can be supposed to have great property in the funds. Yet the connections of the members may be so great with the proprietors, as to render them more tenacious of public faith, than prudence, policy, or even justice, strictly speaking, requires. And perhaps too, our foreign enemies may be so politic as to discover, that our safety lies in despair, and may not, therefore, show the danger, open and barefaced, till it be inevitable. The balance of power in EUROPE, our grandfathers, our fathers, and we, have all deemed too unequal to be preserved without our attention and assistance. But our children, weary of the struggle, and fettered with incumbrances, may sit down secure, and see their neighbours oppressed and conquered; till, at last, they themselves and their creditors lie both at the mercy of the conqueror. And this may properly enough be denominated the *violent death* of our public credit.

---

61. I have heard it has been computed, that all the creditors of the public, natives and foreigners, amount only to 17,000. These make a figure at present on their income; but in case of a public bankruptcy, would, in an instant, become the lowest, as well as the most wretched of the people. The dignity and authority of the landed gentry and nobility is much better rooted; and would render the contention very unequal, if ever we come to that extremity. One would incline to assign to this event a very near period, such as half a century, had not our fathers' prophecies of this kind been already found fallacious, by the duration of our public credit so much beyond all reasonable expectation. When the astrologers in FRANCE were every year foretelling the death of HENRY IV. *These fellows,* says he, *must be right at last.* We shall, therefore, be more cautious than to assign any precise date; and shall content ourselves with pointing out the event in general.

33. These seem to be the events, which are not very remote, and which reason foresees as clearly almost as she can do any thing that lies in the womb of time. And though the ancients maintained, that in order to reach the gift of prophecy, a certain divine fury or madness was requisite, one may safely affirm, that, in order to deliver such prophecies as these, no more is necessary, than merely to be in one's senses, free from the influence of popular madness and delusion.

10.

Of the Original Contract

1.   As no party, in the present age, can well support itself, without a philosophical or speculative system of principles, annexed to its political or practical one; we accordingly find, that each of the factions, into which this nation is divided, has reared up a fabric of the former kind, in order to protect and cover that scheme of actions, which it pursues.[62] The people being commonly very rude builders, especially in this speculative way, and more especially still, when actuated by party-zeal; it is natural to imagine, that their workmanship must be a little unshapely, and discover evident marks of that violence and hurry, in which it was raised. The one party, by tracing up government to the DEITY, endeavour to render it so sacred and inviolate, that it must be little less than sacrilege, however tyrannical it may become, to touch or invade it, in the smallest article. The other party, by founding government altogether on the consent of the PEOPLE, suppose that there is a kind of *original contract,* by which the subjects have tacitly reserved the power of resisting their sovereign, whenever they find themselves aggrieved by that authority, with which they have, for certain purposes, voluntarily entrusted him. These are the speculative principles of the two parties; and these too are the practical consequences deduced from them.

2.   I shall venture to affirm, *That both these* systems *of speculative principles are just; though not in the sense, intended by the parties:* And, *That both the* schemes *of practical consequences are prudent; though not in the extremes, to which each party, in opposition to the other, has commonly endeavoured to carry them.*

3.   That the DEITY is the ultimate author of all government, will never be denied by any, who admit a general providence, and allow, that all events

---

62. [Hume sketches the differences between the Whigs and Tories in the essay "Of the Parties of Great Britain."]

in the universe are conducted by an uniform plan, and directed to wise purposes. As it is impossible for the human race to subsist, at least in any comfortable or secure state, without the protection of government; this institution must certainly have been intended by that beneficent Being, who means the good of all his creatures: And as it has universally, in fact, taken place, in all countries, and all ages; we may conclude, with still greater certainty, that it was intended by that omniscient Being, who can never be deceived by any event or operation. But since he gave rise to it, not by any particular or miraculous interposition, but by his concealed and universal efficacy; a sovereign cannot, properly speaking, be called his vice-gerent, in any other sense than every power or force, being derived from him, may be said to act by his commission. Whatever actually happens is comprehended in the general plan or intention of providence; nor has the greatest and most lawful prince any more reason, upon that account, to plead a peculiar sacredness or inviolable authority, than an inferior magistrate, or even an usurper, or even a robber and a pyrate. The same divine superintendant, who, for wise purposes, invested a TITUS or a TRAJAN with authority, did also, for purposes, no doubt, equally wise, though unknown, bestow power on a BORGIA or an ANGRIA. The same causes, which gave rise to the sovereign power in every state, established likewise every petty jurisdiction in it, and every limited authority. A constable, therefore, no less than a king, acts by a divine commission, and possesses an indefeasible right.

4.   When we consider how nearly equal all men are in their bodily force, and even in their mental powers and faculties, till cultivated by education; we must necessarily allow, that nothing but their own consent could, at first, associate them together, and subject them to any authority. The people, if we trace government to its first origin in the woods and desarts, are the source of all power and jurisdiction, and voluntarily, for the sake of peace and order, abandoned their native liberty, and received laws from their equal and companion. The conditions, upon which they were willing to submit, were either expressed, or were so clear and obvious, that it might well be esteemed superfluous to express them. If this, then, be meant by the *original contract,* it cannot be denied, that all government is, at first, founded on a contract, and that the most ancient rude combinations of mankind were formed chiefly by that principle. In vain, are we asked in what records this charter of our liberties is registered. It was not written on parchment, nor yet on leaves or barks of trees. It preceded the use of writing and all the other civilized arts of life. But we trace it plainly in the nature of man, and in the equality, or something approaching equality, which we find in all the individuals of that species. The force, which now

prevails, and which is founded on fleets and armies, is plainly political, and derived from authority, the effect of established government. A man's natural force consists only in the vigour of his limbs, and the firmness of his courage; which could never subject multitudes to the command of one. Nothing but their own consent, and their sense of the advantages resulting from peace and order, could have had that influence.

5.   Yet even this consent was long very imperfect, and could not be the basis of a regular administration. The chieftain, who had probably acquired his influence during the continuance of war, ruled more by persuasion than command; and till he could employ force to reduce the refractory and disobedient, the society could scarcely be said to have attained a state of civil government. No compact or agreement, it is evident, was expressly formed for general submission; an idea far beyond the comprehension of savages: Each exertion of authority in the chieftain must have been particular, and called forth by the present exigencies of the case: The sensible utility, resulting from his interposition, made these exertions become daily more frequent; and their frequency gradually produced an habitual, and, if you please to call it so, a voluntary, and therefore precarious, acquiescence in the people.

6.   But philosophers, who have embraced a party (if that be not a contradiction in terms) are not contented with these concessions. They assert, not only that government in its earliest infancy arose from consent or rather the voluntary acquiescence of the people; but also, that, even at present, when it has attained full maturity, it rests on no other foundation. They affirm, that all men are still born equal, and owe allegiance to no prince or government, unless bound by the obligation and sanction of a *promise*. And as no man, without some equivalent, would forego the advantages of his native liberty, and subject himself to the will of another; this promise is always understood to be conditional, and imposes on him no obligation, unless he meet with justice and protection from his sovereign. These advantages the sovereign promises him in return; and if he fail in the execution, he has broken, on his part, the articles of engagement, and has thereby freed his subject from all obligations to allegiance. Such, according to these philosophers, is the foundation of authority in every government; and such the right of resistance, possessed by every subject.

7.   But would these reasoners look abroad into the world, they would meet with nothing that, in the least, corresponds to their ideas, or can warrant so refined and philosophical a system. On the contrary, we find, every where, princes, who claim their subjects as their property, and assert their independent right of sovereignty, from conquest or succession. We find also, every

where, subjects, who acknowledge this right in their prince, and suppose themselves born under obligations of obedience to a certain sovereign, as much as under the ties of reverence and duty to certain parents. These connexions are always conceived to be equally independent of our consent, in PERSIA and CHINA; in FRANCE and SPAIN; and even in HOLLAND and ENGLAND, wherever the doctrines above-mentioned have not been carefully inculcated. Obedience or subjection becomes so familiar, that most men never make any enquiry about its origin or cause, more than about the principle of gravity, resistance, or the most universal laws of nature. Or if curiosity ever move them; as soon as they learn, that they themselves and their ancestors have, for several ages, or from time immemorial, been subject to such a form of government or such a family; they immediately acquiesce, and acknowledge their obligation to allegiance. Were you to preach, in most parts of the world, that political connexions are founded altogether on voluntary consent or a mutual promise, the magistrate would soon imprison you, as seditious, for loosening the ties of obedience; if your friends did not before shut you up as delirious, for advancing such absurdities. It is strange, that an act of the mind, which every individual is supposed to have formed, and after he came to the use of reason too, otherwise it could have no authority; that this act, I say, should be so much unknown to all of them, that, over the face of the whole earth, there scarcely remain any traces or memory of it.

8.   But the contract, on which government is founded, is said to be the *original contract;* and consequently may be supposed too old to fall under the knowledge of the present generation. If the agreement, by which savage men first associated and conjoined their force, be here meant, this is acknowledged to be real; but being so ancient, and being obliterated by a thousand changes of government and princes, it cannot now be supposed to retain any authority. If we would say any thing to the purpose, we must assert, that every particular government, which is lawful, and which imposes any duty of allegiance on the subject, was, at first, founded on consent and a voluntary compact. But besides that this supposes the consent of the fathers to bind the children, even to the most remote generations, (which republican writers will never allow) besides this, I say, it is not justified by history or experience, in any age or country of the world.

9.   Almost all the governments, which exist at present, or of which there remains any record in story, have been founded originally, either on usurpation or conquest, or both, without any pretence of a fair consent, or voluntary subjection of the people. When an artful and bold man is placed at the head of an army or faction, it is often easy for him, by employing,

sometimes violence, sometimes false pretences, to establish his dominion over a people a hundred times more numerous than his partizans. He allows no such open communication, that his enemies can know, with certainty, their number or force. He gives them no leisure to assemble together in a body to oppose him. Even all those, who are the instruments of his usurpation, may wish his fall; but their ignorance of each other's intention keeps them in awe, and is the sole cause of his security. By such arts as these, many governments have been established; and this is all the *original contract,* which they have to boast of.

10. The face of the earth is continually changing, by the encrease of small kingdoms into great empires, by the dissolution of great empires into smaller kingdoms, by the planting of colonies, by the migration of tribes. Is there any thing discoverable in all these events, but force and violence? Where is the mutual agreement or voluntary association so much talked of?

11. Even the smoothest way, by which a nation may receive a foreign master, by marriage or a will, is not extremely honourable for the people; but supposes them to be disposed of, like a dowry or a legacy, according to the pleasure or interest of their rulers.

12. But where no force interposes, and election takes place; what is this election so highly vaunted? It is either the combination of a few great men, who decide for the whole, and will allow of no opposition: Or it is the fury of a multitude, that follow a seditious ringleader, who is not known, perhaps, to a dozen among them, and who owes his advancement merely to his own impudence, or to the momentary caprice of his fellows.

13. Are these disorderly elections, which are rare too, of such mighty authority, as to be the only lawful foundation of all government and allegiance?

14. In reality, there is not a more terrible event, than a total dissolution of government, which gives liberty to the multitude, and makes the determination or choice of a new establishment depend upon a number, which nearly approaches to that of the body of the people: For it never comes entirely to the whole body of them. Every wise man, then, wishes to see, at the head of a powerful and obedient army, a general, who may speedily seize the prize, and give to the people a master, which they are so unfit to chuse for themselves. So little correspondent is fact and reality to those philosophical notions.

15. Let not the establishment at the *Revolution* deceive us, or make us so much in love with a philosophical origin to government, as to imagine all others monstrous and irregular. Even that event was far from corresponding to these refined ideas. It was only the succession, and that only in the regal

part of the government, which was then changed: And it was only the majority of seven hundred, who determined that change for near ten millions. I doubt not, indeed, but the bulk of those ten millions acquiesced willingly in the determination: But was the matter left, in the least, to their choice? Was it not justly supposed to be, from that moment, decided, and every man punished, who refused to submit to the new sovereign? How otherwise could the matter have ever been brought to any issue or conclusion?

16. The republic of ATHENS was, I believe, the most extensive democracy, that we read of in history: Yet if we make the requisite allowances for the women, the slaves, and the strangers, we shall find, that that establishment was not, at first, made, nor any law ever voted, by a tenth part of those who were bound to pay obedience to it: Not to mention the islands and foreign dominions, which the ATHENIANS claimed as theirs by right of conquest. And as it is well known, that popular assemblies in that city were always full of licence and disorder, notwithstanding the institutions and laws by which they were checked: How much more disorderly must they prove, where they form not the established constitution, but meet tumultuously on the dissolution of the ancient government, in order to give rise to a new one? How chimerical must it be to talk of a choice in such circumstances?

17. The ACHÆANS enjoyed the freest and most perfect democracy of all antiquity; yet they employed force to oblige some cities to enter into their league, as we learn from POLYBIUS.[63]

18. HARRY the IVth and HARRY the VIIth of ENGLAND, had really no title to the throne but a parliamentary election; yet they never would acknowledge it, lest they should thereby weaken their authority. Strange, if the only real foundation of all authority be consent and promise!

19. It is in vain to say, that all governments are or should be, at first, founded on popular consent, as much as the necessity of human affairs will admit. This favours entirely my pretension. I maintain, that human affairs will never admit of this consent; seldom of the appearance of it. But that conquest or usurpation, that is, in plain terms, force, by dissolving the ancient governments, is the origin of almost all the new ones, which were ever established in the world. And that in the few cases, where consent may seem to have taken place, it was commonly so irregular, so confined, or so much intermixed either with fraud or violence, that it cannot have any great authority.

20. My intention here is not to exclude the consent of the people from being one just foundation of government where it has place. It is surely

63. Lib. ii. cap. 38.

the best and most sacred of any. I only pretend, that it has very seldom had place in any degree, and never almost in its full extent. And that therefore some other foundation of government must also be admitted.

21. Were all men possessed of so inflexible a regard to justice, that, of themselves, they would totally abstain from the properties of others; they had for ever remained in a state of absolute liberty, without subjection to any magistrate or political society: But this is a state of perfection, of which human nature is justly deemed incapable. Again; were all men possessed of so perfect an understanding, as always to know their own interests, no form of government had ever been submitted to, but what was established on consent, and was fully canvassed by every member of the society: But this state of perfection is likewise much superior to human nature. Reason, history, and experience shew us, that all political societies have had an origin much less accurate and regular; and were one to choose a period of time, when the people's consent was the least regarded in public transactions, it would be precisely on the establishment of a new government. In a settled constitution, their inclinations are often consulted; but during the fury of revolutions, conquests, and public convulsions, military force or political craft usually decides the controversy.

22. When a new government is established, by whatever means, the people are commonly dissatisfied with it, and pay obedience more from fear and necessity, than from any idea of allegiance or of moral obligation. The prince is watchful and jealous, and must carefully guard against every beginning or appearance of insurrection. Time, by degrees, removes all these difficulties, and accustoms the nation to regard, as their lawful or native princes, that family, which, at first, they considered as usurpers or foreign conquerors. In order to found this opinion, they have no recourse to any notion of voluntary consent or promise, which, they know, never was, in this case, either expected or demanded. The original establishment was formed by violence, and submitted to from necessity. The subsequent administration is also supported by power, and acquiesced in by the people, not as a matter of choice, but of obligation. They imagine not, that their consent gives their prince a title: But they willingly consent, because they think, that, from long possession, he has acquired a title, independent of their choice or inclination.

23. Should it be said, that, by living under the dominion of a prince, which one might leave, every individual has given a *tacit* consent to his authority, and promised him obedience; it may be answered, that such an implied consent can only have place, where a man imagines, that the matter depends on his choice. But where he thinks (as all mankind do who are born under

established governments) that by his birth he owes allegiance to a certain prince or certain form of government; it would be absurd to infer a consent or choice, which he expressly, in this case, renounces and disclaims.

24. Can we seriously say, that a poor peasant or artizan has a free choice to leave his country, when he knows no foreign language or manners, and lives from day to day, by the small wages which he acquires? We may as well assert, that a man, by remaining in a vessel, freely consents to the dominion of the master; though he was carried on board while asleep, and must leap into the ocean, and perish, the moment he leaves her.

25. What if the prince forbid his subjects to quit his dominions; as in TIBERIUS'S time, it was regarded as a crime in a ROMAN knight that he had attempted to fly to the PARTHIANS, in order to escape the tyranny of that emperor?[64] Or as the ancient MUSCOVITES prohibited all travelling under pain of death? And did a prince observe, that many of his subjects were seized with the frenzy of migrating to foreign countries, he would doubtless, with great reason and justice, restrain them, in order to prevent the depopulation of his own kingdom. Would he forfeit the allegiance of all his subjects, by so wise and reasonable a law? Yet the freedom of their choice is surely, in that case, ravished from them.

26. A company of men, who should leave their native country, in order to people some uninhabited region, might dream of recovering their native freedom; but they would soon find, that their prince still laid claim to them, and called them his subjects, even in their new settlement. And in this he would but act conformably to the common ideas of mankind.

27. The truest *tacit* consent of this kind, that is ever observed, is when a foreigner settles in any country, and is beforehand acquainted with the prince, and government, and laws, to which he must submit: Yet is his allegiance, though more voluntary, much less expected or depended on, than that of a natural born subject. On the contrary, his native prince still asserts a claim to him. And if he punish not the renegade, when he seizes him in war with his new prince's commission; this clemency is not founded on the municipal law, which in all countries condemns the prisoner; but on the consent of princes, who have agreed to this indulgence, in order to prevent reprisals.

28. Did one generation of men go off the stage at once, and another succeed, as is the case with silk-worms and butterflies, the new race, if they had sense enough to choose their government, which surely is never the case with men, might voluntarily, and by general consent, establish their

---

64. TACIT. Ann. vi. cap. 14.

own form of civil polity, without any regard to the laws or precedents, which prevailed among their ancestors. But as human society is in perpetual flux, one man every hour going out of the world, another coming into it, it is necessary, in order to preserve stability in government, that the new brood should conform themselves to the established constitution, and nearly follow the path which their fathers, treading in the footsteps of theirs, had marked out to them. Some innovations must necessarily have place in every human institution, and it is happy where the enlightened genius of the age give these a direction to the side of reason, liberty, and justice: but violent innovations no individual is entitled to make: they are even dangerous to be attempted by the legislature: more ill than good is ever to be expected from them: and if history affords examples to the contrary, they are not to be drawn into precedent, and are only to be regarded as proofs, that the science of politics affords few rules, which will not admit of some exception, and which may not sometimes be controuled by fortune and accident. The violent innovations in the reign of HENRY VIII. proceeded from an imperious monarch, seconded by the appearance of legislative authority: Those in the reign of CHARLES I. were derived from faction and fanaticism; and both of them have proved happy in the issue: But even the former were long the source of many disorders, and still more dangers; and if the measures of allegiance were to be taken from the latter, a total anarchy must have place in human society, and a final period at once be put to every government.

29. Suppose, that an usurper, after having banished his lawful prince and royal family, should establish his dominion for ten or a dozen years in any country, and should preserve so exact a discipline in his troops, and so regular a disposition in his garrisons, that no insurrection had ever been raised, or even murmur heard, against his administration: Can it be asserted, that the people, who in their hearts abhor his treason, have tacitly consented to his authority, and promised him allegiance, merely because, from necessity, they live under his dominion? Suppose again their native prince restored, by means of an army, which he levies in foreign countries: They receive him with joy and exultation, and shew plainly with what reluctance they had submitted to any other yoke. I may now ask, upon what foundation the prince's title stands? Not on popular consent surely: For though the people willingly acquiesce in his authority, they never imagine, that their consent made him sovereign. They consent; because they apprehend him to be already, by birth, their lawful sovereign. And as to that tacit consent, which may now be inferred from their living under his dominion, this is no more than what they formerly gave to the tyrant and usurper.

30. When we assert, that all lawful government arises from the consent of the people, we certainly do them a great deal more honour than they deserve, or even expect and desire from us. After the ROMAN dominions became too unwieldly for the republic to govern them, the people, over the whole known world, were extremely grateful to AUGUSTUS for that authority, which, by violence, he had established over them; and they shewed an equal disposition to submit to the successor, whom he left them, by his last will and testament. It was afterwards their misfortune, that there never was, in one family, any long regular succession; but that their line of princes was continually broken, either by private assassinations or public rebellions. The *prætorian* bands, on the failure of every family, set up one emperor; the legions in the East a second; those in GERMANY, perhaps, a third: And the sword alone could decide the controversy. The condition of the people, in that mighty monarchy, was to be lamented, not because the choice of the emperor was never left to them; for that was impracticable: But because they never fell under any succession of masters, who might regularly follow each other. As to the violence and wars and bloodshed, occasioned by every new settlement; these were not blameable, because they were inevitable.

31. The house of LANCASTER ruled in this island about sixty years; yet the partizans of the white rose seemed daily to multiply in ENGLAND. The present establishment has taken place during a still longer period. Have all views of right in another family been utterly extinguished; even though scarce any man now alive had arrived at years of discretion, when it was expelled, or could have consented to its dominion, or have promised it allegiance? A sufficient indication surely of the general sentiment of mankind on this head. For we blame not the partizans of the abdicated family, merely on account of the long time, during which they have preserved their imaginary loyalty. We blame them for adhering to a family, which, we affirm, has been justly expelled, and which, from the moment the new settlement took place, had forfeited all title to authority.

32. But would we have a more regular, at least a more philosophical, refutation of this principle of an original contract or popular consent; perhaps, the following observations may suffice.

33. All *moral* duties may be divided into two kinds.[65] The *first* are those, to which men are impelled by a natural instinct or immediate propensity, which operates on them, independent of all ideas of obligation, and of all

---

65. [See EPM, appendix 3, for a full discussion of this division of moral duties.]

views, either to public or private utility. Of this nature are, love of children, gratitude to benefactors, pity to the unfortunate. When we reflect on the advantage, which results to society from such humane instincts, we pay them the just tribute of moral approbation and esteem: But the person, actuated by them, feels their power and influence, antecedent to any such reflection.

34. The *second* kind of moral duties are such as are not supported by any original instinct of nature, but are performed entirely from a sense of obligation, when we consider the necessities of human society, and the impossibility of supporting it, if these duties were neglected. It is thus *justice* or a regard to the property of others, *fidelity* or the observance of promises, become obligatory, and acquire an authority over mankind. For as it is evident, that every man loves himself better than any other person, he is naturally impelled to extend his acquisitions as much as possible; and nothing can restrain him in this propensity, but reflection and experience, by which he learns the pernicious effects of that licence, and the total dissolution of society which must ensue from it. His original inclination, therefore, or instinct, is here checked and restrained by a subsequent judgment or observation.

35. The case is precisely the same with the political or civil duty of *allegiance,* as with the natural duties of justice and fidelity. Our primary instincts lead us, either to indulge ourselves in unlimited freedom, or to seek dominion over others: And it is reflection only, which engages us to sacrifice such strong passions to the interests of peace and public order. A small degree of experience and observation suffices to teach us, that society cannot possibly be maintained without the authority of magistrates, and that this authority must soon fall into contempt, where exact obedience is not payed to it. The observation of these general and obvious interests is the source of all allegiance, and of that moral obligation, which we attribute to it.

36. What necessity, therefore, is there to found the duty of *allegiance* or obedience to magistrates on that of *fidelity* or a regard to promises, and to suppose, that it is the consent of each individual, which subjects him to government; when it appears, that both allegiance and fidelity stand precisely on the same foundation, and are both submitted to by mankind, on account of the apparent interests and necessities of human society? We are bound to obey our sovereign, it is said; because we have given a tacit promise to that purpose. But why are we bound to observe our promise? It must here be asserted, that the commerce and intercourse of mankind, which are of such mighty advantage, can have no security where men pay no regard

to their engagements. In like manner, may it be said, that men could not live at all in society, at least in a civilized society, without laws and magistrates and judges, to prevent the encroachments of the strong upon the weak, of the violent upon the just and equitable. The obligation to allegiance being of like force and authority with the obligation to fidelity, we gain nothing by resolving the one into the other. The general interests or necessities of society are sufficient to establish both.

37. If the reason be asked of that obedience, which we are bound to pay to government, I readily answer, *because society could not otherwise subsist:* And this answer is clear and intelligible to all mankind. Your answer is, *because we should keep our word.* But besides, that no body, till trained in a philosophical system, can either comprehend or relish this answer: Besides this, I say, you find yourself embarrassed, when it is asked, *why we are bound to keep our word?* Nor can you give any answer, but what would, immediately, without any circuit, have accounted for our obligation to allegiance.

38. But *to whom is allegiance due? And who is our lawful sovereign?* This question is often the most difficult of any, and liable to infinite discussions. When people are so happy, that they can answer, *Our present sovereign, who inherits, in a direct line, from ancestors, that have governed us for many ages;* this answer admits of no reply; even though historians, in tracing up to the remotest antiquity, the origin of that royal family, may find, as commonly happens, that its first authority was derived from usurpation and violence. It is confessed, that private justice, or the abstinence from the properties of others, is a most cardinal virtue: Yet reason tells us, that there is no property in durable objects, such as lands or houses, when carefully examined in passing from hand to hand, but must, in some period, have been founded on fraud and injustice. The necessities of human society, neither in private nor public life, will allow of such an accurate enquiry: And there is no virtue or moral duty, but what may, with facility, be refined away, if we indulge a false philosophy, in sifting and scrutinizing it, by every captious rule of logic, in every light or position, in which it may be placed.

39. The questions with regard to private property have filled infinite volumes of law and philosophy, if in both we add the commentators to the original text; and in the end, we may safely pronounce, that many of the rules, there established, are uncertain, ambiguous, and arbitrary. The like opinion may be formed with regard to the succession and rights of princes and forms of government. Several cases, no doubt, occur, especially in the infancy of any constitution, which admit of no determination from the

laws of justice and equity: And our historian RAPIN pretends, that the controversy between EDWARD the Third and PHILIP DE VALOIS was of this nature, and could be decided only by an appeal to heaven, that is, by war and violence.

40. Who shall tell me, whether GERMANICUS or DRUSUS ought to have succeeded to TIBERIUS, had he died, while they were both alive, without naming any of them for his successor? Ought the right of adoption to be received as equivalent to that of blood, in a nation, where it had the same effect in private families, and had already, in two instances, taken place in the public? Ought GERMANICUS to be esteemed the elder son because he was born before DRUSUS; or the younger, because he was adopted after the birth of his brother? Ought the right of the elder to be regarded in a nation, where he had no advantage in the succession of private families? Ought the ROMAN empire at that time to be deemed hereditary, because of two examples; or ought it, even so early, to be regarded as belonging to the stronger or to the present possessor, as being founded on so recent an usurpation?

41. COMMODUS mounted the throne after a pretty long succession of excellent emperors, who had acquired their title, not by birth, or public election, but by the fictitious rite of adoption. That bloody debauchee being murdered by a conspiracy suddenly formed between his wench and her gallant, who happened at that time to be *Prætorian Præfect;* these immediately deliberated about choosing a master to human kind, to speak in the style of those ages; and they cast their eyes on PERTINAX. Before the tyrant's death was known, the *Præfect* went secretly to that senator, who, on the appearance of the soldiers, imagined that his execution had been ordered by COMMODUS. He was immediately saluted emperor by the officer and his attendants; chearfully proclaimed by the populace; unwillingly submitted to by the guards; formally recognized by the senate; and passively received by the provinces and armies of the empire.

42. The discontent of the *Prætorian* bands broke out in a sudden sedition, which occasioned the murder of that excellent prince: And the world being now without a master and without government, the guards thought proper to set the empire formally to sale. JULIAN, the purchaser, was proclaimed by the soldiers, recognized by the senate, and submitted to by the people; and must also have been submitted to by the provinces, had not the envy of the legions begotten opposition and resistance. PESCENNIUS NIGER in SYRIA elected himself emperor, gained the tumultuary consent of his army, and was attended with the secret good-will of the senate and people of ROME. ALBINUS in BRITAIN found an equal right to set up his claim; but SEVERUS, who governed PANNONIA, prevailed in the end above

both of them. That able politician and warrior, finding his own birth and dignity too much inferior to the imperial crown, professed, at first, an intention only of revenging the death of PERTINAX. He marched as general into ITALY; defeated JULIAN; and without our being able to fix any precise commencement even of the soldiers' consent, he was from necessity acknowledged emperor by the senate and people; and fully established in his violent authority by subduing NIGER and ALBINUS.[66]

43. *Inter hæc Gordianus CÆSAR* (says CAPITOLINUS, speaking of another period) *sublatus a militibus.* Imperator *est appellatus, quia non erat alius in præsenti.*[67] It is to be remarked, that GORDIAN was a boy of fourteen years of age.

44. Frequent instances of a like nature occur in the history of the emperors; in that of ALEXANDER'S successors; and of many other countries: Nor can any thing be more unhappy than a despotic government of this kind; where the succession is disjointed and irregular, and must be determined, on every vacancy, by force or election. In a free government, the matter is often unavoidable, and is also much less dangerous. The interests of liberty may there frequently lead the people, in their own defence, to alter the succession of the crown. And the constitution, being compounded of parts, may still maintain a sufficient stability, by resting on the aristocratical or democratical members, though the monarchical be altered, from time to time, in order to accommodate it to the former.

45. In an absolute government, when there is no legal prince, who has a title to the throne, it may safely be determined to belong to the first occupant. Instances of this kind are but too frequent, especially in the eastern monarchies. When any race of princes expires, the will or destination of the last sovereign will be regarded as a title. Thus the edict of LEWIS the XIVth, who called the bastard princes to the succession in case of the failure of all the legitimate princes, would, in such an event, have some authority.[68] Thus the will of CHARLES the Second disposed of the whole SPANISH

---

66. HERODIAN, lib. ii.

67. ["In the meantime Gordian Caesar was lifted up by the soldiers and hailed emperor (that is, Augustus), there being no one else at hand." Julius Capitolinus, *Maximus and Balbinus,* §14, in *Scriptores Historiae Augustae,* translated by David Magie.]

68. It is remarkable, that, in the remonstrance of the duke of BOURBON and the legitimate princes, against this destination of LOUIS the XIVth, the doctrine of the *original contract* is insisted on, even in that absolute government. The FRENCH nation, say they, chusing HUGH CAPET and his posterity to rule over them and their posterity, where the former line fails, there is a tacit right reserved to choose a new

monarchy. The cession of the ancient proprietor, especially when joined to conquest, is likewise deemed a good title. The general obligation, which binds us to government, is the interest and necessities of society; and this obligation is very strong. The determination of it to this or that particular prince or form of government is frequently more uncertain and dubious. Present possession has considerable authority in these cases, and greater than in private property; because of the disorders which attend all revolutions and changes of government.

46.   We shall only observe, before we conclude, that, though an appeal to general opinion may justly, in the speculative sciences of metaphysics, natural philosophy, or astronomy, be deemed unfair and inconclusive, yet in all questions with regard to morals, as well as criticism, there is really no other standard, by which any controversy can ever be decided. And nothing is a clearer proof, that a theory of this kind is erroneous, than to find, that it leads to paradoxes, repugnant to the common sentiments of mankind, and to the practice and opinion of all nations and all ages. The doctrine, which founds all lawful government on an *original contract,* or consent of the people, is plainly of this kind; nor has the most noted of its partizans, in prosecution of it, scrupled to affirm, *that absolute monarchy is inconsistent with civil society, and so can be no form of civil government at all;*[69] and *that the supreme power in a state cannot take from any man, by taxes and impositions, any part of his property, without his own consent or that of his representatives.*[70] What authority any moral reasoning can have, which leads into opinions so wide of the general practice of mankind, in every place but this single kingdom, it is easy to determine.

47.   The only passage I meet with in antiquity, where the obligation of obedience to government is ascribed to a promise, is in PLATO's *Crito:* where

---

royal family; and this right is invaded by calling the bastard princes to the throne, without the consent of the nation. But the Comte de BOULAINVILLIERS, who wrote in defence of the bastard princes, ridicules this notion of an original contract, especially when applied to HUGH CAPET; who mounted the throne, says he, by the same arts, which have ever been employed by all conquerors and usurpers. He got his title, indeed, recognized by the states after he had put himself in possession: But is this a choice or contract? The Comte de BOULAINVILLIERS, we may observe, was a noted republican; but being a man of learning, and very conversant in history, he knew that the people were never almost consulted in these revolutions and new establishments, and that time alone bestowed right and authority on what was commonly at first founded on force and violence. See *Etat de la France,*Vol. III. [Henri de Boulainvilliers, *État de la France (State of France)*, 3 vols. (London, 1727).]

69. See LOCKE on Government, chap. vii. § 90.

70. Id. chap. xi. § 138, 139, 140.

SOCRATES refuses to escape from prison, because he had tacitly promised to obey the laws. Thus he builds a *tory* consequence of passive obedience, on a *whig* foundation of the original contract.

48. New discoveries are not to be expected in these matters. If scarce any man, till very lately, ever imagined that government was founded on compact, it is certain, that it cannot, in general, have any such foundation.

49. The crime of rebellion among the ancients was commonly expressed by the terms νεωτερίζειν, *novas res moliri.*[71]

---

71. [Both of these terms mean to make innovations, especially political changes.]

Of Passive Obedience

1. In the former essay, we endeavoured to refute the *speculative* systems of politics advanced in this nation; as well the religious system of the one party, as the philosophical of the other. We come now to examine the *practical* consequences, deduced by each party, with regard to the measures of submission due to sovereigns.

2. As the obligation to justice is founded entirely on the interests of society, which require mutual abstinence from property, in order to preserve peace among mankind; it is evident, that, when the execution of justice would be attended with very pernicious consequences, that virtue must be suspended, and give place to public utility, in such extraordinary and such pressing emergencies. The maxim, *fiat Justitia & ruat Cœlum,* let justice be performed, though the universe be destroyed, is apparently false, and by sacrificing the end to the means, shews a preposterous idea of the subordination of duties. What governor of a town makes any scruple of burning the suburbs, when they facilitate the approaches of the enemy? Or what general abstains from plundering a neutral country, when the necessities of war require it, and he cannot otherwise subsist his army? The case is the same with the duty of allegiance; and common sense teaches us, that, as government binds us to obedience only on account of its tendency to public utility, that duty must always, in extraordinary cases, when public ruin would evidently attend obedience, yield to the primary and original obligation. *Salus populi suprema Lex,* the safety of the people is the supreme law. This maxim is agreeable to the sentiments of mankind in all ages: Nor is any one, when he reads of the insurrections against Nero or Philip the Second, so infatuated with party-systems, as not to wish success to the enterprize, and praise the undertakers. Even our high monarchical party, in spite of their sublime theory, are forced, in such cases, to judge, and feel, and approve, in conformity to the rest of mankind.

3.   Resistance, therefore, being admitted in extraordinary emergencies, the question can only be among good reasoners, with regard to the degree of necessity, which can justify resistance, and render it lawful or commendable. And here I must confess, that I shall always incline to their side, who draw the bond of allegiance very close, and consider an infringement of it, as the last refuge in desperate cases, when the public is in the highest danger, from violence and tyranny. For besides the mischiefs of a civil war, which commonly attends insurrection; it is certain, that, where a disposition to rebellion appears among any people, it is one chief cause of tyranny in the rulers, and forces them into many violent measures which they never would have embraced, had every one been inclined to submission and obedience. Thus the *tyrannicide* or assassination, approved of by ancient maxims, instead of keeping tyrants and usurpers in awe, made them ten times more fierce and unrelenting; and is now justly, upon that account, abolished by the laws of nations, and universally condemned as a base and treacherous method of bringing to justice these disturbers of society.

4.   Besides we must consider, that, as obedience is our duty in the common course of things, it ought chiefly to be inculcated; nor can any thing be more preposterous than an anxious care and solicitude in stating all the cases, in which resistance may be allowed. In like manner, though a philosopher reasonably acknowledges, in the course of an argument, that the rules of justice may be dispensed with in cases of urgent necessity; what should we think of a preacher or casuist, who should make it his chief study to find out such cases, and enforce them with all the vehemence of argument and eloquence? Would he not be better employed in inculcating the general doctrine, than in displaying the particular exceptions, which we are, perhaps, but too much inclined, of ourselves, to embrace and to extend?

5.   There are, however, two reasons, which may be pleaded in defence of that party among us, who have, with so much industry, propagated the maxims of resistance; maxims, which, it must be confessed, are, in general, so pernicious, and so destructive of civil society. The *first* is, that their antagonists carrying the doctrine of obedience to such an extravagant height, as not only never to mention the exceptions in extraordinary cases (which might, perhaps, be excusable) but even positively to exclude them; it became necessary to insist on these exceptions, and defend the rights of injured truth and liberty. The *second,* and, perhaps, better reason, is founded on the nature of the BRITISH constitution and form of government.

6.   It is almost peculiar to our constitution to establish a first magistrate with such high pre-eminence and dignity, that, though limited by the laws, he is, in a manner, so far as regards his own person, above the laws, and can neither be questioned nor punished for any injury or wrong, which may be committed by him. His ministers alone, or those who act by his commission, are obnoxious to justice; and while the prince is thus allured, by the prospect of personal safety, to give the laws their free course, an equal security is, in effect, obtained by the punishment of lesser offenders, and at the same time a civil war is avoided, which would be the infallible consequence, were an attack, at every turn, made directly upon the sovereign. But though the constitution pays this salutary compliment to the prince, it can never reasonably be understood, by that maxim, to have determined its own destruction, or to have established a tame submission, where he protects his ministers, perseveres in injustice, and usurps the whole power of the commonwealth. This case, indeed, is never expressly put by the laws; because it is impossible for them, in their ordinary course, to provide a remedy for it, or establish any magistrate, with superior authority, to chastise the exorbitancies of the prince. But as a right without a remedy would be an absurdity; the remedy in this case, is the extraordinary one of resistance, when affairs come to that extremity, that the constitution can be defended by it alone. Resistance therefore must, of course, become more frequent in the BRITISH government, than in others, which are simpler, and consist of fewer parts and movements. Where the king is an absolute sovereign, he has little temptation to commit such enormous tyranny as may justly provoke rebellion: But where he is limited, his imprudent ambition, without any great vices, may run him into that perilous situation. This is frequently supposed to have been the case with CHARLES the First; and if we may now speak truth, after animosities are ceased, this was also the case with JAMES the Second. These were harmless, if not, in their private character, good men; but mistaking the nature of our constitution, and engrossing the whole legislative power, it became necessary to oppose them with some vehemence; and even to deprive the latter formally of that authority, which he had used with such imprudence and indiscretion.

12.

Idea of a Perfect Commonwealth

1.   IT is not with forms of government, as with other artificial contrivances; where an old engine may be rejected, if we can discover another more accurate and commodious, or where trials may safely be made, even though the success be doubtful. An established government has an infinite advantage, by that very circumstance of its being established; the bulk of mankind being governed by authority, not reason, and never attributing authority to any thing that has not the recommendation of antiquity. To tamper, therefore, in this affair, or try experiments merely upon the credit of supposed argument and philosophy, can never be the part of a wise magistrate, who will bear a reverence to what carries the marks of age; and though he may attempt some improvements for the public good, yet will he adjust his innovations, as much as possible, to the ancient fabric, and preserve entire the chief pillars and supports of the constitution.

2.   The mathematicians in EUROPE have been much divided concerning that figure of a ship, which is the most commodious for sailing; and HUYGENS, who at last determined the controversy, is justly thought to have obliged the learned, as well as commercial world; though COLUMBUS had sailed to AMERICA, and Sir FRANCIS DRAKE made the tour of the world, without any such discovery. As one form of government must be allowed more perfect than another, independent of the manners and humours of particular men; why may we not enquire what is the most perfect of all, though the common botched and inaccurate governments seem to serve the purposes of society, and though it be not so easy to establish a new system of government, as to build a vessel upon a new construction? The subject is surely the most worthy curiosity of any the wit of man can possibly devise. And who knows, if this controversy were fixed by the universal consent of the wise and learned, but, in some future age, an opportunity might be afforded of reducing the theory to practice, either by a dissolution of some old government, or by the combination of men to form a new one,

in some distant part of the world? In all cases, it must be advantageous to know what is most perfect in the kind, that we may be able to bring any real constitution or form of government as near it as possible, by such gentle alterations and innovations as may not give too great disturbance to society.

3.   All I pretend to in the present essay is to revive this subject of speculation; and therefore I shall deliver my sentiments in as few words as possible. A long dissertation on that head would not, I apprehend, be very acceptable to the public, who will be apt to regard such disquisitions both as useless and chimerical.

4.   All plans of government, which suppose great reformation in the manners of mankind, are plainly imaginary. Of this nature, are the *Republic* of PLATO, and the *Utopia* of Sir THOMAS MORE. The OCEANA is the only valuable model of a commonwealth, that has yet been offered to the public.

5.   The chief defects of the OCEANA seem to be these. *First,* Its rotation is inconvenient, by throwing men, of whatever abilities, by intervals, out of public employments. *Secondly,* Its *Agrarian* is impracticable. Men will soon learn the art, which was practised in ancient ROME, of concealing their possessions under other people's name; till at last, the abuse will become so common, that they will throw off even the appearance of restraint. *Thirdly,* The OCEANA provides not a sufficient security for liberty, or the redress of grievances. The senate must propose, and the people consent; by which means, the senate have not only a negative upon the people, but, what is of much greater consequence, their negative goes before the votes of the people. Were the King's negative of the same nature in the ENGLISH constitution, and could he prevent any bill from coming into parliament, he would be an absolute monarch. As his negative follows the votes of the houses, it is of little consequence: Such a difference is there in the manner of placing the same thing. When a popular bill has been debated in parliament, is brought to maturity, all its conveniencies and inconveniencies, weighed and balanced; if afterwards it be presented for the royal assent, few princes will venture to reject the unanimous desire of the people. But could the King crush a disagreeable bill in embryo (as was the case, for some time, in the SCOTTISH parliament, by means of the lords of the articles, the BRITISH government would have no balance, nor would grievances ever be redressed: And it is certain, that exorbitant power proceeds not, in any government, from new laws, so much as from neglecting to remedy the abuses, which frequently rise from the old ones. A government, says MACHIAVEL, must often be brought back to its original principles. It appears then, that, in the OCEANA, the whole legislature may be said to rest

in the senate; which HARRINGTON would own to be an inconvenient form of government, especially after the *Agrarian* is abolished.

6.   Here is a form of government, to which I cannot, in theory, discover any considerable objection.

7.   Let GREAT BRITAIN and IRELAND, or any territory of equal extent, be divided into 100 counties, and each county into 100 parishes, making in all 10,000. If the country, proposed to be erected into a commonwealth be of more narrow extent, we may diminish the number of counties; but never bring them below thirty. If it be of greater extent, it were better to enlarge the parishes, or throw more parishes into a county, than encrease the number of counties.

8.   Let all the freeholders of twenty pounds a-year in the county, and all the householders worth 500 pounds in the town parishes, meet annually in the parish church, and chuse, by ballot, some freeholder of the county for their member, whom we shall call the county *representative.*

9.   Let the 100 county representatives, two days after their election, meet in the county town, and chuse by ballot, from their own body, ten county *magistrates,* and one *senator.* There are, therefore, in the whole commonwealth, 100 senators, 1100 county magistrates, and 10,000 county representatives. For we shall bestow on all senators the authority of county magistrates, and on all county magistrates the authority of county representatives.

10.   Let the senators meet in the capital, and be endowed with the whole executive power of the commonwealth; the power of peace and war, of giving orders to generals, admirals, and ambassadors, and, in short, all the prerogatives of a BRITISH King, except his negative.

11.   Let the county representatives meet in their particular counties, and possess the whole legislative power of the commonwealth; the greater number of counties deciding the question; and where these are equal, let the senate have the casting vote.

12.   Every new law must first be debated in the senate; and though rejected by it, if ten senators insist and protest, it must be sent down to the counties. The senate, if they please, may join to the copy of the law their reasons for receiving or rejecting it.

13.   Because it would be troublesome to assemble all the county representatives for every trivial law, that may be requisite, the senate have their choice of sending down the law either to the county magistrates or county representatives.

14.   The magistrates, though the law be referred to them, may, if they please, call the representatives, and submit the affair to their determination.

15. Whether the law be referred by the senate to the county magistrates or representatives, a copy of it, and of the senate's reasons, must be sent to every representative eight days before the day appointed for the assembling, in order to deliberate concerning it. And though the determination be, by the senate, referred to the magistrates, if five representatives of the county order the magistrates to assemble the whole court of representatives, and submit the affair to their determination, they must obey.

16. Either the county magistrates or representatives may give, to the senator of the county, the copy of a law to be proposed to the senate; and if five counties concur in the same order, the law, though refused by the senate, must come either to the county magistrates or representatives, as is contained in the order of the five counties.

17. Any twenty counties, by a vote either of their magistrates or representatives, may throw any man out of all public offices for a year. Thirty counties for three years.

18. The senate has a power of throwing out any member or number of members of its own body, not to be re-elected for that year. The senate cannot throw out twice in a year the senator of the same county.

19. The power of the old senate continues for three weeks after the annual election of the county representatives. Then all the new senators are shut up in a conclave, like the cardinals; and by an intricate ballot, such as that of VENICE or MALTA, they chuse the following magistrates; a protector, who represents the dignity of the commonwealth, and presides in the senate; two secretaries of state; these six councils, a council of state, a council of religion and learning, a council of trade, a council of laws, a council of war, a council of the admiralty, each council consisting of five persons; together with six commissioners of the treasury and a first commissioner. All these must be senators. The senate also names all the ambassadors to foreign courts, who may either be senators or not.

20. The senate may continue any or all of these, but must re-elect them every year.

21. The protector and two secretaries have session and suffrage in the council of state. The business of that council is all foreign politics. The council of state has session and suffrage in all the other councils.

22. The council of religion and learning inspects the universities and clergy. That of trade inspects every thing that may affect commerce. That of laws inspects all the abuses of law by the inferior magistrates, and examines what improvements may be made of the municipal law. That of war inspects the militia and its discipline, magazines, stores, &c. and when the republic is in war, examines into the proper orders for generals. The coun-

cil of admiralty has the same power with regard to the navy, together with the nomination of the captains and all inferior officers.

23. None of these councils can give orders themselves, except where they receive such powers from the senate. In other cases, they must communicate every thing to the senate.

24. When the senate is under adjournment, any of the councils may assemble it before the day appointed for its meeting.

25. Besides these councils or courts, there is another called the court of *competitors;* which is thus constituted. If any candidates for the office of senator have more votes than a third of the representatives, that candidate, who has most votes, next to the senator elected, becomes incapable for one year of all public offices, even of being a magistrate or representative: But he takes his seat in the court of competitors. Here then is a court which may sometimes consist of a hundred members, sometimes have no members at all; and by that means, be for a year abolished.

26. The court of competitors has no power in the commonwealth. It has only the inspection of public accounts, and the accusing of any man before the senate. If the senate acquit him, the court of competitors may, if they please, appeal to the people, either magistrates or representatives. Upon that appeal, the magistrates or representatives meet on the day appointed by the court of competitors, and chuse in each county three persons; from which number every senator is excluded. These, to the number of 300, meet in the capital, and bring the person accused to a new trial.

27. The court of competitors may propose any law to the senate; and if refused, may appeal to the people, that is, to the magistrates or representatives, who examine it in their counties. Every senator, who is thrown out of the senate by a vote of the court, takes his seat in the court of competitors.

28. The senate possesses all the judicative authority of the house of Lords, that is, all the appeals from the inferior courts. It likewise appoints the Lord Chancellor, and all the officers of the law.

29. Every county is a kind of republic within itself, and the representatives may make bye-laws; which have no authority 'till three months after they are voted. A copy of the law is sent to the senate, and to every other county. The senate, or any single county, may, at any time, annul any bye-law of another county.

30. The representatives have all the authority of the BRITISH justices of peace in trials, commitments, &c.

31. The magistrates have the appointment of all the officers of the revenue in each county. All causes with regard to the revenue are carried ultimately by appeal before the magistrates. They pass the accompts of all the officers;

but must have their own accompts examined and passed at the end of the year by the representatives.

32. The magistrates name rectors or ministers to all the parishes.

33. The Presbyterian government is established; and the highest ecclesiastical court is an assembly or synod of all the presbyters of the county. The magistrates may take any cause from this court, and determine it themselves.

34. The magistrates may try, and depose or suspend any presbyter.

35. The militia is established in imitation of that of SWISSERLAND, which being well known, we shall not insist upon it. It will only be proper to make this addition, that an army of 20,000 men be annually drawn out by rotation, paid and encamped during six weeks in summer; that the duty of a camp may not be altogether unknown.

36. The magistrates appoint all the colonels and downwards. The senate all upwards. During war, the general appoints the colonel and downwards, and his commission is good for a twelvemonth. But after that, it must be confirmed by the magistrates of the county, to which the regiment belongs. The magistrates may break any officer in the county regiment. And the senate may do the same to any officer in the service. If the magistrates do not think proper to confirm the general's choice, they may appoint another officer in the place of him they reject.

37. All crimes are tried within the county by the magistrates and a jury. But the senate can stop any trial, and bring it before themselves.

38. Any county may indict any man before the senate for any crime.

39. The protector, the two secretaries, the council of state, with any five or more that the senate appoints, are possessed, on extraordinary emergencies, of *dictatorial* power for six months.

40. The protector may pardon any person condemned by the inferior courts.

41. In time of war, no officer of the army that is in the field can have any civil office in the commonwealth.

42. The capital, which we shall call LONDON, may be allowed four members in the senate. It may therefore be divided into four counties. The representatives of each of these chuse one senator, and ten magistrates. There are therefore in the city four senators, forty-four magistrates, and four hundred representatives. The magistrates have the same authority as in the counties. The representatives also have the same authority; but they never meet in one general court: They give their votes in their particular county, or division of hundreds.

43. When they enact any bye-law, the greater number of counties or divisions determines the matter. And where these are equal, the magistrates have the casting vote.

44. The magistrates chuse the mayor, sheriff, recorder, and other officers of the city.

45. In the commonwealth, no representative, magistrate, or senator, as such, has any salary. The protector, secretaries, councils, and ambassadors, have salaries.

46. The first year in every century is set apart for correcting all inequalities, which time may have produced in the representative. This must be done by the legislature.

47. The following political aphorisms may explain the reason of these orders.

48. The lower sort of people and small proprietors are good judges enough of one not very distant from them in rank or habitation; and therefore, in their parochial meetings, will probably chuse the best, or nearly the best representative: But they are wholly unfit for county-meetings, and for electing into the higher offices of the republic. Their ignorance gives the grandees an opportunity of deceiving them.

49. Ten thousand, even though they were not annually elected, are a basis large enough for any free government. It is true, the nobles in POLAND are more than 10,000, and yet these oppress the people. But as power always continues there in the same persons and families, this makes them, in a manner, a different nation from the people. Besides the nobles are there united under a few heads of families.

50. All free governments must consist of two councils, a lesser and greater; or, in other words, of a senate and people. The people, as HARRINGTON observes, would want wisdom, without the senate: The senate, without the people, would want honesty.

51. A large assembly of 1000, for instance, to represent the people, if allowed to debate, would fall into disorder. If not allowed to debate, the senate has a negative upon them, and the worst kind of negative, that before resolution.

52. Here therefore is an inconvenience, which no government has yet fully remedied, but which is the easiest to be remedied in the world. If the people debate, all is confusion: If they do not debate, they can only resolve; and then the senate carves for them. Divide the people into many separate bodies; and then they may debate with safety, and every inconvenience seems to be prevented.

53. Cardinal RETZ says, that all numerous assemblies, however composed, are mere mob, and swayed in their debates by the least motive. This we find confirmed by daily experience. When an absurdity strikes a member, he conveys it to his neighbour, and so on, till the whole be infected. Separate this great body; and though every member be only of middling sense, it is not probable, that any thing but reason can prevail over the whole. Influence and example being removed, good sense will always get the better of bad among a number of people.

54. There are two things to be guarded against in every *senate:* Its combination, and its division. Its combination is most dangerous. And against this inconvenience we have provided the following remedies. 1. The great dependence of the senators on the people by annual elections; and that not by an undistinguishing rabble, like the ENGLISH electors, but by men of fortune and education. 2. The small power they are allowed. They have few offices to dispose of. Almost all are given by the magistrates in the counties. 3. The court of competitors, which being composed of men that are their rivals, next to them in interest, and uneasy in their present situation, will be sure to take all advantages against them.

55. The division of the senate is prevented, 1. By the smallness of their number. 2. As faction supposes a combination in a separate interest, it is prevented by their dependence on the people. 3. They have a power of expelling any factious member. It is true, when another member of the same spirit comes from the county, they have no power of expelling him: Nor is it fit they should; for that shows the humour to be in the people, and may possibly arise from some ill conduct in public affairs. 4. Almost any man, in a senate so regularly chosen by the people, may be supposed fit for any civil office. It would be proper, therefore, for the senate to form some *general* resolutions with regard to the disposing of offices among the members: Which resolutions would not confine them in critical times, when extraordinary parts on the one hand, or extraordinary stupidity on the other, appears in any senator; but they would be sufficient to prevent intrigue and faction, by making the disposal of the offices a thing of course. For instance, let it be a resolution, That no man shall enjoy any office, till he has sat four years in the senate: That, except ambassadors, no man shall be in office two years following: That no man shall attain the higher offices but through the lower: That no man shall be protector twice, &c. The senate of VENICE govern themselves by such resolutions.

56. In foreign politics the interest of the senate can scarcely ever be divided from that of the people; and therefore it is fit to make the senate absolute with regard to them; otherwise there could be no secrecy or refined policy.

Besides, without money no alliance can be executed; and the senate is still sufficiently dependant. Not to mention, that the legislative power being always superior to the executive, the magistrates or representatives may interpose whenever they think proper.

57. The chief support of the BRITISH government is the opposition of interests; but that, though in the main serviceable, breeds endless factions. In the foregoing plan, it does all the good without any of the harm. The *competitors* have no power of controlling the senate: They have only the power of accusing, and appealing to the people.

58. It is necessary, likewise, to prevent both combination and division in the thousand magistrates. This is done sufficiently by the separation of places and interests.

59. But lest that should not be sufficient, their dependence on the 10,000 for their elections, serves to the same purpose.

60. Nor is that all: For the 10,000 may resume the power whenever they please; and not only when they all please, but when any five of a hundred please, which will happen upon the very first suspicion of a separate interest.

61. The 10,000 are too large a body either to unite or divide, except when they meet in one place, and fall under the guidance of ambitious leaders. Not to mention their annual election, by the whole body of the people, that are of any consideration.

62. A small commonwealth is the happiest government in the world within itself, because every thing lies under the eye of the rulers: But it may be subdued by great force from without. This scheme seems to have all the advantages both of a great and a little commonwealth.

63. Every county-law may be annulled either by the senate or another county; because that shows an opposition of interest: In which case no part ought to decide for itself. The matter must be referred to the whole, which will best determine what agrees with general interest.

64. As to the clergy and militia, the reasons of these orders are obvious. Without the dependence of the clergy on the civil magistrates, and without a militia, it is in vain to think that any free government will ever have security or stability.

65. In many governments, the inferior magistrates have no rewards but what arise from their ambition, vanity, or public spirit. The salaries of the FRENCH judges amount not to the interest of the sums they pay for their offices. The DUTCH burgo-masters have little more immediate profit than the ENGLISH justices of peace, or the members of the house of commons formerly. But lest any should suspect, that this would beget negligence

in the administration (which is little to be feared, considering the natural ambition of mankind), let the magistrates have competent salaries. The senators have access to so many honourable and lucrative offices, that their attendance needs not be bought. There is little attendance required of the representatives.

66. That the foregoing plan of government is practicable, no one can doubt, who considers the resemblance that it bears to the commonwealth of the United Provinces, a wise and renowned government. The alterations in the present scheme seem all evidently for the better. 1. The representation is more equal. 2. The unlimited power of the burgo-masters in the towns, which forms a perfect aristocracy in the DUTCH commonwealth, is corrected by a well-tempered democracy, in giving to the people the annual election of the county representatives. 3. The negative, which every province and town has upon the whole body of the DUTCH republic, with regard to alliances, peace and war, and the imposition of taxes, is here removed. 4. The counties, in the present plan, are not so independent of each other, nor do they form separate bodies so much as the seven provinces; where the jealousy and envy of the smaller provinces and towns against the greater, particularly HOLLAND and AMSTERDAM, have frequently disturbed the government. 5. Larger powers, though of the safest kind, are intrusted to the senate than the States-General possess; by which means, the former may become more expeditious, and secret in their resolutions, than it is possible for the latter.

67. The chief alterations that could be made on the BRITISH government, in order to bring it to the most perfect model of limited monarchy, seem to be the following. *First,* The plan of CROMWELL's parliament ought to be restored, by making the representation equal, and by allowing none to vote in the county elections who possess not a property of 200 pounds value. *Secondly,* As such a house of Commons would be too weighty for a frail house of Lords, like the present, the Bishops and SCOTCH Peers ought to be removed: The number of the upper house ought to be raised to three or four hundred: Their seats not hereditary, but during life: They ought to have the election of their own members; and no commoner should be allowed to refuse a seat that was offered him. By this means the house of Lords would consist entirely of the men of chief credit, abilities, and interest in the nation; and every turbulent leader in the house of Commons might be taken off, and connected by interest with the house of Peers. Such an aristocracy would be an excellent barrier both to the monarchy and against it. At present, the balance of our government depends in some measure on the

abilities and behaviour of the sovereign; which are variable and uncertain circumstances.

68. This plan of limited monarchy, however corrected, seems still liable to three great inconveniencies. *First,* It removes not entirely, though it may soften, the parties of *court* and *country. Secondly,* The king's personal character must still have great influence on the government. *Thirdly,* The sword is in the hands of a single person, who will always neglect to discipline the militia, in order to have a pretence for keeping up a standing army.

69. We shall conclude this subject, with observing the falsehood of the common opinion, that no large state, such as FRANCE or GREAT BRITAIN, could ever be modelled into a commonwealth, but that such a form of government can only take place in a city or small territory. The contrary seems probable. Though it is more difficult to form a republican government in an extensive country than in a city; there is more facility, when once it is formed, of preserving it steady and uniform, without tumult and faction. It is not easy, for the distant parts of a large state to combine in any plan of free government; but they easily conspire in the esteem and reverence for a single person, who, by means of this popular favour, may seize the power, and forcing the more obstinate to submit, may establish a monarchical government. On the other hand, a city readily concurs in the same notions of government, the natural equality of property favours liberty, and the nearness of habitation enables the citizens mutually to assist each other. Even under absolute princes, the subordinate government of cities is commonly republican; while that of counties and provinces is monarchical. But these same circumstances, which facilitate the erection of commonwealths in cities, render their constitution more frail and uncertain. Democracies are turbulent. For however the people may be separated or divided into small parties, either in their votes or elections; their near habitation in a city will always make the force of popular tides and currents very sensible. Aristocracies are better adapted for peace and order, and accordingly were most admired by ancient writers; but they are jealous and oppressive. In a large government, which is modelled with masterly skill, there is compass and room enough to refine the democracy, from the lower people, who may be admitted into the first elections or first concoction of the commonwealth, to the higher magistrates, who direct all the movements. At the same time, the parts are so distant and remote, that it is very difficult, either by intrigue, prejudice, or passion, to hurry them into any measures against the public interest.

70. It is needless to enquire, whether such a government would be immortal. I allow the justness of the poet's exclamation on the endless projects

of human race, *Man and for ever!*[72] The world itself probably is not immortal. Such consuming plagues may arise as would leave even a perfect government a weak prey to its neighbours. We know not to what length enthusiasm, or other extraordinary movements of the human mind, may transport men, to the neglect of all order and public good. Where difference of interest is removed, whimsical and unaccountable factions often arise, from personal favour or enmity. Perhaps, rust may grow to the springs of the most accurate political machine, and disorder its motions. Lastly, extensive conquests, when pursued, must be the ruin of every free government; and of the more perfect governments sooner than of the imperfect; because of the very advantages which the former possess above the latter. And though such a state ought to establish a fundamental law against conquests; yet republics have ambition as well as individuals, and present interest makes men forgetful of their posterity. It is a sufficient incitement to human endeavours, that such a government would flourish for many ages; without pretending to bestow, on any work of man, that immortality, which the Almighty seems to have refused to his own productions.

72. [The identity of this poet has not been established.]

Essays

The Composition, Reception, and Early Influence of Hume's *Essays* and *Enquiry Concerning the Principles of Morals*

MARK G. SPENCER

David Hume (1711–1776) is widely known as one of the most influential philosophers of the Western tradition. That renown rests largely on his authorship of *A Treatise of Human Nature* (1739–40). There are many good reasons for this elevated reputation, including what Hume had to say in the *Treatise* on abstract philosophical topics related to epistemology, such as his theory of ideas, and his thoughts on causality, belief, ethics, and self-identity.[1] But if we are better to understand Hume historically, then we need to remember that along with being a talented philosopher and abstract thinker, Hume was also what the eighteenth century knew as an enlightened "man of letters." Yes, he aimed to reach elite and eminent scholars who often in their works wrote for one another, but he also strove to make a living by writing for an expanding audience of general readers (including women) to whose diverse interests he catered. Hume's writing life was very much linked to the growing world of print that was a central pillar of the Age of Enlightenment. As Hume put it near the beginning of his short autobiography, "My Own Life," his life's story was "little more than the History of my Writings; as, indeed, almost all my life has been spent in literary pursuits and occupations."[2] What he left out of the piece was a not-insignificant, if short, career as a diplomat and under-secretary of state, activities that also informed Hume's life as an observer and writer on human nature. Hume's contributions to the history of ideas are best appreciated when his writings are approached not as isolated texts but alongside Hume's other publications, contemporary reactions to them, and as part of the author's life as a whole.

This chapter attempts to situate the primary texts of *David Hume on Morals, Politics, and Society* in the context of Hume's life and intellectual development, as well as in some of their wider historical and historiographical settings. The essay sketches the composition of Hume's moral and political *Essays* and his *Enquiry Concerning the Principles of Morals* (some of his moral and political essays were published before, and some after, that work). It also aims to illuminated the early reception of these works, in part by drawing on Hume's impact on important Enlightenment writers such as Henry Home (1696–1782; after 1752, Lord Kames), Adam Ferguson (1723–1816), Adam Smith (1723–1790), Jeremy Bentham (1748–1832), and, in America, James Madison (1751–1836), but also by considering some of the broader parameters of the impact of Hume's moral, political, and social thought in the eighteenth- and early nineteenth-century British Atlantic world.

Hume's Early Life and Writings

Hume was born in Edinburgh, Scotland, on 26 April 1711, to Joseph Hume of Ninewells (1680–1713) and Katherine Falconer (d. 1745), daughter of Lord President Sir David Falconer.[3] Much of his early youth was spent in Edinburgh and, with his older brother, John, and sister, Katherine, in the Scottish countryside at the smallish Hume estate, Ninewells, at Chirnside in Berwickhire on the banks of the Whiteadder, close to the border with England. The direct impact of Joseph Hume, a minor laird, on his son was minimal because Joseph died in 1713 when David was only two. His mother's influence was longer lasting and more significant, although also difficult to measure, as these things often are. She did not remarry following the death of her husband and raised David and his siblings in what appears to have been the typically strict Calvinist environment of her time and place. Her youngest son came to reject that religion, but he hung on to ideas about determinism, the contingency of things, and our inability to know God, who if he was to be real for us, is made so through faith alone.

Having spent some time at the local school, Hume attended the University of Edinburgh with John, who was older by four years. Hume matriculated on 27 February 1723 but had entered the college the previous academic year, at the age of ten, young even by the standards of eighteenth-century Britain, which often saw boys beginning college at age twelve or earlier. He would later maintain: "My studious disposition, my sobriety, and my industry, gave my family a notion that the law was a proper profession for me; but I found an unsurmountable aversion to every thing but the pursuits of philosophy and general learning; and while they fancied I was poring upon Voet and Vinnius, Cicero and Virgil were the authors which I was secretly devouring."[4] We might think of the future "man of letters" taking shape even at this young age, although we also need to be cautious in believing everything about the self-image that Hume endeavored to create in an autobiography penned for posterity as his life was coming to an end.

Leaving college in 1725, aged fourteen – without a degree (as many did who did not see a need for taking one) – Hume had no settled course for his life. Resident in Edinburgh for a time, he studied law at the university; it did not do much for him, although it may have furthered a burgeoning friendship with Henry Home and planted seeds for future study, some of which resulted in the texts reprinted in this volume. Feeling somewhat defeated and uncertain of his future, Hume returned to Ninewells to collect his thoughts.

It is from this period that his first letter survives. Hume wrote to his friend Michael Ramsay on 4 July 1727: "I receivd all the Books you writ of . . . just now I am entirely confind to my self & Library for Diversion."[5] Hume was reading much and beginning, perhaps, even to know that he had something to say himself. But it was not easy going. As he put it in his letter to Ramsay, "All the progress that I made is but drawing the Outlines, in loose bits of Paper; here a hint of passion, there a Phenomenon in the mind accounted for, in another the alteration of these accounts; sometimes a remark upon an Author I have been reading. And none of them worth to any Body & I believe scarce to my self."[6] Hume was making notes but did not yet have a system to apply them to, in part because he had left his philosophy courses with little respect for the logic and metaphysics taught there.

Hume was working so hard in his solitary studies that it was beginning to take a toll on his health. Reading in solitude for long hours, challenging long-held beliefs of important thinkers, including ones related to the God and religion of his upbringing, but still uncertain of what exactly he had to say and unclear about what direction his life would take, with no gainful employment – it all proved too much. In 1729, like many a young man before and since, the adolescent Hume had a breakdown. He later wrote of himself to an unnamed physician whose advice he sought:

About the beginning of Septr 1729, all of my Ardor seem'd in a moment to be extinguisht, & I cou'd no longer raise my Mind to that pitch, which formerly gave me such excessive Pleasure. I felt no Uneasyness or Want of Spirits, when I laid aside my Book; &

therefore never imagined there was any bodily Distemper in the Case, but that my Coldness proceeded from a Laziness of Temper, which must be overcome by redoubling my Application. In this Condition I remain'd for nine Months.[7]

In February 1734, desperate for a change of scenery and for a different pace of life – and perhaps urged by family impatience at his lack of direction – Hume traveled south to Bristol to take up employment in the office of a sugar-merchant. That, too, did not go well although he made at least one lasting friend there, James Birch, about whom little is now known besides what Hume wrote about him in an early letter. Soon, Hume looked even further afield, this time to France. From France, he wrote to provide Birch with an account of his travels, as his friend also had "a design of coming thither, for Study & Diversion."[8] Hume remained in France for three years, reading, writing, and mixing with new company first for a short time in Paris, then in Reims, and finally, at La Flèche the site of a Jesuit College where René Descartes (1596–1650) had earlier been a student. All of that contributed to Hume's developing ideas, in part by introducing him to the works of new authors. On returning to Britain from France, an invigorated Hume was ready to publish the first volumes of his first major work, *A Treatise of Human Nature: Being an Attempt to Introduce the Experimental Method of Reasoning into Moral Subjects* (1739–40).

The *Treatise* comprised three books: "Of the Understanding" and "Of the Passions," both published in 1739, and "Of Morals," which was published in 1740. By any measure the *Treatise* was deeply, even densely, philosophical. In the eighteenth century, the *Treatise* was read by important figures in the scholarly world, where it was also reviewed in the learned journals, but it did not reach nearly as wide an audience as would Hume's later rewrite of it and his more popular essays on morals, politics, and society. Immediately, Hume was apprehensive about how the *Treatise* would be received and then increasingly disappointed with its muted reception, so much so that he even published a short pamphlet in an effort to raise more interest in the book.[9] In his autobiography, Hume wrote of the reception of the *Treatise:* "Never literary attempt was more unfortunate than my Treatise of Human Nature. It fell *dead-born from the press,* without reaching such distinction, as even to excite a murmur among the zealots. But being naturally of a cheerful and sanguine temper, I very soon recovered the blow, and prosecuted with great ardour my studies in the country."[10]

The works reprinted in this volume are largely the fruit of those labors and Hume's assessment that his "want of success in publishing the Treatise

. . . had proceeded more from the manner than the matter."[11] Hume's post-*Treatise* writings (his essays on topics related to morals, politics, and society; his philosophical enquiries; and his historical writings) should not be thought of as separate from the aspirations of Hume's formal and abstract philosophy as presented in his *Treatise*. As originally conceived, that work was to have sections on taste and politics as well. Moreover, the "science of man" that Hume defined in the introduction to his *Treatise* was to be further developed in his later works but always with an eye to making it accessible to many beyond the learned few and in such ways that philosophy remained connected to daily life. As Hume memorably put it: "Be a philosopher; but, amidst all your philosophy, be still a man."[12]

Hume's Post-*Treatise* Writings

Most of Hume's polite essays and post-*Treatise* philosophy, including most of what is published in this collection, were written and first published in the dozen years from 1740 to 1752.[13] His first volume of essays was published in London in 1741 as *Essays, Moral and Political*.[14] That work, he said, "was favourably received, and soon made me entirely forget my former disappointment."[15] Of the essays reprinted here, that first volume of essays contains "Of the Liberty of the Press," "That Politics May Be Reduced to a Science," "Of the First Principles of Government," and "Of Parties in General." These essays encompass some of Hume's best-known statements on politics, including his observation that it is "on opinion only that government is founded" – a formulation guaranteed to annoy divine-rights theorists just as much as believers in the contractual origins of government, and even those whose theories sanctioned what had been inherited as legitimate and right.[16]

Another volume with the same title followed in 1742. Some of Hume's essays represented new fields of inquiry for him, but he had certainly not given up on ideas first expressed in the *Treatise*. Hume wished to recast much of what he had written there in a manner that was more easily accessible to a wider audience. So, in 1748 he published his *Philosophical Essays Concerning Human Understanding,* the work that is now more recognized by its revised title of 1758, *An Enquiry Concerning Human Understanding,* and known by Hume scholars simply as his first *Enquiry.* The work contains twelve chapters on different aspects of philosophy, from the "Origin of Ideas" and "Probability" to "Liberty and Necessity," "Sceptical Philosophy," and Hume's infamous critique "Of Miracles." With the publication of that piece, Hume's eighteenth-century readers knew him as an unbeliever who had taunted "that the CHRISTIAN religion not only was at first attended with miracles, but even at this day cannot be believed by any reasonable person without one."[17]

Hume continued to offer volumes of miscellaneous essays–some old but revised, some new–to the reading public. One suspects that Hume knew that he was on to a good thing. Earlier, in 1742, Hume had written to Henry Home that he hoped his *Essays* would "prove like dung with marl, and bring forward the rest of my Philosophy, which is of a more durable, though of a harder and more stubborn nature."[18] In 1748 he published *Three Essays, Moral and Political*. Those essays–"Of National Characters," "Of the Original Contract," and "Of Passive Obedience"–are all reprinted in this volume. A few years later, in 1752, Hume published yet another volume of essays, his *Political Discourses*, a work Hume says was his only publication "successful on first publication."[19] Several important essays included in this volume were first published there: "Of Commerce," "Of Refinement in the Arts" (originally published as "Of Luxury"), "Of Public Credit," and "Idea of a Perfect Commonwealth."

Looking at Hume's essay production as a whole as it stood in 1752, one is struck by an overriding theme of "improvement." There are widening contexts in which Hume's essays might be situated and against which his concerns with improvement are underscored. As Roger L. Emerson has argued, when we consider what Hume had to say on political economy in particular, those considerations must surely include elements of the locality in which he was born and raised: "Hume was a farm boy who grew up knowing the value of new agricultural techniques, new crops and the value of expanding markets, better roads and better marketing facilities."[20] His eye for such matters stayed with him throughout his life and informed his work as an historian as well.

Beyond that local biographical setting is a larger Scottish context. Mid eighteenth-century Scotland was the scene of considerable improvement projects, especially in the Lowlands, and Hume, like other writers of the Scottish Enlightenment, was deeply aware that he lived in times witnessing material change for the better.[21] Also relevant, and again as Emerson has argued, was the context of attempted improvements to the conditions of those living in the Scottish Highlands. With the failure of yet another Scottish rebellion in 1745, there were rigorous efforts to make sure others did not follow. Mitigating measures included punishments and prohibitions of various sorts, largely aimed at clanship, but also planned improvement projects. Hundreds of miles of roads were surveyed and built, better bridges were designed and installed, innovative agricultural plans were formulated and disseminated. How best to achieve stability in the Highlands? How to counteract backwardness with forward thinking? As Emerson writes, "Hume's *Political Discourses* appeared while that debate was still ongoing and the new Commissioners for the Annexed Estates Commission were being chosen. . . . When Hume wrote the *Political Discourses* he surely hoped to influence an ongoing debate both in Edinburgh and in London."[22] And these biographical and local Scottish settings might themselves be situated in an even wider context related to the improvement that Hume and other literati sought, globally, in the Age of Enlightenment.

Hume's essays as a whole are meant to offer a defense of a world of expanding commerce and increased industry and sociability, material well-being, refined knowledge and manners, and political freedom. Indeed, for Hume the individual items on that list were not goals to be sought on their own – they were all intimately, even interactively, connected. He put much of this succinctly in a memorable passage in his essay "Of Refinement in the Arts." The passage is worth quoting here at length for what it tells us about Hume's central aspirations as a "man of letters":

The same age, which produces great philosophers and politicians, renowned generals and poets, usually abounds with skillful weavers, and ship-carpenters. We cannot reasonably expect, that a piece of woolen cloth will be wrought to perfection in a nation, which is ignorant of astronomy, or where ethics are neglected. The spirit of the age affects all the arts; and the minds of men, being once roused from their lethargy, and put into a fermentation, turn themselves on all sides, and carry improvements into every art and science. Profound ignorance is totally banished, and men enjoy the privilege of rational creatures, to think as well as to act, to cultivate the pleasures of the mind as well as those of the body.

The more these refined arts advance, the more sociable men become: nor is it possible, that, when enriched with science, and possessed of a fund of conversation, they should be contented to remain in solitude, or live with their fellow-citizens in that distant manner, which is peculiar to ignorant and barbarous nations. They flock into the cities; love to receive and communicate knowledge; to show their wit or their breeding; their taste in conversation or living, in clothes or furniture. Curiosity allures the wise; vanity the foolish; and pleasure both. Particular clubs and societies are every where formed: Both sexes meet in an easy and sociable manner; and the tempers of men, as well as their behaviour, refine apace. So that, besides the improvements which they receive from knowledge and the liberal arts, it is impossible but they must feel an encrease of humanity, from the very habit of conversing together, and contributing to each other's pleasure and entertainment. Thus *industry, knowledge,* and *humanity,* are linked together by an indissoluble chain, and are found, from experience as well as reason, to be peculiar to the more polished, and, what are commonly denominated, the more luxurious ages.[23]

It is difficult to find in all that Hume wrote any one passage that more aptly summarizes the essence of his thinking on morals, politics, and society. Indeed, the passage is useful as a contemporary summary of what the eighteenth-century Enlightenment meant to many of the Scots (and others) at its center.[24]

Hume, however, was not often as prescriptive in his writing as he is here. Perhaps because of that it is often difficult to ascertain his precise position on one topic or another. He had a tendency to look at issues from multiple perspectives, including ones that differed from the common ones of his time. His goal was not always to draw clear conclusions but rather to provide his readers with suggestive signposts and rough roadmaps as guides for them to reach their own conclusions on one topic or another. Hume's contemporary readers did not always know what to make of his directions, and readers today often do not agree on how best to interpret what Hume wrote. Indeed, few writers have been interpreted in such widely varying ways as has Hume. Philosophers, political scientists, economists, historians, and other scholars continue to debate the degree to which Hume was a sceptic, or not; the nature of his religious belief, if any; his precise thoughts on progress and commercial development; if he was a Whig or a Tory; a conservative or liberal thinker.[25] Many of those, and other competing understandings, can be explained if Hume is seen as inviting his readers to engage in debates of that sort. If it is true that one of Hume's aims was to encourage informed and active debate of questions rather than to instill passive knowledge of answers, it is tempting to imagine him looking back with some satisfaction at the debates that continue to swirl around his thought more than 250 years on.

The year before he published the passage quoted above from "Of Refinement in the Arts," Hume sent to press another part of the recasting of his *Treatise*—his *Enquiry Concerning the Principles of Morals* (1751), or what has become known simply as his second *Enquiry*. He had been writing that book since 1749. It is reprinted in this volume in its entirety, as it most certainly should be. Hume wrote of the second *Enquiry:* "In my opinion (who ought not to judge on that subject)," it "is of all my writings, historical, philosophical, or literary, incomparably the best."[26] Although not all of Hume's earliest readers agreed with that assessment (some of them are introduced below), many did.

One of the distinguishing features of the second *Enquiry* is Hume's concerted effort to avoid technical jargon. Hume explained it this way in an important appendix to the work: "Throughout this enquiry, we always consider in general, what qualities are a subject of praise or of censure, without entering into all the minute differences of sentiment, which they excite. . . . These sciences are but too apt to appear abstract to common readers, even with all the precautions which we can take to clear them from superfluous speculations, and bring them down to every capacity."[27]

The 1740s and 1750s were years in which Hume continued to revise his essays previously published, releasing them in corrected editions and new formats. The most important of these was his *Essays and Treatises on Several Subjects,* a collection of Hume's various essays and both *Enquiries*. The first edition of that work was published in 1758 but many others followed.[28] Sometimes new pieces would be included. His essay "Of the Jealousy of Trade," for instance, was the first to be added, even appearing in some late printings of the 1758 edition of *Essays and Treatises*. Hume's essay "Of the Origin of Government" was written last of all of the works appearing in the present volume. It was first published in the posthumous edition of the *Essays and Treatises* of 1777, a volume that Hume had prepared while nearing his death in 1776.

In the 1750s and 1760s, Hume was publishing other things for which he would be remembered, not least of which was his six-volume *The History of England from the Invasion of Julius Caesar to the Revolution in 1688* (1754–62).[29] The *History* may have been the most widely circulated of any of Hume's works in the eighteenth and nineteenth centuries, and its popularity helped to bolster the reputation and readership of the works reprinted in this volume. Hume had become a bestselling author. As one recent assessment has put it, by this point in his career, Hume's name was now one "that stirred the booksellers."[30] Writing of his situation, Hume remarked, "I returned to Edinburgh in 1769, very opulent (for I possessed a revenue of 1000 l. a-year), healthy, and though somewhat stricken in years, with the prospect of enjoying long my ease, and of seeing the increase of my reputation."[31]

Hume's Early British Reception

Measuring the early influence of Hume's publications as a whole is difficult, but recent scholarly research has begun to give more attention to his works' early reception.[32] That research sheds light on Hume's intentions and shows that contemporaries were aware of the widening appeal of his writings. In particular, many of Hume's eighteenth- and early nineteenth-century readers in the British Atlantic Enlightenment, seeing past Hume's reputation as a skeptical philosopher and religious doubter, were able to absorb his (often very practically oriented) ideas on morals, politics, and society. Often, as in revolutionary America, they did so with lasting effect for the modern world.

Important review essays of Hume's works offer a point of departure. In its lead essay for January 1752 for instance, the *Monthly Review,* one of the most important literary journals of eighteenth-century Britain, reviewed Hume's *Enquiry Concerning the Principles of Morals.* There, William Rose (1719–1752), a Scot working in London, wrote of Hume that the "reputation this ingenious author has acquir'd as a fine and elegant writer, renders it unnecessary for us to say any thing in his praise. We shall only observe in general, that clearness and precision of ideas on abstracted and metaphysical subjects, and at the same time propriety, elegance and spirit, are seldom found united in any writings in a more eminent degree than in those of Mr. *Hume.*" Rose suggested that Hume's *Enquiry* would appeal to a large audience: "The work now before us will, as far as we are able to judge, considerably raise the reputation; and, being free from that sceptical turn which appears in his other pieces, will be more agreeable to the generality of Readers."[33]

In the next essay in the journal, Rose reviewed Hume's *Political Discourses.* Again, Rose was flattering: "FEW writers are better qualified, either to instruct or entertain their readers, than Mr. *Hume.* On whatever subject he employs his pen, he presents us with something new; nor is this his only merit, his writings (as we observed in the preceeding article) receive a farther recommendation from that elegance and spirit which appears in them, and that clearness of reasoning, which distinguishes them from most others." Rose went on to say that Hume's *Political Discourses* "are upon curious and interesting subjects; abound with solid reflections;

and shew the author's great knowledge of ancient and modern history, and his comprehensive views of things."[34]

Reviews of a similar nature appeared elsewhere, such as in the *Scots Magazine* and the *Critical Review*. By 1760, the latter, in praising a new volume of Hume's political essays, could write that it

> reflects credit on the good sense, moderation, and public spirit of the elegant writer. Mr. Hume's writings will admit of no abstract, as it would not be possible to couch his meaning in less compass than he has allowed it, without losing much of the strength and beauty of his reasoning. WE shall therefore close this article with observing, that the author runs no hazard of diminishing the reputation he has deservedly acquired of a refined, manly, and free inquirer, by this addition to his political works.[35]

But along with their praise, contemporaries were also often cautious in accepting all that Hume wrote. Even generally positive reviewers such as Rose would often strike a circumspect tone. The opening lines of Rose's 1757 review of Hume's *Four Dissertations* is illustrative:

> THERE are but few of our modern Writers, whose works are so generally read, as those of Mr. Hume. And, indeed, if we consider them in one view, as sprightly and ingenious compositions, this is not at all to be wondered at: there is a delicacy of sentiment, an original turn of thought, a perspicuity, and often an elegance, of language, that cannot but recommend his writings to every Reader of taste. It is to be regretted, however, that such a genius should employ his abilities in the manner he frequently does. In his attacks upon the religion of his country, he acts not the part of an open and generous enemy, but endeavours to weaken its authority by oblique hints, and artful insinuations. In this view his works merit little, if any, regard; and few Readers, of just discernment, we apprehend, will envy him any honours his acuteness, or elegance, can possibly obtain, when they are only employed in filling the mind with the uncomfortable fluctutations of scepticism, and the gloom of infidelity.[36]

The impact of Hume's writings on morals, politics, and society with his Scottish Enlightenment contemporaries was similarly broad and multifaceted, if more complicated. One of those on whom Hume had an impact was Adam Ferguson, sometimes referred to as "the father of modern sociology." Ferguson, a longtime friend of Hume's and the one who would also succeed him as keeper of the Advocates' Library in Edinburgh, published his

An Essay on the History of Civil Society in 1767.[37] There, Ferguson traced the development of civil society from its "rude" origins to its "polished" conclusions. That broad storyline was one that may have owed something to Hume's way of seeing things in his *Essays,* but scholars have most often concentrated on the differences between Hume's thought and Ferguson's, of which there are many. Ferguson believe in providential design, but the fortuitous, uneven, and unforeseen ways in which causes and effects played out in Ferguson's account of human society's development is something that he shared with Hume.

Hume's impact on Ferguson's *Essay* is evident in more tangible ways too, such as in its several references to Hume's *History of England* and when Ferguson drew on Hume's essay "Of the Populousness of Ancient Nations." In his section "On Population and Wealth," Ferguson cited Hume approvingly: "'When nations were divided into small territories, and petty commonwealths, where each man had his house and his field to himself, and each country had its capital free and independent; what a happy situation for mankind,' says Mr Hume, 'how favourable to industry and agriculture, to marriage and to population!'"[38] It should also be pointed out that Hume always had significant reservations about Ferguson's book. Reading the manuscript before it was published, Hume remarked in a letter to their mutual friend Hugh Blair:

> I have perus'd Ferguson's Papers more than once, which had been put into my hands, some time ago at his desire. I sat down to read them with great Prepossession, founded on my good Opinion of him, on a Small Specimen I had seen of them some Years ago, and on yours & Dr Robertson's Esteem of them: But I am sorry to say it, they have no-wise answer'd my Expectation. I do not think them fit to be given to the Public, neither on account of the Style nor the Reasoning; the Form nor the Matter.[39]

He thought no more highly of the book that was published.[40]

Hume's impact on other thinkers of the Scottish Enlightenment was demonstrably more pronounced and intimate. That was the case with Robert Wallace (1697–1771), for instance, who engaged Hume's essay on the populousness of ancient nations in his book *A Dissertation on the Numbers of Mankind* (1753), and with James Steuart (1712–1780), whose *An Inquiry into the Principles of Political Economy* (1767) took up a number of Hume's economic essays. A more significant engagement is evident in the case of Henry Home.

In 1779, in the third edition of Henry Home's (by then Lord Kames) *Essays on the Principles of Morality and Natural Religion*, one finds several borrowings from and allusions to Hume's work, including an extended debate with Hume that Kames had initiated in the first edition of his book, published in 1751, twenty-eight years earlier.[41] From the beginning, Kames had been critical of aspects of Hume's account of "justice." Now, in a completely new additional chapter, "Various Opinions Concerning the Foundation of Morality," Kames provided what he took to be a point-by-point refutation of his friend's system.

The crux of Kames's critique is that Hume in the *Enquiry Concerning the Principles of Morals* was too smart for his own good. Kames maintained that Hume's book "shows uncommon genius exerted in a pleasing stile," and that he "has given great scope to invention," but that sadly he "has been little attentive to the facts and principles." The streamlined nature of his second *Enquiry* that we have seen Hume took to be a good thing, Kames considered a fatal flaw: "Love of simplicity has betrayed him into the error . . . of founding morality upon a single principle, overlooking the complex nature of man, composed of many principles."[42] For Kames, that was the mistake that had led Hume to deny "that we have any original sense of justice," which is wrongly cast as "an artificial virtue." It is also worth noting that Kames's chapter concludes with a defense of his (by 1779, deceased) friend:

> Will the reader indulge me a few words more, to express some concern I feel for myself. The arguments urged in the Enquiry, appear inferior to the other productions of an author, who was justly esteemed the greatest philosopher of his time. . . . Whatever prejudice I may have against the doctrines of the Enquiry, my conscience acquits me of any prejudice against the author. Our friendship was sincere while he lived, without ever a difference, except in matters of opinion.

Kames ends, "I never was addicted to controversy; and would have avoided the attacking a gentleman who had both my love and esteem, had it been consistent with the plan of the present work."[43]

Perhaps with none of his Scottish contemporaries did Hume have a closer friendship or more of an impact on the topics of morals, politics, and society than with Adam Smith. Smith was familiar with Hume's works from an early date, probably from Smith's student days at Oxford University in the early 1740s.[44] It is not known when the men met for the first time, but it was probably sometime around 1748, and the two quickly became closest of friends. In early 1752, only a couple of weeks after the foundation of the Glasgow Literary Society with which Smith was involved, we find him reading a paper on an "account of some of Mr David Hume's Essays on Commerce."[45] From the early 1750s the two friends were frequent correspondents, and that exchange of letters gives us a sense of their familiarity with one another's works. Writing to Smith in September 1752, Hume was even eager to have Smith's improvements for a new edition of his *Essays:* "I am just now diverted for a Moment by correcting my Essays moral & political, for a new Edition. If any thing occur to you to be inserted or retrench'd, I shall be obliged to you for the Hint. In case you shou'd not have the last Edition by you, I shall send you a Copy of it."[46]

When he came to publish his own ideas, Smith cited Hume's works frequently – including in his two most important books, *The Theory of Moral Sentiments* (1759) and his widely read, then and now, *An Enquiry into the Nature and Causes of the Wealth of Nations* (1776). D. D. Raphael and A. L. Macfie – the editors of *The Theory of Moral Sentiments* for the Glasgow Edition of the Works of Adam Smith – find that "among contemporary thinkers Hume had the greatest influence." Commentators have shown, for instance, how in *The Theory of Moral Sentiments,* Smith enlisted the concept of "a spectator" as an impartial judge to help in formulating his theory of morals, much as Hume (and Francis Hutcheson [1694–1747] before him) had.[47] But Smith did not accept all that Hume wrote. Far from it; according to Raphael and Macfie, "Smith rejects or transforms Hume's ideas far more often than he follows them, but his own views would have been markedly different if he had not been stimulated to disagreement with Hume."[48] In Smith's discussion "Of the Amiable and Respectable Virtues," for instance, we see a Humean influence but one tempered by Smith's leanings toward Stoicism, something Hume rejected. And like Kames, Smith was highly critical of Hume's theory of justice.

Smith, then, did not imitate Hume slavishly, and even often disagreed with him in significant ways, but Hume's publications provided Smith with several points of departure. Hume's overall impact on Smith is wonderfully summarized by Smith's modern biographer Ian Simpson Ross:

> Pondering the development of thought here from Hume to Smith, we can see that the foundation of their friendship, perhaps, was the recognition by the younger man (b. 1723) of the brilliance of the older (b. 1711), and a willingness to take his ideas and challenge them, then push them further, to advance major ideals of the Enlight-

enment which they held in common, namely, expansion of natural liberty within the framework of law, through an understanding of the principles of human nature and the outcome of social forces, with a view to maximizing human welfare.[49]

Perhaps nothing demonstrates their closeness more than Smith's offer to correct the proofs of the final edition of the dying Hume's *Essays and Treatises on Several Subjects.* Smith wrote from his home in Kirkcaldy in August 1776: "I shall likewise, if you will give me leave, correct the Sheets of the new edition of your works, and shall take care that it shall be published exactly according to your last corrections."[50] It is difficult to imagine Hume trusting anyone else to such a task. As Hume's final days approached, it was Smith to whom he turned to assure the posthumous publication of his *Dialogues Concerning Natural Religion* and his autobiographical "My Own Life."

In March 1777 Smith contributed the important introductory material – a preface and a letter about Hume's character – to William Strahan's edition of *The Life of David Hume, Esq. Written by Himself.* There, Smith praised Hume's "constant pleasantry," the result of his "good-nature and good-humour, tempered with delicacy and modesty," and infamously concluded, "Upon the whole, I have always considered him, both in his lifetime and since his death, as approaching as nearly to the idea of a perfectly wise and virtuous man, as perhaps the nature of human frailty will permit."[51] Smith's involvement here signifies more than their close friendship. As Richard B. Sher aptly summarizes, "Together, 'My Own Life' and Smith's letter showed off the camaraderie that prevailed among the Scottish literati of Hume's day at the same time that they humanized and glorified an author whose writings were frequently viewed as harmful to morality and society."[52] Others in the eighteenth century who were on less intimate terms with Hume nonetheless took his ideas in various directions and far beyond the Scottish Enlightenment.

The English utilitarian thinker Jeremy Bentham offers an illustrative example. In his *A Fragment on Government* (1776), Bentham claimed that it was after reading Hume on the principle of utility that he formulated his utilitarian theory (Bentham wrote, "I felt as if scales had fallen from my eyes"). That is not to say that there is a simple and direct trajectory to be drawn from Hume to Bentham, but that Hume's writing inspired Bentham's utilitarianism seems irrefutable.[53]

Perhaps Hume's most significant contribution to the study of morals, society, and especially politics was rooted in his efforts to approach those topics historically, from the perspective of experience. Only then might one hope to make a science of politics.[54] That lesson was one that had an impact not only with Hume's contemporary readers in Britain and Europe but also on the other side of the Atlantic, where some of Hume's eighteenth-century readers were in the midst of their own political experiment, the creation of the American republic.

Hume's Early American Reception

Hume's publications we now know – including those reprinted in this volume – circulated widely in America during the eighteenth century.[55] Americans not only read Hume's works for the pleasures they contained; they cited them often on particular points being debated in the newspapers, pamphlets, and books of the day.[56] On topics ranging from the liberty of the press and the opinion of right, to the idea of a perfect commonwealth, the political maxim that every man must be supposed a knave, and calls for freer trade and balanced constitutions, Hume was a cited authority. Unfortunately, Hume's infamous footnote to his essay "Of National Characters" – Hume there wrote, "I am apt to suspect the negroes to be naturally inferior to the whites" – was also in play. Some, like Edward Long (1734–1813) in his *The History of Jamaica* (1774) and Richard Nisbet in *Slavery Not Forbidden by Scripture* (1773), quoted Hume's line with approval. Others, such as Benjamin Rush (1746–1813) and the anonymous author of *Personal Slavery Established* (1773), defied Hume's suspicions.[57] But Hume's most lasting impact in America is found elsewhere. It is not to be gathered in any catalogue of particular lessons that Americans discovered – or challenged – on his pages. It is realized in the cumulative effect on those, like James Madison, who internalized so much of what Hume wrote. As was the case with others who read Hume carefully, Madison came to believe that "political and social theory always needed to be tested against, and refined by, historical experience and contemporary practice."[58]

In 1787 Madison joined with Alexander Hamilton (1757–1804) and John Jay (1745–1829) to produce *The Federalist*. Originally published as a series of eighty-five newspaper essays that aimed, pragmatically, to defend the U.S. Constitution of 1787, *The Federalist* succeeded, timelessly, to present in the voice of Publius the core principles of eighteenth-century American political thought. Here, the American Founding Fathers' debt to Hume was stated more clearly than is usually the case when it comes to noting intellectual influence. In the concluding paragraph to Federalist no. 85–the concluding paper of the entire collection–Publius identified Hume as a "solid and ingenious" writer who provided "judicious reflections" for Americans in the midst of creating their new, experimental state. That founding process had not come to its conclusion with the end of the American War of Independence in 1783 or with the ratification of the U.S. Constitution in 1787. Indeed, in defense of the plan of government established in that Constitution, Publius quoted a passage from Hume's "Of the Rise and Progress of the Arts and Sciences":

> To balance a large state or society (says he), whether monarchical or republican, on general laws, is a work of so great difficulty that no human genius, however comprehensive, is able, by the mere dint of reason and reflection, to effect it. The judgments of many must unite in the work; EXPERIENCE must guide their labor; TIME must bring it to perfection, and the FEELING of inconveniences must correct the mistakes which they *inevitably* fall into in their first trials and experiments.[59]

Here, then, is a significant role for Hume far beyond the composition, reception, and early influence of Hume's *Essays* and *Enquiry Concerning the Principles of Morals*.

By the early decades of the nineteenth century, Hume's reputation as an enlightened "man of letters" was firmly established, and his moral, political, and social thought continued to circulate widely. In America, Hume's *Essays and Treatises on Several Subjects* and *History of England* were now incorporated into college libraries and curriculums, and informed debates in print and in various learned associations, including student societies. An important publication in this regard was Thomas Ewell's (1785–1826) two-volume edition, in 1817, of Hume's "collected works," entitled *Philosophical Essays on Morals, Literature, and Politics; by David Hume*.[60] There, in a book Ewell proudly cast as a "FIRST AMERICAN EDITION," Hume's nineteenth-century students had access in one place to all of the writings that are again published together in *David Hume on Morals, Politics, and Society*.

NOTES

1. A good point of entry for students interested in this vast historiography is the journal *Hume Studies,* published since 1975. It is fully indexed.
2. David Hume, "My Own Life," in David Hume, *The History of England from the Invasion of Julius Caesar to The Revolution in 1688,* 6 vols., ed.

William B. Todd (Indianapolis: Liberty Fund, 1983), 1:xxvii. This piece it-self was very much cast for the eighteenth century's growing audience of readers. It was first published by William Strahan (1715–1785) as *The Life of David Hume, Esq. Written by Himself* (London, 1777), accompanied by a letter about Hume's last days written by Adam Smith (1723–1790), Hume's close friend and a fellow member of the Scottish Enlightenment. Smith and his role in Strahan's publication of Hume's *Life* are discussed below.

3. Two standard modern biographies are Ernest Campbell Mossner, *The Life of David Hume* (Edinburgh: Thomas Nelson and Sons, 1954; revised edition, Ox-ford: Clarendon Press, 1980), and Roderick Graham, *The Great Infidel: A Life of David Hume* (East Lothian, Scotland: Tuckwell Press, 2004). Here, I have drawn on both, and others, such as A. J. Ayer's short volume for the Past Mas-ters series, *Hume* (Oxford: Oxford University Press, 1980). As the accounts of Hume intellectual life in all of these biographies are defective, students of Hume will welcome the new intellectual biography by James Harris, *Hume: An Intellectual Biography* (Cambridge: Cambridge University Press, 2015). Two recent essays are also useful for what they tell us about Hume's intellectual biography: M. A. Stewart, "Hume's Intellectual Development, 1711–1752," in *Impressions of Hume,* ed. Marina Frasca-Spada and P. J. E. Kail (Oxford: Oxford University Press, 2005), 11–58, and Roger L. Emerson, "Hume's Intel-lectual Development: Part II," chapter 6 in Roger L. Emerson, *Essays on David Hume, Medical Men and the Scottish Enlightenment: "Industry, Knowledge and Humanity"* (Farnham, England: Ashgate, 2009), 103–25.

4. Hume, "My Own Life," xxvii.

5. See J. Y. T. Greig, ed., *The Letters of David Hume,* 2 vols. (1932; reprint edi-tion Oxford: Oxford University Press, 2011), 1:9. For other published Hume letters, students might consult Raymond Klibansky and Ernest C. Mossner, eds., *New Letters of David Hume* (Oxford: Oxford University Press, 1954), and, more recently, Felix Waldmann, *Further Letters of David Hume* (Edin-burgh: Edinburgh Bibliographical Society, 2014). David Raynor is preparing for publication an edition of Hume's complete correspondence.

6. Greig, *Letters,* 1:9.

7. Greig, *Letters,* 1:13.

8. Greig, *Letters,* 1:22.

9. See Hume's *An Abstract of a Book Lately Published; Entitled, "A Treatise of Human Nature," &c. Wherein the Chief Argument of That Book Is Far-ther Illustrated and Explained* (London, 1740). For a modern reprinting, see *An Abstract of a "Treatise of Human Nature" 1740: A Pamphlet Hitherto Unknown by David Hume,* ed. J. M. Keynes and P. Sraffa (Cambridge: Cam-bridge University Press, 1938). See also Mark G. Spencer, "Another 'Curious

Legend' about Hume's *An Abstract of a Treatise of Human Nature," Hume Studies* 29 (April 2003): 89–98.

10. Hume, "My Own Life," xxviii.

11. Hume, "My Own Life," xxix.

12. That passage comes near the beginning of Hume's *Enquiry Concerning Human Understanding;* see Tom L. Beauchamp's edition (Oxford: Clarendon Press, 2000), 7.

13. The first surviving reference to what would become the *Essays* may be in Hume's letter to Henry Home of 1 June 1739: "You see I am better than my word, having sent you two papers instead of one. I have hints of two or three more, which I shall execute at my leisure." Greig, *Letters,* 1:30. A month later, on 1 July 1739, he wrote again: "I hope you always esteem yourself more obliged to me when I send you papers I do not approve of, than when I send you those I think more tolerable; since there may be a share of vanity in the latter case, which can have no part in the former. I have a strong suspicion against the present packet. One of the papers will be found very cold; and the other be esteemed somewhat sophistical." Greig, *Letters,* 1:31.

14. It contained fifteen essays, some of which work at his original plan to write about taste and politics. All were "moral" in the eighteenth-century meaning of that term, as pertaining to the actions of men. The essays were (1) "Of the Delicacy of Taste and Passion"; (2) "Of the Liberty of the Press"; (3) "Of Impudence and Modesty"; (4) "That Politicks May Be Reduc'd to a Science"; (5) "Of the First Principles of Government"; (6) "Of Love and Marriage"; (7) "Of the Study of History"; (8) "Of the Independency of Parliament"; (9) "Whether the British Government Inclines More to Absolute Monarchy, or to a Republick"; (10) "Of Parties in General"; (11) "Of the Parties of Great Britain"; (12) "Of Superstition and Enthusiasm"; (13) "Of Avarice"; (14) "Of the Dignity of Human Nature"; and (15) "Of Liberty and Despotism." For a more complete publishing history of Hume's various essays, see Eugene Miller's foreword to his edition of Hume's *Essays.* See David Hume, *Essays Moral, Political and Literary,* ed. Eugene F. Miller (Indianapolis: Liberty Classics, 1985), xi–xviii.

15. Hume, *Essays,* ed. Miller, xxxiv.

16. Ryu Susato, *Hume's Sceptical Enlightenment* (Edinburgh: University of Edinburgh Press, 2015), offers the latest discussion of this topic, placing Hume's ideas in their historical context.

17. Hume, *An Enquiry Concerning Human Understanding,* ed. Beauchamp, 99.

18. Hume to Henry Home, 13 June 1742, in Klibansky and Mossner, *New Letters of David Hume,* 10.

19. Hume, "My Own Life," xxx.

20. Roger L. Emerson, "A Note on Hume and Political Economy," in Emerson, *Essays on David Hume,* 155–62, 160 (quotation). See also Roger L. Emerson, "The Scottish Contexts for David Hume's Political-Economic Thinking," in *David Hume's Political Economy,* ed. Carl Wennerlind and Margaret Schabas (New York: Routledge, 2008), 10–30, and in the same volume, Ian Simpson Ross, "Emergence of Hume as Political Economist: A Biographical Perspective," 31–48. For an attempt to sketch some aspects of the Scottish background on the topic, see the essays in N. T. Phillipson and Rosalind Mitchison, eds., *Scotland in the Age of Improvement* (Edinburgh: Edinburgh University Press, 1970).

21. On this wider Scottish context, see David Allan, *Scotland in the Eighteenth Century: Union and Enlightenment* (London: Longman, 2002), esp. 85–103.

22. Emerson, "A Note on Hume and Political Economy," 159. That Highland improvement (or lack thereof) was still on Hume's mind in the mid-1750s is evident from his correspondence. See Hume to John Wilkes, 8 October 1754: "If your time had permitted, you should have gone into the Highlands. You woud there have seen human Nature in the golden Age, or rather, indeed, in the Silver: For the Highlanders have degenerated somewhat from the primitive Simplicity of Mankind." Greig, *Letters,* 1:195.

23. David Hume, *Essays, Moral, Political and Literary,* Essay 8, paragraphs 4–5. For a useful essay connecting Hume's *Political Discourses* and his *History of England* to his *Treatise* on the topic of commercialization, see Carl Wennerlind, "David Hume's Political Philosophy: A Theory of Commercial Modernization," *Hume Studies* 28 (2002): 247–70. On this wider topic, see also Christopher Berry's recent book *The Idea of Commercial Society in the Scottish Enlightenment* (Edinburgh: Edinburgh University Press, 2013).

24. The universality of Hume's *Political Discourses* helps to explain the work's wide circulation outside of Scotland. On its significant circulation in eighteenth-century France, for instance, see Gilles Robel, "Hume's *Political Discourses* in France," in *The Edinburgh History of the Book in Scotland,* vol. 2, *Enlightenment and Expansion, 1707–1800,* ed. Stephen W. Brown and Warren McDougall (Edinburgh: Edinburgh University Press, 2012), 221–32.

25. The debate on Hume as a conservative or liberal thinker has been especially fruitful. Compare, for instance, Donald W. Livingston, "David Hume and the Conservative Tradition," *The Intercollegiate Review* 44 (2009): 30–41, with John B. Stewart, "The Public Interest vs. Old Rights," *Hume Studies* 21 (1995): 165–88.

26. Hume, "My Own Life," xxx.

27. David Hume, *An Enquiry Concerning the Principles of Morals,* appendix 4, note 78.

28. For a recent and informative history of those editions, see Lorne Falkenstein and Neil McArthur, introduction to *Essays and Treatises on Philosophical Subjects: David Hume,* ed. Lorne Falkenstein and Neil McArthur (Peterborough, Ontario: Broadview Editions, 2013), 15–44.

29. For a recent collection of essays approaching the *History* from an interdisciplinary perspective, see Mark G. Spencer, ed., *David Hume: Historical Thinker, Historical Writer* (University Park: Pennsylvania State University Press, 2013).

30. See Stephen W. Brown and Warren McDougall, introduction to Brown and McDougall, eds., *The Edinburgh History of the Book in Scotland,* 2:21.

31. Hume, "My Own Life," xxxiii.

32. See, for instance, the primary sources collected together in James Fieser, ed., *Early Responses to Hume,* 10 vols. (1999; second, revised edition, Bristol, England: Thoemmes Continuum, 2005), and Mark G. Spencer, ed., *Hume's Reception in Early America,* 2 vols. (Bristol, England: Thoemmes Press, 2002). See also Peter Jones, ed., *The Reception of David Hume in Europe* (Bristol, England: Thoemmes Continuum, 2005); David Allan, *Making British Culture: English Readers and the Scottish Enlightenment, 1740–1830* (New York: Routledge, 2008); and Mark R. M. Towsey, *Reading the Scottish Enlightenment: Books and Their Readers in Provincial Scotland, 1750–1820* (Leiden: Brill, 2010). This trend of giving increased attention to an author's contemporary reception is not specific to Hume or to authors of the Scottish Enlightenment. Historiographically, the trend might be thought to harken back to a broadening of the history of ideas to include their social components. See, for instance, Robert Darnton, "In Search of the Enlightenment: Recent Attempts to Create a Social History of Ideas," *Journal of Modern History* 43 (1971): 113–32.

33. William Rose, "ART. I. *An Enquiry Concerning the Principles of Morals.* By David Hume, Esq; 12mo. 3s. Millar," *Monthly Review* 6 (January 1752): 1–19, 1 (quotation).

34. William Rose, "ART. II. *Political Discourses.* By David Hume, Esq; 8vo. 3s. Printed at Edinburgh; for Kincaid and Donaldson," *Monthly Review* 6 (January 1752): 19–43, 19 (quotation).

35. [Anon.], "Art. 18. *Two New Essays,* by David Hume, Esq; 1st. *Of the Jealousy of Trade.* 2d. *Of the Coalition of Parties,*" *Critical Review* 9 (1760): 493.

36. William Rose, "*Four Dissertations. 1. The Natural History of Religion. 2. Of the Passions. 3. Of Tragedy. 4. Of the Standard of Taste.* By David

Hume, Esq; 12mo. 3s. Millar," *Monthly Review* 16 (1757): 122–139, 122 (quotation).

37. On Ferguson and his *An Essay on the History of Civil Society,* see Duncan Forbes's introduction to his edition for Edinburgh University Press (1966). See also David Kettler, *The Social and Political Thought of Adam Ferguson* (Columbus: Ohio State University Press, 1965); David Allan, *Adam Ferguson* (Aberdeen: Arts and Humanities Research Council Centre for Irish and Scottish Studies, 2006); and Iain McDaniel, *Adam Ferguson in the Scottish Enlightenment: The Roman Past and Europe's Future* (Cambridge, Mass.: Harvard University Press, 2013).

38. Ferguson, *An Essay on the History of Civil Society,* 141.

39. Hume to Hugh Blair, 11 February 1766, in Greig, *Letters,* 2:11–12.

40. Hume wrote to Blair on 1 April 1767 to say that the "success" of Ferguson's book gave him "great Satisfaction, on account of my sincere Friendship for the Author; and so much the rather, as this Success was to me unexpected. I have since begun to hope, and even to believe, that I was mistaken; and in this Perswasion have several times taken it up and read Chapters of it: But to my great Mortification and Sorrow, I have not been able to change my Sentiments." Greig, *Letters,* 2:133.

41. For a modern reprinting of the 1779 edition with accompanying textual apparatus, see Henry Home, Lord Kames, *Essays on the Principles of Morality and Natural Religion: Corrected and Improved, in a Third Edition. Several Essays Added Concerning the Proof of a Deity,* ed. Mary Catherine Moran (Indianapolis: Liberty Fund, 2005). My quotations are from that edition.

42. Kames, *Essays on the Principles of Morality,* 82.

43. Kames, *Essays on the Principles of Morality,* 94–95. Their earlier friendship had been hardened when they were attacked together on charges of infidelity, including ones brought on by George Anderson in *An Estimate of the Profit and Loss of Religion, Personally and Publicly Stated: Illustrated with Reference to Essays on Morality and Natural Religion* (Edinburgh, 1753). That Hume did not think much of Anderson is evident from his correspondence. He wrote to Alan Ramsay in 1752: "Anderson, the godly, spiteful, pious, splenetic, charitable, unrelenting, meek, persecuting, Christian, inhuman, peace-making, furious Anderson, is at present very hot in pursuit of Lord Kames." See Hume to Allan Ramsay, n.d., in Greig, *Letters,* 1:224.

44. See D. D. Raphael, "'The True Old Humean Philosophy' and Its Influence on Adam Smith," in *David Hume Bicentenary Papers,* ed. G. P. Morice (Edinburgh: Edinburgh University Press, 1977), 23–38.

45. See Ian Simpson Ross, "Adam Smith's 'Happiest' Years as a Glasgow Profes-

sor," in *The Glasgow Enlightenment,* ed. Andrew Hook and Richard B. Sher (East Lothian, Scotland: Tuckwell Press, 1995), 73–94, 80 (quotation).

46. Hume to Adam Smith, 24 September 1752, in Greig, *Letters,* 1:168.

47. For an introduction to the complicated relationship between the philosophy of Hutcheson, Hume, and Smith, see John Robertson, "The Scottish Contribution to the Enlightenment," in *The Scottish Enlightenment: Essays in Reinterpretation,* ed. Paul Wood (Rochester, N.Y.: University of Rochester Press, 2000), 37–62.

48. D. D. Raphael and A. L. Macfie, introduction to Adam Smith, *The Theory of Moral Sentiments* (Indianapolis: Liberty Classics, 1982; an exact photographic reproduction of the edition published by Oxford University Press in 1976 and reprinted with minor corrections in 1979), 10.

49. Ian Simpson Ross, "The Intellectual Friendship of David Hume and Adam Smith," in *New Essays on David Hume,* ed. Emilio Mazza and Emanuele Ronchetti (Manilo, Italy: FancoAngeli, 2007), 345–63, 346 (quotation). More recently, see Ross's *The Life of Adam Smith* (Oxford: Clarendon Press, 1995), esp. chapter 16, "Euge! Belle! *Dear Mr Smith,*" 270–88.

50. Adam Smith to Hume, 22 August 1776, in *The Correspondence of Adam Smith,* ed. Ernest Campbell Mossner and Ian Simpson Ross (Indianapolis: Liberty Classics, 1987), 206.

51. Smith's letter circulated widely, not only in Strahan's pamphlet but also when it was appended to most posthumous editions of Hume's *Essays and Treatises on Several Subjects* and *History of England.* The sections of it quoted in this essay are from the 1778 edition of the *History,* ed. Todd, 1:xxxix–xl. On Strahan, see J. A. Cochrane, *Dr. Johnson's Printer: The Life of William Strahan* (London: Routledge and Kegan Paul, 1964).

52. Richard B. Sher, *The Enlightenment and the Book: Scottish Authors and Their Publishers in Eighteenth-Century Britain, Ireland, and America* (Chicago: University of Chicago Press, 2006), 56.

53. The connection has long been noted in the scholarship and was summarized in Albee Ernest's *A History of English Utilitarianism* (London: Allen and Unwin, 1901). More recently, see Douglas G. Long, "'Utility' and the 'Utility Principle': Hume, Smith, Bentham, Mill," *Utilitas* 12 (1990): 12–39, and Stephen Darwall, "Hume and the Invention of Utilitarianism," in *Hume and Hume's Connexions,* ed. M. A. Stewart and John P. Wright (University Park: Pennsylvania State University Press, 1995), 58–82, who concludes, "Thus did Hume open up a space for philosophical utilitarianism even if he did not himself occupy it" (76). Annette C. Baier, *A Progress of Sentiments: Reflections on Hume's "Treatise"* (Cambridge, Mass.: Harvard University

Press, 1991), argues persuasively that Hume's "emphasis on pleasure as the good for the sake of which we endorse enlightened versions of morality, is what Bentham found so enlightening in Hume's writings. . . . But Bentham blunts Hume's distinction between the useful and the agreeable, distorting the agreeable into cash utility" (204).

54. See James Moore, "The Social Background of Hume's Science of Human Nature," in *McGill Hume Studies,* ed. David Fate Norton, Nicholas Capaldi, and Wade L. Robison (San Diego: Austin Hill Press, 1976), 12–41. Moore writes, "And the experimental nature of the rules and conventions of society was to become Hume's point of departure for a science of politics in which forms of government and politics were themselves regarded as experiments, as uncertain trails of judgment by which politicians have attempted to contrive a world consistent with the uniform interests and passions, the needs and wants of human beings" (40–41).

55. See Mark G. Spencer, *David Hume and Eighteenth-Century America* (Rochester, N.Y.: University of Rochester Press, 2005). See also James Moore, "Hume's Political Science and the Classical Republican Tradition," *Canadian Journal of Political Science* 10 (1977): 809–39.

56. For a pioneering study on citation as a key to influence, see Donald S. Lutz, "The Relative Influence of European Writers on Late Eighteenth-Century American Political Thought," *American Political Science Review* 78 (1984): 189–97.

57. See Spencer, *David Hume and Eighteenth-Century America,* 72–74. For the wider Scottish context, see Iain Whyte, "'The Upas Tree, Beneath Whose Pestiferous Shade All Intellect Languishes and All Virtue Dies': Scottish Perceptions of the Slave Trade and Slavery, 1756–1833," in *Recovering Scotland's Slavery Past: The Caribbean Connection,* ed. T. M. Devine (Edinburgh: Edinburgh University Press, 2015), 187–206.

58. See Mark G. Spencer, "Hume and Madison on Faction," *William and Mary Quarterly,* 3rd series, 59 (2002): 869–96, 896 (quotation).

59. Publius, "Federalist No. 85," in *The Federalist Papers,* ed. Clinton Rossiter (New York: New American Library, 1961), 56–57.

60. Ewell's edition added some further apparatus, as his full title indicates: *Philosophical Essays on Morals, Literature, and Politics; by David Hume. To Which Is Added, the Answer to His Objections to Christianity, by Dr. Campbell. Also, an Account of Mr. Hume's Life, an Original Essay, and a Few Notes.* Two imprints from 1817 are known: Philadelphia and Georgetown, D.C.

For their helpful comments on drafts of this chapter, the author is grateful to Roger L. Emerson and Mark Hanvelt; the volume's editors, Angela Coventry and Andrew Valls; and his anonymous readers for Yale University Press.

How Hume Influenced Contemporary Moral Philosophy

ELIZABETH S. RADCLIFFE

Hume's impact on the course of moral theory is immeasurable. He wrote in the era known as the Enlightenment, characterized by rejection of the theocentric medieval worldview and substitution of nature-based perspectives in science, humanities, social and political science, philosophy, and other areas. One of the major intellectual and practical advances of the seventeenth century was the development of a distinct scientific method. Hume's project was to implement this newly developed method in an empirical study of human nature. He has subsequently been regarded as a pioneer in the program of "experimental" philosophy, which emphasizes the use of empirical data to inform conceptual analyses. Hume's endeavors produced theoretical innovations in moral philosophy (and other areas), and his proposals concerning how morality originates from human nature have continually been revisited and revised in the centuries since he wrote. His impact on moral theory has been wide-ranging, persistent, and–in a few ways–paradoxical.

Hume offers a moral epistemology, a theory of how we make moral distinctions, one that is foundational to moral naturalism. He rejects attempts to portray morality as accessible by rational intuition of specifically moral facts or through theological channels. Chief among Hume's influential theses are (1) that reason is inert to produce action without the assistance of passion (motivational anti-rationalism), (2) that the moral distinctions we make depend on sentiments of approval (moral sentimentalism), and (3) that conclusions about what we ought to do cannot be inferred from claims about what is the case (the is-ought gap, sometimes called "Hume's Law" or "Hume's Guillotine"). Each of these theses has inspired its own large body of literature, the first on the Humean theory of motivation, the second on Humean sentimentalism, and the last on the relation between facts and values. Ironically, some non-naturalists and advocates of the "autonomy" of morality (morality as an area independent from anything we study in the natural world) have pointed to Hume's remarks on the logical gap between "is" and "ought" as providing grounds for their position. And surprisingly, some contemporary scholars have argued that Hume's theory of motivation and practical reasoning is actually significantly different from the contemporary theory that bears his name.[1] Moreover, in normative ethics, many contemporary virtue theorists claim Hume as progenitor,[2] but some consequentialists do as well.[3]

So, pieces of Hume's ethical theory lend themselves to conflicting traditions, and it is an intriguing question which positions can legitimately make claim to his arguments as their foundation. Is Hume's moral legacy one of confusion or one of a multifaceted, complex, but consistent morality? In the following, I discuss the various strands in ethical theory that each of these three theses has motivated, starting with motivational anti-rationalism, moving to the "is-ought" gap, and then concluding with moral sentimentalism. Along the way, I offer some observations about various interpretations of Hume and his impact on directions in contemporary ethics. Hume first advanced his moral theory in book 3 of *A Treatise of Human Nature* (1740) and then reformulated it for more popular presentation in his later *Enquiry Concerning the Principles of Morals* (1751). As some critics have noted, he may have changed his mind about some of the details of his sentimentalist theory in the intervening years, but his fundamental views about the inertness of reason and the necessity of sentiment to morality did not change.[4] Hume's *Essays* also anticipate certain themes in the moral theory of the second *Enquiry*.

Motivational Anti-Rationalism

The classical arguments defending the "belief-desire" model of motivation integral to contemporary naturalism are usually attributed to Hume. However, in fact, Francis Hutcheson first advanced arguments about the inertness of reason in *Illustrations on the Moral Sense* (1728): he argues that all truths are discovered by reason, but any truths that appear to excite us to action ("exciting" reasons) presuppose affections for objects to which those truths refer.[5] But Hume's formulation of the arguments are almost universally referenced in current discussions of motivation and practical reason, because he gives a sustained, systematic defense of his theory, one grounded in principles of empirical psychology and science (T 2.3.3.3; EPM, app. 1).[6]

Hume's thesis that reason alone cannot motivate is actually vague, and its meaning has been subject to much discussion. It in fact provides a step in a larger argument against the seventeenth-century rationalists Ralph Cudworth and Samuel Clarke (among others). Clarke argues that there are eternal relations and fitnesses in the universe that determine our obligations and "make it fit and reasonable for creatures to so act."[7] Cudworth, at least in his later writings, promotes the view that morality, if it exists, must be necessary, eternal, and immutable, in the way the truths of math and logic are.[8] In response, Hume offers a two-stage argument to combat the conclusion that morality is constituted by rational relations and is discerned by reason on its own. The first stage defends the view that reason cannot motivate action on its own, and the second concludes that morality cannot be derived from reason alone. The second follows from the first, given Hume's observation that morality concerns practice and does motivate on its own (T 2.3.3, 3.1.1; EPM, 1.7–8, app. 1).

Hume argues in *A Treatise of Human Nature* that reason functions to discover truth and falsity, via either demonstration or causal (probable) reasoning. Demonstration is about conceptual relations, so it cannot motivate us to action (on its own), since action has to do with changing the way the world is. Causal reasoning does not originate motives either: "It can never in the least concern us to know, that such objects are causes, and such other effects, if both the causes and effects be indifferent to us" (T 2.3.3.3). In the *Enquiry Concerning the Principles of Morals,* Hume affirms this claim: "Utility is only a tendency to a certain end; and were the end totally indifferent to us, we should feel that same indifference toward the means" (EPM, app. 1.3). He there encapsulates his argument about the inertness of reason by pointing out that reasoning and speculation can offer us representations of virtue and vice.

However, inferences of the understanding "have no hold of the affections" and do not "set in motion the active powers of men." Hume writes, "What is intelligible, what is evident, what is probable, what is true, procures only the cool assent of the understanding; and gratifying a speculative curiosity, puts an end to our searches" (EPM, 1.7). What is necessary to engage us are the passions, which arise upon our reflecting on sources of pleasure and pain (although some passions are also instinctual[9]); the use of reflection, however, does not imply that reason produces the passions. Hume notes, "the ultimate ends of human action can never, in any case, be accounted for by *reason,* but recommend themselves entirely to the sentiments and affections of mankind." (EPM, app. 1.18). If we ask a person why she exercises, she replies that she desires to be healthy; if asked why she wants to be healthy, she says that sickness is unpleasant. Hume observes that it is impossible to give an explanation why anyone hates pain. Avoidance of pain is an ultimate end for which no reason can be given (EPM, app. 1.18). Ultimately, the passions are a matter of taste, not reason, since what one finds pleasurable or painful is due to one's constitution.

Contemporary Humeans about motivation (Simon Blackburn, Mark Schroeder, Neil Sinhababu, Michael Smith, and Bernard Williams,[10] among others) take it that Hume is here defending the view that a passion (specifically desire) separate from belief, the product of reason, is necessary for motivation. Whether Hume actually means to say this is a matter of debate. Smith's argument for Humeanism makes the claim that reference to a desire-state is necessary in order to explain what it is for someone to have a motivating reason, a reason that explains one's action. (Although Hume himself does not countenance reasons for action, he would regard what Smith considers a motivating reason as a cause or an explanation.) Smith draws on Elizabeth Anscombe's description of belief and desire in terms of "direction of fit" to explain his view: beliefs aim to fit the world, and true beliefs succeed in doing so; desires aim to fit the world with themselves, and it is no fault in a desire if it is not realized in the world.[11] When the desire is paired with a belief about the means to the end, contemporary Humeans say that we have a motivating reason for action, but that the reason has two distinct elements, belief and desire.

Some opponents to Humeanism reply that it is possible for one mental state to have both directions of fit, to serve as belief and desire at the same time. So-called besires are purported to be cognitive states that prompt behavior. John McDowell says, for instance, that a virtuous person's cognitions about goodness motivate certain behavior. For instance, a person's conception of another as shy makes the virtuous person behave in ways that would make the shy person comfortable in public situations.[12] Smith's reply, however, is that for any belief state about good (in a virtuous person or not), we can conceive of one who is in that mental state but lacks the relevant desire. Saying this is not enough, I think, to get at just what is compelling about this reply. For one might object that while Smith's point demonstrates that beliefs and desires are not conceptually the same, it might be the case that they have the same referent – like Clark Kent and Superman. The problem with this objection is that we have no way to determine what it would be like to find a belief posing or functioning as a desire. We can only identify a belief-state by its role in our mental life, its role of representing the world to us in a certain way, and a desire-state by its role of providing an impetus to change the world in a certain respect. So, there is no way to discover that a motive (a desire) is also a representation (a belief). The criterion of identity requires me to recognize the belief and desire states separately, and it would feel no differently to me if the belief and desire had the same referent than if they were two different states occurring to me simultaneously.[13]

While Hume has influenced discussions in motivational psychology in a significant way, some critics have recently questioned whether Hume actually meant to be arguing for the Humean theory of motivation. The idea behind this suggestion is that while Hume clearly thinks that reason alone does not motivate, beliefs (or some beliefs) and reason are not identical. Different critics have offered various renditions of how Hume's account unfolds in this regard: (1) beliefs about sources of pleasure and pain are non-inferential and so are not produced by reason; thus, they can motivate even though reason cannot;[14] or (2) beliefs about sources of pleasure and pain can motivate, even though other beliefs cannot, because pleasure and pain are "active";[15] or (3) just because the reasoning process itself cannot produce motivating passions does not mean that the products of reason, namely beliefs, cannot produce motivating passions;[16] or (4) the faculty of reason, producing only ideas, never has a passion or an action as a product, but this does not imply that beliefs do not produce passions or actions.[17] However, readers should be cautious in accepting the suggestion that what Hume says about the inertness of reason really does not apply to beliefs.

There is a natural way to understand Hume's account that does not rely on the view that beliefs about the causes of pleasure and pain have motivating force on their own. I have an experience of pleasure from an object that I know has certain features—for instance, a deep red cabernet with chocolate overtones. So, I then desire wines with that deep and chocolaty cabernet essence because I have experienced the pleasure they bring. Reason yields the belief that another wine, which I have not experienced, has similar characteristics. Since I desire those features, this wine holds for me the prospect of pleasure, and I acquire a desire for it. Desire originates from the impression of pleasure I have experienced in the past and gets transferred to future objects via reasoning. The motivation is not originating in a belief but in a sentiment of pleasure. This interpretation is consistent with Hume's declaring in the *Enquiry,* "Taste, as it gives pleasure or pain, and thereby constitutes happiness or misery, becomes a motive to action, and is the first spring or impulse to desire and volition" (EPM, app. 1.21). There are, I believe, systematic reasons as well to think that Hume regards beliefs without passions as inert. One of these reasons is the difficulty in explaining how beliefs and passions compete to cause action. Passions, for Hume, have causal strength and no content; beliefs have content and are held with degrees of conviction. Competition would require a common parameter, but it is hard to say what that might be. I have no space to say more, but I have discussed such matters elsewhere.[18]

In present-day discussions on the topic of reason, morality, and action, the rationalists against whom Humeans argue are not typically subscribers to a Clarkeian or Cudworthian view, but rather to an ethics inspired by eighteenth-century philosopher Immanuel Kant. The Humean-Kantian debate in ethics and action theory has focused on the nature of practical reason—whether and how reason can formulate recommendations for action—in addition to assessing representations of the world. Most parties to the discussion assume that if reason is practical, then in judging an action worthy, reason can give rise directly to non-cognitive, intentional states that motivate the action thought best. Those philosophers who argue that reason can evaluate the ends of action, and that rational agents necessarily have a motive to pursue those assessed as morally or prudentially required, have a Kantian orientation—for instance, Stephen Darwall, Alan Donagan, Alan Gewirth, Christine Korsgaard, and Thomas Nagel.[19] Of course, the details of their theories differ from each other and from Kant's.

On the other hand, naturalists typically defend Humean instrumentalism, the view that reason cannot evaluate the appropriateness of ends but can evaluate the suitability of proposed means to our ends. On the instrumentalist conception of practical rationality, agents are rational insofar as they take the necessary and sufficient means to their ends, but the ends are not subject to rational assessment. Contemporary instrumentalism traces its roots to Hume's arguments about the inertness of reason and to famous texts, such as Hume's declaration that "reason is, and ought only to be the slave of the passions, and can never pretend to any other office than to serve and obey them" (T 2.3.3.4). The theory draws on Hume's naturalistic characterization of reason as the activity of discovering what is true and false: it "instructs us in the pernicious or useful tendencies of qualities and actions" but does not originate sentiments of approval or disapproval (EPM, app. 1.3). Reason so characterized can give us beliefs about the best means to our ends, but it cannot originate the conative states that prompt action: "Reason, being cool and disengaged . . . directs only the impulse received from appetite and inclination, by showing us the means of attaining happiness or avoiding misery" (EPM, app. 1.27). Yet, it is clear that Hume himself was not an instrumentalist, even though he provides the basis for the instrumentalist claims. Hume's own arguments imply that it makes no sense to judge people as irrational when they fail to take the means to their ends. Judgments of rationality for Hume, technically speaking, do not apply to action, since actions are not true or false. In his view, reason never gives us a belief of the form, "If I desire A, I ought to do act α"; rather, it gives us beliefs of the form, "Act α is a means to A." So, contemporary instrumentalists differ from Hume in their insistence that a plausible version of practical rationality has as its standard that we ought to take the necessary and sufficient means to our ends. Still, instrumentalists continually point to Hume as their inspiration.

Kantians are united in rejecting the instrumentalist conception of practical reason, arguing that we have no rational obligation to take the means to ends that are not themselves justified by reason.[20] Humean instrumentalism treats all desires as equally normative for action, saying as it does that we ought to take the means to our ends, whatever they may be. Critics argue that a theory of practical reasoning must be able to judge some desires – for instance, self-destructive whims – as non-justifying. In response, some present-day Humeans have made it their project to develop a theory of reasons for action that answers this objection. On one such account, we act from reasons only when we act on desires that cohere in a consistent set – that is, desires whose mutual fulfillment is possible in the long run.[21] This suggestion supposedly secures the heart of Humeanism, since it does not impose standards on action outside of the agent's own set of motivations. On another account, we act on reasons only when we act on desires that do not undermine our values, where values are defined in terms of those desires that we wish to retain on reflection.[22] To what degree these attempts succeed is debatable, and working out the details of these approaches is difficult.[23] But that the contemporary Humean model of motivation is continually under revision or refinement is evidence of the deep and wide-ranging impact Hume's insights have had in moral and motivational psychology.

"Is" and "Ought"

Hume makes the connection between motivational anti-rationalism and moral sentimentalism obvious, since his conclusion that morality does not depend on reason alone but also requires sentiment is derived from the inability of reason to motivate us by itself (T 1.1.1–2). However, his thesis on "is" and "ought" is, to some readers' minds, not connected in any plain way to the other theses. J. L. Mackie and Jonathan Harrison in classic works have called the paragraph from the *Treatise* in which Hume offers it an "afterthought,"[24] since it is presented as an added observation after rigorous arguments for the conclusion that morality cannot be derived from reason alone and immediately after a comparison of moral qualities to secondary qualities.[25] But it is hardly a trivial postscript: it follows, with some added premises, from his strict separation of the roles of reason and passion in both the *Treatise* and the second *Enquiry*, and it underprops his arguments for sentimentalism in both works as well.[26] I say more about this later.

As far as I can tell, little attention was paid specifically to Hume's remarks on "is" and "ought" in the eighteenth and nineteenth centuries. Jeremy Bentham was an exception. He thought obligations were independent of factual matters and agreed with what he took to be the import of the is-ought passage. Yet, in *The Rationale of Judicial Evidence* (1827), he makes an observation about a purported inconsistency in Hume's own approach:

> The Propensity on the part of writers to attach to the idea of practice the idea of obligation . . . silently and without notice . . . , and the confusion spread by it . . . was first noticed by Hume, in his Treatise on Human Nature [*sic*]. But such is the force of habit and prepossession, after pointing out the cause of error, he continued himself to be led astray by it. On some occasions the principle of utility was recognized by him as the criterion of right and wrong, and in this sense the efficient cause of obligation. But on other occasions the *ipse dixit* principle, under the name of the moral sense, was, with the most inconsistent oscitancy, seated by his own hands on the same throne.[27]

Apparently, Bentham does not think that regarding utility as the source of obligation is problematic, perhaps because he regards utility as a matter of value, rather than as a matter of fact. He takes reference to reactions of the moral sense to be reference to factual matters.[28] Contemporary philosophers have also accused Hume of violating his own dictum, both by offering a theory on which what is virtuous or vicious can be inferred from facts about the feelings of certain spectators, or by offering a theory of justice on which observations about human practices justify obligations to keep promises, respect property, and so on.[29] On the other hand, Alasdair MacIntyre,[30] Geoffrey Hunter,[31] and Annette Baier[32] have argued that Hume never intended to be condemning a move from "is" to "ought." Instead, he was asking for an explanation of the move (Hunter, Baier), or showing us how the move can legitimately be made – that is, not by reference to theological concerns, but by reference to human interests (MacIntyre). And J. L. Mackie argues that Hume really meant to be defending moral non-cognitivism in his thesis about "is" and "ought": Moral judgments never follow from factual claims about the world, since they are not factual claims but expressions of feelings.[33]

As I have noted, "Hume's Law" has been affirmed by rational intuitionists like Henry Sidgwick and G. E. Moore. Moore famously argued that when morality is defined by reference to something like happiness production or human approval, one can still ask whether actions with the relevant quality are really good. He concluded that the fact-value gap implies that moral qualities are indefinable and moral truths are rationally intuited necessary truths.[34] There are also noteworthy attempts to show Hume's Law is simply wrong. In 1960 A. N. Prior published a seminal paper in which he demonstrated just with the use of the disjunctive operator in logic that a conclusion about morality can be deduced from non-moral premises.[35] And in 1964 John Searle published his widely discussed article "How to Derive 'Ought' from 'Is,'" arguing that the act of promising by its very nature places one under an obligation. Since it is an analytic truth that when one has an obligation, one ought to fulfill it, it follows that Jones's saying "I promise to pay Smith $100" entails that Jones ought to pay Smith a hundred dollars.[36] It is remarkable that one paragraph of uncertain meaning has had such a deep impact on discussions of moral naturalism and non-naturalism.

Of all the commentaries on offer, however, Nicholas Sturgeon's 2001 paper, "Moral Skepticism and Moral Naturalism in Hume's *Treatise*," exhibits Hume most in the spirit of the Enlightenment and naturalistic thought and, I think, does most justice to the text.[37] On Sturgeon's interpretation, it is no coincidence that Hume invokes the analogy with secondary qualities just prior to making his observation on "is" and "ought." Hume has argued that vice and virtue consist neither in demonstrable relations nor in matters of fact that are discerned by causal reasoning. They are facts accessible by feeling, so that when we pronounce an action or character vicious, we mean that we have "a sentiment of blame" when contemplating it. And then Hume writes, "Vice and virtue, therefore, may be compar'd to sounds, colours, heat and cold, which, according to modern philosophy, are not qualities in objects, but perceptions in the mind" (T 3.1.1.26). On Sturgeon's reading, Hume's skepticism about our ability to infer an "ought" from an "is" parallels the skepticism found in John Locke and other early moderns about our ability to infer what secondary qualities an object will have from observing its primary qualities or the primary qualities of its constituent parts. The corpuscular theory of physics from Robert Boyle supports an account of qualities whereby the characteristics of the unobservable constituent parts determine what we perceive. The distinction between primary and secondary qualities is, among other things, a distinction between qualities in objects whether perceived or not (the primary, such as size, figure, and mass) and qualities imputed to objects in virtue of how they are perceived (the secondary, such as colors, shapes, and smells). The source of Locke's skepticism about our ability to infer secondary qualities from primary ones has to do with the distinctive phenomenal characters of secondary-quality perceptions, which seem to have no inferential or imaginable connection with their physical causes: for instance, the perception of redness does not "resemble" (whatever that means) the size, texture, or configuration of the physical parts that cause the perception of redness. Locke finds the explanation of the perception of pleasures and pains especially problematic in this regard. Likewise, Hume (on Sturgeon's interpretation) thinks that how a moral spectator would feel could never be inferred from the idea of an action or its motive, that is, from the description of an action's features.

I find many aspects of this reading significant. Understanding the is-ought gap depends on accepting Hume's arguments (in T 3.1.1, and EPM, 1.7–9, and appendix 1) that morality is not accessible by reasoning but discovered by and defined in terms of natural sentiments. This reading implies that the is-ought skepticism Hume highlights is addressed neither by the use of logical operators nor by pointing to the nature or semantics of promising and obligation, since it relies on the thesis, for which Hume has argued, that moral judgments are perceptual. It is not a skepticism about "basing" morality on natural facts but about how we discover a connection between the two – not by demonstration and not by experience of external perceptions connected by conditioning in causal inferences. It requires experience of internal perceptions, or perceptions of reflection, which are, not coincidentally, motivating. It is also not about whether moral judgments are cognitions. Moreover, when Hume's thesis on "is" and "ought" is understood in this way, Hume is not an inconsistent naturalist. Even though we might infer the content of morality from facts about feelings, this is only because the moral content originates in feelings rather than in reason. That Hume allows in his theory of justice that our social interactions become normative through practice is no problem either, since the normativity derives from our approval of the practices, not from any inferences from the features of the practices. As Frederick G. Whelan notes in his essay in this volume, "Advocacy of certain social arrangements . . . rest in part on empirical assessments of feasibility and predicted consequences as well as on the sentiments of approval or disapproval that ultimately determine moral judgment."[38]

With the is-ought paragraph lifted from the context of Hume's project of implementing the new science in a study of human nature, it has been elevated to a "law" and interpreted in a way that Hume probably never intended. I want to suggest that the real lesson of Hume's caution about facts and values is this: that all moral naturalists are committed to a sentimentalism in their metaethics, which allows the move from factual observations to value conclusions. This point is supported in the second *Enquiry,* which seems to presuppose the is-ought paragraph, even though no analogous passage appears there.[39] Hume's project there is to show the respective contributions of reason and sentiment in determining what we count as personal merit or virtue, which are natural qualities of a person. His conclusion is that reason can determine the effects of people's qualities, but the fact that certain qualities are virtues (those useful or agreeable to the self or to others) is due entirely to a sentiment of approval toward them, common to all human beings (EPM, 9.1–7). Mere inference cannot give us the categories of virtue and vice.

Now, some critics argue, contrary to Hume, that Humean passions are defined not by how they feel but by the circumstances under which they are experienced. For example, pride is a feeling of pleasure experienced when one considers a pleasant object related to the self. And if all sentiments and passions are so identifiable, this means that we can infer after all from the circumstances what one will feel (perhaps unlike secondary qualities, which are distinguished by the experiential phenomenon).[40] So, in their view, Hume would be wrong to hold that we cannot infer moral sentiments from the features of an action (even if we cannot infer secondary quality perceptions from the primary).[41] However, if I am correct that Hume's aim is to show that naturalists must be sentimentalists of some sort, *this* point remains intact. That our moral distinctions depend on feelings will still hold true, even if we are able to infer what those feelings will be without experiencing them in every instance.

Moral Sentimentalism: Metaethical and Normative Approaches

Even though Hume was not the first sentimentalist, he is probably the most influential. The idea that we make moral discernments by experiencing a certain feeling (passion, sentiment) was advanced by eighteenth-century moralists like Anthony Ashley Cooper, Lord Shaftesbury, and Francis Hutcheson and has found a revival in twenty-first century metaethics, with contributions from Michael Slote,[42] Justin D'Arms,[43] and Jesse Prinz,[44] among others. For Hume, sentimentalism implies not only that morality is known by feeling but that the constitution of morality itself depends on mental states of spectators (spectators who assume a general, unbiased perspective). "Moral realism" is very much a term of art, but if moral realism is the view that moral qualities exist independent of the mind, then Hume is antirealist. This does not necessarily mean that he denies that there are moral qualities (although perhaps he does), but at a minimum, he thinks moral qualities are response-dependent. Some philosophers see the latter view as a form of realism about morality too, since human responses are part of nature (and I tend to agree). Hume himself, however, was not trying to answer what he thought were incoherent metaphysical questions; his project was to formulate a moral epistemology by use of the experimental method.

Hume's sentimentalism has sometimes been taken as the basis for emotivism, a contemporary metaethical theory that characterizes moral judgments as non-cognitive (no-content) expressions of feelings. Hume's texts at times lend support to that view; for instance, he writes, "to have a sense of virtue, is nothing but to *feel* a satisfaction of a particular kind from the contemplation of a character. The very *feeling* constitutes our praise or admiration" (T 3.1.2.3). Since emotivism came on the scene with the linguistic turn in the mid-twentieth century, it obviously was not on Hume's mind.[45] Recent proponents of moral non-cognitivism defend their view, not on semantic grounds but on metaphysical grounds, to avoid commitments to peculiar moral properties they think would be necessary to make a moral judgment true or false. According to J. L. Mackie, such properties would have to be prescriptive and descriptive at the same time, and nothing in nature is like that.[46] Recently, Simon Blackburn[47] and Allan Gibbard[48] (among others) have advanced a more sophisticated form of non-cognitivism – namely, expressivism – which portrays moral judgments as expressions of evaluative attitudes but also tries to account for the realist-sounding aspects of moral judgments. For instance, moral judgments seem to contradict one another and can function as premises in valid arguments. On the expressivist line, moral judgments have meaning, but it is determined by the mental states (e.g., approval or disgust) that those judgments serve to express. Blackburn's expressivism is part of his "quasi-realist" program and is coupled with moral projectivism, a view which he explicitly traces to Hume.[49] Quasi-realism is an attempt to avoid the realist's metaphysical commitments while pointing to special features of normative judgments that justify our treating them *as though* they are true or false. Moral projectivism is a psychological thesis about why we act as though moral qualities exist in the world, when in fact they are a product of our own feelings, and Blackburn finds this view articulated in Hume. The idea is that while our moral distinctions are a product of our own reactions to others' actions or characters, we project those feelings back onto the world as though they came from the outside world and represent something there. Hume writes,

> Thus, the distinct boundaries and offices of *reason* and of *taste* are easily ascertained. The former conveys the knowledge of truth and falsehood. The latter gives the sentiment of beauty and deformity, vice and virtue. The one discovers objects, as they really stand in nature, without addition or diminution. The other has a productive faculty, and gilding or staining all natural objects with the colours, borrowed from internal sentiment, raises, in a manner, a new creation. (EPM, app. 1.21)

Whether Hume himself can, all things considered, be read as a projectivist and quasi-realist is again a disputable matter, but his arguments on the purview of reason and sentiment have been the impetus to one of the most influential metaethical programs in contemporary philosophy.

SENTIMENTALISM AND UTILITY AS A NORM

Hume's sentimentalism was closely aligned in many eighteenth- and nineteenth-century commentaries with a normative ethics that has utility as the standard. Some contemporary philosophers also regard Hume a utilitarian of a sort, even though the relation between sentimentalism and utility as a norm is far from clear.

In 1751 Henry Home (Lord Kames) offered a somewhat uneven critique of Hume in which he first criticizes Hume's focus on utility: "Love of simplicity has betrayed him into the . . . error . . . of founding morality on a single principle, overlooking the complex nature of man, composed of many principles."[50] But then he continues, "Utility indeed is not made the sole foundation of morality; for it is admitted that benevolence is founded on a moral sense."[51] His chief complaint seems to be that public utility is made the foundation of justice in Hume's theory of artificial virtue, when in fact, Kames thinks, we have a natural sense that approves of and motivates us to respect for property, promise-keeping, and so on.

But Adam Smith (1759) does not focus only on Hume's theory of justice when reading Hume as proposing utility as the foundation of all moral and aesthetic approval. To Hume's view that spectators sympathize with the pleasure a house owner gets from its useful features, Smith responds that many luxuries do not bring happiness to the owner, who may toil over maintaining them; yet, we still approve them. The spectator "does not even imagine that they [wealthy owners] are really happier than other people: but he imagines that they possess more means of happiness. And it is the ingenious and artful adjustment of those means to the end for which they were intended, that is the principal source of his admiration."[52] Likewise, we do not approve of social institutions for their actual benefits but for a design we conceive to be aimed at the public good. In the case of natural morality, Smith argues that our approval is due to a sense of rightness or propriety, not to sympathy with the actual effects of an action on others.[53] But Jeremy Bentham praises Hume for founding virtue on utility. Upon reading relevant parts of the *Treatise,* he writes, "I felt as if scales had fallen from my eyes."[54]

Perhaps Hume's account of justice, along with his classification of the virtues, especially in the second *Enquiry,* as traits useful to the self, useful to others, agreeable to the self, and agreeable to others, is reminiscent of some sort of utility standard. In section 5 of the *Enquiry,* "Why Utility Pleases," Hume offers an analysis of why the public utility of the social virtues engages our approving sentiments. Certainly none of these features alone is a basis for attributing to Hume the view that maximizing happiness is the chief moral principle. Smith was simply mistaken to think that Hume focused on actual consequences. We approve the system of justice not because each action has the best outcome but because of our tendency to imagine the overall results of rule-following behavior, which is in our enlightened self-interest. This theme is prefigured in Hume's essays "Of the First Principles of Government" and "Of the Origin of Government." Hume remarks on the surprising ease with which the many submit their passions to government by the few: because of human frailty, people institute magistrates to oblige people "to consult their own real and permanent interests."[55] Furthermore, unlike utilitarianism, when there is a conflict between qualities useful or agreeable to the self and qualities useful or agreeable to others, there is nothing in Hume's theory requiring that the latter should be given priority. But in the twentieth century, John Rawls promoted the idea that Hume's sentimentalism leads to utilitarianism. He argues classical utilitarianism "is closely related to the concept of the impartial sympathetic spectator."[56] He continues, "This special pleasure [approval] is the result of sympathy. In Hume's account it is quite literally a reproduction in our experience of the satisfactions and pleasures which we recognize to be felt by others. Thus, an impartial spectator experiences this pleasure in contemplating the social system in proportion to the net sum of pleasure felt by those affected by it."[57] In the forward to John Rawls's *Lectures on the History of Political Philosophy,* Samuel Freeman writes that in his political philosophy course, Rawls taught Henry Sidgwick, along with Hume and J. S. Mill, "to give students an idea of (what he regarded as) the three major utilitarian philosophers."[58]

Rawls, like Smith, neglects to acknowledge Hume's account of our reliance on general rules, which implies that, as spectators, we do not always reproduce the feelings of others. Because we take actions as signs of characters, we sympathize with the effects a character trait would usually have, even though the trait might lack that effect in a particular instance. Furthermore, Hume recognizes our psychological limitations and observes that our sympathies as spectators are limited to "the narrow circle," those immediately and directly affected by an agent. We simply cannot sympathize with the long-term consequences of an action, which presumably would be required if Hume's moral sentimentalism yielded classical utilitarian results. Of course, utilitarianism has assumed many shapes and forms, and I cannot say for sure that Hume's theory cannot be configured as one of them. It is safe to say, however, that Hume was a key figure in the development of the classical utilitarian view. With the reintroduction of hedonistic and humanistic concerns into moral theory but with an emphasis on the non-egoistic side of human nature, conditions are set for utilitarian theory to flourish. And it does.

SENTIMENTALISM AND VIRTUE

Virtue ethics is rooted in the theories of Plato and especially Aristotle, who supports his account of the virtues by appeal to teleology and a theory of the good life. In medieval philosophy, the dominance of Christianity orients ethics to authority and law. Thomas Reid comments, "The Ancients commonly arranged . . . [morals] under the four cardinal virtues of prudence, temperance, fortitude, and justice. Christian writers . . . under the heads of duty we owe to God, to ourselves, and to others."[59] Jerome Schneewind writes, "It is no surprise to find that there is a commonly accepted understanding of virtue and virtues in the seventeenth century which makes them secondary to laws or rules."[60] He quotes Locke here: "By whatever standard soever we frame in our minds the ideas of virtues and vices . . . their rectitude or obliquity, consists in the agreement with those patterns prescribed by some law."[61] Schneewind comments that natural law philosophers, who largely ignored virtue in favor of duties, dominated moral thinking in the seventeenth and early eighteenth centuries.[62]

It is sometimes said that sentimentalism, at least in the sympathy-based form that Hume offers, must be consequentialist (even if not utilitarian), for the very reasons offered by Rawls's analysis of the spectator. Any moral system can refer as "virtues" to the traits that motivate the actions promoted by the theory; hence, consequentialists and deontologists can formulate their lists of virtues and vices, even though theirs is not a "virtue ethics." But I think Hume is a virtue theorist for the following reasons. He sees character traits, not actions, as the primary objects of evaluation. He also posits "national" characters in addition to those particular to individuals, with the former a product of the close interactions among those in one political body ("Of National Characters").[63] He offers an explanation why particular traits are valuable and ought to be cultivated, and on his theory, the virtues and vices exist in the agents, not as projections of spectators.[64] Since as an experimental philosopher Hume sees virtues as determined by our practices – by our admiration of others when we take up a common point of view – he strips virtue ethics of teleology. This does not mean, however, that the virtues and vices are inexplicable, or that Hume has no notion of better and worse lives. Because our natural sympathy, or our "fellow feeling" as Hume puts it in EPM, allows the sharing of pleasures and pains, we take pleasure in traits that are generally useful and agreeable to agents and to others (EPM, 8n50).[65] We also take pride (a form of pleasure) in our own congenial and useful traits. Hume builds his notion of the good life out of human experience, rather than supposing an idealized, Aristotelian conception of human good from the start.[66] He writes that the best character is one that can adapt to use caution or to use enterprise, depending on the purpose and circumstances. "He is happy, whose circumstances suit his temper; but he is more excellent, who can suit his temper to any circumstances" (EPM, 6.9). And in "Of Refinement in the Arts," Hume proposes that education, practices, and example promote happiness when they inculcate "a relish for action and pleasure."[67] More contentious is the claim that virtues, for Hume, are in the actors, rather than a product of projected feelings of spectators. I do not think that Hume was concerned with the ontology of the virtues but rather with how we distinguish them from the vices. Yet, given contemporary concerns about the status of morality, we need only see Hume's virtues and vices as powers of traits in the agents to evoke certain sentiments in observers in order to understand them as dependent on observers but existing in agents. I cannot defend this view in detail here, but others like Christine Swanton have.[68]

Schneewind argues that Hume turned the natural law theorists' distinction between perfect and imperfect duties into a distinction between artificial and natural virtue.[69] Hume himself speaks the language of duties in his essay "Of the Original Contract," where he notes the difference between ethical actions toward which we are motivated by natural propensities (like benevolence), on the one hand, and by a sense of obligation to support society on the other.[70] Perfect duties in natural law are those that must be carried out if society is to survive. Analogously, the Humean artificial virtues of justice, fidelity to promises, and allegiance to government are required for institutional stability. Imperfect duties improve the quality of life but are not necessary to societal survival. Hume's natural virtues, which include generosity, humanity, compassion, friendship, gratitude, and others, similarly enhance and elevate our lives. I want to note two other contributions Hume makes to the development of virtue ethics. First, he introduces the spectator-based conception of virtue, which allows us to articulate a list of the virtues without first offering a contentious theory of the good life. Second, Hume's theory, using the details of the sympathy mechanism, describes moral assessment of traits in terms of their effects, a feature of his theory that may very well give virtue consequentialists reason to claim Hume as an eighteenth-century proponent of their theory.[71]

CONTEMPORARY SENTIMENTALISM

I want to mention two approaches among contemporary sentimentalists who take their inspiration from Hume. Jesse Prinz and others represent the experimentalist school in contemporary philosophy, approaching ethics through empirical psychological studies of the origin of values and moral distinctions.[72] Prinz's project is purely descriptive, accepting a strict division between "is" and "ought" and appealing to G. E. Moore's open question argument. Prinz's contribution to the Humean project suggests that morality is a construction from our sentiments and real in the way human constructions are. In his view, since it is possible for two observers to agree on the facts but have different emotive responses to them, we must acknowledge a wide divergence in moral systems, which indicates that morality is relative. For instance, systems emphasizing autonomy and rules about justice and rights have taken hold in individualistically oriented Western culture, while some Eastern cultures place an emphasis on community and often advance rules about rank and sex. But all of these systems are sentimentally based. About normative theories, Prinz writes, "classic normative ethical theories are not vindicated by anything I've said, nor are they refuted. These theories stand as worthy recommendations for action. Perhaps a steady commitment to moral progress will ultimately lead us to adopt some components of the classic theories."[73]

Humean sentimentalism has also evolved into an ethics of compassion or care in the twentieth and twenty-first centuries, advanced by philosophers like Nel Noddings and Michael Slote.[74] Such a theory treats sentimentalism both as a metaethics and as a normative theory, and makes the move from spectator to agent insofar as sympathy (or empathy, their preferred term) possessed by the moral spectator is a desirable agent trait. Slote acknowledges that his view requires the possession of a second-order empathy about having empathy. The moral directive of his moral sentimentalism is "that it is morally wrong to act – that one has an obligation not to act – in ways that express or exhibit a lack of fully developed empathy."[75]

Conclusion

To the question whether Hume's legacy in moral philosophy is one of confusion or one of a complex and multifaceted moral theory, my answer is this: Because Hume's arguments are sophisticated in the range of moral phenomena for which they account and compelling for their logical rigor, Hume has inspired many a movement in ethics. He need not be a subscriber to all the views his works have encouraged. It is a testament to his genius that he has been cited as the source for the Humean theory of motivation, instrumentalism about practical reason and other accounts of Humean practical reasoning, various interpretations of the is-ought gap, differing versions of moral non-cognitivism, the contemporary quasi-realist program, utilitarian theory, a version of virtue ethics, and contemporary versions of moral sentimentalism. I am confident in describing Hume himself as a thorough-going naturalist who recognized the proper roles of passion and reason in motivation and whose works offer a spectator theory of morality and an empirically grounded account of the virtues and vices. Hume has not left a legacy of confusion but rather a rich reservoir of observations about human nature, action, and moral judgment and practice. That

Hume's approach has reinvigorated moral theory in the twenty-first century speaks volumes about his influence.[76]

NOTES

I am very grateful to Angela Coventry and Andrew Valls for their helpful comments on an earlier draft of this paper. A shorter version was presented as part of a panel on "Hume's Enlightenment Legacy" at the 41st International Hume Society Conference at Portland State University in July 2014. I thank the conferees, the organizers, and my fellow panelists, Michael Gill and John Wright, for discussion and encouragement.

1. See Rachel Cohon, *Hume's Morality: Feeling and Fabrication* (New York: Oxford University Press 2008), 73–77; Peter Kail, *Projectivism and Realism in Hume's Philosophy* (Oxford: Oxford University Press, 2007), 189–203; David W. D. Owen, "Reason, Belief and the Passions," in *The Oxford Handbook of David Hume,* ed. Paul Russell (New York: Oxford University Press, 2016), 133–55; and Charles R. Pigden, "If Not Non-Cognitivism, Then What?" in *Hume on Motivation and Virtue,* ed. Charles R. Pigden (Basingstoke, England: Palgrave Macmillan, 2009), 80–104.

2. See, for instance, Julia Driver, "Pleasure as the Standard of Virtue in Hume's Moral Philosophy," *Pacific Philosophical Quarterly* 85, no. 2 (2004): 173–94; Lorenzo Greco, "Toward a Humean Virtue Ethics," in *Aristotelian Ethics in Contemporary Perspective,* ed. Julia Peters (New York: Routledge, 2013), 210–23, and "The Self as Narrative in Hume," *Journal of the History of Philosophy* 53, no. 4 (2015): 699–722, esp. section 7; Christine Swanton, "Can Hume Be Read as a Virtue Ethicist?" *Hume Studies* 33, no. 1 (2007): 91–113; and Jacqueline Taylor, "Virtue and the Evaluation of Character," in *Blackwell Guide to Hume's* Treatise, ed. Saul Traiger (Oxford: Blackwell, 2006), 276–95.

3. See, for instance, Ronald Glossip, "Is Hume a Classical Utilitarian?" *Hume Studies* 2, no. 1 (1976): 1–16; John Rawls, *A Theory of Justice* (Cambridge, Mass.: Harvard University Press, 1971), 32–33; and Jordon Howard Sobel, "Hume's Utilitarian Theory of Right Action," *Philosophical Quarterly* 47, no. 186 (1997): 55–72.

4. See, for instance, Jacqueline Taylor, "Hume's Later Moral Philosophy," in *The Cambridge Companion to Hume,* 2nd ed., ed. David Fate Norton and Jacqueline Taylor (Cambridge: Cambridge University Press, 2008), 311–40; and Annette Baier, *"Enquiry Concerning the Principles of Morals:* Incomparably the Best?" in *A Companion to Hume,* ed. Elizabeth S. Radcliffe (Malden, Mass.: Blackwell, 2008), 293–320.

5. Francis Hutcheson, *Illustrations on the Moral Sense* (1728), ed. Bernard Peach (Cambridge, Mass.: Harvard University Press, 1971), 120–22.

6. Citations are to David Hume, *A Treatise of Human Nature* (1739–40), ed. David Fate Norton and Mary J. Norton (Oxford: Clarendon Press, 2007), book, part, section, and paragraph numbers (hereafter T), and to Hume, *Enquiry Concerning the Principles of Morals,* section and paragraph number or appendix and paragraph number (hereafter EPM).

7. Samuel Clarke, *A Discourse Concerning the Unchangeable Obligations of Natural Religion* (1705), in *Moral Philosophy from Montaigne to Kant,* ed. J. B. Schneewind (Cambridge: Cambridge University Press, 1990), 1:295.

8. Ralph Cudworth, *A Treatise Concerning Eternal and Immutable Morality with a Treatise of Freewill,* ed. Sarah Hutton (Cambridge: Cambridge University Press, 1996).

9. Among the instinctual passions are benevolence, resentment, love of life, kindness to children, desire of punishment to our enemies and of happiness to our friends, bodily appetites, and the sentiments of morality and beauty (T 2.3.3.8, 2.3.9.8).

10. Simon Blackburn, "Practical Tortoise Raising," *Mind* 104, no. 416 (1995): 695–711, and *Ruling Passions* (New York: Oxford University Press, 1998); Mark Schroeder, *Slaves of the Passions* (New York: Oxford University Press, 2007); Neil Sinhababu, "The Humean Theory of Motivation Reformulated and Defended," *Philosophical Review* 118, no. 4 (2009): 465–500, and "The Belief-Desire Account of Intention Explains Everything," *Nous* 47, no. 4 (2013): 680–96; Michael Smith, *The Moral Problem* (Oxford: Blackwell, 1994); Bernard Williams, "Internal and External Reasons" (1980), in B. Williams, *Moral Luck* (Cambridge: Cambridge University Press, 1981), 101–13.

11. G. E. M. Anscombe, *Intention* (1957; 2nd edition, Oxford: Basil Blackwell, 1963), 55–57; Smith, *The Moral Problem,* 116.

12. John McDowell, "Are Moral Requirements Hypothetical Imperatives?" *Proceedings of Aristotelian Society* Supplement 52 (1978): 18–22. Mark van Roojen also defends the existence of besires in "Humean Motivation and Humean Rationality," *Philosophical Studies* 79, no. 1 (1995): 37–57.

13. I borrow this argument from my "The Humean Theory of Motivation and Its Critics," in Radcliffe, ed., *A Companion to Hume,* 477–92.

14. Pigden, "If Not Non-Cognitivism, Then What?"

15. Kail, *Projectivism and Realism in Hume's Philosophy,* 189–203.

16. Cohon, *Hume's Morality,* 63–95.

17. Owen, "Reason, Belief and the Passions."

18. Most recently, see "The Inertness of Reason and Hume's Legacy," *Canadian Journal of Philosophy* 42, no. S1 (2012): 117–33.

19. Stephen Darwall, *Impartial Reason* (Ithaca, N.Y.: Cornell University Press, 1983); Alan Donagan, *The Theory of Morality* (Chicago: University of Chicago Press, 1977); Alan Gewirth, *Reason and Morality* (Chicago: University of Chicago Press, 1978); Christine Korsgaard, *The Sources of Normativity* (Cambridge: Cambridge University Press, 1996), and *The Constitution of Agency: Essays on Practical Reason and Moral Psychology* (Oxford: Oxford University Press, 2008); Thomas Nagel, *The Possibility of Altruism* (Princeton, N.J.: Princeton University Press, 1970).

20. See especially Christine Korsgaard, "The Normativity of Instrumental Reason," in *Ethics and Practical Reason,* ed. Garrett Cullity and Berys Gaut (Oxford: Clarendon Press, 1997), 213–54.

21. See, for instance, Alan Goldman, *Reasons from Within: Desires and Values* (Oxford: Oxford University Press, 2009).

22. See, for instance, Donald Hubin, "Desires, Whims, and Values," *Journal of Ethics* 7, no. 3 (2003): 315–35.

23. For some critique, see Elizabeth Radcliffe, "Reasons from the Humean Perspective," *Philosophical Quarterly* 62, no. 249 (2012): 777–96.

24. Jonathan Harrison, *Hume's Moral Epistemology* (Oxford: Clarendon Press, 1976), 69; J. L. Mackie, *Hume's Moral Theory* (London: Routledge and Kegan Paul, 1980), 60.

25. The famous passage is the following: "I cannot forbear adding to these reasonings an observation, which may, perhaps, be found of some importance. In every system of morality, which I have hitherto met with, I have always remark'd, that the author proceeds for some time in the ordinary way of reasoning, and establishes the being of a God, or makes observations concerning human affairs; when of a sudden I am surpriz'd to find, that instead of the usual copulations of propositions, *is,* and *is not,* I meet with no proposition that is not connected with an *ought,* or an *ought not.* This change is imperceptible; but is, however, of the last consequence. For as this *ought,* or *ought not,* expresses some new relation or affirmation, 'tis necessary that it shou'd be observ'd and explain'd; and at the same time that a reason should be given, for what seems altogether inconceivable, how this new relation can be a deduction from others, which are entirely different from it. But as authors do not commonly use this precaution, I shall presume to recommend it to the readers; and am persuaded, that this small attention wou'd subvert all the vulgar systems of morality, and let us see, that the distinction of vice and virtue is not founded merely on the relations of objects, nor is perceiv'd by reason" (T 3.1.1.27).

26. On this point, see also Stephen Buckle, *Hume's Enlightenment Tract: The Unity and Purpose of an* Enquiry Concerning Human Understanding (Oxford: Oxford University Press, 2001), 233n6.

27. Jeremy Bentham, *The Rationale of Judicial Evidence,* book 1, chapter 7, in *Early Responses to Hume's Moral, Political and Literary Writings,* ed. James Fieser (Bristol, England: Thoemmes Continuum Press, 2005), 1:303.

28. And interestingly, he assumes utility and the moral sense as a source of value are competing normative theories, when many of us would understand reference to a moral sense as a metaethical theory compatible with other normative theories.

29. See, for instance, Wade Robison, "Much Obliged," in *Hume on* Is *and* Ought, ed. Charles C. Pigden (Basingstoke, England: Palgrave Macmillan, 2010), 65–75.

30. Alasdair MacIntyre, "Hume on 'Is' and 'Ought,'" *Philosophical Review* 68, no. 4 (1959): 451–68; reprinted in V. C. Chappell, ed., *Hume: A Collection of Critical Essays* (London: Macmillan, 1968) 240–64, and W. D. Hudson, ed., *The Is-Ought Question* (London: Macmillan, 1969), 35–50.

31. Geoffrey Hunter, "Hume on *Is* and *Ought,*" *Philosophy* 37, no. 140 (1962): 148–52.

32. Annette Baier, *A Progress of Sentiments* (Cambridge, Mass.: Harvard University Press, 1991), 176–77; Baier, "Hume's Own 'Ought' Conclusions," in Pigden, ed., *Hume on* Is *and* Ought, 49–64.

33. Mackie, *Hume's Moral Theory,* 70.

34. G. E. Moore, *Principia Ethica* (New York: Cambridge University Press, 1903), section 10, paragraph 3.

35. A. N. Prior, "The Autonomy of Ethics," *Australasian Journal of Philosophy* 38, no. 3 (1960): 199–206.

36. John Searle, "How to Derive 'Ought' from "Is,'" *Philosophical Review* 73, no. 1 (1964): 43–58.

37. Nicholas Sturgeon, "Moral Skepticism and Moral Naturalism in Hume's *Treatise,*" *Hume Studies* 27, no. 1 (2001): 3–83.

38. Frederick G. Whelan, "Political Science and Political Theory in Hume's *Essays,*" in this volume.

39. Stephen Buckle suggests that the is-ought thesis is supposed in appendix 1 of EPM; see *Natural Law and the Theory of Property: Grotius to Hume* (Oxford: Clarendon Press, 1991), 280–83, and *Hume's Enlightenment Tract,* 233n6. This is speculation on my part, but perhaps no analogous paragraph appears in EPM because EPM was aimed at a public audience, while the passage on "is" and "ought" was aimed at philosophers who made such arguments.

40. See, for example, Philippa Foot, "Hume on Moral Judgment," in *Virtues and Vices and Other Essays in Moral Philosophy* (Oxford: Clarendon Press, 2002), 74–80; and Donald Davidson, "Hume's Cognitive Theory of Pride," *Journal of Philosophy* 73, no. 19 (1976): 744–57.

41. Sturgeon thinks something like this and so he thinks Hume is mistaken to compare moral qualities to secondary qualities with regard to the non-inferential nature of the latter.

42. Michael Slote, *Moral Sentimentalism* (New York: Oxford University Press, 2010).

43. For instance, Justin D'Arms, "Two Arguments for Sentimentalism," *Philosophical Issues* 15, no. 1 (2005): 1–21. D'Arms has numerous articles on the topic.

44. Jesse Prinz, *The Emotional Construction of Morals* (Oxford: Oxford University Press, 2007).

45. The turn to linguistic analysis was initiated by philosophers like A. J. Ayer in *Language, Truth, and Logic* (1936; Harmondsworth, England: Penguin, 1971).

46. J. L. Mackie, *Ethics: Inventing Right and Wrong* (Middlesex, England: Pelican, 1977), 38.

47. Simon Blackburn, *Essays in Quasi-Realism* (Oxford: Oxford University Press, 1993).

48. Allan Gibbard, *Wise Choices, Apt Feelings* (Cambridge, Mass.: Harvard University Press, 1990).

49. Mackie also finds projectivism in Hume. See *Hume's Moral Theory,* 72.

50. Henry Home, Lord Kames, *Essay on the Principles of Morality and Natural Religion* (1751; 2nd revised edition, 1779), in Fieser, ed., *Early Responses,* 1:18.

51. Kames, *Essay on the Principles of Morality,* 18.

52. Adam Smith, *The Theory of Moral Sentiments* (1759), part 4, section 1, in Fieser, ed., *Early Responses,* 1:121.

53. Henry Sidgwick later agrees with Smith, asking why we do not simply feel moral approval of all useful things (chairs, trees, etc.), citing Hume's mixture of "intellectual gifts" with "proper excellences" among the virtues as an instance of the problem. *Outline of the History of Ethics* (1886; 5th edition, 1902), in Fieser, ed., *Early Responses,* 1:394–400.

54. Jeremy Bentham, *A Fragment on Government* (1776), in Fieser, ed., *Early Responses,* 1:151. Dugald Stewart writes that justice as an artificial virtue, for Hume, derives all of its obligations from "the political union" and "from utility." He actually thought that this characterization of justice cannot help to distinguish natural and artificial virtue, since the natural virtues, founded

on "blind impulses," could not be virtues in the first place. Rather, we approve of benevolence and justice because we believe them to be duties. *The Philosophy of the Active and Moral Powers of Man* (1828), in Fieser, ed., *Early Responses,* 1:343.

55. Essay 5.3.

56. Rawls, *A Theory of Justice,* 184.

57. Rawls, *A Theory of Justice,* 185–86.

58. Samuel Freeman, foreword to John Rawls, *Lectures on the History of Political Philosophy,* ed. Samuel Freeman (Cambridge, Mass.: Harvard University Press, 2007), xi.

59. Thomas Reid, *Essay on the Active Powers of Man* (1788), ed. Knud Haakossen and James A. Harris (Edinburgh: Edinburgh University Press, 2010), book 5, chapter 2.

60. Jerome Schneewind, "The Misfortunes of Virtue," in *Virtue Ethics,* ed. Roger Crisp and Michael Slote (New York: Oxford University Press, 1997), 181.

61. John Locke, *Essay Concerning Human Understanding,* ed. Peter H. Nidditch (New York: Oxford University Press, 1979), book 2, chapter 28, section 14.

62. Among these natural law theorists, in addition to John Locke, are Sir Edward Coke (1552–1634), Hugo Grotius (1583–1645), and Samuel von Pufendorf (1632–1694).

63. Essay 6.9.

64. Christine Swanton insists on the last in her essay "Can Hume Be Read as a Virtue Ethicist?"

65. Fellow feeling in the second *Enquiry* may be a different sentiment from the product of sympathy in the *Treatise.* The reference to this feeling may signal a change in Hume's theory from a culturally conditioned sympathy to a universal sentiment that allows us to share in others' emotional reactions.

66. In this connection, see Greco, "Toward a Humean Virtue Ethics," 216–18.

67. Essay 11.3.

68. Swanton, "Can Hume Be Read as a Virtue Ethicist?" 93–100.

69. Schneewind, "The Misfortunes of Virtue," 185–89.

70. Essay 14.33–34.

71. For instance, see Julia Driver, *Uneasy Virtue* (Cambridge: Cambridge University Press, 2001); Judith Thompson, "The Right and the Good," *Journal of Philosophy* 94, no. 6 (1997): 273–98; and Linda Zagzebski, *Virtues of the Mind: An Inquiry into the Nature of Virtue and the Ethical Foundations of Knowledge* (New York: Cambridge University Press, 1996).

72. Prinz, *The Emotional Construction of Morals* (among other works); D'Arms, "Two Arguments for Sentimentalism"; Shaun Nichols, *Sentimental Rules:*

On the Natural Foundations of Moral Judgment (New York: Oxford University Press, 2004).

73. Prinz, *The Emotional Construction of Morals,* 305.

74. For instance, Nel Noddings, *Caring, a Feminine Approach to Ethics and Moral Education* (Berkeley: University of California Press, 1984).

75. Slote, *Moral Sentimentalism,* 91.

Political Science and Political Theory in Hume's *Essays*

FREDERICK G. WHELAN

This essay offers a commentary on the political essays by David Hume that are included in this volume, along with an interpretation of Hume's approach to political theory. The emphasis is on the manner in which Hume weaves together normative arguments with the findings of his descriptive or empirical political science. First, however, let us situate the material covered here within Hume's work as a whole.

The program of Hume's philosophy was announced in the introduction to his first work, where he states that he will pursue the "science of man" or of human nature, based on "experience and observation," as the foundation of all knowledge, and that this science will include logic, morals, criticism, and politics.[1] Traditionally the study of Hume has been dominated by philosophers, who often focus on Hume's "logic," or his account of what he also terms the "understanding." This subject is beyond the scope of this volume, but we should note that it includes an important analysis of causation and our belief in the causal regularity of the natural and social worlds, which underlies the rest of Hume's science of man. Also of interest to philosophers (and political theorists) is Hume's account of moral judgment and the virtues, or his ethical doctrine, which is presented in his *Enquiry Concerning the Principles of Morals.* Under "criticism" we may include Hume's writings on aesthetics, religion, and culture, the latter including the essay "Of Refinement in the Arts," which is considered below. That brings us to Hume on politics, the central theme of this interpretive essay.[2]

One aspect of the contemporary "rethinking" of Hume has been a growth in interest in Hume's political thought in contrast to his more purely (or technically) philosophical positions (which of course also continue to be debated).[3] Important parts of Hume's political theory fall under "morals" and may be studied in his second *Enquiry:* these include his analysis of the virtues of justice and allegiance; the general basis of "political society"; and our obligation to respect property, keep promises, and obey government. Additional elements are found in several dozen political essays, which typically address more specific and concrete topics. Some of the essays are devoted to economic subjects or to what was then called political economy and treated as a branch of morals and politics.[4] One should add that Hume went on to write a politically oriented *History of England,* adding historiography to his science of man.[5] One disadvantage in studying Hume's political theory is that it is not summed up in a single book; on the other hand, Hume cultivated a lively and readable style when he wrote the shorter works contained in this volume. He did so because his intentions as a moral and political writer were practical as well as philosophical and scientific: he hoped that his arguments would promote such values as social utility, political moderation, legal and constitutional government, free trade and industry, and the civility and refinement of modern society. The fact that such values guided Hume's intellectual efforts bears out the main theme of this essay.

The Method of Humean Science

In contrast to present academic practice, Hume does not distinguish between political science – confined to the observation of facts, the formulation of descriptive generalizations, causal explanation, and the empirical confirmation of hypotheses – and political theory, understood as addressing normative or evaluative issues that arise in political life. "Political theory" in Hume's case is best understood broadly as embracing value judgments based on standards derived from his moral philosophy as well as scientific and historical analysis. Hume famously declared that one cannot strictly deduce ought-claims from factual ones, but he does not deny that the realms of "is" and "ought" are connected in our thinking.[6] Advocacy of certain social arrangements and approval of certain courses of conduct rest in part on empirical assessments of feasibility and predicted consequences as well as on the sentiments of approval or disapproval that ultimately determine moral judgment. Although as a philosopher he maintains a somewhat detached and critical view of the topics he takes up, Hume typically offers moral and political judgments in close relation to the findings of his political science as well as to actual practice, historical experience, and the common opinions of ordinary people. Hume's political theory thus incorporates a scientific aspiration, and this theme offers a point of entry into a consideration of the politics of his essays.

In his *Treatise of Human Nature,* in which Hume announced his program as the development of a "science of man," he also sets forth the basic assumptions of the scientific outlook and method. These include the "natural beliefs" (not themselves rationally provable but perfectly serviceable) that every event has a cause, that similar causes regularly produce similar effects, that the course of nature continues uniformly, and thus that, with respect to particular causal relations, the future resembles the past. Hume also famously develops the logic of inductive or causal inference. He denies that we can perceive causality directly or know intuitively what might cause what, and he insists that causality can be ascribed only through the careful observation of the "constant conjunction" of objects of similar types. Apart from our immediate perceptions and memory, causality is the basis of all our factual knowledge and scientific explanation, whether we infer the causes of observed effects or predict the effects of causal factors, both in the natural and social worlds. Some of Hume's principles of causal knowledge become problematic in social science, where the interactions of numerous causes and actors produce complexity and novelty and where controlled experiments are usually not possible: as we shall see, there are often insufficient similar cases to establish causation by the strict standard of constant conjunction, and in matters of concern to history-writing the future rarely resembles the past.[7]

In his moral philosophy Hume often proposes psychological accounts of the operation of human passions including the moral sentiments that are expressed, for example, in our sense of the duties of justice and allegiance and of ensuing conduct. This bridge from human nature to political theory is extended in Hume's essays, where the "science of man" encompasses many social, political, and economic phenomena. It is, for example, because "effects will always correspond to causes" in the realm of human behavior that legislators can confidently "regulate the administration of public affairs" by a system of laws, as Hume argues in "That Politics May Be Reduced to a Science" (Essay 2.12). Most of "Of the Liberty of the Press" (Essay 1) attempts to explain (rather than justify) this unusual British institution by reference to Britain's equally unusual mixed government (on which more below).

Hume's scientific ambitions are an expression of the confidence of his period – the Enlightenment – in the growth of knowledge and the potential advances in human happiness expected to flow from it.[8] At the same time, Hume called himself a skeptic. This was partly because he denied the possibility of rational insight into causal relations apart from observation and empirical confirmation and into moral truth apart from our sentiments. It was also because he sought to emphasize that accurate knowledge was acquired only through careful investigation and that most people were overly "credulous," or prone to adopt unfounded beliefs with undue conviction. This theme of intellectual caution occasionally appears in Hume's political writings, since even scientific reasoning is imperfect. The philosopher's business is to study the "general course of things"; his conclusions therefore may fail in particular cases of domestic politics, which depend on "the concurrence of a multitude of causes," while foreign politics, which depend on "the caprices of a few persons," are even less amenable to scientific explanation (Essay 7.2). Unusual cases should not detract from general observations; they are "to be taken as proofs, that the science of politics affords few rules, which will not admit of some exception, and which may not sometimes be controuled by fortune and accident" (Essay 10.28). Skeptical disclaimers point to acknowledged limitations of Hume's science but do not deter the enterprise.

The Science of "National Characters"

It was stated above that elements of Hume's normative theory – evaluative judgments embodying his own moral choices – are frequently intermingled with his descriptive and explanatory efforts. A good place to start, however, is "Of National Characters," a relatively straightforward exercise in social science. Hume accepts as a given the popular view that nations and some professional groups have traits that are widely shared by their members and that distinguish them from other groups. These traits are treated as effects that are assumed to have consistent causes, a general account of which is the topic of the essay. Hume concludes that moral and political causes such as customs, education, laws, and forms of government are responsible, along with the mutual influence or "contagion" of emotions and attitudes among the members of a continuously interacting population, grounded in the important psychological mechanism of sympathy. Hume's main effort is directed to refuting the alternative hypothesis that national characters are shaped by physical causes such as climate and terrain – an influential idea that was defended by Montesquieu among others.[9] The logic of Hume's scientific method is best seen in his nine counterarguments, such as that a constant climate cannot explain character variations in adjacent nations, or that climate variations cannot explain observed uniformities in large countries like China or the common character of dispersed groups like Jews or Jesuits.

The study of national characters was a prominent branch of social science until it went out of fashion around the mid-twentieth century (after which studies of political culture addressed overlapping issues). One reason it went out of fashion is evident in Hume's essay: the generalized traits that were to be explained were contentious and sometimes invidious, often little more (as Hume admits) than popular stereotypes or prejudices, whereas the objects of scientific study must be better defined and agreed upon among impartial observers. The problem of defining and delimiting the objects of study, which is more difficult in the social than in the natural sciences, does not detract from the logic of Hume's study, an early effort in social analysis.

With respect to scientific objectivity one should note Hume's comments on hypocrisy as a structural defect (not a personal failing) of the clerical profession, a point in which Hume's personal anticlericalism merges with causal analysis. One should also not gloss over Hume's footnote on race, in which Hume repeats a conventional racist view of Africans. This passage is unique in Hume's writings as well as anomalous in this essay, since it suggests an element of physical (or biological) determinism. Hume's rejection of reports of the talented Jamaican appears to be an unscientific dismissal of evidence contrary to his general thesis; it is better understood, however, as an expression of another of Hume's methodological principles – that testimony regarding an unusual deviation from a general pattern should be discounted as probably mistaken. Some were beginning to be consider race as a scientific category in Hume's period, although a judgment of "inferiority" such as we find here is not a scientific claim.

The Science of Constitutionalism

Hume's scientific ambition is clearly expressed in the title of "That Politics May Be Reduced to a Science," which offers several propositions that he holds to be well-founded. We should recall that in political science the phenomena being studied are often complex due to many interacting causal chains, and the evidence for the topics that interest Hume is often drawn from history. In this essay and elsewhere Hume has no choice but to generalize from a small number of cases, even though in his own philosophy causal claims are strengthened – or their probability increased – by repeated observations of similar "conjunctions." Many modern political scientists prefer to work with large data sets often collected to test a particular hypothesis. Hume would not have objected to this, but like other Scottish Enlightenment thinkers, he was attracted to larger historical questions typically having a limited body of evidence.[10]

Hume's first proposition is that direct democracy leads to disorder and anarchy (as in ancient Rome), in contrast to more sedate representative assemblies. The second is that nobles without vassals acting in government as a corporate body (as in Venice) are preferable to nobles with vassals (as in Poland) – that is, a feudal nobility, which historically obstructed the growth of effective central government. The third is that a hereditary chief executive is more stable, especially as regards succession, than an elective one. These claims reflect interesting factual analysis bearing on European political history and institutions. What stands out, however, is that each also includes normative analysis (explicitly marked by words like "preferable") and recommendations in favor of one of the alternatives in each pair. Value judgments are based directly on scientific conclusions along with Hume's evident approval of political order, stability, and governmental effectiveness. Furthermore, these three propositions taken together clearly refer to the British constitution of Hume's period, which included a hereditary monarch, a House of Lords comprising a post-feudal nobility, and an elected House of Commons, which Hume sometimes calls the "republican" or "democratic" part of the system (Essay 1.1). Hume's political science findings are thus deployed in defense of a particular form of government, a constitutional and parliamentary monarchy.[11]

The constitutionalism that we glimpse here is one of the major themes in Hume's normative political theory in his *Essays;* it is also evident in his *History of England,* where the emergence of the eighteenth-century constitution from previous political conflicts is the central theme. The version of constitutional doctrine implied here derives from the ancient doctrine of "mixed government," in which the best regime was held to combine monarchical, aristocratic, and democratic elements, all of which had to concur in legislation. A more familiar version posits a horizontal division of authority among executive, legislative, and judicial branches of government. Hume also endorses this model, at least with respect to the importance of separating executive and legislative authority. In either version, these constitutional theories call for the separation of governmental powers into different branches or institutions, and both envision the operation of checks and balances – or what Hume often calls "checks and controls" (Essay 2.3) – within government, in order to limit its overall power and to prevent abuses by officials. Constitutional government so conceived, along with the goals of limited government and broad representation of social interests, is a central ingredient of what is now termed the "classical liberal" tradition that was prominent in eighteenth-century thought, a tradition to which Hume, like the American constitutional framers, belonged.[12]

Explaining and Appraising Liberty

Since the mixed constitution was the British status quo by the 1740s, Hume's stance in upholding it is in one sense conservative. At the same time, British Whigs often praised their government (usually in contrast to the absolute monarchy of France) with reference to Britain's hard-won liberties.[13] These included both the personal liberties that were secured under "general and inflexible laws" (Essay 1.4) and limited government, and the political liberty inherent in representative government itself. Liberty in either of these senses is a potentially important value in political life, and its ranking by theorists in relation to other values is also a matter for normative judgment.

In "Of the Liberty of the Press" Hume considers the press freedom, including the freedom to criticize the policies of the king and his ministers, that was conspicuous in eighteenth-century England in contrast to other European states. Hume argues that this liberty is attributable to Britain's mixed government and to the balance – or "watchful jealousy" – between the "republican" and monarchical parts of the government, and in particular to the interest of Parliament (and the people it represents) in resisting arbitrary acts by the executive (Essay 1.4). This is a descriptive argument that attempts to explain the unique phenomenon of British press freedom by reference to Britain's equally unique form of government. However, in Hume's own analysis of causality (in which a "necessary connection" is inferred from "constant conjunction"), it is impossible to establish causation between unique phenomena by repeated observations of similar events. Instead, Hume elaborates a possible chain of causal links that include motivational mechanisms posited for the key actors. Although Hume does not propound this method in his philosophical account of causality, it is one that is plausible for much political and historical explanation. The conclusion, however, should be understood as a hypothesis whose scientific standing would be strengthened by confirming observations in similar cases, should they arise. The logic of the argument is also strengthened by the fact that Hume has in mind a large set of European governments and press regimes, with the British case alone varying in both respects. He might also have pointed to close temporal priority (another criterion of cause-and-effect relations): press freedom followed soon after the consolidation of the mixed government in 1689.

In addition to its political-science explanation of the existence of British press freedom, this essay implicitly raises the normative issue of the value of liberty in one of its more important forms. As a philosopher, Hume certainly valued the liberty to express his sometimes controversial ideas, and we can infer from other statements that he largely approved of existing press freedom, although his opening description of it here as "extreme" suggests possible reservations. A normative analysis, however, is not pursued in "Of the Liberty of the Press," the focus of which is explanatory.

Hume's most direct normative statement on liberty occurs in "Of the Origin of Government" (Essay 4). Here he contrasts liberty and authority as two fundamental features of any government, pointing out that they occur in varying proportions and that there is a perpetual struggle for dominance between them in all regimes. Then, characterizing a free government as one having a "partition of power" (that is, a constitutional structure) and acting by "general and equal laws" (the rule of law), Hume asserts that "liberty is the perfection of civil society; but still authority must be acknowledged essential to its very existence" (Essay 4.7). This may be read as stating the fairly obvious point that for liberty to be enjoyed under the laws of a constitutional state, there first must be a state with sufficient authority to enforce the law. Stated differently, the problem of assuring peaceful social order through adequate state institutions must be solved before one can expect to build free institutions, such as a constitutional democracy. Alternatively, however, Hume's statement may imply that liberty and authority in a political system each tend to expand at the expense of the other, causing tension or conflict, and that Hume's general ranking of authority as the more fundamental quality indicates another conservative tendency in his thought.

Institutional Design as a Republican Strategy

A further aspect of Hume's constitutional thought is evident in his "Idea of a Perfect Commonwealth" (Essay 12). While the constitutional doctrines discussed so far refer mainly to the historical English government, this essay offers a speculative exercise in constitutional design. Hume here exhibits an uncharacteristic fascination with the details of an imaginary state; the main overall point, however, is to bring out the importance of carefully designed institutions and decision-making procedures in order to ensure good laws and policy outcomes without reliance on good motives on the part of the political actors involved. This is the idea Hume clearly states in an earlier essay where he dismisses attacks on the character of a recent British prime minister, arguing that a well-ordered constitution (such as most people believed Britain to have) would not have allowed such a bad man to rule for so long, or would have provided an institutional "remedy against mal-administration" (Essay 2.18). By the same token, the political system should function smoothly even without great leaders, and constitutional continuity obviates dangers that might otherwise be feared from a change of ministries. The quality of an absolute government depends on its good (or bad) administration, but institutional forms are crucial for "republican and free governments," especially the "checks and controuls, provided by the constitution," which make it the "interest, even of bad men, to act for the public good" (Essay 2.3). Well-designed constitutional procedures eliminate the need for virtue in public officials, such as other political theories have prescribed – although public spirit when present is an extra benefit.

Beyond this general theme, it is noteworthy that Hume's proposal in his "Idea of a Perfect Commonwealth" is for a "commonwealth," here a synonym for a republic, in two important eighteenth-century (and still relevant) senses: it has an elected chief executive (a "Protector") rather than a hereditary monarch (although Hume had no quarrel with the existing constitutional monarchy of Great Britain), and it has a popularly elected representative legislature. Notably the Senate in the bicameral legislature is also elected rather than composed of hereditary nobles. These elements were all included in the definition of "republic" adopted by the U.S. founders, who were quite familiar with Hume's *Essays;* in particular, the American *Federalist Papers* most explicitly define a republic as a representative government in a constitutional framework. For both Hume and most of the U.S. framers, a third conception of a republic – the classical idea of a regime resting on the civic virtue or public spirit of active citizens – is implicitly abandoned. Instead, Hume's constitutional engineering emphasizes an elaborate system of indirect and equal representation, annual elections, arrangements to promote deliberation, term limits for executive officials, and a complex legislative system involving checks and balances. Perhaps the oddest feature of Hume's scheme to modern eyes is that the elected legislature remains dispersed in the counties rather than convening in a central assembly. As with his preference for representative over direct democracy expressed in "That Politics May Be Reduced to a Science," this reflects Hume's worries about mob rule in the capital city, but it would probably have the questionable effect of keeping politics highly localized.

In a concluding suggestion famously taken up by James Madison in Federalist no. 10, Hume indicates that such an elaborate plan, by "refin[ing] the democracy" (Essay 12.69), would permit representative or republican government to be established in a large country such as Great Britain (or the United States), contrary to the prevailing view that republics could only exist in small states. It should be kept in mind, however, that Hume's "Perfect commonwealth" is a purely theoretical exercise. He adds disclaimers about the difficulty of wholesale and radical political change, and he certainly did not mean to recommend the dismantling of Britain's established constitution – although his ideas may have inspired such thoughts in others.

The Aims of Political Economy

Political economy, another branch of Hume's program for a science of society, was a field to which eighteenth-century Scots made major contributions, notably Adam Smith as well as Hume himself earlier in a number of essays. The growing prominence of this subject reflected modern economic growth and the fact, as Hume remarked elsewhere, that trade had become a central state concern, in the past century. Political economy included the early phases of today's discipline of economics, which studies such topics as money, prices, markets, commerce, and the levels and distribution of wealth in and among societies. Eighteenth-century political economy was also interested in the historical development of societies in these respects, the political and legal institutions that established the background conditions for different economic systems, and the varying effects of state economic policies.[14]

The leading British political economists adopted what today would be termed a liberal perspective, favoring the growth of commerce and manufacturing through free markets and trade and opposing policies that sought to protect the interests of special groups or to strengthen the state by direct control of trade. Such policies were to be found to some degree in all European states, including Great Britain. Nevertheless, free or representative government favors commerce because property is secure there under the law, because commercial interests (and not just the landed nobility) can influence policy, and perhaps because there is a link between political liberty and the spirit of free enterprise; conversely, the aristocratic culture of monarchies disdains trade. For Hume as a social scientist these claims are factual observations or hypotheses, yet this linkage joins two major institutions – free government and commercial freedom – that Hume also clearly endorses as socially beneficial and desirable. In this vein the three economic essays included here are good examples of the mixture of descriptive economic analysis and normative judgments – including policy recommendations – in Hume's political thought.

In "Of Commerce" (Essay 7) Hume defends two crucial theses that together provide strong support for freedom of commerce in advanced states like Great Britain. First, Hume opposes the common belief that the rise of manufacturing and commerce, located in cities, works to the detriment of agriculture and rural areas. Although the growth of the commercial sector means that agriculture occupies a relatively smaller share of a modern economy, agriculture continues and expands to feed the growing population. Indeed, Hume argues, the two sectors are complementary and mutually beneficial: commercial cities offer an expanding market for the products of commercialized agriculture, giving the rural population a higher income with which they can purchase manufactured goods, including luxuries (Essay 7.14). At the same time manufacturing provides jobs for the surplus rural population, an important point given Hume's assumption that the productive employment of labor is the fundamental source of national wealth. Thus the economy as a whole grows, and everyone's standard of living rises. This argument is an application of political economists' general confidence in this period that free-market transactions constitute not a zero-sum game but rather a system of mutual advantage, or that when every group pursues its own particular interest, the common good is indirectly advanced as well. More specifically, this argument implicitly opposes protectionist policies, such as agricultural price supports, of the sort enacted through the influence of landowners in parliament – policies that for Hume (and Smith) inhibited overall economic growth.

Second, Hume argues that there is no conflict between what he calls the "greatness of a state" (or sometimes "the sovereign") and the "happiness of its subjects" (Essay 7.4). The greatness of the sovereign is the power of the state, particularly military power that can be projected outward as the state pursues its national interests in rivalries with other states. Historically, Hume suggests, sovereigns have sought such "greatness" in two ways, both of which are contrary to the happiness of ordinary people, which is usually simply to enjoy a peaceful and materially comfortable private life. It is noteworthy that Hume uses the economic term "consumption" in characterizing this way of life: in a political-economy perspective (though not generally in Hume's philosophy), the consumption of private goods or "commodities" may be taken as an index of well-being or happiness.

First, sovereigns have often drafted their subjects into large armies, seemingly the source of state power. The extreme case of this was the ancient city-states, especially militaristic Sparta, where the entire male population was trained and available for military service. Some of Hume's contemporaries (notably Jean-Jacques Rousseau) admired the ancients, and Sparta in particular, for its disciplined and patriotic civic spirit. Not so Hume, who writes that the Spartan way of life could be sustained only by "violent" and "peculiar" laws whose rigor was contrary to human nature as normally displayed (Essay 7.7–8). No contemporary person would choose to live under such laws, and modern rulers would find it extremely difficult to introduce them, given the profound change from ancient to modern manners. This passage is a clear indication that Hume's values and political theory are modernist–oriented to modern life, not to ancient or classical models. Luckily for modern people, modern rulers prefer small, well-trained professional armies to mass conscription–an example of another economic concept, the superior efficiency of the division of labor or occupational specialization. Such armies, which Hume calculates require only 1 percent of the population, are easily supported from the economic surplus produced by the rest, and especially the commercial sector, a state of affairs that Hume and (he assumes) most people find entirely satisfactory.

Second, rulers have typically embraced an economic regime called mercantilism, one of the main targets of Smith and to an extent of Hume as well. Mercantilist policies regulated economic life in ways that were thought to enhance the state's military power and the economic resources that underlie military strength, for example by hoarding precious metals, maintaining a favorable trade balance, restricting trade in any goods having military or naval uses, seeking colonies, monopolizing trade routes, and chartering privileged trading companies subject to political supervision. All such regulations interfered with free commerce; to that extent they hampered economic growth and therefore the well-being of the people. They were also misguided, according to political economy, since they failed to grasp the point that economic freedom generates greater wealth and thus, indirectly, greater national strength as well as private happiness. Modern political science reveals that in the modern world the greatness of states and the prosperity of societies are perfectly compatible.

This theme is extended in another essay, "Of the Jealousy of Trade" (not included in this volume), a defense of free international trade against the erroneous mercantilist attitude that one's own commerce is to be jealously protected against that of other nations, which are to be regarded as rivals and potential enemies. Hume's policy recommendation (couched in openly evaluative language) rests on an economic analysis that points to the mutual advantages of trade in several respects. Free trade between nations, like voluntary market transactions between individuals, is entered into only if both parties expect to benefit. All trade, including foreign, stimulates the division of labor in domestic production, a key to social wealth. Further, international commerce embodies a form of division of labor among different nations, as each specializes in industries appropriate to its resources (as in what today is termed the theory of comparative advantage), with similar results. And export industries provide extra employment opportunities for labor, which is basic to prosperity. As among the different classes in a national society, so also among different trading nations, there is an ultimate harmony of interests that Hume, like other Enlightenment thinkers, believed would be conducive to more peaceful international relations.

"Of Refinement in the Arts" was included in Hume's collection of economic essays (the *Political Discourses*) although, as its title implies, its subject matter is broader. We return to it later in considering Hume's general appreciation of modern life; for the moment we may note the occurrence here, as in "Of Commerce," of the economic terms "consumption" (by private individuals) of "commodities" (goods produced for sale in the market) as among the ingredients of the happiness enjoyed by most ordinary people in a prosperous society (Essay 8.6). Most striking, however, is Hume's treatment of the idea of "luxury," with which the essay begins. In a neutral economic sense, luxuries are goods that are valued and enjoyed over and above the necessities of life, whether these are understood in a literal or a cultural sense, as the components of a minimally acceptable standard of living. Hume recognizes that most of the goods manufactured in modern societies and traded in commerce are luxury goods in this sense, so an assessment of modern economies is connected to one's view of luxury. As Hume points out, the word "luxury" has inescapable moral connotations, as something judged good or bad (and therefore cannot well serve as a scientific term). In fact, the more usual sense of luxury in the traditional moral outlook was pejorative, or as Hume says, "blameable": luxuries were goods whose enjoyment implies an excessive and frivolous indulgence in material pleasures, a way of life available to the idle rich and at variance with moral character and social responsibility. This was the perspective both of what Hume terms "severe" Christian moralists and of those who admired the ancient Romans or Spartans, whose way of life was austere as well as disciplined and public-spirited. The notion that luxury is contrary to virtue thus calls into question the modern project of economic progress that was studied – and promoted – by political economy. Hume, then, as a defender of modernity and commerce strives to change the way his readers react to this word – or, indeed, to replace it with the more positive "refinement" in many contexts. Conceding that there may be "vicious" forms of luxury, he affirms that in the prevailing patterns of consumption in the modern world, the moderate enjoyment of luxury goods is not only "innocent" and widely available but a mark of the rising living standards that are an index of general welfare.

The final political-economy essay in this collection – one in which the political dimension is prominent – is "Of Public Credit" (Essay 9). A regular and continuous British national debt, based on the sale of treasury bonds to government creditors and organized through the newly established Bank of England, had existed for a half century at the time of Hume's writing. It was patronized by the new and growing commercial and financial classes, who were willing to lend money because they had confidence in a parliamentary regime in which their interests were represented. The government's ability to borrow at low interest, primarily to finance successful wars against France, gave Britain an advantage over the ostensibly powerful "absolute" monarchy and thus contributed to Britain's rising great-power and imperial status.

It is evident from this sketch that the national debt was a political expression of the commercial world and its institutions, hence a natural subject for economic analysis. At the same time, the debt was directly linked to the modernization of the state and its finances as well as to its growing power and capacity to defend its national interest. The debt itself and the complex financial system of which it was a part – and the financial wealth of its investors – were novel phenomena that were misunderstood and mistrusted by many people of a more old-fashioned outlook, not to mention those (such as landowners) who did not profit from the debt but were taxed to pay the interest on it. Given the debt's modernity and connection to commerce, it is surprising to find that Hume strongly opposes public credit, at least in its current form, siding on this issue with more conservative and anticommercial opinion in contrast to his usual modernist stance. A common conservative attitude (typical of the landed gentry), for example, was distrust of the loyalty of financiers, whose mobile wealth was not tied to any particular country (Essay 9.23).

Hume's economic point is that an ever-expanding debt will at some point prove disastrous to the economy and cause a public bankruptcy, with dire consequences; this is obviously true, though Hume does not try to specify or predict the crisis point, as contemporary analysts do when they warn of the danger that exists when the national debt equals the gross domestic product. Hume also argues that the taxes that must ultimately pay for the debt depress consumption to the detriment of most classes of the population.

Hume's more cogent arguments, however, are political and concern the reasons why such a debt, once established, tends to keep growing. It is all too easy, Hume suggests, for government ministers who seek fame through ambitious enterprises to launch expensive projects when they can borrow money rather than raise taxes – "to mortgage the public revenues, and to trust that posterity will pay off the incumbrances" (Essay 9.2). Such projects often included wars enjoying popular support. Hume also believed that political leaders' ability to stir up nationalistic and other mass emotions was a weakness of free governments (including England's). While he supported limited wars to uphold the European balance of power, he was generally averse to military exploits. An advocate of peaceful international trade, he was especially opposed to wars to expand Britain's empire, the most expensive of which, the Seven Years' War, occurred a few years after this essay appeared. Thus "Of Public Credit" conforms to the pattern we have been observing. It identifies tendencies and makes projections based on analysis in the spirit of social science, although factual evidence of economic ruin is lacking, and Hume admits that it is "difficult to foretel the effects which will result from any untried measure" (Essay 9.22). Still, Hume's own evaluative judgments and criticisms of existing policies with their inevitable "abuses" are even more evident.

Analysis of Parties

A final theme in Hume's political science is his analysis of political parties, both generally and in Britain, to which "Of Parties in General" is one of several contributions (Essay 5). As in the case of his treatment of "luxury," however, we immediately notice a terminological ambiguity that brings evaluative connotations into the analysis. The title refers neutrally to "parties," but in the text of the essay Hume begins by referring first to "sects" and then frequently to "factions," the latter apparently synonymous with parties. In eighteenth-century usage a faction was a political combination of persons who pressed a special interest to the detriment of the public good and often did so in a disruptive manner; it was thus a purportedly descriptive term that clearly included a negative judgment on the phenomenon it identified. ("Sect" connotes a splinter group from a major religion and was often also pejorative.) By using these words and joining in the standard condemnation, Hume appears to share this perspective. As he remarks elsewhere, "When men act in a faction, they are apt, without shame or remorse, to neglect all the ties of honour and morality, in order to serve their party" (Essay 4.3). On the other hand, by shifting to "party" and using that word more prominently, Hume seems to seek greater objectivity – or even to reverse the traditional judgment, since a move from a pejorative to a neutral term can imply a favorable evaluation.

Much of this essay is devoted to a classification of different types of parties (or factions) with historical examples. Such an analytic breakdown of a phenomenon into subcategories is a normal part of the scientific method, but Hume adds an openly normative judgment that one type – parties based on interest – are the "most reasonable, and the most excusable." By "interest" Hume appears to mean the various material or economic interests of different social groups or "distinct orders of men," of which he mentions the nobles, the (common) people, soldiers, merchants, and the "*landed* and *trading* part[s] of the nation" (Essay 5.9). (As he argues in "Of Commerce," Hume comments that the interests of the last two groups are not really opposed.) Parties that represent material interests are "reasonable" because such interests, though sometimes in conflict, can be balanced or compromised in a modern, representative government. Hume evidently assumes that an interest-based politics is normal and benign, remarking elsewhere that "the chief support of the BRITISH government is the opposition of interests," even though this breeds factions (Essay 12.57). The contrast is with other factions based on personality, sentiment, or principle, which are less "excusable" or more dangerous because potentially more extremist. As is the pattern in his political theory, Hume moves readily from his "science of man" to practical lessons.[15]

Hume's principal descriptive or causal claim is that parties flourish under a free government as a result of political liberty itself (presumably free speech and association, parliamentary representation, and elections) combined with certain features of human nature, such as people's natural tendency to embrace a variety of competing interests, both material and ideological. (Hume's analysis of the structural and motivational causes of parties resembles and probably influenced James Madison's analysis of what he unequivocally calls "factions" in Federalist no. 10.) From these facts as established by political science, however, it follows that there is no point in condemning parties in a free country like Great Britain. Indeed, someone like Hume who values free government should embrace them.

One practical lesson that flows from this conclusion is that a well-designed constitution should prevent the dangerous excesses of partisanship through its "checks and controuls" on power. Another is that a reasonable and public-spirited person should support moderate parties and oppose their extreme manifestations – "to draw a lesson of moderation with regard to the parties into which our country is at present divided." A "zeal" for liberty and the public good should be encouraged over zeal for party (Essay 2.14). This was a role that Hume, as a philosopher rather than a scientist, took upon himself, and these were goals that many of his essays were intended to serve.

Governmental Legitimacy: Consent versus Utility

The subject of parties brings us to Hume's most famous political essay, "Of the Original Contract," along with its shorter companion piece, "Of Passive Obedience." Like the other essays we have surveyed, these may be read on two levels.

First, Hume tells us at the outset that he is addressing what today would be termed the ideologies of the two British parties of his time, the Whigs and Tories. Parties under these names dated from the end of the seventeenth century but encompassed earlier ideas and attitudes. Reflecting the constitutional upheavals of that century, the Tories upheld the divine and hereditary right of kings (and of the Stuart dynasty) as well as the related principle that resistance to a legitimate monarch is never permissible. The Whigs responded with the claim that the English government was founded on an "original contract" that registered "the consent of the PEOPLE" (Essay 10.1) and enshrined ancient liberties, that kings who violated this contract (like James II) could be resisted and if necessary replaced, and that all legitimate governments should rest on similar principles. The Whigs had prevailed in 1689, when parliament officially proclaimed the doctrine of an "original compact between king and people," and again in 1715 when the direct Stuart line was replaced by George I, but this outcome was not yet fully accepted at the time of Hume's writing (1748). In Hume's view the ideological claims of the two parties were both extreme and implausible, and thus the basis of much needless (and occasionally dangerous) partisan conflict that threatened constitutional government. Both parties, in other words, exemplified the "parties from principle" that Hume says he finds "the most extraordinary and unaccountable *phenomenon*" in "Of Parties in General" (Essay 5.11) – terms that suggest either that Hume judges such behavior to be unreasonable or that he cannot explain its occurrence empirically. In these essays Hume argues that both "systems of speculative principles" (Essay 10.2) are partially valid. Obedience to government is the norm, but no one really rules out resistance to extreme oppression in all cases; both the rule and the exceptions, Hume argues, are explained and justified by "public utility," Hume's standard for moral appraisal of social practices (Essay 11.2). On the other hand, although popular consent (when present) is indeed "one just foundation" – indeed the best title – to authority (Essay 10.20), the notion of an actual, original founding contract was a historical myth (as Hume was to demonstrate in his *History of England*). Hume's aim is clearly to undermine both extreme claims, reduce "party-zeal," find common ground, and thereby promote the more moderate politics he favored.

In pursuing this project Hume advances two claims of his political science. One thesis is stated at the outset of "Of the Original Contract": "No party, in the present age, can well support itself, without a philosophical or speculative system of principles, annexed to its political or practical one" (Essay 10.1). This applies to all parties, but it applies with special force to "parties from principle," which by definition embrace a set of "abstract speculative principle[s]" (Essay 5.11) used to organized and justify their program. Hume's concern is that this dynamic may favor extreme over moderate parties, but the analyst's question is why this pattern is observed. An answer is suggested by a second thesis, Hume's well-known argument that it is "on opinion only that government is founded" (Essay 3.1). People's support for government, Hume says, may be based on their opinions regarding the public interest or property, but the most important factor – and the most relevant in accounting for the Whig and Tory ideologies – is opinion about the "right to power" itself or opinion regarding the ruler's legitimacy or title to rule. Authoritarian governments may appear to rule simply by force, but even they depend on favorable opinion among key social groups or military officers and officials. In modern times, however, the supportive opinion on which governments rest is increasingly the public opinion of the educated and politically active classes. Under a representative government like Britain's this opinion is mobilized and organized into competing segments by political parties, and ideologies are the means by which parties attract and energize their supporters. The prominence of ideas like "original contract" and "divine right of kings" – and ensuing conflicts – are thus explained in Hume's political science by the importance of broad-based popular opinion in a modern society and under a particular form of government.

The second level on which we may read "Of the Original Contract" is as a contribution to normative political theory, in particular to the issue of governmental legitimacy and the problem of people's obligation to obey the laws and other commands issued by government. These two matters are correlative: if a government possesses legitimate authority, or in Hume's terminology a rightful title to rule, then its subjects have a moral obligation to obey, or what Hume often terms a "duty of allegiance" (EPM, 4.1). When Hume considers opinions regarding the right to power and their importance in upholding governments, he is engaged in a descriptive analysis of certain general facts of political life. In his normative theory of this subject Hume presents his own view of the proper criteria of legitimate authority and criticizes opposing views, in particular that found in the contractarian theory of government and the more general consent theory of political obligation of which it is an example. (Hume does not seriously consider the theory of "divine right" as privileging certain rulers.)

Hume's criticism of the "original contract" is directed in the first instance against the popular or Whig theory that a contract between king and people in which the people promise to obey in exchange for protection both establishes and limits governmental authority. His arguments also apply, however, to the more interesting social contract theory as expounded by "philosophers" (Essay 10.6) such as John Locke in connection with the Revolution of 1688, whose ideas were followed by the Scottish philosopher Francis Hutcheson in the generation before Hume. This theory held that free individuals agreed or contracted with one another to establish a civil society and to obey the authority vested in it; they (or a majority of them) then proceeded to establish a government of limited powers to exercise this collective authority on a regular basis. Locke thus envisioned not only government and its legitimate power but society itself and people's membership in society as deriving from an original social contract.

To this Hume replies that governments might indeed have originated in the distant past by some such process (though probably not a formal contract), as roughly equal primitive people "in the woods and desarts" chose war chieftains and lawgivers (Essay 10.4; Essay 4.6). This conjecture about the remote beginnings of government, however, has little or no relevance in the present, when most existing governments, Hume says, "have been founded originally either on usurpation or conquest, or both, without any pretence of a fair consent, or voluntary subjection of the people" (Essay 10.9). These governments have come to be accepted over time if they proved to be stable and beneficial. To this the contract theorist could simply respond that all existing governments are illegitimate insofar as they fail to satisfy the contract standard. For Hume, though, such a radical implication indicates the implausibility of the theory. What is needed is a standard that is both more realistic and more in line with most people's belief that they ought – in most cases – to obey the existing government regardless of its less-than-pristine origins.

Hume points to another difficulty in social contract theory. Even if civil society were originally established by a voluntary agreement among a set of people, how do members of subsequent generations who had no part in the original contract acquire social membership and political obligation? For this, Locke adds a procedural supplement that reflects the larger principle that legitimate government must be based on the consent of the governed. Each new member should ideally give his or her "express consent" to the terms of the social contract, or at least demonstrate "tacit consent" to the existing arrangements by remaining in the country; alternatively, Locke argues that any individual upon attaining maturity may choose to leave the country of his or her birth and form or join a different civil society elsewhere. This would be a clear expression of the freedom of choice that liberal theory prizes.

To this point Hume argues (plausibly) that it is unreasonable to infer tacit consent to government from a person's failure to leave, since emigration is costly and beyond the reach of "a poor peasant or artizan," or indeed most people (Essay 10.24). More generally, most people do not have any real opportunity to register consent (or dissent) and would deny that such consent is the necessary condition of being obligated to obey the law. Most people accept the notion that a duty of allegiance stems from one's birth and upbringing in a particular country. If we press further, moreover, we find that people's belief in the legitimacy of government depends principally on time and custom: the longer a government or regime has ruled, the deeper is popular allegiance or sense of duty likely to be. "They imagine not, that their consent gives their prince a title: But they willingly consent, because they think, that, from long possession, he has acquired a title, independent of their choice" (Essay 10.22). This is likely to be true, at least, so long as the established government meets the test of utility or serves the public good, as the *Enquiry Concerning the Principles of Morals* emphasizes. Such a view, for Hume, accords with the normal continuity and generational overlap of human society (Essay 10.28).

These arguments contain a number of descriptive generalizations about political life and psychology: most governments do not originate in contracts or agreements yet are nevertheless usually accepted by their subjects; most people do not believe that their duty to obey depends on their having signed a contract or given their express consent; continuity and duration, backed up by habit and tradition, are the strongest factors in stabilizing governments. These are scientific claims about popular beliefs or opinion regarding legitimacy and obligation, and yet Hume appears to accord these conclusions normative force as well, in opposition to contract theory. Much of this essay, in other words, embodies a movement in Hume's thought from "is" to "ought." Or, stated differently, Hume evidently wishes to embrace a normative theory regarding the moral duty of allegiance that is sufficiently realistic to support the position of most stable and effective governments, and such a theory will not deviate very far from actual practice and opinion. Thus, while Hume may be classified (in today's terms) as a liberal in his defense of free or constitutional government and free commerce, "Of the Original Contract" reveals another, conservative side of his political theory, in two senses: by insisting that valid, normative principles should not stray far from actual opinion, the theory would normally uphold the political status quo, at least in stable periods; and by accepting the normal inclination to venerate longstanding regimes, it endorses a legitimizing criterion of tradition and precedent. Such a theory, we may add, would offer little guidance in times of revolution or upheaval, and Hume would face a dilemma when established practice and traditional opinion were in opposition to the liberal institutions that he elsewhere defends.

The best-known philosophical argument in "Of the Original Contract" may suggest how Hume would approach such a tension. Political contract and consent theories, Hume points out, seek to derive political obligation from promising. A contract is a mutual or multilateral promise, and to consent is implicitly or explicitly to promise to do something. "But why are we bound to observe our promises?" Hume's moral philosophy offers an extensive answer to this question: promising is a useful social practice, and "fidelity to promises," or promise-keeping, which for Hume forms part of justice, is a virtue whose obligatory nature derives from its tendency to promote "peace and social order" or the overall benefit of the individuals who engage in the practice and of society as a whole. But for Hume, government too is an institution that is necessary for the well-being of society, and hence the virtue and duty of allegiance may be defended in the same way, as grounded in its tendency to promote public or social utility. Hence there is no need to reduce allegiance to a contract or a promise, and "we gain nothing by resolving the one into the other." The duty to keep promises (or contracts) and the obligation to obey the law rest on the same basis (Essay 10.33–36).

A minor criticism of this argument might be that promise-keeping is regarded by many people as a core moral duty, as contractarians evidently assume, and even in Hume's philosophy justice is sometimes treated as being prior to and more fundamental than government. (This is evident in the structure of the argument of sections 2–3 of the *Enquiry.*) In "Of the Original Contract," however, as also throughout the *Enquiry,* we see another side of Hume's normative moral and political theory – his appeal to utility (or social welfare) as the appropriate standard for justifying social practices and institutions. Combining this principle with others in the essay, we may surmise that Hume endorses "long possession" as a criterion of legitimacy, and the popular belief that long-established governments should be obeyed, on utilitarian grounds, as factors that bring social stability and other benefits. Likewise, Hume supports free government and free commerce because he believes these institutions also serve the overall welfare and prosperity of society.

In Hume's philosophy of human nature, custom – both mental and social – is a powerful force in our cognitive and moral lives, and it is people's propensity to rely on custom that leads them to respect old institutions and regimes. Utility, however, is a forward-looking principle, since we assess the relative utilities of alternative actions and practices by considering their future consequences for the well-being of society.[16] A tension between past-oriented custom and future-oriented utility runs deep in Hume's moral philosophy. This tension, however, is not a defect but rather a creative element in Hume's thought, one that is true to the reality of human nature and ordinary life.

Hume's Realist Modernism

Hume's critique of the "original contract" and his substitution of alternative standards for evaluating governments are the best-known components of his political theory. We may conclude with two related, and pervasive, normative themes from his essays.

"Idea of a Perfect Commonwealth" (Essay 12) indicates by its title an affinity (unique in Hume's writings) to the utopian tradition of political theory. In this approach a theorist such as Plato or Thomas More (whom Hume mentions) depicts an ideal state, sometimes as a guide to practical reform but more often as a moral model designed to reveal the gap between what is and what ought to be. The idealism of such writings appears to contrast with the usual realism of Hume's theory, evident in "Of the Original Contract" and other essays. For philosophers in the Platonic tradition, the perfection of a state lies in the end that it seeks to attain, such as a just ordering of society or the virtuous character of the citizens. Hume proposes no such ideal goal. Rather, his "perfect commonwealth" is a streamlined republic with an elected executive and an elaborate system of representation, one that is more egalitarian than the existing British House of Commons. This commonwealth has what Hume calls a "free" and constitutional government, features that he values, but the emphasis is on procedural and institutional design and administrative efficiency, not the ethical quality of the regime. Hume's closing remark that such a well-modeled commonwealth could function in a large country is also a practical consideration, not an ideal.

Two further themes also bring out Hume's distance from the utopian tradition. First, Hume tells us that the "only valuable model" offered by his predecessors is James Harrington's fictional republic, Oceana.[17] Like Hume, Harrington focuses on institutions, but Hume emphasizes the point that Harrington's scheme, unlike Plato's, does not presuppose or aim at any "great reformation in the manners of mankind" – in effect, a change in human nature as it is usually observed (Essay 12.4). The hallmark of a true utopian is the "imaginary" hope of altering human motivation through education and laws, replacing self-interest, for example, with an internalized disposition to just or virtuous conduct. For a liberal (and skeptical) constitutionalist like Hume, such a project – which aims at something that is contrary to all past experience – is fanciful; a more feasible goal is to enjoy personal and political liberty under a constitutional government that takes people as they are and channels their actions toward the public good.

Second, Hume conspicuously disclaims at the outset any radical intentions in pursuing a merely speculative exercise, repeating more explicitly than in "Of the Original Contract" the conservative argument that "An established government has an infinite advantage, by that very circumstance of its being established; the bulk of mankind . . . never attributing authority to any thing that has not the recommendation of antiquity." Hume underlines this view by saying that a "wise magistrate" will keep any innovations as close as possible to the "ancient fabric" of the constitution (Essay 12.1). Thus, while "Idea of a Perfect Commonwealth" expresses some of Hume's values and recommendations, it is far removed from the kind of ideal theory or revolutionary proposal that might be suggested by the title.

Finally, we should recognize Hume's general approval of the modern society that had emerged in advanced countries like England (and was advancing in Scotland) as the context for his more specific political positions. This form of life was often referred to at the time as "commercial society," or the commercial stage of social development, because of the prominence of the relatively new commercial sector, which Hume thoroughly endorsed. Representative government, liberty of the press, personal freedom under the law, secularism, and an enterprising spirit of individualism were also components of this modernity, contrasting with ancient, primitive, and medieval ways of life. Another important dimension is captured in the favorite Humean word "refinement," as in "Of Refinement in the Arts," though the idea of refinement applies not only to the arts and culture but also to science and technology, the material standard of living, philosophy and enlightenment, and the manners and morals of everyday life. Hume and other modernists believed that all these were interconnected, were improving, and were encouraged by free and lawful government and economic growth. Hume's admiration of commercial culture is expressed in his comment that it "rouses men from their indolence; and . . . raises in [those who can afford luxuries] a desire of a more splendid way of life than what their ancestors enjoyed" (Essay 8.15). Critics like Rousseau held that such affluence was limited to a few and that commerce increased the inequality between rich and poor. Like other political economists who believed free markets increased opportunities and employment broadly, Hume doubted this critique, and his normative judgment reflects his confidence: "A too great disproportion among the citizens weakens any state. Every person, if possible, ought to enjoy the fruits of his labour, in a full possession of all the necessaries, and many of the conveniencies of life. No one can doubt, but such an equality is most suitable to human nature" (Essay 7.17).

Another criticism was that modern life promoted self-seeking and competitive attitudes, destroying communal ties and repudiating the values of earlier moral codes, such as classical republican public-spiritedness or the virtues enjoined by Christianity. Indeed, some held that modernity had abandoned the quest for virtue altogether in its materialism. Hume's strategy in the face of such criticisms is not to try to reclaim traditional values but to assert that commercial society promotes a new (and better) set of virtues. Some of these, including justice, allegiance, and benevolence, resemble and overlap with traditional virtues; others, including civility, politeness, and other "useful" and "agreeable" qualities, Hume holds to be distinctive of advanced modern nations. Most directly, Hume argues that "ages of refinement are both the happiest and most virtuous," and he singles out "*industry, knowledge,* and *humanity*" as the typical and interlinked virtues associated with modern prosperity (Essay 8.2–5). Industry here means the industriousness or work-ethic of commerce and manufacturing; knowledge refers to the modern flourishing of philosophy and science, including the knowledge that supports free and moderate government; and humanity denotes an aversion to cruelty and a sympathetic sharing in others' pleasures that generates a form of sociability. Hence commerce, refinement, constitutional government, and their associated virtues define a way of life in terms that convey unmistakable approval.

Conclusion

Throughout his essays, then, we find Hume pursuing his "science of man" in the domain of society and politics. His factual descriptions and analyses of causation, however, often lead to conclusions having normative overtones and sometimes to explicit evaluative judgments. Even when Hume addresses an ethical question, such as the basis of political obligation or the moral status of luxury and refinement, his arguments make reference to historical facts, to findings of political science, and to political economy. In approving what is both desirable and at the same time feasible, Hume's political thought mixes science with advocacy and combines conservative teachings with positions that were (in his time) both liberal and progressive.

NOTES

1. David Hume, *A Treatise of Human Nature,* ed. David Fate Norton and Mary J. Norton (Oxford: Clarendon Press, 2007), introduction (subsequent citations are by book, chapter, and paragraph).
2. A useful overview of Hume's doctrines in all these areas is Claudia M. Schmidt, *David Hume: Reason in History* (University Park: Pennsylvania State University Press, 2003).
3. Recent works on Hume's political theory include John B. Stewart, *Opinion and Reform in Hume's Political Philosophy* (Princeton, N.J.: Princeton University Press, 1992); Knud Haakonssen, "The Structure of Hume's Political Theory," in *The Cambridge Companion to Hume,* ed. David Fate Norton (Cambridge: Cambridge University Press, 1993), 182–221; Neil McArthur, *David Hume's Political Theory: Law, Commerce and the Constitution of Government* (Toronto: University of Toronto Press, 2007); and Frederick G.

Whelan, *The Political Thought of Hume and His Contemporaries,* 2 vols. (London: Routledge, 2015).

4. Hume was a friend of Adam Smith's and influenced the latter's major exposition of political economy, *The Wealth of Nations,* which appeared in the year of Hume's death (1776). Hume's essays appeared in many editions from 1741 onward. His economic essays were published as *Political Discourses* in 1752.

5. Two recent works that draw on Hume's *History of England* to illuminate his political thought are Frederick G. Whelan, *Hume and Machiavelli: Political Realism and Liberal Thought* (Lanham, Md.: Lexington Books, 2004), and Andrew Sabl, *Hume's Politics: Coordination and Crisis in the History of England* (Princeton, N.J.: Princeton University Press, 2012).

6. Hume, *Treatise,* 3.1.2.

7. If the social future always resembled the past, there would be neither history nor political events worth taking notice of, both of which involve innovation and change, even if micro-causal links are regular. Explanations of unusual events are sought in some natural sciences outside the laboratory, although the effects of human agency as well as interactive causes complicate matters in the social world.

8. For a convincing interpretation of Hume's place in the Enlightenment, see Dennis C. Rasmussen, *The Pragmatic Enlightenment: Recovering the Liberalism of Hume, Smith, Montesquieu, and Voltaire* (New York: Cambridge University Press, 2014).

9. The climate theory was famously stated in Montesquieu's *The Spirit of the Laws,* a major Enlightenment work that probably influenced Hume's later writings. In this case, however, Hume's "Of National Characters" appeared in the same year as Montesquieu's book (1748). Since the climate theory was also advanced in a scientific spirit, the physical-versus-moral cause controversy was a dispute within the social science of the period.

10. On the Scottish branch of the Enlightenment, in which Hume was a key early figure, see Christopher J. Berry, *The Social Theory of the Scottish Enlightenment* (Edinburgh: Edinburgh University Press, 1997).

11. This regime had its proximate origins in the English Revolution of 1688–89, which resulted in parliamentary supremacy and a limited monarchy, and in the "Protestant succession" implemented in 1715, which excluded the Catholic and allegedly absolutist Stuart dynasty from the throne. The victorious regime was still controversial when this essay was published (1741), and armed rebellions in favor of the Stuarts ended only in 1745. Hence, "That Politics May Be Reduced to a Science" may be read, along with several other

of Hume's essays, as part of a campaign to uphold the existing government and constitutional settlement, in addition to their theoretical interest.

12. The influence of Hume's essays on the American constitutional framers and the authors of *The Federalist Papers* was extensive. See Whelan, *Hume and Machiavelli,* 325–38, and Mark G. Spencer, *David Hume and Eighteenth-Century America* (Rochester, N.Y.: University of Rochester Press, 2005). See also Robert A. Manzer, "Hume's Constitutionalism and the Identity of Constitutional Democracy," *American Political Science Review* 90 (1996): 488–96.

13. The Whigs – in contrast to the Tories – were the more progressive party, aligned more to commerce than to landowners and agriculture. The Whigs also led the Revolution of 1688–89. Hume called himself a Whig, thereby signaling his approval of the revolution as well as its constitutional results.

14. See the essays in Carl Wennerlind and Margaret Schabas, eds., *David Hume's Political Economy* (New York: Routledge, 2008), for detailed studies. For an overview, see Andrew Skinner, "David Hume: Principles of Political Economy," in Norton, ed., *Cambridge Companion to Hume,* 222–54. On the context, see Istvan Hont and Michael Ignatieff, eds., *Wealth and Virtue: The Shaping of Political Economy in the Scottish Enlightenment* (Cambridge: Cambridge University Press, 1982), and Istvan Hont, *Jealousy of Trade: International Competition and the Nation-State in Historical Perspective* (Cambridge, Mass.: Harvard University Press, 2004).

15. Hume finds uncompromising "parties from principle," both ideological and religious, to be especially worrisome. On the latter, see Jennifer A. Herdt, *Religion and Faction in Hume's Moral Philosophy* (Cambridge: Cambridge University Press, 1997). Party ideologies are discussed below.

16. Hume's dual commitment to science and to the ethical criterion of utility are fundamentally connected by their reliance on causality – causal explanation in science and the causal prediction of the consequences of action in moral reasoning.

17. Less well known today than his seventeenth-century compatriots Hobbes and Locke, Harrington contributed to the republican tradition that flourished during the English Civil War and Interregnum of the 1640s and 1650s.

Hume on Decisions, Convention, and Justice

PETER VANDERSCHRAAF AND ANDREW VALLS

Modern interpreters rightly credit Hume as being an important intellectual ancestor of modern rational choice theory, but the multifaceted nature of Hume's analysis of decision is perhaps less well appreciated.[1] Like most of Hume's work, his analysis of decision is primarily explanatory. Hume is more concerned with how humans actually make decisions than with a normative analysis of decision-making. Yet his analysis of individual decision-making does inform his moral and political thought, particularly his views of justice and property. Hence Hume's views of individual decision-making and of cooperation and coordination are important in themselves, and constitute part of the foundation of his moral and political thought.

Decisions, Rationality, and Utility

Hume is frequently thought of both as having been an early utilitarian and as having proposed the first account of goal-directed or "instrumental rationality." Nevertheless, Hume's relationships with both utilitarianism and instrumental rationality as they are understood in our time are not so transparent as surface appearances suggest. Hume does not present anything like a set of principles of rational choice, although he would allow that in many everyday cases individuals choose in a manner conforming roughly to maximizing expected utility. And despite some affinities with utilitarian theory as it has come to be developed, Hume cannot be considered a utilitarian.

Textbook expositions of decision theory typically focus on the deliberations of a single agent, who must choose from among a set of alternative acts, which together with a set of relevant states define the possible outcomes. Robinson Crusoe deciding how to allocate his labor given what "Nature" might deal him is a common metaphor for single-agent decision theory. Hume seldom discusses specific examples of this sort of canonical decision-theoretic problem. This may seem surprising, given both the fame of his general observations on human choices and his many examples where the decisions of multiple agents interact. In fact, Hume's emphasis on interactive decisions flows quite naturally from his concern for explaining why we humans think and act as we do. Hume maintains that humans are so interdependent that seldom does anyone act without reference to the actions of others.[2] For Hume, Crusoe-like decisions are the exceptions, even if many modern decision theorists treat them as fundamental. Hume gives examples of the interactive decisions he takes to be more typical, mainly in his analysis of convention, which we discuss further in the next section.

There is at least one case where Hume examines an individual's decision without reference to the actions of others. In *An Enquiry Concerning the Principles of Morals,* appendix 1, Hume considers the case of a man who exercises. If one asks the man why he takes exercise, Hume says the man may answer that he desires to maintain health, and if pressed as to why he desires health, the man may respond that he hopes to avoid the pain of illness and expect no further questioning. Or he may respond that health is a prerequisite to his being able to earn an income, which in turn is a means toward pleasure, and again expect no further questioning. Hume's point here is simply that one's decisions are rooted in some end one regards as desirable in and of itself, pleasure being one such end. This blocks the absurdity of an infinite regress of reasons one might otherwise be pressed to give for one's acts.[3]

However, examples like this reveal only one facet of Hume's views on human decisions. Hume never extrapolates from these examples any general principles for rational decision. Hume in fact shows little interest in developing a normative analysis of rational choice. In particular, he does not give either any general constraints on preferences or anything like a principle of maximizing expected utility, either with reference to the individual or to an entire community. This may seem odd given how often Hume is associated with utilitarianism. Hume uses the term "utility" so frequently and so prominently in his moral writings that it would seem obvious he must be a utilitarian of some stripe. But Hume would likely resist being classified as a proto-utilitarian in the classical or contemporary sense. Hume does argue frequently that utility, by which he means general usefulness, produces pleasure.[4] And he states that "the pain or pleasure, which arises from the general survey or view of any action or quality of the mind, constitutes its vice or virtue."[5] However, Hume does not equate utility with pleasure or pleasure-producing properties in general.[6] And nowhere does Hume clearly endorse any principle of acting with the aim of maximizing aggregate happiness or pleasure or aggregate utility. And it is likely that Hume knew of such a principle, namely, the proto-utilitarian principle of Hume's own teacher Francis Hutcheson.[7] Indeed, given his shrewd observations regarding the typical individual's tendencies toward partiality and self-conceit, Hume may have thought that a utilitarian standard like that of Jeremy Bentham or J. S. Mill is surely beyond the reach of humans as we are.[8]

Hume also never proposes anything like a principle of maximizing expected utility derived from one's personal preferences. In fact, while Hume gives extensive discussions of utility and probability in his works, he does not directly incorporate either probabilities or utilities in his discussions of decisions. This is not so surprising given that Hume views his as a predominantly explanatory project. Hume would be the first to point out that an individual going about her everyday affairs seldom if ever runs through a process of deriving cardinal utilities from her preferences, computing weighted averages of these utilities and probabilities, and then finally choosing an alternative that maps to the highest of these weighted averages.

Perhaps no claim of Hume's is more famous, or more scandalous, than "Reason is, and ought only to be the slave of the passions, and can never pretend to any other office than to serve and obey them."[9] One of Plato's core positions in the *Republic* is that the rational part of the soul should regulate the appetitive and spirited parts. One way to read Hume's analysis of how reason and the passions interact is that Hume would stand Plato on his head.[10] Certainly Hume thinks that two received views in moral philosophy are that reason and the passions are in conflict and that reason should have superiority in the regulation of conduct, and he sets himself to refute these views. Hume famously and controversially argues that reason and the passions cannot be in direct conflict since reason can never give rise to what a passion alone can produce, namely a volition, though reason does do what passions do not, namely judge what is true or false regarding relations of ideas and matters of fact. Hume allows that a volition can be the product of a combination of passions and the judgments of reason, but that in fact reason plays a subordinate role by ascertaining the true states of the world relative to one's choice or by evaluating alternative means toward achieving one's desired ends. But any desired end is in principle compatible with reason.

> 'Tis not contrary to reason to prefer the destruction of the whole world to the scratching of my finger. 'Tis not contrary to reason for me to chuse my total ruin, to prevent the least uneasiness of an *Indian* or person wholly unknown to me. 'Tis as little contrary to reason to prefer even my acknowledg'd lesser good to my greater, and to have a more ardent affection for the former than the latter.[11]

Hume's position regarding ends is formally similar to that of his predecessor Thomas Hobbes, who states that anything a person desires is what this person will call "good" and even defines deliberation in terms of a sequence of alternating desires and aversions.[12] But Hobbes in effect adds additional structure to his account of what is good by arguing that there are universally desired ends, such as a universal desire for peace,[13] and universal desires for greater quantities of certain powers, such as wealth and physical strength, that are means to obtaining other future desired ends.[14] Hume does not deny there are ends that most or even all people desire, but he makes no effort to identify such ends as part of his analysis of volition. And Hume expressly states that it need not contravene reason to prefer one's lesser good over one's greater good. Hobbes's and Hume's views here are not necessarily at odds, but they are employed in fundamentally different projects. Hobbes uses his own account of what is good in building his system of natural moral law and normative political theory. Hume is trying to identify at the deepest level the structure of human choices.

One reason for thinking that Hume's theory of choice is an instrumental rationality theory is his willingness to entertain preferences over any set of alternative ends as data for his analysis. A second reason is that it appears to follow straightforwardly from his analysis that one can evaluate the rationality of a choice only in terms of how well this choice serves as a means toward achieving a desired end. For Hume a preference for a particular end can be opposed to reason only in a derivative way, either when this preference is based on false judgments or when it leads one to choose means insufficient for the desired end.[15] Hume would say that had the story of *The Ox-Bow Incident* related actual events, the posse members could sensibly admit that their desire to lynch their captives was unreasonable, but only because this desire was based on their belief that their captives were guilty of the murder and cattle theft that they learned only later had never occurred.[16] Hume would accept Napoleon's admission that the decision to invade Saint-Domingue was great folly but only because Napoleon concluded in the end that diplomacy would have served to fulfill his wish more effectively than military force, not because his wish was to see Saint-Domingue restored to French rule. Hume would add that in such cases, which illustrate how we in fact do express judgments of decisions and passions as being rational or not, speaking of an unreasonable passion or volition is technically speaking improperly.[17]

Reason can and in fact does regulate our choices and even our passions, but on the back end of the deliberative process, so to speak, where this process starts with some motivating passion. In Hume's own words,

> The moment we perceive the falsehood of any supposition, or the insufficiency of any means our passions yield to our reason without any opposition. I may desire any fruit as of an excellent relish; but whenever you convince me of my mistake, my longing ceases. *I may will the performance of certain actions as means of obtaining any desir'd good; but as my willing of these actions is only secondary, and founded on the supposition, that they are causes of the propos'd effect;* as soon as I discover the falsehood of that supposition, they must become indifferent to me.[18]

The italicized part of this passage reads practically like a definition of instrumental rationality. And a number of contemporary philosophers propose accounts of instrumental rationality that they acknowledge are inspired by Hume but that they argue augment what they take to be Hume's own too-thin instrumental rationality.[19] Hume himself would contend that nothing need or should be added to his account of decision-making insofar as this account explains the process of any actual decision. Hume might accept the mantle of being a forerunner of contemporary accounts of instrumental rationality, but he would no doubt insist that this is but a part, and not the main part, of his overall analysis. One might evaluate a decision, whether executed or not, as reasonable or not given certain beliefs regarding relevant facts, but one might not have these beliefs at the moment of decision. Hume might grant that one can evaluate a choice as instrumentally rational given that the chooser bases her decision on sound, relevant beliefs, with the obvious caveat that determining which relevant beliefs are even minimally sound can prove quite a challenge, particularly given his own skeptical doubts regarding the possibility of justifying inductive inferences. But he would maintain that one can sensibly make such a judgment only from a perspective external to the actual decision itself, such as that of a bystander trying to understand the underlying rationale for this decision or that of oneself when one examines one's own choices retrospectively.

Hume is especially interested in analyzing a decision at its most fundamental level, namely as an act of the mind. Viewed at this level, a decision is similar to a passion or desire in that a decision is an original, self-contained mental event that by itself is not subject to reason:

> Reason is the discovery of truth or falsehood. Truth or falsehood consists in an agreement or disagreement either to the *real* relations of ideas, or to *real* existence and matter of fact. Whatever, therefore, is not susceptible of this agreement or disagreement, is incapable of being true or false, and can never be an object of our reason. Now 'tis evident our passions, volitions, and actions, are not susceptible of any such agreement or disagreement; being original facts and realities, compleat in themselves, and implying no reference to other passions, volitions and actions. 'Tis impossible, therefore, they can be pronounced either true or false, and be either contrary or conformable to reason.[20]

Hume classifies passions and desires as "impressions," albeit secondary impressions that are partly based on various ideas.[21] Precisely because they are impressions, passions and desires lack propositional content and are consequently not proper subject matter for reason, which deals with the correspondence of ideas to truth or falsehood. Hume maintains that at bottom, decisions are part of the same general family of mental events.[22] And at bottom decisions have the same status as other impressions in that they are orthogonal to reason. In particular, a decision is never opposed to reason given the agent's actual beliefs at the time of this mental act. Hume points out that people frequently act knowingly against their own interests, and he thinks the explanation for this is no mystery. An immediate violent passion can produce an overriding desire for an end such as vengeance that can be against one's own known interests. Conversely a more calm passion such as the love for life or general appetite for good can curb a more violent passion and lead one to choose according to one's interests. It is the passions that can come into conflict, and when they do conflict, the passions that prevail in the end and underwrite one's actual decision, which will vary according to one's general character or present disposition.[23]

Where does Hume's analysis of decision leave us in the end? Hume gives an account of how an action can on a surface level be an instrumentally rational choice. Again, it is the beliefs regarding the relevant facts that can render a decision rational or not in an indirect way. But at their core, decisions are neither rational nor irrational. Some of Hume's recent interpreters have argued that Hume is not in fact proposing or defending instrumental rationality as an account of practical reason.[24] Hume does not even require that one's preferences be coherent, the usual minimal standard of modern accounts of instrumental rationality. For Hume's main purpose in studying decisions is not to give an account of practical reason but rather to explain the psychological process of choice.

One can read Hume's theory of individual decision as an informal behavioral decision theory.[25] And this part of Hume's project does not serve merely to sow skeptical doubts regarding the possibility of a fully satisfactory account of rational choice. Hume's explanatory analysis of decision-making turns out to be an important part of his larger analysis of morality. Hume concludes that properly speaking, choices and actions cannot be rational or irrational. But choices and actions can be laudable or blameworthy.[26] Hume is trying to identify the root source of the moral distinctions people actually make, and he argues famously that this source must be rooted in the particular feelings that acts and the characters regarded as praiseworthy or blameworthy produce.[27] Hume's analysis of decisions dovetails with this general conclusion. Hume is issuing a clarion call to moral philosophers to turn their focus on what he has identified as the real foundations of decisions and of moral approbation and censure. As he puts it, "Extinguish all the warm feelings and prepossessions in favour of virtue, and all disgust or aversion to vice; Render men totally indifferent towards these distinctions; and morality is no longer a practical study, nor has any tendency to regulate our lives and actions."[28]

Cooperation, Convention, and Justice

Philosophers have discussed conventions and their possible roles in social life even before Socrates. Democritus is said to have argued that things have their names by convention rather than by nature.[29] The thesis that justice is convention evidently had currency in the Athens of Plato's and Aristotle's time.[30] Plato himself presents for consideration at least two versions of this thesis in *Gorgias* and the *Republic*.[31] But what are conventions? And how do conventions originate? Over many centuries, philosophers mulled over which parts of social life are ruled by convention without trying to answer these questions in depth. In the eighteenth century Hume proposed an original analysis of convention that is one of his monumental contributions to philosophy. Several of the giants of early modern moral philosophy, including Hugo Grotius, Thomas Hobbes, Samuel von Pufendorf, and John Locke, foreshadowed Hume's analysis by arguing that specific natural law requirements can be understood as conditionally binding given one's beliefs regarding others' conduct.[32] Yet Hume's treatment of convention is pioneering because he gives general conditions that characterize conventions together with a highly original account of their origins. Hume argues that a convention is a special system of reciprocal expectations that guide conduct in a community. Hume also argues that conventions need not always arise from explicit agreement and can in fact come from certain inductive inferences. Given Hume's analysis, one can understand many of the requirements of morality as well as morally indifferent social rules as conventions, and indeed Hume views the natural moral law as a system of distinguished conventions.[33] Hume's analysis of convention is also another milestone in decision theory, since this analysis explicitly incorporates *interactive* decisions where individuals predicate their own choices on the choices of others. In his account of convention Hume presents an early and informal interactive decision theory that would in the twentieth century be reformulated mathematically as game theory.[34]

In the *Enquiry,* appendix 3, Hume summarizes the core of this analysis:

If by convention be meant a sense of common interest, which sense each man feels in his own breast, which he remarks in his fellows, and which carries him, in concurrence with others, into a general plan or system of actions, which tends to public utility; it must be owned, that, in this sense, justice arises from human conventions. For if it be allowed (what is, indeed, evident) that the particular consequences of a particular act of justice may be hurtful to the public as well as to individuals; it follows that every man, in embracing that virtue, must have an eye to the whole plan or system, and must expect the concurrence of his fellows in the same conduct and behaviour. . . .

Thus two men pull the oars of a boat by common convention, for common interest, without any promise or contract. Thus gold and silver are made the measures of exchange; thus speech and words and language are fixed, by human convention and agreement. Whatever is advantageous to two or more persons, if all perform their part; but what loses all advantage if only one perform, can arise from no other principle. There would otherwise be no motive for any one of them to enter into that scheme of conduct.[35]

Hume characterizes a convention in terms of a rule or practice people follow for mutual benefit. He indicates in his discussion of some other conventions that he does not insist that all involved conform with an established convention all of the time.[36] General conformity suffices, meaning roughly that most individuals involved conform at least most of the time. What Hume does require is that given the choice between conforming or not conforming, a given involved individual serves her interests better by conforming on condition that the others involved generally conform as well. So for Hume a convention is a stable as well as a mutually beneficial practice. Yet Hume clearly recognizes that the members of a community might fail to follow such a practice even if all recognize that the practice, if generally followed, would be stable and mutually beneficial. Hume argues that mutual expectations of conformity are what underwrite actual conformity with the practice. Indeed, Hume concludes that the "sense of common interest," that is, the fact that the practice is mutually beneficial and stable, together with its mutual expression, that is, each individual expressing that she knows this fact and intends to conform, are what really characterize a convention. For the general sense of common interest together with its mutual expression generate the mutual expectations of conformity that produce actual conformity.

Where do the mutual expectations of conformity come from? One might naturally suppose that the individuals who follow a convention generate the requisite expectations by exchanging promises to conform. However, Hume denies that conventions are generally established in this manner. Indeed, Hume maintains that promises themselves are practices arising from certain conventions, so for Hume this purported explanation of the origins of conventions is circular.[37] Hume's own explanation of the origins of conventions relies on learning from experience:

> Men's inclination, their necessities, lead them to combine; their understanding and experience tell them that this combination is impossible where each governs himself by no rule, and pays no regard to the possessions of others: and from these passions and reflections conjoined, as soon as we observe like passions and reflections in others, the sentiment of justice, throughout all ages, has infallibly and certainly had place to some degree or other in every individual of the human species. In so sagacious an animal, what necessarily arises from the exertion of his intellectual faculties may justly be esteemed natural.[38]

Hume argues that people who interact repeatedly can learn to follow a convention via some trial-and-error process by which their expectations regarding each other gradually converge and characterize the convention they follow. Elsewhere, Hume gives more detailed explanations of how certain conventions first emerge. For example, Hume argues that people frequently start to acquire certain sorts of property through *accession,* that is, by associating some connection between a good that one already possesses and another good that is connected to the former and in some sense inferior to the former. According to Hume, accession explains how one becomes the owner of goods such as the produce of one's garden or the offspring of one's livestock, even before one takes possession of these goods.[39] The important point to note here is that Hume maintains that members of society learn to follow conventions via inductive inferences. This is quite remarkable, given that Hume famously maintains that while people routinely make inductive inferences, at a deep level there is no rational justification of such inferences.[40] Moreover, Hume argues that members of a society continually reinforce the mutual expectations that characterize a convention by following the stable and mutually beneficial practice of this convention. Put another way, members of society mutually express the common sense of interest associated with an incumbent convention by actually following the practice of this convention in their interactions.

A remarkable variety of social phenomena can be viewed as Humean conventions. Hume identifies many of these phenomena himself.[41] In some of the underlying coordination problems Hume discusses, such as settling on a monetary currency, adopting words and languages, or moving smoothly in traffic, the interests of all involved evidently coincide perfectly. These are problems of pure coordination. Hume gives as one of his pure coordination examples the case of wagoners passing each other on the road.[42] Neither driver wants to crash into the other. Both want to pass without incident. Hume mentions a number of rules that develop to prevent crashes and determine who should yield to the other, such as "that the lighter machine yield to the heavier, and, in machines of the same kind, that the empty yield to the loaded," and "that those who are going to the capital take place of those who are coming from it."[43] Similarly, people passing each other on the sidewalk need conventions to prevent "jostling, which peaceable people find very disagreeable and inconvenient."[44] In all such cases, the interests of the parties are the same and converge on the need for conventional rules to regulate their interaction. They are fairly indifferent about the content of the rules but merely need some rules to prevent wagon crashes in the road and jostling on the sidewalk.

Hume's analysis of convention goes far beyond pure coordination interactions.[45] Hume discusses problems of inheritance, dividing a limited quantity of a good, obedience to a government, and even adopting rules of warfare and murder.[46] Hume regards problems of these sorts as problems having elements of both coordination and conflict. Hume gives a particularly striking analysis of conventions of property. As with other coordination problems, Hume thinks that the incumbent conventions community members follow that resolve questions of property may seem fickle upon analysis and even analogous to superstitions. But, he adds,

> there is this material difference between *superstition* and *justice,* that the former is frivolous, useless, and burdensome; the latter is absolutely requisite to the well-being of mankind and existence of society. When we abstract from this circumstance (for it is too apparent ever to be overlooked) it must be confessed, that all regards to right and property, seem entirely without foundation, as much as the grossest and most vulgar superstition.[47]

So, for Hume the rules of justice that regulate property are conventions. Their content can vary widely, but what is essential is that there must be some rules determining ownership. For any given good, an individual can either claim this good as her own property or leave this good for others to claim. If two people claim the same good, this is a recipe for conflict. Figure 1 summarizes just such a problem of establishing ownership over a good.

The figure 1 matrix characterizes the Property Game with two players, Claudia and Laura, who can each follow either of two pure strategies: claim the good at stake as her own property (G_i) or concede the good to the other (M_i).[48] The players' preferences over the outcomes resulting

Figure 1. Property Game

Laura

		M_2	G_2
Claudia	M_1	(1, 1)	(1, 2)
	G_1	(2, 1)	(0, 0)

M_i = concede, G_i = claim, $i \in \{1, 2\}$

from their chosen pure strategies are reflected by the payoff vectors in each cell of the matrix, where the first (second) component of each payoff vector is Claudia's (Laura's) payoff at this outcome. Their preferences over outcomes conflict, because (G_1, M_2) is Claudia's most preferred outcome where she becomes owner and Laura concedes, and similarly (M_1, G_2) is Laura's most preferred outcome where she becomes owner. And if both claim in hopes of becoming the owner, at the resulting outcome (G_1, G_2) they fight without resolving their problem, the worst outcome for both. The two outcomes (G_1, M_2) and (M_1, G_2) are stable in the sense that M_1 is Claudia's best response to Laura's following G_2, and M_2 is Laura's best response to Claudia's following G_1, that is, these outcomes are "Nash equilibria" of the Property Game.[49]

If Laura and Claudia are to coordinate, exactly one of them must concede. Who shall it be? Given their conflicting preferences, neither is indifferent to the content of the rules that will determine who owns what. Both also have an interest in avoiding their least-preferred outcome of conflict, which is likely to arise in the absence of any rules whatsoever. There are a bewildering variety of possible conventions that might resolve this problem by determining who owns what, and Hume discusses several. One such convention to which Hume devotes special attention is the convention of *first possession*. This Humean convention can be summarized game-theoretically. If both know who is first possessor, then to implement the first possession convention, Laura and Claudia can follow the contingency strategy: Claim G_i if I am first possessor and concede (M_i) otherwise. With ω_1 and ω_2 denoting the respective possible worlds where Claudia is first possessor and Laura is first possessor, the Humean first possessor convention for the Property Game is summarized in figure 2.

By their both following this contingency strategy, Claudia and Laura alternate between (G_1, M_2) and (M_1, G_2) according to the possible worlds ω_1 and ω_2. When both follow this contingency strategy, at each possible world each follows her best response to the other. So they are at an equilibrium of their Property Game.[50] But this is not the only equilibrium available to them. Hume argues that such a first possessor convention regulates property acquisition in many contexts because *first* possession captures the attention of the parties involved in a way that other successive possessions do not, because a rule of first possession solves questions of initial ownership quickly, and because such a rule is typically, though not always, unambiguous.[51] But there is no *a priori* reason for not following some other rule for establishing initial property rights, and Hume himself discusses some of these other rules.[52] Moreover, Hume points out that there can be a variety

Figure 2. First Possessor Convention of Property Game

Laura

		M_2	G_2
Claudia	M_1	(1, 1)	$(1, 2)^{\omega_2}$
	G_1	$(2, 1)^{\omega_1}$	(0, 0)

M_i = concede, G_i = claim, $i \in \{1, 2\}$

ω_1 = Claudia is first possessor, ω_2 = Laura is first possessor.

of different first possessor conventions, depending on what those involved regard as genuine possession.[53] A community follows a first possessor convention in certain contexts simply because the rules of this convention capture the imagination in a special way. Long before the introduction of the mathematics and technical vocabulary of game theory, Hume anticipated the concept of an equilibrium of a game in his account of convention. In terms of this contemporary vocabulary, a Humean convention is one of many distinct available equilibria the parties involved follow given their reciprocal expectations that all follow *this* equilibrium.

In addition to possession, Hume's account of conventions also explains social cooperation and exchange, and his account anticipated large parts of game theory dealing with interactions having a sequential structure and interactions repeated over time. The Prisoner's Dilemma is the most famous of all mathematical games. Figure 3 depicts the payoff matrix of a Prisoner's Dilemma.

Each player in the Prisoner's Dilemma can either cooperate (C_i) or defect (D_i). Both fare better if both cooperate than if both defect, that is, (C_1, C_2) is *Pareto superior* to (D_1, D_2). But D_i is each player's *strictly dominant* strategy, that is, D_i is each player's unique rational strategy, no matter what conjecture he has regarding the other. (D_1, D_2) is both the unique Nash equilibrium and the only strategy profile compatible with the players being rational and knowing the game's payoff structure. Philosophers and social

Figure 3. Prisoner's Dilemma

Ryan

		C_2	D_2
Thomas	C_1	(2, 2)	(0, 3)
	D_1	(3, 0)	(1, 1)

C_i = cooperate, D_i = defect, $i \in \{1, 2\}$

scientists use the Prisoner's Dilemma to model interactions ranging from public-good provisions to economic exchange to arms races. Once again Hume presents a number of the ideas that today are linked with the Prisoner's Dilemma in an informal manner. In *Treatise,* Hume presents an example that appears to cast doubt on the rationality of economic exchange:

> Your corn is ripe today; mine will be so tomorrow. 'Tis profitable for us both, that I shou'd labour with you to-day, and that you shou'd aid me to-morrow. I have no kindness for you, and know you have as little for me. I will not, therefore, take any pains on your account; and should I labour with you upon my own account, in expectation of a return, I know I shou'd be disappointed, and that I shou'd in vain depend upon your gratitude. Here then I leave you to labour alone: You treat me in the same manner. The seasons change; and both of us lose our harvests for want of mutual confidence and security.[54]

This game is sometimes called "Sequential Prisoner's Dilemma" since it is structurally like the Prisoner's Dilemma except for the fact that one player moves after observing his partner's initial move. In this game, Thomas moves first and can cooperate by helping Ryan or defect by withholding his help, and Ryan can then either cooperate or defect himself. According to Hume's analysis, Thomas concludes that if he were to cooperate, Ryan would then defect. Thomas's unique rational choice is therefore to defect, and similarly for Ryan if he goes first.

Hume wants to explain why so much actual economic exchange occurs, especially given the doubts that his own example raises. He concludes that cooperative conduct in exchange makes sense for each party in the context of repeated interaction. When one promises to provide some good or service to another, she indicates her intention to actually provide this good or service as promised and expects not to be trusted again if she fails to keep her promise.[55] Indeed, Hume thinks that promises themselves are instances of a form of convention and that they serve to raise appropriate expectations regarding one's conduct in an interaction.[56] One keeps one's promise to do one's part in an exchange in order to maintain one's good standing in the community of exchangers:

> I learn to do a service to another, without bearing him any real kindness; because I forsee, that he will return my service, in expectation of another of the same kind, and in order to maintain the same correspondence of good offices with me or with others. And accordingly, after I have serv'd him, and he is in possession of the advantage arising from my action, he is induc'd to perform his part, as foreseeing the consequences of his refusal.[57]

Hume's argument here foreshadows the analysis of history-dependent strategies in repeated games. Quite early in the history of game theory, its practitioners recognized that a huge number of different equilibria are possible in an indefinitely repeated game when the players can use history-dependent strategies. This insight spurred a body of research on repeated games that continues to develop. In an experimental study run by the Rand Corporation in the early 1950s, subjects who engaged in a sequence of Prisoner's Dilemma games with a fixed partner frequently converged into a pattern of mutual cooperation. John Nash argued that this apparent anomaly was easily explained if one supposed the subjects had adopted the history-dependent strategy of cooperating with a partner who has never been the first to defect in the sequence of Prisoner's Dilemmas and defecting otherwise. This is a strategy that punishes a partner for deviating first from a pattern of mutual cooperation. If both players follow this strategy in a repeated Prisoner's Dilemma, then they will cooperate at every period of play since neither will defect first. Nash proved that a pair who follows this history-dependent strategy can be at an equilibrium of a Prisoner's Dilemma repeated over an indefinite time horizon and conjectured that the subjects in the Rand experiment might be trying to follow their parts of this equilibrium. Nash's "folk theorem" for a fixed pair of players who engage in a repeated Prisoner's Dilemma suggests that cooperative conduct in repeated games can be supported via community enforcement.[58]

Hume presents the idea of community enforcement informally himself. Individual members of a given community might meet, attempt to exchange, and then try to repeat this process, possibly with new partners. When exchanges have the structure of an ordinary Prisoner's Dilemma or Sequential Prisoner's Dilemma, one history-dependent strategy such community members might follow is to cooperate with those who have a record of cooperating and not with those who don't. One can think of this as a Humean strategy since Hume observes that one should expect to lose the trust of those in her community if she breaks her promise to cooperate. A variety of folk theorems of community enforcement have been proved showing that the members of a community can be at an equilibrium of the system of repeated Prisoner's Dilemma games they play if all follow some Humean strategies.[59] This shows analytically that Humean strategies can indeed sustain norms of cooperation in exchange. A growing body of field research, experimental games, and computer simulation studies explores how such community enforcement norms can emerge and endure in actual communities.[60] Once again, Hume's original proto-game-theoretic insights continue to be explored and developed in our own time.

Hume's informal community enforcement argument is similar to Hobbes's response in *Leviathan* to the Foole, an individual who directly challenges the rationality of keeping promises when he can profit by breaking his promise.[61] Hobbes and Hume both argue that in fact individuals like the Foole cannot expect to profit from breaking their promises given how much damage breaking a promise is liable to wreak on one's reputation.[62] In the *Enquiry,* Hume considers his own direct challenge against the rationality of keeping promises:

> A sensible knave, in particular incidents, may think that an act of iniquity or infidelity will make a considerable addition to his fortune, without causing any considerable breach in the social union and confederacy. That *honesty is the best policy,* may be a good general rule, but is liable to many exceptions; and he, it may perhaps be thought, conducts himself with most wisdom, who observes the general rule, and takes advantage of all the exceptions.[63]

Taken by itself, the second part of the Knave's remark seems rather innocuous. The Knave appears to be recommending simply that one obey a general rule when obedience serves this rule's good purpose, and to break this rule in the exceptional cases where obedience fails to serve this purpose. But when he applies his general recommendation to the rule he states in the first part of his remark, the Knave's conclusion is anything but harmless. In

Treatise Hume argues that members of society must honor the requirements of justice even when particular circumstances tempt them to deviate from these requirements, or else confusion and chaos will follow.[64] If the Knave is right, then those who accept this piece of common wisdom and who do try to follow the rules of justice without exception are simply mistaken.

Hume's words are seldom so passionate as they are in his response to his Knave's challenge. In one part of this response, Hume extols the advantages an honest person has over people who are like the Sensible Knave:

> Such a one has, besides, the frequent satisfaction of seeing knaves, with all their pretended cunning and abilities, betrayed by their own maxims; and while they purpose to cheat with moderation and secrecy, a tempting incident occurs, nature is frail, and they give into the snare; whence they can never extricate themselves, without a total loss of reputation, and the forfeiture of all future trust and confidence with mankind.

> But were they ever so secret and successful, the honest man, if he has any tincture of philosophy, or even common observation and reflection, will discover that they themselves are, in the end, the greatest dupes, and have sacrificed the invaluable enjoyment of a character, with themselves at least, for the acquisition of worthless toys and gewgaws.[65]

Hume's analysis of the Knave's challenge marks an important turn in Hume's thinking regarding the prudential motivations for being just. In *Treatise* Hume bases his direct warning against breaking a promise entirely on reputational effects. In the response to the Knave's challenge in *Enquiry,* Hume gives inward peace of mind and satisfaction with one's own character at least as important a role as reputation.[66] In *Enquiry,* Hume is relying on what Henry Sidgwick in *The Methods of Ethics* would later dub "internal sanctions" as well as the external sanctions associated with reputation as reasons to develop a response to this challenge.[67]

Why did Hume make this turn? We think an answer to this question lies in the power of the challenge Hume sets himself in *Enquiry.* The Knave claims he can choose between two alternatives: (1) be honest, and in particular keep one's promises without exception, or (2) be honest except for special "perfect opportunities" where dishonest conduct will add substantially to one's personal fortune and will result in no negative external sanctions. The Knave acknowledges that the first alternative may serve him well as a general policy, but claims that the second will serve him better. Here Hume recognizes the possibility of a distinction that became prominent in twentieth-century moral philosophy, namely, that between "rule consequentialism" and "act consequentialism." The Knave's background assumptions are that he can know, at least sometimes, when a perfect opportunity arises, and that the anticipated external good of augmenting his material fortune is the only good of significance with respect to his choice. Hume realizes that if the Knave is granted these background assumptions then no response will satisfy the Knave himself.[68] The Knave can argue that the second alternative weakly dominates the first, since by hypothesis in all circumstances he never fares worse and in some circumstances he fares better when he chooses the second over the first. Weak dominance is another important decision-theoretic concept Hume may have been the first to present, this time in the words of his Knave. And the Knave can argue further that if there is any positive probability that he will encounter a situation he knows to be a perfect opportunity, then rationality requires him to adopt the second alternative. But Hume can also argue that, fortunately, very few individuals are both so good at identifying perfect opportunities for dishonesty and so incapable of appreciating the internal positive sanctions of a good character that following the Knave's advice would be their rational choice. For the rest of we more ordinary folk, Hume's analysis goes far in explaining how being honest without expectation is really the rational choice.

NOTES

1. Robert Sugden argues that Hume's theory of decision anticipates contemporary decision theory in "Hume's Non-Instrumental and Non-Propositional Decision Theory," *Economics and Philosophy* 22 (2006): 365–91. Some of the authors who attribute game-theoretic insights to Hume include Jean Hampton, *Hobbes and the Social Contract Tradition* (Cambridge: Cambridge University Press, 1986); Robert Sugden, *The Economics of Rights, Co-operation and Welfare,* 2nd ed. (New York: Palgrave Macmillan, 2004); Peter Vanderschraaf, "The Informal Game Theory in Hume's Account of Convention," *Economics and Philosophy* 14 (1998): 215–47; and Ken Binmore, *Natural Justice* (Oxford: Oxford University Press, 2005).

2. David Hume, *An Enquiry Concerning Human Understanding,* ed. Tom L. Beauchamp (Oxford: Oxford University Press, 2000), 8.1.17 (hereafter EHU, cited by section, part, and paragraph numbers).

3. Hume, *Enquiry Concerning the Principles of Morals,* appendix 1.18–20 (hereafter EPM, cited by section or appendix and paragraph number).

4. See, for example, EPM, 5, and David Hume, *A Treatise of Human Nature,* ed. David Fate Norton and Mary J. Norton (Oxford: Clarendon Press, 2007),

2.1.10.3, 2.3.10.5, 3.3.5.4 (hereafter *Treatise,* cited by book, part, section, and paragraph numbers).

5. *Treatise,* 3.3.5.1.

6. Hume regards utility as one source of pleasure distinct from others such as beauty. See, for example, EPM, 5, and *Treatise,* 2.1.10.3, 2.3.10.5, 3.3.5.4. So Hume's view differs from that of Bentham, who defines utility as a general family of pleasure-producing properties in *An Introduction to the Principles of Morals and Legislation,* in *The Collected Works of Jeremy Bentham,* ed. J. H. Burns and H. L. A. Hart (Oxford: Clarendon Press, 1996), chapter 1.3.

7. Francis Hutcheson, *An Enquiry Concerning Moral Good and Evil,* in *British Moralists, 1650–1800,* vol. 1, *Hobbes–Gay,* ed. D. D. Raphael (Oxford: Oxford University Press, 1969), 262–99. See also *An Essay on the Nature and Conduct of the Passions and Affections, with Illustrations on the Moral Sense,* in Raphael, ed., *British Moralists,* 1:300–321.

8. *Treatise,* 3.2.2.5, 8; EPM, 3.6, 3.23.

9. *Treatise,* 2.3.3.4.

10. My thanks to Gerasimos Santas for suggesting this metaphor. Santas gives a fine discussion of how Hume's own views can be understood as a challenge to the Platonic position in *Understanding Plato's Republic* (Chichester, United Kingdom: Wiley-Blackwell, 2010), §5.5.

11. *Treatise,* 2.3.3.6.

12. Thomas Hobbes, *Leviathan,* ed. Noel Malcolm (Oxford: Clarendon Press, 2014), 6:7, 49.

13. Hobbes, *Leviathan,* 15:40.

14. Hobbes, *Leviathan,* 11:2; 10:1, 2.

15. *Treatise,* 2.3.3.6.

16. Walter Van Tilburg Clark, *The Ox-Bow Incident* (1940; New York: Modern Library, 2004).

17. *Treatise,* 2.3.3.4, 6.

18. *Treatise,* 2.3.3.7; emphasis added.

19. See especially David Gauthier, *Morals by Agreement* (Oxford: Clarendon Press, 1986), chapter 2; Edward McClennen, *Rationality and Dynamic Choice: Foundational Explorations* (Cambridge: Cambridge University Press, 1990); and Robert Nozick, *The Nature of Rationality* (Princeton, N.J.: Princeton University Press, 1993).

20. *Treatise,* 3.1.1.9.

21. *Treatise,* 1.1.2, 2.1.1.1, 2.3.3.5.

22. In *Treatise,* 2.3.9.2, Hume actually classifies volitions as direct passions. In *Treatise,* 2.3.1.2, Hume also says that will is an internal impression, even though the will is not a passion properly speaking. In a fine critical study,

David Owen argues that for Hume the will is a faculty and as such is not itself a passion; rather, its products, which are volitions, are passions. See David Owen, "Hume and the Mechanics of Mind: Impressions, Ideas, and Association," in *The Cambridge Companion to Hume,* 2nd ed., ed. David Fate Norton and Jacqueline Taylor (Cambridge: Cambridge University Press, 2008), 70–104. John Connolly gives another illuminating discussion of Hume's view of decisions as mental events in "David Hume and the Concept of Volition: The Will as Impression," *Hume Studies* 13 (1987): 276–305.

23. *Treatise,* 2.3.3.8–10.

24. See, for example, Christine Korsgaard, "Skepticism about Practical Reason," *Journal of Philosophy* 83 (1986): 5–25; Elijah Millgram, "Was Hume a Humean?" *Hume Studies* 21 (1995): 75–93; and Sugden, "Hume's Non-Instrumental and Non-Propositional Decision Theory."

25. This is in fact how Robert Sugden reads Hume in "Hume's Non-Instrumental and Non-Propositional Decision Theory."

26. *Treatise,* 3.1.1.10.

27. *Treatise,* 3.1.1–2.

28. EPM, 1.8.

29. Proclus attributes such arguments to Democritus. Francesco Ademello quotes these arguments from *Platonis Cratylum,* XVI, 6:20:7:6, and gives an English translation in *The Cratylus of Plato: A Commentary* (Cambridge: Cambridge University Press, 2011), 92.

30. Nicholas Denyer documents this in "The Origins of Justice," *Suzetesis: Studi offerti a Marcello Gigante* (Naples: G. Macchiaroli, 1983), 133–52.

31. *Gorgias* (483a–484b) and *Republic* (358e–359b), in *Plato: Complete Works,* ed. John M. Cooper (Indianapolis: Hackett, 1997).

32. Some representative examples include Hugo Grotius, *The Rights of War and Peace,* ed. Richard Tuck (Indianapolis: Liberty Fund, 2005), 1.1:7; Hobbes, *Leviathan,* 14:4–5; Samuel Pufendorf, *On the Law of Nature and of Nations,* in *The Political Writings of Samuel Pufendorf,* ed. Craig Carr (Oxford: Oxford University Press, 1994), 2.3:13; and John Locke, *Second Treatise of Government,* in *Locke: Two Treatises of Government,* ed. Peter Laslett (Cambridge: Cambridge University Press, 1988), §20.

33. *Treatise,* 3.2.1–6.

34. See note 1.

35. EPM, appendix 3.7–8. See also *Treatise,* 3.2.2.10, 3.2.2.22, 3.2.3.4–11, 3.2.5.11.

36. EPM, 9.22; *Treatise,* 3.2.5.9–10. Here Hume refers to a convention where others withdraw their trust in case one breaks a promise, which obviously indicates that a convention of promise-keeping remains in force even if some occasionally violate this convention.

37. *Treatise,* 3.2.2.10, 3.2.5.1. In EPM, appendix 3.9, Hume also expressly denies that conventions can be identified with promises.

38. EPM, appendix 3.9. See also *Treatise,* 3.2.2.10.

39. *Treatise,* 3.2.3.10; EPM, appendix 3.10n76.

40. Perhaps the best known statements of these claims are in EHU, 4.2.3, 4.2.21.

41. Russell Hardin identifies twenty-two distinct classes of coordination problems Hume discusses in his writings. See Russell Hardin, *David Hume: Moral and Political Theorist* (Oxford: Oxford University Press, 2007), 85.

42. EPM, 4.19.

43. EPM, 4.19n22.

44. EPM, 4.19n22.

45. See Sugden, *The Economics of Rights,* 33–35, and Peter Vanderschraaf, "Knowledge, Equilibrium, and Convention," *Erkenntnis* 49 (1998): 337–69, for further discussion on this point.

46. *Treatise,* 3.2.3.10n5; Hume, "Of the First Principles of Government" (Essay 3); EPM, 4.20.

47. EPM, 3.38. See also EPM, 3.35–37, and *Treatise,* 3.2.3.4n1.

48. This game is also known as Hawk-Dove in much of the game-theoretic literature.

49. In a game a strategy combination is a "Nash equilibrium" if each agent engaged in the game gains her highest expected payoff by following the strategy that is her part of this combination, given that the others also follow their parts of this combination.

50. This alternation scheme is a "correlated equilibrium," since the two players tie their choices to the same set $\Omega = \{\omega_1, \omega_2\}$ of possible worlds. Robert Aumann developed the formal account of correlated equilibrium in "Subjectivity and Correlation in Randomized Strategies," *Journal of Mathematical Economics* 1 (1974): 67–96, and "Correlated Equilibrium as an Expression of Bayesian Rationality," *Econometrica* 55 (1987): 1–18. The correlated equilibrium concept includes Nash equilibrium as a special case.

51. *Treatise,* 3.2.3.6–8.

52. *Treatise,* 3.2.3.

53. *Treatise,* 3.2.3.7.

54. *Treatise,* 3.2.5.8.

55. EPM, 9.24; *Treatise,* 3.2.5.10.

56. *Treatise,* 3.2.5.1–2, 10–11. See also EPM, appendix 3.7.

57. *Treatise,* 3.2.5.9.

58. Nash did not publish this result. Nash's results and related results for history-dependent strategies in repeated games are known as folk theorems because

early game theorists knew of and discussed such results informally long before any such results were first published.

59. George Mailath and Larry Samuelson summarize many of the results of the community enforcement literature in *Repeated Games and Reputations: Long-Run Relationships* (Oxford: Oxford University Press, 2006). Robert Sugden and Michihiro Kandori proved some of the first folk theorems of community enforcement. See Sugden, *The Economics of Rights,* chapter 6, and Michihiro Kandori, "Social Norms and Community Enforcement," *Review of Economic Studies* 59 (1992): 63–80.

60. The literature of this research has grown so large that no single resource or set of resources adequately summarizes it. Two of the now classic studies on community enforcement are Robert Axelrod, *The Evolution of Cooperation,* revised ed. (New York: Basic Books, 2006), and Elinor Ostrom, *Governing the Commons: The Evolution of Institutions for Collective Action* (Cambridge: Cambridge University Press, 1990).

61. Hobbes, *Leviathan,* 15:4–5.

62. Hobbes gives his response to the Foole in *Leviathan,* 15:5. Robert Sugden and Brian Skyrms were perhaps the first to clearly draw a connection between folk theorems in game theory and Hobbes's response to the Foole. See Sugden, *The Economics of Rights,* 165–69, and Brian Skyrms, "The Shadow of the Future," in *Rational Commitment and Social Justice: Essays for Gregory Kavka,* ed. Jules Coleman and Christopher Morris (Cambridge: Cambridge University Press, 1998), 12–22.

63. EPM, 9.22.

64. *Treatise,* 3.2.6.9. See also *Treatise,* 3.2.2.22, and EPM, appendix 3.3–6, 10.

65. EPM, 9.24–25.

66. In the concluding section of *Treatise* Hume asserts that having inner peace and being satisfied with one's own character, as well as having the high regard of others, depends on one strictly observing the social virtues, and that these goods are more valuable than any increase in fortune one gains by breaching these virtues. *Treatise,* 3.3.6.6. But in *Treatise* Hume does not make his point regarding inner peace and satisfaction with one's own character in the context of his conventionalist analysis of promises. And indeed Hume gives the impression that he speaks of these goods as an afterthought, since he deliberately refrains from insisting on this point and speculates that discussing this point fully would require another work beyond the scope of *Treatise.*

67. Henry Sidgwick, *Methods of Ethics,* 7th ed. (Indianapolis: Hackett, 1981), book 2, chapter 5.

68. Hume admits as much in EPM, 9.23.

Index

Rethinking the Western Tradition